This very comprehensive and well-written guide
ment is clearly based on a great wealth of knowled
working on many projects worldwide. Case studie
tive approaches and the latest thinking on practical solutions to address difficult issues. The book will be of particular use to practitioners involved with the
detailed planning and implementation of resettlement and livelihood restoration
measures.
Ted Pollett, International Social Development and Resettlement Advisor &
Former Principal Social Development Specialist, IFC

This book is a marvellous compendium of all the important elements of resettlement and economic displacement, and more importantly it is a practical guide
to actually undertaking the work. Aimed primarily at social performance practitioners and project managers, the language and structure of the book makes for
easy reading and comprehension. Its currency flows from the field experience of
the writers, very evident in its many case examples. Currency is enhanced through
up-to-date cross-referencing to Equator Bank and other international standards.
This is an essential resource for everybody involved in or about to embark on the
resettlement and displacement of land-connected people.
Bruce Harvey, Director, Resolution88

This book is clearly written by practitioners. The project examples, tools, templates
and frameworks could not be shaped other than through years of experience. The
book firmly establishes land access and resettlement as a discipline that involves
a comprehensive set of activities. It should end the discussion with those who
still think that resettlement is just about building new houses. Many thanks for
this fantastic contribution!
Luc Zandvliet, author of *Getting it Right: Making Corporate Community*
Relations Work

The Guide is a welcome and timely addition to the existing guidance on such a
challenging issue. The fact that it is done by practitioners for practitioners makes
it particularly useful. The Guide also articulates a strong "business case" for
private companies and governments to get it right. I can see practitioners around
the world using the Guide as a key tool and to engage clients and other stakeholders in dealing with such a complex issue more effectively.
Jorge Villegas, Social Development Specialist

While there is a number of guidelines for the development of resettlement action
plans, this book provides practical considerations and tools to assist project teams
involved in resettlement action plan implementation. This is supported by the
use of real-life examples of good practice and challenges encountered during
implementation.
Jan Grobler, Principal Technical Expert for Land Acquisition and Resettlement,
Royal Dutch Shell

This book is a must-read for everyone in resource development. It provides the business case for relocation, provides common-sense advice, and debunks the myths associated with developing robust social plans.

Ross Gallinger, former Executive Director of PDAC and CSR Professional

Corporate leaders, project managers and social practitioners involved in delivering resettlement programmes will find this "how-to" guide an invaluable resource for carrying out resettlement on large infrastructure projects. This book goes beyond policy and principles to explain in detail the practical steps required to engage with communities, negotiate mutually acceptable arrangements for land access and resettlement, and successfully implement. This is a significant contribution to advancing resettlement practice.

Robert Barclay, International Resettlement Practitioner

This book provides a comprehensive, well-organised and practical guide to the complex issue of land access and resettlement, with particular relevance to the extractives sector. Drawing on a wealth of professional experience and a series of benchmark surveys, the authors have created a much-needed reference guide that bridges the gap between international resettlement policies and how these are executed on the ground in the private sector context.

Justin Pooley, Resettlement Specialist, IFC

This is an essential handbook for governments and developers that are working in instances where resettlement cannot be avoided and are committed to reducing the harm associated with physical, economic and social displacement. The authors draw on their vast international experience to present practical, accessible steps to manage the resettlement process.

Dr Ana Maria Esteves, Director, Community Insights Group

LAND ACCESS
AND
RESETTLEMENT
A GUIDE TO BEST PRACTICE

LAND ACCESS
AND
RESETTLEMENT
A GUIDE TO BEST PRACTICE

Gerry Reddy, Eddie Smyth and **Michael Steyn**

Greenleaf
PUBLISHING

Published by
Greenleaf Publishing Limited
Aizlewood's Mill, Nursery Street
Sheffield S3 8GG, UK
www.greenleaf-publishing.com

Printed in the United Kingdom
Printed and bound by CPI Group (UK) Ltd, Croydon, CR0 4YY

Cover by LaliAbril.com
Photographs by the authors

British Library Cataloguing in Publication Data:
A catalogue record for this book is available from the British Library.
ISBN-13: 9781783532131 [paperback]
ISBN-13: 9781783532339 [hardback]
ISBN-13: 9781783531752 [PDF ebook]
ISBN-13: 9781783531769 [ePub ebook]

Contents

Preface

The natural resources sector, including the mining, oil and gas industries, large-scale infrastructure projects such as dams, and other activities requiring large-scale land acquisition such as biofuel projects, are operating in a context of increased awareness and regulation regarding the potential social impacts of their activities, particularly in developing countries. At the same time, companies increasingly appreciate the business case for 'getting social right', and the benefits of creating shared value.

Projects are increasingly located in areas where land access and land use are major issues for both the project and communities. Land access and resettlement is concerned with managing these challenging processes to minimise impacts on communities, mitigate any impacts that do occur, and ideally leave communities better off than before, through appropriate resettlement, restoration of livelihoods and other initiatives. The ideal result should be mutual gains for communities, companies and governments.

The authors, Gerry Reddy, Eddie Smyth and Michael Steyn, have worked on land access and resettlement projects for many years across the world and each has equally contributed to the production of this book. However, a time came when we felt there was a need for a firm whose main focus was land access and resettlement. We therefore set up Intersocial Consulting in 2010 with the express aim to be one of the leading firms worldwide in advising and assisting companies on land access, resettlement and related issues. Our vision is to support companies and communities in delivering mutually beneficial natural resource and infrastructure projects, creating win–win scenarios. Intersocial and its directors and team members have planned, implemented and reviewed over 50 land access and resettlement projects in more than 30 countries internationally, and conducted benchmarking exercises on more than 60 projects for a variety of clients in the mining, oil and gas sectors.

Based on this experience relating to over 100 projects in more than 40 countries, we felt that writing a practical and accessible guide to land access and resettlement processes would be invaluable in helping companies successfully address social issues and implement projects, based on extensive experience of what works and what does not. There is plenty of existing literature available on land access and resettlement, including the International Finance Corporation, World Bank and a myriad of other standards and guidelines, which set the broad context for good practice in the area. What is missing is an up-to-date, accessible and practical guide on how to optimally plan for, implement and review land access and resettlement projects, and avoid pitfalls, based on the main lessons that have been learned on the ground over the past decade or so.

The book does not aim to be an academic discussion of land access and resettlement. It focuses on demystifying the land access and resettlement process, putting forward the business case for doing it right, and draws on lessons learned from real project experience in outlining the key steps to take and tools to use in planning, implementing and reviewing projects, and how to avoid the inevitable pitfalls along the way.

Our objective was to write a book that provides a practical roadmap for corporate leaders, project managers and practitioners, but also academia, government, affected communities and civil society, for planning and implementing successful land access and resettlement. We hope the book will sit dog-eared and well used on desks for years to come.

Acknowledgements

The authors would like to thank all the staff, past and present, of Intersocial Consulting. This book is as much a product of their expertise, diligence and commitment to best practice on projects as it is a product of the authors.

We would like to thank our families, true partners in this venture, not least for their understanding that to do the work on the ground means long periods away from home.

Thanks go to our valued clients, and the communities in which they operate. It is a constant privilege to be invited to work with great people on interesting projects in some of the most interesting places in the world, and get to know the people who live there.

Particular thanks go to Alex Armitage and Ellen De Keyser for their inputs to Chapter 7 on impact assessment; Joana Cameira for illustrating key aspects of resettlement site and housing design; and Andrew McQuillan of ExactlyDesigns and Aithche Smyth (aithche.com) for their assistance with graphic design.

Sincere thanks to our publishers, Greenleaf Publishing, for their guidance, assistance and encouragement.

1

Introduction

> I don't know much about land access and resettlement, but from what I do know, it will cost way more than you think, something will go hideously wrong, and it will take a lot longer than planned
>
> Project manager of a major mining project

Why is a best practice guide to land access and resettlement important?

Many natural resource projects have experienced commu-nity protests, significant delays or have not been completed, due to poorly planned and implemented approaches to land access and resettlement, with consequent negative impacts on communities, inflated project costs and corporate repu-tational damage.

Land access and resettlement is challenging, but it is possible to do it right

Poorly planned infrastructure projects, including dams and transport routes, often underestimate social impacts and can have devastating effects on communities.

Other attempts to relocate people for environmental or social benefit, such as in the protection of national parks or resettlement of refugees or internally displaced people, often result in winners and losers, and therefore unsustainable and temporary solutions.

At the same time, companies and governments increasingly appreciate the business case for 'getting social right'.

Based on extensive experience of what works and what does not, a practical and accessible guide to land access and resettlement processes is invaluable in helping project proponents successfully address social issues and implement projects.

This book focuses on:

- Demystifying the land access and resettlement process
- Putting forward the business case for undertaking land access and resettlement in a comprehensive and best practice manner
- Highlighting the key components, issues, challenges and risks in the land access and resettlement process
- Pointing to lessons learned from real project experience
- Discussing guiding principles, useful tools and key points to bear in mind for tackling challenges
- Alerting practitioners to the key measures that need to be taken to avoid problems and enable success

Who should read this book?

The book provides a practical roadmap for corporate leaders, project managers, practitioners, academia, government and civil society for planning and implementing successful land access and resettlement. We also hope that affected communities will find it useful.

Although the main focus of the book is on natural resource project related resettlement, the multiple complex issues and considerable impacts arising from such projects mean that much of the guidance is equally applicable to projects concerned with infrastructure, disaster-related, post-conflict or conservation-related resettlement. The book also highlights specific issues connected with these types of resettlement where relevant.

What exactly is land access and resettlement?

Natural resource projects and major infrastructure projects can have considerable impacts on local communities, chiefly due to the need to acquire large areas of land. When projects are located in developing and middle-income economies the impacts are most keenly felt, as it often requires displacement of large, often rural, populations with predominately land-based livelihoods.

Land access and resettlement can also be required to **protect ecologically sensitive areas** from human activities, or to rehouse populations affected by **conflict or natural disasters**.

Land access and resettlement is concerned **with managing these challenging processes to minimise impacts** on communities, mitigate any impacts that do occur, and ideally leave communities better off, through appropriate resettlement, restoration of livelihoods and related initiatives. The ideal result should be mutual gains for communities, companies and governments.

Land access and resettlement therefore refers both to:

- **Physical displacement**: where there is loss of shelter and assets resulting from project-related acquisition of land and/or restrictions on land use that requires the affected persons to move to another location

- **Economic displacement**: where there is a loss of assets or access to assets that leads to loss of income sources or other means of livelihoods as a result of project-related land acquisition and/or restrictions on land use

When resettlement is practically unavoidable it must be:

- Carefully and systematically planned from an early stage

- Undertaken with the informed and active participation of displaced persons and other relevant stakeholders

The goal of a land access and resettlement project is not just to achieve access to the land, but to form a lasting and meaningful partnership with local communities, government and all relevant stakeholders in order to ensure the future success of a project and benefits for all.

This can be particularly challenging when there are no clear project benefits in terms of large-scale employment, and existing livelihoods may be curtailed, such as in the case of resettlement from national parks in the interests of protecting sensitive ecosystems.

Regardless of whether resettlement is involuntary or voluntary, the overall objectives, guiding principles, approach and desired outcomes should not be different.

> Process is as important as outcome

Key concepts

It is important at this point to have a clear understanding of some key concepts that are mentioned and discussed throughout the book. These include the following:

- **Land access/acquisition**: this includes not just outright purchases of property, but also acquisition of access rights, e.g. rights of way

- **Resettlement**: resettlement is the process of not just compensating and moving, but also re-establishing, people who live or work on the land required for a project

- **Physical displacement**: where there is loss of shelter and assets resulting from project-related acquisition of land and/or restrictions on land use that requires the affected persons to move to another location
- **Economic displacement**: where there is a loss of assets or access to assets that leads to loss of income sources or other means of livelihoods as a result of project-related land acquisition and/or restrictions on land use
- **Involuntary resettlement**: when affected people do not have the right to refuse land acquisition or restrictions on land use that result in physical or economic displacement. This arises in situations involving lawful expropriation, temporary or permanent restrictions on land use, or negotiated settlements in which the buyer can resort to expropriation or impose legal restrictions on land use if negotiations with the seller fail
- **Voluntary resettlement**: this arises when people are not obliged to move and the land acquirer cannot resort to expropriation or other compulsory procedures if negotiations fail
- **Livelihoods**: the full range of means that individuals, households and communities utilise to make a living
- **Vulnerable people**: these are people who by virtue of gender, ethnicity, age, physical or mental disability, economic disadvantage or social status may be more adversely affected by displacement than others, and who may be limited in their ability to claim or take advantage of resettlement assistance and related development benefits

A **glossary of key terms** is also provided at the back of the book.

What are the key components of the land access and resettlement process?

The key steps in the land access and resettlement process can be grouped into the following interrelated areas:

- Stakeholder engagement
- Assessment
- Planning
- Implementation
- Monitoring and evaluation

In practice these areas are overlapping and iterative. The exact timing and make-up of each element will vary from project to project. An example of how some of these key processes might interrelate on a typical mining project is shown in Figure 1.1. Within these simple elements the process can be further broken down into the following important components:

Figure 1.1: Key processes on a typical mining project.

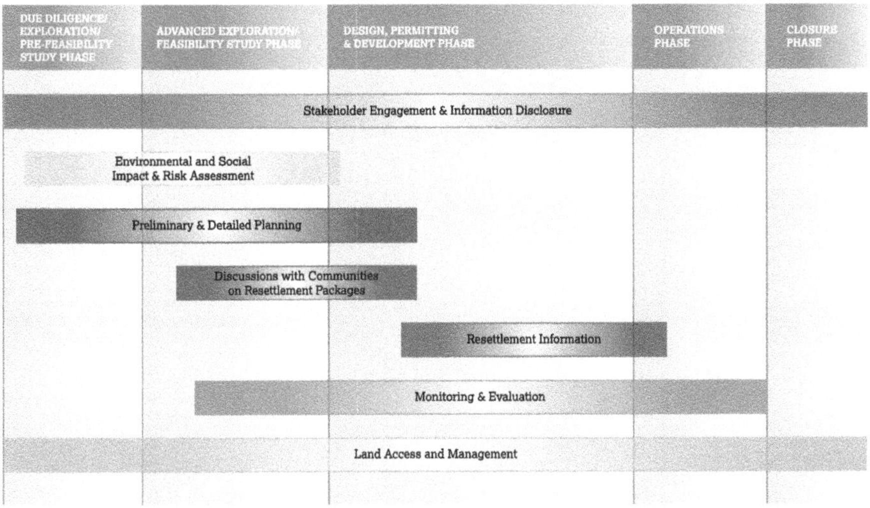

DUE DILIGENCE/ EXPLORATION/ PRE-FEASIBILITY STUDY PHASE	ADVANCED EXPLORATION/ FEASIBILITY STUDY PHASE	DESIGN, PERMITTING & DEVELOPMENT PHASE	OPERATIONS PHASE	CLOSURE PHASE

Stakeholder Engagement & Information Disclosure

Environmental and Social Impact & Risk Assessment

Preliminary & Detailed Planning

Discussions with Communities on Resettlement Packages

Resettlement Information

Monitoring & Evaluation

Land Access and Management

Stakeholder engagement
- Broad stakeholder engagement
- The negotiation process (internal and external)

Assessment
- Review of best practice and institutional and legal frameworks
- Baseline data collection and analysis
- Assessing project impacts and minimising displacement
- Risk and opportunity assessments

Planning
- Project planning and preparation
- Development of compensation frameworks
- Physical resettlement planning
- Livelihood restoration planning
- Consideration of vulnerable persons
- Considerations of cultural heritage

Implementation
- Compensation payments process
- Resettlement implementation and moves
- Livelihood restoration
- Measures to support vulnerable persons

Figure 1.2: The land access and resettlement process.

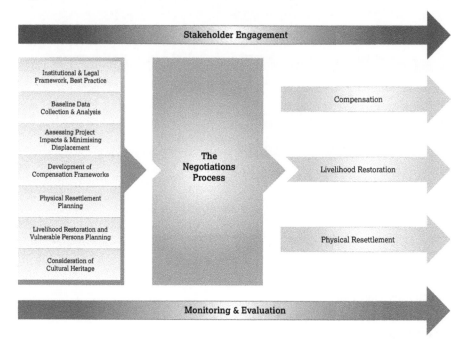

Monitoring, evaluation and reporting

- Internal monitoring and evaluation
- External monitoring and evaluation
- Reporting
- Completion audits

These components also form the essential parts of any resettlement action plan, the key management tool required to plan the land access and resettlement process. This book also follows the logic of this project cycle.

While the overall process can be regarded as one ongoing engagement with all stakeholders on land access, the negotiations with communities and key stakeholders can be seen as the centrepoint around which the process itself revolves, with planning and preparations in advance of the negotiations, and implementation of the project thereafter. This is shown graphically in Figure 1.2.

What are the key challenges, issues and risks?

Projects worldwide are increasingly facing a number of common and overarching challenges:

There is a growing pressure to develop projects in a socially responsible manner. This pressure comes from increased awareness of local communities, shareholder concerns, local, regional and national governments, and other external stakeholders including national and international NGOs (non-governmental organisations) and international regulatory bodies.

The bar is being raised. This can be seen in the form of higher standards and laws, both in terms of more stringent national laws, and international laws and standards such as the Performance Standards of the IFC (International Finance Corporation). These were updated in 2012, while the World Bank introduced a new draft E&S Framework in 2014 and the EBRD (European Bank for Reconstruction and Development) also reviewed its own Performance Requirements in 2012.

There are often high community and government expectations. Communities and governments expect not only that affected households are treated with respect and that the negative impacts of projects are mitigated, but that projects should result in individuals, households and communities benefiting significantly, i.e. that they are left in a better economic situation as a result of the project.

Projects are increasingly located in challenging and sensitive areas. Mining, oil and gas prospects are increasingly found in areas which are environmentally sensitive, or where there are challenging social issues, often actually due to previous negative experiences of such projects in the area. At the same time, resettlement projects are increasingly seen as a solution to the encroachment of communities on sensitive habitats where there is severe competition for resources.

There is often a lack of realism about the effort, time and cost to undertake resettlement properly. While the social departments of companies are often keenly aware of the time and resources required to obtain a social licence to operate and achieve timely land access, other key personnel may not realise this and insufficient time and resources will be applied at the outset of projects. This can result in much more costly delays and negative impacts and publicity later.

There is an increasing risk of speculative activities. There can be a significant influx of people into project areas in anticipation of benefits from the project proponent. This can result in speculative building of structures or planting of crops in anticipation of compensation or resettlement. Where this is not well managed it can result in projects quickly becoming uneconomic or very costly to develop.

Resettlement planning cannot be done like other aspects of project planning: communities must be involved. Companies as a whole need to be clear that communities need to be involved at every step of resettlement planning, and every detail of resettlement planning must be discussed and agreed. Where resettlement planning occurs in isolation, such as in anticipation of saving time, the risk is that disagreements will arise later which will result in costly delays.

Projects often suffer from a legacy of broken promises and lack of community trust. This often occurs because community relations, stakeholder engagement and issues such as control of expectations are not taken seriously at the outset of projects, such as during the exploration stage of natural resource projects, but equally it can be because previous commitments made in earlier phases are not met, which can affect the development of projects.

There is often limited capacity of communities/government. In many of the locations where project opportunities occur, the capacity of communities and government to interact with the project as meaningful stakeholders may be limited. Communities may require significant capacity-building before they can meaningfully negotiate and discuss project benefits, while local government may have few resources and personnel to meet their stipulated objectives and allow development of common approaches to development, and may find it difficult or impossible to become meaningful development partners.

Projects cannot simply rely on joint-venture partners or government to do resettlement for projects, but must work with them. On some projects the temptation may be to devolve as much of the responsibility surrounding resettlement to partners or government as early as possible in the process, especially if they appear to be willing partners, or have a statutory obligation to undertake the resettlement process. However, in reality, as highlighted above, their capacity and resources will sometimes be extremely limited, and any shortfall in delivery will still remain the responsibility of the project proponent. At the same time, it is important to involve government and partners effectively, and ensure that eventual handover of responsibilities to government, such as in relation to resettlement sites, is planned for from the outset.

Leaders may not be truly representative. It is often tempting for projects to focus on engagement with community leaders in order to fast-track community consultation. However, in many locations recent developments such as urbanisation or in-migration may mean that traditional leaderships are not representative of the entire population, or for many they may have lost their institutional relevance. In other instances, they may be seen as unpopular or corrupt. It is crucial not only to effectively assess the leadership systems in host communities, but also not to rely on them as a substitute for more comprehensive stakeholder engagement.

Restoration of livelihoods, let alone improving them, is difficult. Projects can no longer address impacts by restoring pre-existing standards of living or livelihood strategies, but must show that the project has improved the livelihood mechanisms and economic situation of project-affected persons. This is not only increasingly demanded by communities and governments, but is highlighted by international standards governing land acquisition and resettlement. This poses a significant challenge, given that restoration of past levels of livelihood is, in itself, often not easy to achieve.

Finding replacement land is increasingly challenging. Mining projects are occurring in areas where there is not just a significant resident population to be resettled but, often more challenging, there is a need to find sufficient replacement farmland, or indeed access to fishing areas, which often reflects the predominant livelihoods in the area.

Resettlement involves multiple negotiations. While consultation, trust-building and negotiation with communities are the most obvious aspects of project negotiations, and the most time-consuming, negotiations also take place with various levels of government and other key stakeholders. Negotiations also need to occur internally with other project and corporate departments as well as with senior management, who may need to be persuaded of the business case for undertaking resettlement properly, and to make compromises in terms of resettlement packages as well as project schedules and implementation.

Meeting standards appropriate to site in a practical way. While international and internal company standards relating to resettlement may be consistent globally, every site is different. Standards must be adhered to but applied in a practical way, appropriate to each site: a 'cookie-cutter' approach will not work.

Making sure schedule and budget are realistic. The time and cost required to do resettlement should be understood and reflected in the overall schedule and budget at the outset of the project. Any attempts to unrealistically reduce the budget or time-scales at this stage will only result in inaccurate and unrealistic planning.

What is the format of this best practice guide to land access and resettlement?

The chapters of the book follow the logic of the project life-cycle, with up-to-date case studies provided, outlining key lessons and best practice guidance. The book is designed so it can either be read from start to finish, or a particular aspect of the process can be consulted in a stand-alone chapter.

1. For each key component of the project cycle, the book asks:
   - What is the objective?
   - What are the key issues, challenges and risks?
   - What are the guiding principles?
   - What are the key components of the process?

   What is the objective of the negotiation process?

   Mining, oil and gas and infrastructure projects cannot take place without securing access to land. However, this objective cannot be met unless land is accessed in a manner that adequately engages affected people to hear their concerns and include their thoughts in the development of mitigation measures and other planning aspects.
   Therefore the objective of negotiations is to enable the conclusion of **suitable agreements** with project-affected persons that:

2. Each section then goes through the most common questions and issues arising for each component, including what to plan for.

   What preparations are required before starting negotiations?

   During the period prior to the commencement of negotiations, the project negotiation team will need to undertake extensive preparations in order to be ready. These need to include the following:
   - Undertake **stakeholder identification and analysis**, taking into account the results of a displacement impact assessment. This involves assessing community organisation, power relations and divisions; conflict within and between the communities; the potential effects of external stakeholder groups; project displacement and other impacts; community issues and concerns, posturing, and strengths and weaknesses.

3. Case studies highlighting lessons learned, both good and bad, are included at key points.

   Project example

   A project in Eastern Europe commenced negotiations without adequate planning. A comprehensive agenda was not prepared, and there was no work plan, schedule or negotiation strategy. As a result, negotiations took place in an uncoordinated manner and lasted much longer than originally anticipated.

   Project example

   A project in Latin America undertook extensive prenegotiation planning, including preparation of a detailed negotiation plan, work plan and schedule. A number of planning workshops were held to inform the planning process. As a result, the project was able to conduct negotiations in a structured and well co-ordinated manner.

4. Each section concludes with a checklist of key considerations to bear in mind.

   The negotiation process: key considerations

   - **Start early**: you will need the time. Be realistic about how long negotiations will take.
   - Before you commence planning, **reflect on lessons learned** on other projects and during your earlier project phases.
   - **Make sure you have right team**: land access and resettlement negotiations are not for the faint hearted, inexperienced or unprepared.
   - No land acquisition and resettlement negotiations should be undertaken without first developing explicit overall **objectives and guiding principles**, as well as a comprehensive **negotiation strategy and plan** (including opening, fallback and

A helpful **glossary of key terms**, found at the back of the book, explains key terms and concepts used.

What is included in the guide?

The chapters follow the key aspects of the project life-cycle as outlined above, and are discussed briefly below.

The business case for getting social right

Chapter 2 seeks to assist practitioners in addressing a key issue, namely ensuring a proper appreciation for detailed planning of land access and resettlement projects among internal stakeholders in a company or government, by putting forward the business case for undertaking land access and resettlement projects in a detailed and proper manner, with adequate time, budget and resources.

Putting the business case for getting social right means talking the language of project financiers and engineers to demonstrate that undertaking projects with due attention to all social issues isn't just the right choice ethically, but will benefit the bottom line for projects in terms of projects being successfully delivered on time and cost, and with a meaningful relationship developed with all stakeholders which ensures continued success.

The business case needs to demonstrate that the cost of getting social right is dwarfed by the cost of getting it wrong.

Best practice and institutional and legal frameworks

There is a myriad of best practice guidance in relation to land access and resettlement, albeit that much of this is necessarily general in nature. **Chapter 3** outlines the key guidance and how this should be taken into account in project planning. In particular, how national laws, regulations and guidance may need to be considered alongside international standards, and how to ensure all stakeholders are satisfied with the process.

Project planning and preparation

Chapter 4 seeks to demystify the project planning process and outline a logical framework for ensuring project teams are properly prepared for land access and resettlement projects. It is important that the social considerations of a project are managed as professionally as any engineering aspect, and indeed that planning is integrated with the planning of engineers and managers so that the entire team appreciates the time-scales, the project requirements and the social challenges and opportunities.

It is fair to say that, traditionally, the planning of social aspects of projects was not always undertaken with professional rigour due to a combination of under-resourcing and a reliance on non-specialist personnel, where project time-scales and the need to ensure that all impacts were addressed were not fully appreciated. While planning and management of social considerations has a greater degree of uncertainty due to the human factors involved, it is still possible. It is no longer acceptable for social aspects of projects to be planned in a haphazard and reactive manner, considering the key risks for all stakeholders when things go wrong. This includes proper attention to organisation, resourcing, budgeting and scheduling.

Stakeholder engagement

Chapter 5 details each aspect of the stakeholder engagement process, from initial identification and mapping of all stakeholders to demonstrating how adequate engagement with stakeholders on every aspect of the project, for the lifetime of the project, can be assured. The issue of internal project engagement is also considered, including how to ensure best practice standards are followed when government or a joint-venture partner is responsible for the land access and resettlement process.

Baseline data collection and analysis

Chapter 6 details the necessary data required for projects to be properly planned, assessed and mitigated, and the various methodologies to ensure data is collected in an inclusive, efficient, comprehensive and secure manner.

The approach to analysis of data required for effective resettlement planning and impact mitigation is discussed in detail.

Assessing project impacts and minimising displacement

Based on the effective approaches to stakeholder engagement and data collection and analysis discussed in previous chapters, **Chapter 7** outlines an approach to ensuring all project impacts are identified and assessed, and measures designed to address these, including as a primary goal the minimisation of displacement of communities and households in the first instance.

Compensation frameworks

In light of the key impacts outlined in Chapter 7, **Chapter 8** details the various approaches to compensation for affected households and individuals, particularly the development of eligibility criteria and entitlements in respect of loss of land, crops, housing and other key impacts which can be assessed in monetary terms. Chapter 8 considers when monetary compensation is appropriate or adequate, and when alternative compensation methodologies need to be considered.

Physical resettlement planning

Physical resettlement, namely when households living in the project area are required to move, requires effective identification, design, planning and construction of alternative communities, housing and related facilities, in order to mitigate effectively for physical losses, but also to ensure the future cohesion and success of the communities affected.

Chapter 9 details the planning of resettlement sites, infrastructure and housing in a way which should maximise the success of physical resettlement, including through the effective participation of affected households and communities and due consideration of their real needs and wants. Mention is also given to instances of physical resettlement after conflict or disaster, or related to the protection of ecosystems, and what special considerations are required in these cases.

Livelihood restoration planning

Effective livelihood restoration planning is concerned with those economically impacted through land access projects. This is often manifested in the loss of agricultural land, crops or small businesses, or loss of access to natural resources that sustain local livelihoods. Impacts and losses may be temporary or permanent. Restoration of livelihoods is largely regarded as one of the most challenging aspects of any land access process, let alone leaving affected households better off than before. **Chapter 10** outlines approaches to the assessment of livelihoods, and the development of effective programmes to maximise success.

Vulnerable persons

Chapter 11 gives special consideration to vulnerable persons and households, including how these may be defined, identified and assessed, and what special measures need to be put in place to address impacts on already vulnerable households, or those who may be at risk of vulnerability.

The negotiation process

The negotiation process is the critical central component of the land access and resettlement process. It can be seen as the centrepoint around which the whole land access and resettlement process turns. All planning and field activities up to the point of negotiations are in preparation for the negotiation process. The outcome of negotiations informs all subsequent activities, including compensation, resettlement construction, moves of affected households and livelihood restoration. How effectively the negotiation process is managed will in large part determine the success or failure of a land access and resettlement process. **Chapter 12** discusses planning and implementation of the negotiation process in detail, including key steps to take to maximise the potential for a win–win outcome for all stakeholders.

Compensation and sign-off process

Following on from the preparatory compensation planning outlined in Chapter 8, **Chapter 13** examines the management of the compensation payment and individual household sign-off process following negotiations, including key elements to consider to ensure a fair, transparent and secure process, which addresses all concerns of both the affected households and the project.

Resettlement implementation and moves

Following on from the prenegotiation physical resettlement planning described in Chapter 9, **Chapter 14** discusses the key considerations in the implementation of new sites, housing and community facilities, including how to sensitively manage the moves of affected households, and measures to ensure the success of resettlement communities following a move.

Community investment

While resettlement and livelihood restoration planning and implementation are intended to address the key impacts on directly affected populations, **Chapter 15** recognises that planning of these aspects needs to be undertaken with regard to the wider community investment initiatives of the project, which should seek to address wider impacts, direct and indirect, and maximise opportunities arising from the project for the benefit of all, including the business benefits for the project.

Livelihood restoration and community development implementation

Chapter 16 examines the implementation of agreed livelihood restoration programmes and wider community development initiatives, including vulnerability assistance, and how and by whom programmes should be managed and delivered in order to maximise success and sustainability in the future.

Cultural heritage

Chapter 17 considers issues surrounding cultural heritage, including archaeological and traditionally significant sites, cemeteries and graves. The various possible approaches to management of these sensitive issues are outlined.

Monitoring and evaluation

A key aspect of the land access and resettlement process is effective monitoring and evaluation of the entire process. **Chapter 18** discusses the need to integrate monitoring and evaluation considerations in project planning from day one, in order to be able to answer the question: Is the project a success?

Land management

Projects are often of a scale which may result in progressive periods of land access over time and result in impacts, positive and negative, which may take place over a wide area, well beyond the project boundaries. **Chapter 19** discusses the concept of life-of-project land management planning, which takes into account the need to address potential competition for resources in the area; influx and speculation arising from the project, not just in the period when the project is being planned and implemented, but also during the operations phase and at closure; project plans with respect to broader community and regional investment; and the need to engage effectively with government and other key stakeholders so that plans are integrated fully with local and regional development objectives. Land management planning also offers the opportunity to check that other social management plans are aligned with meeting the objectives of delivering and protecting land for the project, while creating shared value.

Closing thoughts

The guide concludes with a summary of key conclusions and final thoughts on the planning and implementation of successful land access and resettlement projects.

Why are there no specific chapters on human rights, gender or indigenous peoples?

Human rights, gender and indigenous peoples are important aspects of land access and resettlement processes, and particular attention needs to be given to vulnerable and potentially vulnerable groups.

In many instances, women in particular constitute a significant potentially vulnerable group; efforts need to be made to ensure the interests of women are considered in all aspects of a project, and that they are adequately consulted during the process. Women often face a number of disadvantages in terms of public consultation, particularly in the developing world, and at the same time make an essential contribution to a public consultation process, not least because of their intimate knowledge regarding issues such as land management, water resources, etc., which can provide valuable information of relevance to specialist studies. They are also frequently in a good position to identify community needs and priorities that can be taken up in social development programmes.

However, rather than addressing human rights and gender in a specific chapter, this book prefers to mainstream the issues of human rights and gender throughout the book. Therefore all aspects of the land access and resettlement process are considered through the prism of human rights and gender, and where relevant the various chapters of the book outlining the key steps in the process will refer to specific issues of relevance.

Issues that require special treatment in respect of indigenous groups are discussed in the relevant chapters.

What about other resources in addition to this guide?

The book refers to other key resources relevant to the various topics discussed throughout the book, particularly international standards. The bibliography provides a list of references and a list of useful documents that were consulted in the preparation of the book.

2

The business case for getting it right

Ensuring a proper appreciation for detailed planning of land access and resettlement projects among internal stakeholders in a company or government is a key issue for project planners. This can be achieved by putting a business case forward in a detailed and proper manner with adequate time, budget and resources.

Putting forward the business case for getting social right means talking the language of project financiers and engineers as well as social practitioners. This will help demonstrate that undertaking projects with due attention to all social issues isn't just the right choice ethically, but will benefit the bottom line for project proponents in terms of projects being successfully delivered on time and budget, and with a meaningful relationship and reputation developed with all stakeholders which ensures continued success, and delivers clear longer-term business benefits.

Social impacts and particularly land access are a key risk to projects. The business case can demonstrate that the cost of getting social right is dwarfed by the cost of getting it wrong.

> Social issues should be managed as a science, not an art

What is the business case for getting social right?

Companies and governments increasingly appreciate **the business case** for 'getting social right'.

First, adequately addressing key impacts **reduces the risk** of community unrest and conflict, which can result in work stoppages, legal action or withdrawal of licences to operate.

Second, effectively channelling development benefits to local communities can generate a wide range of **direct and indirect business benefits**. The pursuit of these benefits, or 'business drivers', is what can help motivate companies to support properly undertaken resettlement and community investment approaches. Once a company identifies key business drivers, these can then be used to inform the strategy for addressing social issues. For example, local skills training makes sense for the business as well as nearby communities, as local labour will be cheaper than flying in skilled workers from abroad (IFC 2010b).

What are the key issues, challenges and risks?

The following are key social issues, challenges and risks that can be identified as common to most, if not all, projects:

- Projects are increasingly being developed in **locations with significant social issues and risks**, e.g. due to existing population densities
- There are **high community and government expectations**
- There is **increased pressure for localisation** in the spheres of employment and procurement
- **Negative legacy issues** may colour perception of current projects
- There are demands for more **transparency and increased oversight** of projects
- The trend is towards **negotiation** instead of merely consultation or disclosure when dealing with affected communities
- Companies are being asked to do things that were **traditionally the responsibility of government**
- Projects face **increased costs** and **demands to show increased value** for communities and countries in which they are located
- **A lack of project realism** about the complexity of social issues, and the effort, time and cost required to address these properly. This can result in conflict with local communities, government and other stakeholders such as NGOs (non-governmental organisations). This can result in temporary or permanent stoppages, which can dwarf the cost of any social spend.

> The social aspects of projects must be managed in as systematic a manner as other elements of the business

Particularly in a downturn such as that recently experienced in the mining sector, a project can often find itself caught between:

- Rapidly rising costs/fluctuating commodity prices/funding issues

and

- The demands of different stakeholders:
  - Shareholders: demanding an improved return on investment
  - Communities: demanding an increased share of project benefits
  - Governments: demanding an increased share of revenues, while often passing responsibilities traditionally within their purview onto companies

Companies have often responded to this by cutting social spending across the board, as this has been perceived as merely discretionary spending rather than what is required to mitigate impacts, address risks and maximise value. Project managers have often questioned the necessity for essential social spending, instead asking, **'What's the minimum I have to do?'** This short-term thinking does not take account of the legacy and long-term issues and risks which can be created, which may not manifest themselves until during the operations phase of a project.

It is critical to look instead at all **social spending** within the context of a broader evaluation of **how a company or project minimises risk and maximises value**.

> Social issues are not an afterthought or sideline but integral to project success and maximising net present value

How to demonstrate the costs of getting it wrong, and the benefits of getting it right?

Costly social issues can manifest themselves on land access and resettlement projects due to a variety of factors, including:

- Inadequate early project planning
- Creation of unsustainable precedents in early planning/exploration stages
- Inadequate identification of stakeholders
- Poor stakeholder communication and/or inadequate negotiation and agreements
- Inadequate baseline data collection and/or analysis
- Ineffective communication between social and technical teams
- Unrealistic schedules and budgets
- Development of inappropriate solutions, e.g. related to housing or livelihoods
- Not meeting commitments or adhering to agreements made with communities

The cost of getting social wrong can clearly manifest itself in the following ways:

- Immediate protests on key issues by local stakeholders, leading to work stoppages during exploration, construction or operations

- Longer-term protest preventing project development completely, or leading to long-term closures during operation and inability to expand projects
- A legacy of mistrust leading to ongoing disputes and increased costs associated with ongoing engagement and security

The costs of these delays or stoppages will vary from project to project, but there are many examples where projects have been badly affected by social issues in recent times.

What is clear to natural resource companies is that, for example, a delay in exploration drilling of a week may cost thousands of dollars, a delay in project construction of a week may run to hundreds of thousands, while a significant delay in permitting may ultimately cost millions. Of course, all delays will affect production dates, while reputational damage can also have follow-on costs well beyond the project.

What is harder to articulate than the costs when things go wrong, is the benefits to the bottom line of social spend when things go right. Practitioners have often struggled with not just **how best to demonstrate to project planners the cost of getting it wrong** on a project, but also to demonstrate the **value created** by social spending.

As noted by the IFC (International Finance Corporation), not rigorously quantifying the value prevents social managers from:

- Understanding the true benefits of such social spend/investments
- Prioritising social spend
- Integrating social investment into core operational planning processes, impeding cross-functional synergies
- Communicating in a compelling manner to project planners and external stakeholders
- Formulating budget requests that match their needs

The issue of social investment as a mechanism both to minimise risks, as discussed above, and to maximise value to the project, is what the IFC has referred to as **value protection** and **value creation** (www.fvtool.com):

- **Value protection** refers to how much risk may be avoided or mitigated through what the IFC describe as 'Sustainability Investment Projects' (chiefly social spending on stakeholder engagement and community investments, but could also include land access and resettlement costs), by costing out the potential savings resulting from reduced frequency and intensity of negative events (e.g. delays in construction, disruptions in production, conflict, lawsuits, etc.).
- **Value creation** refers to the cost–benefit analysis of each intervention (e.g. value from building sound trust relationships with stakeholders; substituting expensive expatriates with local hires through a local training programme, etc.).

Value Protection (indirect)	**Value Protection (direct)**
The indirect risk mitigation potential of social spend • Value of avoiding costly delays disruptions, lawsuits • Value not readily calculated (e.g. investments in social cohesion, reputation, etc.)	The direct cost-benefit of social spend • Value from input savings or productivity rises • Values that can be readily calculated (e.g. local workforce training enables substituting ex-pats)

Source: Adapted from www.fvtool.com.

This focus on value creation in addition to value protection is similar to the **shared value** advocated by the Shared Value Initiative, a management strategy focused on companies creating measurable business value by identifying and addressing social problems that intersect with their business (www.sharedvalue.org).

The **IFC's FV (Financial Valuation) Tool for Sustainability Investments** seeks to help companies make the business case for strategic stakeholder engagement and community investments by quantifying their value, and can be readily applied in land access and resettlement planning and budgeting.

Specifically, it aims to answer three questions:

• What is the optimal portfolio of social initiatives for a given stage of project exploration, planning and operation?

• How large an economic return in terms of value of risk mitigated can be expected from such a portfolio?

• When is the ideal time-frame for making a specific intervention?

The FV Tool enables company social practitioners to communicate more effectively, and in more rigorous business terms, with company financial teams and corporate managers, and to provide some financial rationale for each intervention in terms of value protection and risk mitigation, as well as direct value creation.

The FV Tool is based on a range of traditional planning activities, such as stakeholder management, risk analysis, cost–benefit analysis and a review of existing and planned programmes. This book will not go into a detailed description of the tool, but sources for the IFC's FV Tool and user guides can be found at www.ifc.org.

Overall, the IFC reports that the FV Tool has shown that investments in land access activities can account for the majority share of value protection.

Demonstrating the value of effective land access planning

The IFC reports that, in terms of land access and resettlement, when **Newmont Mining Corporation** tested the FV Tool, they noted that land access and acquisition was a significant value driver. The company had worked on integrating social practitioners with engineers in a unified project team to plan land access and resettlement (which included the authors of this guide). Trust built in an earlier project paid off, with all learning from the first site applied at a second site. The engineering team worked closely with the social team, and phased construction started six months ahead of schedule. The savings in time and money were attributable to Newmont's reputation of being a fair land access and compensation negotiator. The financial benefits had not been clearly understood and quantified prior to the FV Tool exercise.

A strong correlation was also found between community relations and security spend: Newmont spends less than other mining companies in Ghana on security.

After four months working with the FV Tool, the Newmont controller was defending CSR spend to other managers.

The benefits for Newmont were that:

- They could cost out potential risk consequences (e.g. community unrest, blockades, lawsuits)
- The ability for social managers to articulate the direct value of their interventions and speak from a financial and risk perspective
- Allowed common discussion on land access and social investment approaches and budgets among multidisciplinary teams, preventing the 'silo' approach
- The Tool could assist in improving understanding of social investment's connection to financial drivers.

(www.fvtool.com)

While the FV Tool requires a period of concerted effort by a multidisciplinary team to examine all data related to the project, a project in development could quickly assess the likely risk mitigation potential of social spend by asking itself the following simple questions:

- What is my current social budget, as required to mitigate risks and maximise business benefits?
- What would be the cost to the project of:
  - A one-month delay in a project being permitted?
  - A one-week stoppage of a drill rig?
  - A one-month delay in commencing mine construction?
  - A one-day stoppage of operating mine production?

The social budget that needs to be considered will usually be the budget for any stakeholder engagement, land access and resettlement project activities, plus the annual community investment budget.

Any project can then **develop scenarios** to demonstrate the cost of social spending versus the cost to the project from not effectively addressing social issues.

It will quickly become clear in most cases that the costs of a one-week stoppage could be a considerable proportion of the social budget, which is considered sufficient to mitigate immediate impacts and lay the foundations for ongoing relations with stakeholders and the development of direct and indirect business benefits.

How else can the business case for stakeholder engagement and community investment be incorporated in project planning?

In addition to utilising the IFC's FV Tool, a host of other methodologies and tools may be utilised to focus social spend on the business case.

In terms of community investment, the **IFC's community investment guide** (IFC 2010b) discusses defining the case for community investment with a view to maximising **value creation** by:

- Identifying the company's broad business objectives and the steps necessary to reach them
- For each business objective, identifying the underlying business 'drivers' or 'benefits' that could be facilitated by community investment
- For each driver, considering how community investment could contribute
- Prioritising those areas where community investment is likely to make the biggest contribution to facilitating business strategy and objectives (e.g. skills training)
- Further developing the business case, based on estimated costs versus estimated value of community investment, in helping the company to achieve its specific business objectives

This is further discussed in Chapter 15 concerning community investment.

Other chapters of this book outline the risks at each stage of the land access and resettlement process which may result in significant costs, and the appropriate methodologies to follow to maximise **value protection and creation** throughout the process.

The business case: key considerations

Social spending must have a business case:

- Understand the social issues and risks from the earliest stages of the project
- Prioritise social spending to address key project impacts, risks and potential business benefits
- Involve social personnel in the overall project assessment and planning from day one
- Align social activities with the overall project schedule and milestones

Maximise the business benefits:

- Maximise the use of social budgets: look for opportunities to both minimise risks and maximise business benefits, e.g. spending on capacity-building to increase local hiring and procurement
- Leverage social spend through development of sustainable partnerships with local development actors

Apply more business rigour to social activities:

- The days of social being undertaken by nonexperts are long gone
- Treat social as a science, not an art
- Train social and other personnel to communicate in a common business language
- All social projects must have a clear scope, objective, work plan and schedule, budget and key performance indicators
- The social aspects of projects must be completely integrated with the overall project management, schedules and budgets
- Utilise financial valuation tools such as the IFC's FV Tool

Increase social awareness among project technical teams:

- Make the team understand that social is everyone's responsibility and can contribute to the bottom line
- Develop an appreciation that early project phases can build a solid or weak foundation
- Consider making social performance a bonus criteria for all senior managers, just as is common in the case of health and safety and environmental issues
- Consider disclosing social impact and mitigation information, just as health and safety and environmental data and key performance indicators are released

3

Best practice and institutional and legal frameworks

An important starting point when undertaking land access and resettlement is to fully understand the legislative framework, as well as relevant policies and standards. This chapter aims to provide practitioners with a clear understanding of what to consider, in particular giving project planners a better idea of which organisations have developed standards and what other useful guidance is available.

What are the key issues, challenges and risks?

In the context of the legal and best practice framework within which land access and resettlement occurs, projects face the following issues and challenges:

- There is an increase in legislation in some countries as well as a plethora of good practice standards and guidance being issued by a number of institutions
- With all the standards that have been developed, projects sometimes find it challenging to know which standards to apply; in addition, if there is a significant gap or difference between national legislation and standards, then projects need to determine how to address this, often in a situation where governments may resent or have concerns about the imposition of international standards on their countries
- While standards must be adhered to, they need to be applied in a practical way appropriate to each country and site, as a 'cookie-cutter' approach will not work

> The bar is being raised all the time

What are the guiding principles?

Key guiding principles to bear in mind include:

- **Compliance with laws and standards**: planning and implementation must be based on compliance with applicable laws, policies and standards
- **Think global/act local**, i.e. ensure compliance with standards but remember that, while not diminishing the level of compliance, you will need to tailor on-the-ground measures and solutions to take account of country- and project-specific conditions and circumstances

Are national regulatory requirements sufficient?

Most countries still have limited laws, with these often only dealing with some of the relevant issues, such as compensation, expropriation and building standards. Areas that are often poorly addressed include community engagement, livelihoods, and monitoring, evaluation and reporting.

However, countries are increasingly legislating on how land access and resettlement should be undertaken, for example India, Ghana and Indonesia. Nevertheless, requirements in many countries often still fall below good practice requirements set out in guidance such as the IFC's (International Finance Corporation) Performance Standards on Environmental and Social Sustainability. In addition, legislation often has more to say about what needs to be done, but not much about how it should be planned and actually undertaken.

> Mere compliance with national requirements typically does not enable a project to address key risks

What good practice standards and guidance are available?

A number of different institutions have developed standards and guidance documents on or related to land access and resettlement. These include the following:

- IFC (discussed in more detail below)
- World Bank (discussed in more detail below)
- Asian Development Bank: Safeguards Requirements 2 (ADB 2009: 44-54) and *Handbook on Resettlement: A Guide to Good Practice* (1998)

> There are a number of useful standards and guidance materials available to help optimise land access and resettlement performance

- Inter-American Development Bank: *Involuntary Resettlement: Operational Policy and Background Paper* (OP-710) (1998)
- African Development Bank: *Integrated Safeguards System*, Safeguard 2 (2013: 31-8)
- EBRD (European Bank for Reconstruction and Development) (discussed in more detail below)
- Japan Bank for International Co-operation: *Guidelines for Confirmation of Environmental and Social Considerations: Involuntary Resettlement* (2012)

These standards typically set a higher standard than national legislation. There is increasing convergence between the aforementioned standards, as updates are periodically developed.

International Finance Corporation

The IFC standards are applicable to private-sector clients of the IFC, but are generally regarded as the guiding standard in the natural resource and infrastructure sectors, with many companies committed to complying with them or having modelled their own corporate standards on them.

The IFC has a Sustainability Framework that consists of its Policy and eight Performance Standards on Environmental and Social Sustainability (IFC 2012), and its Access to Information Policy. Of particular relevance to land access and resettlement are the following:

- Performance Standard 1: Assessment and Stakeholder Engagement
- Performance Standard 5: Land Acquisition and Involuntary Resettlement
- Performance Standard 7: Indigenous Peoples
- Performance Standard 8: Cultural Heritage

This chapter does not discuss the Performance Standards in detail, as they are discussed in the other chapters that deal with specific aspects of the land access and resettlement process.

There are supporting **guidance notes** for each Performance Standard. In addition, the IFC has developed a series of **good practice documents** that are designed to help practitioners dealing with land access and resettlement and related issues. These include:

> The IFC standards provide a practical common sense approach for dealing with land access and resettlement

- *Doing Better Business Through Effective Public Consultation and Disclosure* (1998)
- *Investing in People: Sustainable Communities through Improved Business Practice—A Community Development Resource Guide for Companies* (2000)
- *Handbook for Preparing a Resettlement Action Plan* (2002)

- *Good Practice Note: Addressing the Social Dimensions of Private Sector Projects* (2003)
- *Stakeholder Engagement: A Good Practice Handbook for Companies Doing Business in Emerging Markets* (2007)
- *Working Together: How Large-Scale Mining Can Engage with Artisanal and Small-Scale Miners* (2008)
- *Addressing Grievances from Project-Affected Communities: Guidance for Projects and Companies on Designing Grievance Mechanisms (Good Practice Note)* (2009a)
- *Projects and People: A Handbook for Addressing Project-Induced In-Migration* (2009b)
- *Guide to Human Rights Impact Assessment and Management* (2010a)
- *Strategic Community Investment: A Good Practice Handbook for Companies Doing Business in Emerging Markets* (2010b)
- *A Guide to Getting Started in Local Procurement* (2011)
- *Cumulative Impact Assessment and Management: Guidance for the Private Sector in Emerging Markets* (2013a)
- *A Strategic Approach to Early Stakeholder Engagement: A Good Practice Handbook for Junior Companies in the Extractives Industries* (2013b)
- *Addressing Project Impacts on Fishing Based Livelihoods: A Good Practice Handbook—Baseline Assessment and Development of a Fisheries Livelihood Restoration Plan (Draft)* (2014)

For a comprehensive list of IFC guidance documents, see the *IFC Sustainability Resources Brochure 2013* (IFC 2013c), as well as www.commdev.org.

World Bank

World Bank policy in relation to non-private-sector projects is set out in:

- Operational Policy (OP) 4.12—Involuntary Resettlement (2001a)
- Bank Procedure (BP) 4.12—Involuntary Resettlement (2001b)

In addition, the World Bank has published a guidance book called *Involuntary Resettlement Source Book: Planning and Implementation in Development Projects* (2004).

The World Bank released a new draft environmental and social framework in 2014, including E&S Standard 5: Land Acquisition, Restrictions on Land Use and Involuntary Resettlement (World Bank 2014).

European Bank for Reconstruction and Development

The EBRD has put in place an Environmental and Social Policy (2008) and a set of ten Performance Requirements, including the following:

- Performance Requirement 1: Environmental and Social Appraisal and Management
- Performance Requirement 5: Land Acquisition, Involuntary Resettlement and Economic Displacement
- Performance Requirement 7: Indigenous Peoples
- Performance Requirement 8: Cultural Heritage
- Performance Requirement 10: Information Disclosure and Stakeholder Engagement

Commercial banks and the Equator Principles

The Equator Principles (www.equator-principles.com) are a financial industry benchmark for determining, assessing and managing social and environmental risk in project financing. The principles were adopted in June 2003 by ten of the world's leading financial institutions and, as of January 2014, 79 financial institutions had adopted the principles, covering over 70% of international project finance debt in emerging markets. The principles were updated in 2006 to align them with the IFC Performance Standards, and again in 2013.

Adopting institutions undertake not to loan to projects in which the borrower will not, or is unable to, comply with the environmental and social policies and processes outlined in the principles. In the case of non-designated countries, compliance is required with the IFC Performance Standards.

Industry organisations

There are a number of industry-wide organisations, with voluntary membership, designed to represent member interests and improve member performance in key areas, including social performance. In the extractive sector these organisations include:

- **IPIECA** (International Petroleum Industry Environmental and Conservation Association): IPIECA has approximately 36 member companies, comprising all six supermajors, seven national oil companies and 16 member associations, forming a network who represent over 400 oil and gas companies. Its members account for over half of the world's oil production.
- **ICMM** (International Council on Mining & Metals): the ICMM has approximately 21 company members and 33 member associations. Members operate at over 950 sites in approximately 59 countries.
- **PDAC** (Prospectors & Developers Association of Canada): PDAC represents the interests of the Canadian mineral exploration and development industry.

There are approximately **9,000** individual members and **1,254** corporate members. This is important given that the Toronto Stock Exchange (TSX) is the biggest source of junior mining finance in the world.

All of these organisations have developed guidance materials to help deal with social issues, including land access and resettlement.

Corporate policies and standards

Many or most private-sector companies in the extractives sector have formal policies or commitments on how they will deal with social issues, including land access and resettlement. With respect to land access and resettlement, these policies and commitments range from detailed formal policies, standards and procedures through to broad policy statements that reference a commitment to, for example, the IFC Performance Standards.

When are the various standards applicable?

Corporate standards will typically stipulate the scope of their application: for example, companies may limit their application to involuntary resettlement situations (as opposed to voluntary).

The IFC Performance Standards are applicable to private-sector clients of the IFC, but companies and projects may choose to make a formal commitment to their application (or to the application of other standards) even when they do not obtain IFC funding or other forms of IFC involvement. The supporting guidance notes are not mandatory, but do provide useful guidance.

Projects that obtain finance from Equator Principle signatory banks would have to comply with their standards (as would be the case where, for example, the African Development Bank, EBRD or Asian Development Bank provides finance to a project).

As mentioned previously, the IFC standards provide a practical common-sense approach for dealing with land access and resettlement, and are generally regarded as the guiding standard in the natural resource sector and a useful guide to the development of a comprehensive approach to land access and resettlement which can minimise risk and maximise benefits.

What are the key steps to consider?

Key steps to undertake early in the planning stage concerning legal frameworks and standards include:

- Identify and review all applicable laws, policies, standards and guidance
- Use the applicable laws, policies, standards and guidance to help develop the project's land access and resettlement objectives and guiding principles
- If the company lacks a formal land access and resettlement policy, develop one (as part of a broader social management system)
- Prepare a project policy framework as early as possible (for example, at pre-feasibility stage). These are variously called: an LARPF (land access and resettlement policy framework) or RPF (resettlement policy framework) where there is physical and economic displacement; and an LRF (livelihood restoration framework) where there is only economic displacement. An RPF should broadly identify objectives, principles, policies, procedures and organisational arrangements for dealing with land access and resettlement. Such frameworks are particularly useful in two situations:
  - **Pre-feasibility study and feasibility study stages**: particularly to help estimate the time-frame and cost of land acquisition and resettlement
  - **Where there are multiple project components**: if a project has subprojects or multiple components that cannot be identified before project approval or that may be implemented sequentially over an extended period, an RPF can ensure consistency of approach between components and phases. Projects must then prepare management plans, such as resettlement action plans, which are consistent with the RPF to cover each subproject or component.
- As soon as appropriate in the early planning stage, the project will need to develop a formal management plan (resettlement action plan or livelihood restoration plan) to deal with land access and resettlement. This needs to include an institutional and legal framework chapter (which would discuss applicable laws, policies and standards).
- The project needs to ensure that relevant people are capacity built to ensure they fully understand applicable laws, policies and standards. This should include not only project personnel directly involved in land access and resettlement, but also project management and other personnel involved in, for example, determining the project footprint and land take needs, as well as external stakeholders including project-affected persons and government as required.

Figure 3.1: Example of a 'gap analysis' template.

Land Access & Displacement Topic	Host Country Legislation	Corporate Standards	IFC Standards	Gap Analysis	Strategy
E.g. Entitlement Cut-off					
E.g. Livelihood Restoration					
Etc...					

What if there is a gap between national legislation and international standards and best practice?

Another key step that a project needs to undertake early on in the planning process is to determine if there are any gaps between national laws and applicable policies and standards, and what the strategy will be to address those gaps, as necessary. This process should necessarily involve early engagement with government. An example of a template for such a 'gap analysis' is shown in Figure 3.1.

Best practice and legal frameworks: key considerations

- No land access and resettlement planning or implementation should be undertaken without first developing explicit overall **objectives and guiding principles, based on applicable laws, policies and standards**.
- **The IFC standards provide common-sense guidance** on how to manage land access and resettlement. However, they, and other standards, **do not give you all the answers on the ground**.
- **Do not kid yourself about expropriation**: it typically is more complicated and risky, and will take longer than your lawyers may tell you.

4

Project planning and preparation

This chapter seeks to outline a logical framework for ensuring project teams are properly prepared for land access and resettlement projects. Subsequent chapters deal with some of the topics in this chapter in more detail. It is important that social considerations on projects are managed as professionally as any engineering or other aspect of a project, and indeed that social planning is fully integrated with the planning of engineers and managers of other aspects of the overall project, so that the entire team appreciates project requirements and time-scales, and the social issues, challenges, risks and opportunities.

It is fair to say that, traditionally, the planning of social aspects of projects was not always undertaken with adequate professional rigour due to a combination of under-resourcing and a reliance on non-specialist personnel. While planning and management of social aspects has a greater degree of uncertainty due to the human factors involved, good planning and management is still possible. It is therefore no longer acceptable for social aspects of projects to be planned in a haphazard and reactive manner that is disconnected from overall project planning, considering the key risks for all stakeholders when things go wrong.

Chapter 1 has already introduced the key components of the land access and resettlement process, as well as the key challenges, issues and risks. The key graphic illustrating the overall land access and resettlement process is reproduced in Figure 4.1. There is no way that one can apply a 'cookie cutter' or 'one size fits all' process to all land access and resettlement projects. However, there are certain basic planning processes and tools that can and should be used regardless of the project in question. These are discussed below.

Figure 4.1: The land access and resettlement process.

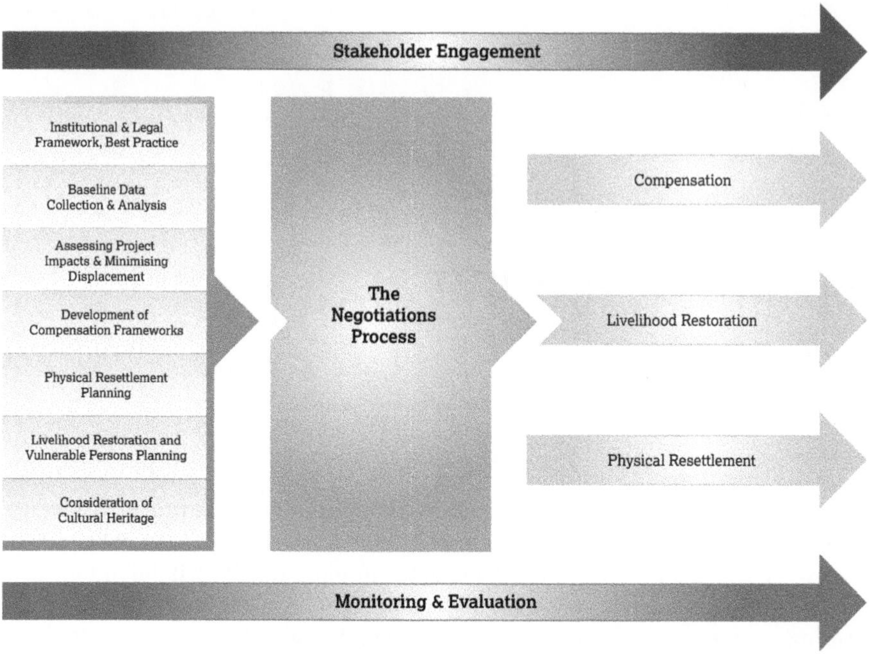

What are the objectives of land access and resettlement early planning and preparation?

The core objective of the overall process, from a project perspective, is to secure land access. However, this objective cannot be met unless **the process of planning land access and related resettlement is undertaken in a thorough and appropriate manner**. The risks of a badly managed resettlement can cause severe hardship for people, but also time, cost and reputational risk for the project.

More specifically, the objectives of early project planning are to:

- Ensure that all components of the land access and resettlement process will be well planned, including assessment, stakeholder engagement, implementation, and monitoring and evaluation

- Ensure that all relevant issues and risks are dealt with, and that the project can secure access to land in a timely manner and within budget

- Minimise land take to the extent possible and avoid, or at least minimise, displacement to the extent practically possible

- Ensure that displacement impacts will be addressed in a manner that meets legal requirements and relevant good practice standards

- Ensure that projects are properly resourced and funded

How to get started?

Important early planning steps include the following:

- Start planning as early as possible
- Plan and hold a kick-off meeting/workshop
- Review applicable laws, standards and practices
- Determine whether or not land transactions and resettlement are voluntary or involuntary
- Carry out a precedent/benchmarking review and identify key lessons (good and bad)
- Determine key guiding objectives and principles
- Determine project footprint and land take requirements (which must include buffer zones required for safety or other reasons where buffer zones will result in displacement of people)
- Review land take requirements and see how displacement of people can be avoided or minimised
- Make key planning assumptions
- Establish and resource the land access and resettlement team
- Establish a commitments/promises register or incorporate promises made into an existing site commitments register
- Prepare reporting formats
- Hold planning workshops and meetings as required (workshops can be particularly useful for bringing people from different project areas and disciplines together to discuss key topics)

 Project example

A project in Africa had previously conducted a successful land access and resettlement process, but realised that there was scope for improvement in the next phase of land access for a project expansion. Accordingly, it commissioned a benchmarking report to compare its performance with other projects internationally. It then conducted a lessons learned workshop to consider the good, the bad and the ugly of past practice, and to identify key areas for future improvement. Critically, the workshop was not only attended by members of the land access and resettlement team, but also external experts and members of the overall project planning team. This process of reflection and improvement enabled the project to successfully undertake two subsequent land take phases with a more planned and streamlined process, that resulted in improved measures to address livelihoods impacts and a reduced overall project time-line and cost compared with the first phase.

Key questions to consider at the outset

Important questions to ask yourself are:

- What is the location, type, nature and extent of the land access and resettlement process that needs to be planned?
- What is the level of planning: exploration, pre-feasibility study or bankable feasibility study?
- Is this a greenfield or brownfield project?
- Is this a life-of-project or phased land take?
- Is physical and/or economic displacement involved?
- Is there linear land take?
- What options are there for securing land access: involuntary or voluntary resettlement?
- Is a joint venture or government leading part of process?
- Are there any legacy issues?

> Understanding the type, nature and extent of the land access and resettlement required for a project is essential as this will help determine the type and extent of planning required

 Project example

On a project in Latin America, land access was required for a range of different facilities, including pipelines, roads and power lines. These facilities would extend over hundreds of kilometres, through different regions, provinces and geographical areas, from mountainous areas to the coast. The project therefore structured its land access and resettlement team to consist of a central management core and teams located along the linear routes across the regions. It was also realised that the magnitude of the land take meant that it was better to focus first on land take in areas where this was critical for the development of initial facilities as determined by the overall project development schedule, rather than trying to secure access to all land at once.

Ensuring a comprehensive approach

Land access and resettlement activities are **part of the larger social and environmental management strategy and system** that a project should establish to address risks and impacts. The management system should contain policies, social and environmental risk and impact assessment mechanisms, management plans/programmes, adequate organisational capacity, training, stakeholder engagement (internal and external), a grievance mechanism, reporting mechanisms, and monitoring and evaluation methods.

Depending on the project and its requirements and issues, management plans may consist of a series of specific plans: for example, to address stakeholder engagement; community health, safety and security; environmental impacts; land access/acquisition and resettlement; in-migration; artisanal/small-scale mining; building and crop speculation; indigenous people; cultural heritage; community development; and monitoring and evaluation.

The key point is that land access and resettlement planning and activities should not be considered in isolation from the broader project and other management areas and plans.

The land access and resettlement process needs to be **carefully aligned with the overall project schedule** and permitting process. It is therefore **important that project personnel involved in land access and resettlement planning are integrated into the overall project team**. Their involvement in overall site planning from an early stage will enhance efforts to avoid or minimise displacement by, for example, involving these personnel in decisions about where best to locate infrastructure and hence the extent and cost of the site land requirements.

Accordingly, land access and resettlement, site planning, exploration/geology, operations, community relations, external relations, legal and other relevant personnel must work closely together to ensure integrated and co-ordinated planning and implementation activities.

Where projects are part of a large corporation with multiple projects internationally, another issue to consider is how to ensure a suitably consistent approach and sharing of information, issues and tools across the group. Formation of a cross-group resettlement working group or similar type body can be a useful way to prevent projects working in silos, 'reinventing the wheel' and making the same mistakes.

A framework for undertaking resettlement planning is set out in Figure 4.2.

Figure 4.2: A framework for undertaking resettlement planning.

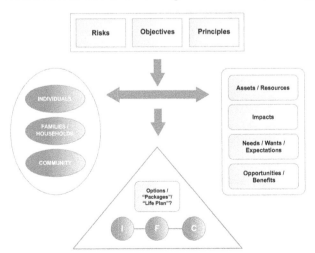

Project example

On project in Latin America, senior management realised the importance of early land access and resettlement planning for project success, so put in place a team to address this from the scoping stage. Overall project planners and the land access and resettlement team worked closely from very early on to find ways to minimise land take and displacement. As early as the pre-feasibility study stage, it became clear that this collaboration had saved potentially millions of dollars in compensation costs, with several project facilities being moved from their originally envisaged locations.

 Project example

On a project in Africa, overall project management sometimes deliberately kept land access and resettlement planners out of overall project discussions on the location of project facilities. This was because there was a perception that they were overestimating the land access challenge. As a result, there was not full alignment on project land take requirements. When project development commenced, the construction team moved into some areas farmed by communities without any community consultation or compensation. This caused major problems with community members. It also subsequently transpired that an important project facility was slated to be built on an area with dense cropping, and hence high compensation costs, when it would have been possible to move the facility and reduce displacement issues considerably. All of this could have been easily avoided by a more integrated approach to project planning.

> Land access and resettlement must be carefully and systematically planned from an early stage, with the informed and active participation of internal and external stakeholders

What are the key components of early project planning?

Key components to be considered at the outset include:

- Structuring and resourcing the team
- Developing a work plan and schedule
- Developing cost estimates and budgets

- Developing scenarios
- Assessment of project impacts, risks and opportunities
- Information management
- Development of planning assumptions and parameters
- Development of a policy framework
- Development of management plans
- Avoidance and minimisation of displacement
- Consideration of early stage land access approaches
- Consideration of legacy issues
- Life-of-project versus phased land takes
- Determining draft compensation packages
- Early and appropriate involvement of stakeholders
- Planning for financing
- Planning for external review
- Planning for processes managed by third parties
- Dealing with multiple languages

These key components are discussed in turn briefly below, with key components expanded on in later chapters.

Structuring and resourcing the team

The land access and resettlement team needs to be made up of suitably skilled and experienced personnel, and the team should be led by a senior person dedicated full time to the role. A variety of skills are required to deal with the various tasks involved in land access and resettlement, including project management; stakeholder engagement (consultation and negotiation); database establishment, data collection and analysis; impact, risk and opportunity assessment; physical and urban planning, engineering and architectural; livelihood restoration and improvement/alternative livelihoods; community development; plan and report writing; legal and financial; and construction and logistical skills.

> Social should not be a dumping ground for people who do not fit in elsewhere in the project team

Given the variety of skills and personnel required to plan and implement land access and resettlement, and the need for such people to work closely together and interact consistently with outside stakeholders, it is fundamentally important that the various staff, consultants and contractors work together as one integrated team, with clearly defined roles and responsibilities, and under the overall supervision of one designated manager.

Factors that require careful consideration when deciding on the make-up of the team is the balance between:

Figure 4.3: Structuring the team.

- **National and expatriate personnel**: there is sometimes the perception that expatriates are softer. There is also sometimes the perception that expatriates are less understanding and perceptive, but this is not always the case when it comes to a comparison between expatriates and nationals from the capital city. Expatriates are naturally typically less attuned to local conditions, but they may also be better able to be objective and more strategic.
- **Local staff and other nationals from elsewhere in the country**: there is sometimes the fear or risk that when local staff form part of the main project negotiating team, due to their links to impacted people, there is a risk of the project's strategy being divulged. On the other hand it is also sometimes the case that nationals from elsewhere, for example 'the big city', are perceived as being arrogant and insensitive to local customs and requirements.

Each project will have different circumstances and considerations, but it is the authors' experience that the project team should have an appropriate mix of national and expatriate personnel (but this mix may evolve over time). The more important issue is whether people have requisite skills and experience: this may require capacity-building.

An example of a resettlement project organisational chart is set out in Figure 4.4.

Figure 4.4: A resettlement project organisational chart.

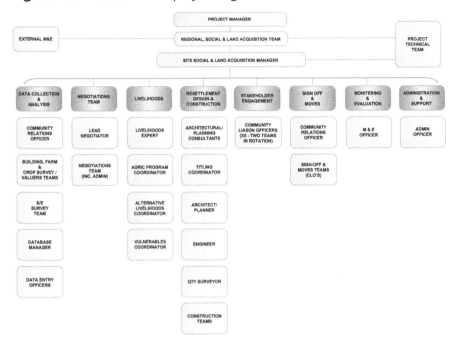

👍 Project example

On a project in Eastern Europe, some of the communities in question were conservative and therefore limited the scope for interaction between project personnel and women in the community. In order to ensure that women were adequately involved in the engagement process, the project ensured that the community relations and land access team included women who could deal directly with the affected women, included holding regular meetings separately.

A key concern of investors and lenders when looking at a project is what is the commitment and capacity of the management team to deliver, and do they have the budget and resources to do it right

Work plan and schedule

A detailed work plan and schedule is a necessary tool to manage the land access and resettlement process (planning and implementation) as projects often under-estimate the time required and are then forced to either delay the overall project or attempt risky and dangerous short cuts. Estimating the duration of the different components of the process is typically not easy, but doing this early on (with subsequent updates) is useful in order to ensure that the project is being realistic and that the land access and resettlement time-line and overall project schedule are aligned.

Project planners should prepare and regularly update a land access and reset-tlement work plan and schedule, bearing in mind the following:

- Pre-feasibility and feasibility studies must include an appropriate level land access and resettlement work plan and schedule

- It is useful in early stage planning to develop base, best- and worst-case options (this is because land access and resettlement can take longer than originally anticipated due to third-party actions)

- It is critical to ensure that the land access and resettlement work plan and schedule are fully integrated into the overall project schedule and linked to the key milestones therein

- It is important to take account of the political situation when planning: it may be advisable to avoid resettlement negotiations or physical moves immediately prior to or after political elections or during other significant events, such as religious holidays or crop-planting seasons.

 Project example

The resettlement team at a mining project in Eastern Europe estimated how long was necessary to thoroughly undertake the land access and resettlement process. However, corporate management informed them that the company was solely reliant on this project and that they had already promised the board of directors, shareholders and the market that land access would be completed and mine construction started by a certain date. Therefore the resettlement team was told to ignore its original schedule and fast-track the process. The project was unable to secure land access in the time-frame demanded by the company.

Cost estimates and budgets

The cost of land access and resettlement is commonly underestimated during the early stages of a project. This is mainly due to the absence of complete infor-mation on the scale of project impacts and inexperienced teams preparing the budgets. Costs such as resettlement site earthworks and the cost of livelihood restoration are commonly underestimated.

Prepare and regularly update cost estimates/budgets (and cash flow estimate), bearing in mind the following:

- Pre-feasibility and feasibility studies must include an appropriate level land access and resettlement budget and cash flow forecast
- It is useful to develop base, best- and worst-case options (this is because land access and resettlement can take longer than originally anticipated due to third-party actions)
- During preliminary planning prior to discussions on resettlement packages with people that will be displaced, it is useful to develop multiple scenarios that are based on different levels of compensation or assistance offered for the key components that make up resettlement packages

 Project example

During the feasibility study for a mining project in Eastern Europe, the community relations team developed a cost estimate for undertaking required land access and resettlement. Despite the team advising that the necessary land take could not be secured for a lesser amount, the feasibility study team decided to significantly lower the estimated land access and resettlement cost included in the feasibility study sent to the board of directors for approval. The comment made at the time was that if a higher amount was included in the cost estimate, then this would threaten the ability of the project to meet the necessary economic hurdle rate for project approval. The board approved the project, but later queried why land access and resettlement costs were significantly higher than the approved budget.

Scenarios

Planning must not only shape a preferred course and plan for this, but, to the extent possible, also consider and plan for alternative scenarios. The project should brainstorm a range of potential scenarios that might arise.

No matter how well a project plans, communities and governments will have their own views, agendas and approach, and a variety of issues may arise that require a review and modification of the project's approach

Project example

On a project in Asia, it was immediately apparent that project development would require very significant land access and resettlement. Even though the project was only at scoping stage, management realised that it was critical to obtain at least an accurate initial high-level estimate of the work required, schedule and cost of such an exercise. Working with project personnel, and using satellite imagery and other existing data, consultants were able to develop work plans, schedules and cost estimates for a number of scenarios (base, best and worst case).

Assessment

Identification and assessment/analysis of impacts, stakeholders, risks and opportunities are very important early steps in any land access and resettlement planning process. While this topic is discussed in more detail in Chapter 7, suffice it to say here that planning that is not based on a thorough assessment process will be in danger of not being grounded in the local and national context and reality.

A useful tool to develop at the early planning stage is an impact and packages matrix (referred to as an entitlement matrix when discussed further in Chapter 8). This allows a project to consider the potential impacts on various stakeholders and assets, and brainstorm potential compensation approaches. An example template is shown in Figure 4.5 (another example is contained in Chapter 8).

Information management

Planning without an adequate database or IMS (information management system) will be much more challenging. While this topic is dealt with in more detail in Chapter 6, it is worth noting that the land access and resettlement team needs an IMS that is established early, is set up with a life-of-project perspective, forms part of the broader social IMS and the broader overall project IMS, and is a tool to help undertake integrated project planning.

The IMS should be able to:

- Operate locally with limited external support, and be capable of evolution and tailoring to meet the requirement of the specific project
- Store and analyse baseline data (with geo-referencing)
- Determine and record individual, household and community impacts and compensation and assistance entitlements
- Enable the running of different planning scenarios (time and cost) based on adjustments to the land take and mix of affected people and assets
- Produce and store sign-off forms related to choices made by impacted persons, payments, moves and handover

Figure 4.5: An impact and packages matrix.

Type of Impact/Loss	Types of Mitigation	Category of PAP	Compensation Package	Eligibility Rules	Key Planning Assumptions
LOSS OF LAND (DEPRIVATION OF USE DUE TO PHYSICAL DISPLACEMENT					
Permanent Loss of Urban Land					
Permanent Loss of Agricultural and Grazing Land (including fallow land)					
Temporary Land Loss (e.g. land required for drilling sites)					
LOSS OF LIVELIHOODS (DUE TO ECONOMIC DISPLACEMENT)					
Farming					
Use of other natural resources (sand/wood etc.)					
Fishing					
Commercial Enterprises					
Employees of Businesses					
Artisanal and Small Scale Miners					
Loss of Rental Income on Residential & Commercial Buildings					
LOSS OF STRUCTURES/BUILDINGS (ONLY IMMOVABLE STRUCTURES IMPACTED BY PHYSICAL DISPLACEMENT					
Houses (Primary Residences)					
Secondary Houses/Farmsteads (not a Primary Residence)					
Residential Annexes/Other Private Structures (including fences and storage sheds)					
Worship Buildings e.g. Churches					
Commercial Buildings					
Fish Ponds					
Public/Institutional Buildings					
Incomplete Structures					
Abandoned/Ruined Structures					

Type of Impact/Loss	Types of Mitigation	Category of PAP	Compensation Package	Eligibility Rules	Key Planning Assumptions
LOSS OF INFASTRUCTURE (IMPACTED BY PHYSICAL DISPLACEMENT)					
Water Facilities					
Electrical Facilities					
Roads & Drainage					
Sanitation Facilities					
LOSS OF ACCESS (IMPACTED BY PHYSICAL DISPLACEMENT AND/OR DEPRIVATION OF USE)					
Watercourses and Water sources/ River diversions					
Forests					
Roads & Pathways					
LOSS OF CULTURAL HERITAGE (IMPACTED BY PHYSICAL DISPLACEMENT AND/OR DEPRIVATION OF USE					
Graves/Cemeteries					
Shrines					
OTHER COMPONENTS					
Vulnerable Persons					
Tenants					
Re-establishment Allowance					
Transportation, Loading & Unloading Assistance for people and their possessions					
Social Disarticulation (Social capital lost through dismantling or debilitation of networks)					
Land Tenure					
Benefit Sharinh					
Bonuses					
Other Assistance					

- Track the overall process of paying and moving affected people and the re-establishment of their livelihoods
- Manage a grievance procedure
- Store stakeholder engagement records
- Provide regular analysis and reports on progress in land access and resettlement implementation, including monitoring and evaluation

 Project example

A large international mining company recognised the need for a high-level IMS to manage a large and complex land access and resettlement exercise. However, the system developed by an external contractor proved to be expensive to maintain, and complicated to evolve and tailor to the requirements of the project in question. More worryingly, it was prone to crashing when required to handle actual compensation payments to project-affected persons. This required the project to run a simple Excel-based database in parallel in order to enable payments to be processed for irate community members.

Planning assumptions and parameters

In order to be able to carry out required planning activities, including accurate scheduling and budgeting, it is important to make certain key planning assumptions, with these being reviewed and updated periodically, as appropriate.

These may include:

- Area of land take required
- Number of displaced people, households and communities (those physically displaced, and those only economically displaced)
- Number of buildings and structures to be physically displaced (with estimates of the number of residential and other types of building or structure)
- Number of rooms and area of buildings and structures to be physically displaced
- Extent of infrastructure and institutional facilities physically displaced and to be provided at resettlement sites
- Area of cropped land (including fallow land) and economic trees to be physically displaced
- Extent of economic displacement

Even at very early assessment and planning stages, such as the pre-feasibility study level, best possible estimates and assumptions should be made in order to enable informed planning and decision-making.

Policy framework

As referred to in Chapter 3, early preparation of an overarching policy framework is important to guide planning activities.

Such frameworks are particularly useful in two situations:

- **Pre-feasibility study and feasibility study stages**: particularly to help estimate the time-frame and cost of land acquisition and resettlement
- **Where there are multiple project components**: if a project has subprojects or multiple components that cannot be identified before project approval or that may be implemented sequentially over an extended period, an RPF (resettlement policy framework) can ensure consistency of approach between components and phases. Projects must then prepare management plans, such as resettlement action plans, which are consistent with the RPF to cover each subproject or component.

The policy framework should broadly identify objectives, principles, policies, procedures and organisational arrangements for dealing with land access and resettlement.

Management plans

Depending on the type of displacement that will be caused by land access, and whether the project has multiple components, different types of management plan may need to be prepared. For example, a **RAP (resettlement action plan)** where there is physical and economic displacement, and an **LRP (livelihood restoration plan)** where there will only be economic displacement.

The applicable management plan (RAP or LRP) is a document in which the project sets out a comprehensive plan to address physical and/or economic displacement of project-affected persons. The management plan must specify the policies the project will adhere to, the procedures that it will follow and the actions that it will take to mitigate adverse impacts, compensate losses and provide development benefits to persons and communities displaced by the project. No displacement of people should occur until the management plan has been finalised, agreed, disclosed and implemented. An example of an outline of a RAP is shown in Figure 4.6.

The preparation of a RAP or LRP should take place through a number of stages that are linked to the overall project development process, along the lines shown in Figure 4.7.

Projects should also have overarching SEPs (stakeholder engagement plans) that plan for co-ordinated project-wide engagement with stakeholders. Within the broad context of the SEP, the RAP or LRP would have a chapter setting out the land access and resettlement-specific related engagement process.

> Plans should be developed early in the overall project planning cycle, ideally starting with draft plans during the pre-feasibility stage, with progressive updating and development thereafter

Figure 4.6: An example RAP outline.

Glossary of Terms
Acronyms and Abbreviations
Preamble
Proponent's Commitment
Executive Summary

1	**Introduction**		**8**	**Relocation and Compensation Packages**
1.1	Purpose of this Document		8.1	IFC Guidance & Country Requirements
1.2	Project Description		8.2	Eligibility and Packages
1.3	Objectives and Principles			
			9	**Livelihood Restoration**
2	**Legal and Policy Framework**		9.1	IFC Guidance & Country Requirements
2.1	International Best Practice		9.2	Key Challenges & Considerations
2.2	Country Institutional Framework		9.3	Key Principles & Objectives
2.3	Country Legal Framework		9.4	Packages
2.4	Land Titling and Registration		9.5	Host communities
2.5	International Standards and Guidance			
2.6	Corporate Policies		**10**	**Temporary Hardship & Vulnerable Households**
2.7	Comparative Analysis of National Laws & IFC Standards		10.1	IFC Guidance & Country Requirements
			10.2	Defining Vulnerability
3	**Baseline Data Collection and Analysis**		10.3	Project Responsibilities
3.1	International Best Practice		10.4	Identifying Vulnerable People
3.2	Baseline Data Collection		10.5	Management of Vulnerability
3.3	Analysis of Baseline Data			
3.4	Thematic Mapping and Survey Analyses		**11**	**Protection of Cultural Heritage**
			11.1	IFC Guidance & Country Requirements
4	**Project Impacts**		11.2	Cultural Context and Ethnicity
4.1	IFC Guidance & Country Requirements		11.3	Assessment of Cultural Heritage
4.2	Physical Impact of the Project		11.4	Cultural Heritage Management Plan
4.3	Identifying Project Impacts			
4.4	Project-Affected Households		**12**	**Management of Resettlement Grievances**
4.5	Project-Affected Public Facilities		12.1	IFC Guidance & Country Requirements
4.6	Project-Affected Public Access		12.2	Grievance Mechanism
4.7	Efforts to Minimize Project Impacts		12.3	Scope of Grievance Mechanism
4.8	Closure and Rehabilitation		12.4	Processing Grievances
			12.5	Assistance to Vulnerable Persons
5	**Consultation and Disclosure**		12.6	Transparency and Confidentiality
5.1	IFC Guidance & Country Requirements		12.7	Monitoring
5.2	Purpose & Objectives of Stakeholder Engagement			
5.3	Approach to Stakeholder Engagement		**13**	**Organizational Framework**
5.4	Stakeholder Identification, Analysis & Overview		13.1	IFC Guidance & Country Requirements
5.5	Stakeholder Engagement to Date		13.2	Land Access & Resettlement Team Structure
5.6	Planned Resettlement Engagement Activities		13.3	Roles & Responsibilities
			13.4	Community Involvement
6	**Compensation Framework**		13.5	Government Involvement
6.1	IFC Guidance & Country Requirements		13.6	Resettlement Committees and Forums
6.2	Key Considerations			
6.3	The Total Value Proposition		**14**	**Monitoring and Evaluation**
6.4	Valuation Methodologies		14.1	IFC Guidance & Country Requirements
6.5	Eligibility and Entitlements		14.2	Key Performance Indicators
			14.3	Internal M&E Process
7	**Resettlement Packages**		14.4	External M&E Process
7.1	IFC Guidance & Country Requirements		14.5	Community Involvement
7.2	Resettlement Sites		14.6	Reporting
7.3	Resettlement Housing and Other Structures			
7.4	Resettlement Lots		**15**	**RAP Budget and Implementation Schedule**
7.5	Public Buildings		15.1	IFC Guidance & Country Requirements
7.6	Churches		15.2	Parameters and Assumptions
7.7	Government Buildings		15.3	Budget Summary
7.8	Businesses		15.4	Project Schedule
7.9	Other Measures			
7.10	Construction, Handover & Maintenance			
7.11	Host Communities			

In addition to the above (both of which will eventually become public documents), preparation of a **negotiation plan** is strongly recommended. The critical difference between a negotiation plan and the other plans is that it would remain a confidential internal project document, containing the project's strategy, tactics and arrangements for reaching agreement with project-affected persons. An example of a negotiation plan outline is shown in Figure 4.8.

Figure 4.7: Preparation stages for a RAP or LRP.

Project Development Stages	RAP/LAP Preparation Stages
Pre-feasability	- Land access and resettlement Scoping and Preparation of Policy Framework (and/or draft Pre-negotiations RAP/LRP [First Version])
Feasability	- Preparation of updated Policy Framework (and draft Pre-negotiation Plan [First or Second Version])
Design, Permitting and Development	- Preparation of Detailed RAP/LRP (For negotiation, finalisation, implementation and disclosure) - Implementation of RAP/LRP and Monitering and Evaluation thereof
Operations	- Monitering and Evaluation of RAP/LRP

Figure 4.8: A negotiation plan outline.

1. Introduction
2. Negotiation participants
3. Negotiation phases and topics
4. Lessons learned, important points to remember and guiding principles
5. Key considerations and questions
6. Critical and noncritical issues
7. Approach to negotiations
8. Proposed negotiations agenda
9. Project negotiating team
10. Project opening, fallback and final positions
11. Preparations and steps for setting the scene
12. Procedural issues
13. Information sharing and capacity-building measures
14. Negotiating style
15. Scenarios
16. Negotiation work plan and schedule
17. Conclusion

 Project example

On a project in Latin America, the company chose to manage the land access and resettlement elements of the process separately. As a result, initial land access discussions with individual landowners was given to a separate team of lawyers to handle, and this process commenced without the development of an overarching RAP (resettlement action plan) or co-ordinated negotiation plan. The consequence was that different landowners were paid different rates of compensation for the same types of land, and people were very unhappy when they discovered this, with some refusing to move even though they had already been paid compensation. Furthermore, some of the impacts of displacement were not dealt with by the legal team, e.g. livelihood restoration and tenants. Subsequently, the land access process became bogged down. After a review of status, management decided to involve the community relations team more closely in the process, and to develop an overarching RAP to plan and undertake the process in a more structured and co-ordinated manner.

Avoidance and minimisation

The project must investigate site design options and take every practically feasible step and measure to minimise displacement of people. A written report setting out the investigations conducted, options considered and measures taken to avoid and minimise displacement should be prepared and approved as part of the early planning process and prior to commencement of any land acquisition and resettlement. Measures to minimise land access and speculative activities are discussed in detail in Chapter 7.

It is useful to remember that avoiding land take may not avoid the need for resettlement, e.g. leaving people *in situ* may not be possible due to other project impacts

Early stage land access

Policies, systems and personnel may not always be in place to undertake early stage land access in a manner that takes account of longer-term project considerations—the rush to secure access can pose future problems for the project, for example with inappropriate compensation being paid and a legacy of mistrust/bad precedents being set.

Projects need to carefully consider the needs for early stage land access and ensure that where at all possible these are planned within the overall project framework and policies.

It is critical to deal with social issues properly from day one as precedents (good or bad) are set that can pose a challenge for the remainder of the project

 Project example

On a project in Latin America, project management failed to clarify guiding objectives and principles for early stage land access. As a result, field geologists fast-tracked initial land access by paying high levels of compensation, failing to take into account the implications of paying such rates for the wider future land take. It later became clear that, when these compensation rates were extrapolated to later project stages, the cost of land access was going to be significantly higher than originally anticipated or necessary. Early preparation of a land access and resettlement policy framework could have helped to avoid this situation.

Legacy issues

Two situations may arise:

- The project proponent may acquire a brownfield site where past land access and resettlement activities were undertaken badly, leaving a legacy of unaddressed impacts and risks and mistrust among communities and other external stakeholders
- Personnel responsible for securing land access and dealing with resettlement may join a project where the process has been ongoing for some time, such as due to a change of personnel, mergers or acquisitions

In these cases, early planning will need to include a review of activities already undertaken by the project in order to ensure they have been done adequately. This may identify the need for retroactive measures to rectify shortfalls, and could entail putting in place measures at a later stage of the process than would normally be the case where this is necessary and possible.

Life-of-project versus phased land takes

Projects that will be developed in different phases over a long period sometimes face a dilemma about whether to acquire all land required for the the life of the project or only for the initial phase. A variety of sometimes contradictory factors and risks need to be considered, including:

- The large upfront cost of acquiring all land versus a higher overall long-term land cost
- The danger of crop, building and other forms of costly speculation if land is not secured early
- The logistical challenges of handling all land access and resettlement at once

 Project example

On a project in Africa the overall project planning team and the land access and resettlement team identified a land area required for a mine expansion. Despite the obvious imminent need for the whole parcel of land in question, the project decided, for financial reasons, to only acquire the piece immediately necessary, taking the view that the balance could be acquired shortly. When the project turned its attention to acquiring the balance of the land a few months later, it transpired that community members and outsiders had used the intervening period to speculate by building a significant number of buildings and planting new crops. This pushed up the cost of accessing this land quite significantly.

- The business risk of building the initial phases of a project but failing to secure land for subsequent phases when the business model and return on investment are ultimately premised on a larger project

Each project will have to consider this based on its particular circumstances and this issue is discussed in more detail in Chapter 7.

Determining packages

This topic is discussed in more detail in Chapter 8. What can be noted here is that the type, nature and extent of compensation measures and other types of assistance and benefit that are provided by a project will depend on the various factors and issues discussed above, such as the types of displacement impact caused, applicable national requirements, applicable standards, benchmarking of other projects, precedents set, the prevailing political context, the respective bargaining positions and negotiating abilities of the parties, and the urgency of when the project requires access to land.

How to appropriately involve external stakeholders

Land access and resettlement is different from a number of other overall project activities in the sense that it cannot simply be planned internally, but requires the active involvement of relevant third parties, in particular affected communities and local government agencies. While third-party involvement is necessary, the timing and extent of this involvement needs to be carefully managed, especially at the early planning stage:

- During the scoping, pre-feasibility study and bankable feasibility study stages of a project most, if not all, planning will take place internally
- Even when third parties are involved, elements of the planning process will necessarily have to remain confidential to project personnel
- While the objective is for different parties to work closely together, they will have their own objectives and agendas and will often not simply be planning together in a neutral manner, but rather engaging in a challenging process of negotiation

It is useful to make a distinction between:

- Early stage project planning before negotiations with communities occur: here most of the planning will be internal

> Based on its particular circumstances, each project will need to determine the appropriate level of community involvement in the planning process, bearing in mind the balance between confidentiality, applicable legal and standard requirements, and the need to involve communities in planning their future as much as possible

- Planning during and after the negotiation process: here communities and other third parties will be far more involved

Ultimately, land access and resettlement cannot be planned solely by the project proponent. Packages and outcomes should be negotiated with affected people.

Stakeholder engagement is discussed in more detail in Chapters 5 and 12.

 Project example

On a project in Africa the Company was keen to engage with the affected communities as much as possible. However, they also needed to prevent the sort of speculation on project lands which had occurred on neighbouring projects in anticipation of benefits. Therefore the Company had to balance the need to be as transparent as possible with the need to keep the project cut-off date as confidential as possible. When the project entitlement cut-off date was announced, and surveys of the area began, a communication plan was rolled out, explaining to traditional leaders and communities the need for confidentiality to protect the projects viability and ensure benefits would only accrue to genuinely affected people. This was accepted by the communities.

Planning for financing

Commercial banks that provide project finance typically have social and environmental standards with which they require compliance—many commercial banks are Equator Principle signatories. The process of engaging with lending institutions, such as the IFC (International Finance Corporation), European Bank for Reconstruction and Development and commercial banks, often takes longer than project proponents envisage.

With respect to land access and resettlement, as with other social and environmental components, lenders will likely require that management plans and other elements planned by the project proponent are reviewed by their own or other

 Project example

On a project in Eastern Europe, management was confident that it could obtain commercial bank finance without getting bogged down in a lengthy process of interaction about how it would handle environmental and social impacts of the project. Accordingly, the overall schedule for developing the project did not adequately take account of the process and time required to engage with bank social experts and modify management plans, including the resettlement action plan, to meet their requirements before any funds would be released.

external experts. Therefore, the planning process, work plan and schedule need to provide time for engagement with lenders (bearing in mind that this will typically involve a negotiation process of its own).

Planning for external review

Given the magnitude of the land access and resettlement challenge, it is increasingly common for projects to be reviewed by external experts hired directly by the project proponent, in addition to external review by lending institutions. Often the idea is that the external reviewer hired by the project will help to ensure not only that land access and resettlement planning is being undertaken appropriately by the designated team, but that the project is ready for discussions with the lender.

External review can be undertaken in a variety of forms, such as by an individual expert or a review panel consisting of two or more experts. Depending on the terms of reference, the role of the external reviewer/panel may have a different emphasis, such as a 'hands off' review, or a review function incorporating participation with the land access and resettlement team in discussing and planning for particular issues and events.

It is important to insist that external reviewers understand that their role is not merely to 'helicopter in' to the project site periodically to tell people what they are doing wrong. The process should also provide practical advice on potential steps and actions worth taking by the project.

 Project example

On a project in Latin America, the company decided to put in place two types of external review related to the land access and resettlement process: an internal panel of experts and an external panel. Depending on the topics in question, the two panels would meet with the on-site land access and resettlement team either separately or together.

Processes managed by third parties

Land access for a project, and related resettlement, is sometimes managed by government or a joint-venture partner. Where this is not a legal requirement, it is sometimes considered advantageous by a project proponent to allow someone else to worry about the land access and resettlement challenge. However, solely relying on someone else is often dangerous, particularly where their standards and capacity are low or limited. At the end of the day, if something goes wrong the problem and related risks will rest with the project.

Where land access and resettlement are the responsibility of government, the IFC advises that:

- The project will collaborate with the responsible government agency to the extent permitted
- Where government capacity is limited, the project will play an active role during planning, implementation and monitoring
- Where the measures envisaged by the government will not meet IFC or applicable corporate standards, the project should prepare a **supplemental resettlement action plan** (where there is physical displacement) and an **environmental and social action plan** (where there will only be economic displacement)

Where processes are managed by third parties, projects should consider specific staff with a focus on government and/or partner relations, who can champion the business case for appropriate standards and interventions from the earliest stages of the project.

An initial social due diligence should be undertaken at the outset of any joint venture (with companies or government) which should identify potential issues in the partner addressing all non-technical risks, particularly in relation to land access, and potential strategies which should be developed to address these potential gaps.

The project should then consider development of a **specific partner engagement strategy**, which needs to accomplish the following with the partner:

- An agreed approach to engagement between the key partners involved
- An appreciation of a project proponent's commitment to international and corporate standards
- A real understanding of the business case for following these standards and why it makes economic sense for the project, and will be quicker in the long run
- An understanding of how gaps in national legislation or traditional approaches can be met, and who will be responsible for this
- An outline of the supplementary actions that may be devised by the project proponent, if possible in partnership, to address these gaps
- An agreed organisational structure which allows shared oversight, planning and implementation of social management and mitigation efforts
- How community expectations will be managed and how supplementary actions will be presented so as not to create unwanted precedents for government
- Means of joint management, and monitoring and evaluation of agreed actions

The key aspect of the above approach would be the ability to persuade partners of the business case for adhering to international best practice and standards.

Languages

Extractive sector and infrastructure projects often take place in locations and with teams where different languages need to be used to interact with local and national stakeholders, as well as corporate offices and financial institutions. The reality often is that it is therefore not possible to conduct all project business in one language. From a planning perspective, this necessitates ensuring that the project has personnel with adequate language skills, and/or that translators are available who can ensure that verbal and written communications and records accurately reflect what is being discussed, done and agreed in the relevant languages.

 Project example

A project in Africa was being developed by a company with a predominantly English-speaking corporate management team. However, local communities spoke a number of different languages, while French was the main language used for commerce and government business. It was agreed to conduct negotiations primarily in French, with translators available at all times to translate into other languages as necessary. All resettlement committee proceedings were audio-recorded, and summary meeting minutes prepared and signed at the next meeting by the chairperson, as well as community, project and government representatives. It was agreed that meeting minutes constituted an acceptable record of agreements reached, with a final overall agreement being signed during a formal closing ceremony, followed by the updating and disclosure of the resettlement action plan.

Project planning and preparation: key considerations

- **Start planning early** as you will need the time
- **Do things properly from day one**: plan social and land access management as professionally as any other aspect of the project
- **Integrate schedules** for land access and resettlement with broader project schedules
- Use an **experienced, skilled and adequately resourced team**, integrated with the overall project team
- No land access and resettlement planning should be undertaken without first **developing explicit overall objectives and guiding principles**

- Before you commence planning, **reflect on the lessons learned on other projects** and during your earlier project phases
- **There is no quick fix and there are no short cuts**
- Prepare **realistic schedules and cost estimates** during the early project stages
- **Integrate** land access, resettlement, broader community development and overall project planning
- **Avoid and minimise displacement** to the extent possible, but have a life-of-project land take perspective
- **Show sensitivity** to local cultural norms
- **Avoid unaffordable precedents**
- Consider the **hidden costs of project delays** when making decisions
- Try to develop a project plan based on **alternative scenarios** so you have flexibility
- Resettlement practitioners need to get better at **showing the business case** for doing it right
- Plan thoroughly, but accept that some **flexibility** may be necessary in the process

5
Stakeholder engagement

This chapter deals with the broad topic of stakeholder engagement. This is a wide subject area, and so discussion of stakeholder engagement in this book is necessarily brief, and concerned specifically with how stakeholder engagement relates to the land access and resettlement process.

Chapter 12 deals specifically with the negotiation process as it pertains to land access and resettlement.

Literature and training courses on stakeholder engagement sometimes tend to focus only on engagement with communities. While affected communities are critical stakeholders, this chapter also looks at other important external and internal stakeholders.

What is stakeholder engagement and why is it important?

Stakeholder engagement is a two-way process of communication between a project and each of its stakeholders. It is an ongoing process throughout the life of a project, consisting of the elements discussed in this chapter.

Stakeholder engagement is an essential basis for:

- Building strong and mutually beneficial relationships with project stakeholders
- Improved understanding and decision-making
- The identification and management of project impacts on communities and related social risks
- The identification and management of project risks in relation to time, budget and reputation
- Maximisation of benefits for all stakeholders

Other reasons that stakeholder engagement is important include:

- You cannot expect co-operation from people if you do not engage and co-operate with them
- Stakeholders may be able to delay or stop your project, increase project costs or tarnish your reputation
- Properly engaging with stakeholders is increasingly a legislative requirement
- The IFC (International Finance Corporation), World Bank, EBRD (European Bank for Reconstruction and Development) and other similar institutions require proper stakeholder engagement as a condition for financing
- Commercial banks are often Equator Principle signatories, and this stipulates stakeholder engagement
- The majority of companies have made commitments to engage with stakeholders as part of their corporate policy commitments

> Perception is reality—if you do not engage then people will create their own reality

Public relations versus stakeholder engagement

It is important to distinguish between public relations and stakeholder engagement. While the two may appear to mean the same thing, in practice public relations often has connotations of an advertising exercise. Some companies, such as in the extractives sector, establish separate community relations and public relations departments, with the former dealing with project site community relations issues, for example, and the latter dealing with the media. However a company chooses to deal with the above, all of the external parties in question need to be considered as stakeholders.

What is very clear is that community relations cannot be dealt with as a public relations exercise that is planned and co-ordinated by a public relations firm from 'the big city', and engagement with stakeholders cannot be just about advertising, i.e. there needs to be more than fancy words.

Project example

Faced with negative feedback from local communities, civil society and the media about its proposed project, a company in Eastern Europe decided to hire a New York public relations firm to plan and co-ordinate its response, even though the firm's personnel would continue to be based in the US. This was despite the warnings of in-country project personnel who emphasised the need for community and other stakeholder relations to be managed in country, with an emphasis on placing staff at the project site, as well as in the national and regional capital cities. After a period during which relations with stakeholders worsened, and it proved extremely difficult to co-ordinate engagement activities, the company decided to restructure matters. The US firm was replaced by a national firm to handle media relations, while community and government relations were allocated to dedicated in-house and in-country departments. All the internal parties had regular meetings to co-ordinate their activities.

Who are stakeholders?

Stakeholders are any and all individuals, groups, organisations and institutions interested in and potentially affected by a project or having the ability to influence a project. Stakeholders are therefore both persons directly affected by a project, and the broader group of people and organisations with an interest in the project (such as government, media, civil society). Key stakeholders are those who can significantly influence the success of the project or who are significantly impacted by it. Determining who the stakeholders are on a particular project, and their respective interests and influence, will require a process of stakeholder identification and analysis.

Potential stakeholders can come from following broad categories:

- Communities, including vulnerable persons, civic organisations and businesses
- Government (local, national and regional), including regulators
- Civil society, including NGOs (non-governmental organisations), CBOs (community-based organisations) and other advocacy groups
- Media and opinion leaders
- Customers, both current and potential
- Internal, including shareholders, board of directors and employees
- Joint-venture partners
- Contractors and suppliers
- Lending institutions, potential investors and analysts

- Academia
- Supranational organisations

'Stakeholders' are increasingly self-legitimising. In other words, those who judge themselves to have an interest in an organisation's operations, value and performance are de facto 'stakeholders' (SustainAbility *et al.* 2002: 8).

What are the standards?

Countries are increasingly legislating the requirement to undertake stakeholder engagement, although the degree to which they specify requirements varies and many still have limited formal requirements. In addition to government regulation, there is a plethora of best practice standards and guides that have been developed by a variety of institutions including banks and industry organisations and associations. As well as the extensive experience of the authors, we draw on these materials, in particular those of the IFC, as we believe they provide a common-sense approach to stakeholder engagement.

IFC PS (Performance Standard) 1 (IFC 2012) provides that:

- The nature, frequency and level of effort of stakeholder engagement may vary considerably and will need to be commensurate with a project's risks and adverse impacts, concerns raised by affected communities, and the project phase.
- The project should undertake a process of consultation in a manner that provides affected communities with opportunities to express their views on project risks, impacts and mitigation measures, and allows the project to consider and respond to them.
- Effective consultation should be a two-way process that:
  - Begins early in the process of identification of environmental and social risks and impacts, and continues on an ongoing basis as risks and impacts arise
  - Is based on prior disclosure and dissemination of relevant, transparent, objective, meaningful and easily accessible information which is in a culturally appropriate local language(s) and format and is understandable to affected communities
  - Focuses inclusive engagement on directly affected people as opposed to those not directly affected
  - Is free of external manipulation, interference, coercion or intimidation
  - Enables meaningful participation, where applicable
  - Is documented.

What are the objectives?

Undertaking stakeholder engagement without clear objectives is no different from developing a project or undertaking any human endeavour without objectives, i.e. efforts will lack focus. It is useful to disaggregate stakeholders and develop engagement objectives for each group.

The overall objective of stakeholder engagement is to obtain and retain broad community and other stakeholder support to enable the project to develop, operate and expand peacefully. Broad community support is a collection of expressions by affected communities, through individuals and their recognised representatives, in support of the project. There may be broad community support even if some individuals or groups object to the project.

An important secondary objective is that, through meaningful engagement, stakeholders can influence the design and implementation of projects for mutual benefit.

> Stakeholder engagement objectives need to be carefully aligned with overall corporate business objectives

What are the key challenges, issues and risks?

Key challenges, issues and risks that projects face include the following:

- Increasing legal requirements
- Increasing community, government and societal expectations
- More media attention, particularly on the extractive sector
- New technologies are making the world increasingly interconnected, including new communication vehicles for community activism
- Turnover of project personnel, meaning that relationships with stakeholders sometimes have to be re-established and prior commitments made need to be carefully recorded
- Companies not getting enough credit for what they are doing well
- Companies need to get better at showing what they are doing well

> Many companies have made major strides in the social arena, including in the extractive sector, but the sector is still perceived in a negative light by many

It is worth quoting from Deloitte's *Tracking the Trends 2014* concerning the mining industry:

mining companies are in the spotlight—as cast not only by international media but also by a growing number of monitoring and standard setting bodies. Social media has elevated these activities to new levels, enabling the instantaneous and global dissemination of negative press in real time. As a result, corporate reputations, access rights to new discoveries and market valuations are all at risk like never before. (Deloitte 2013: 24)

What are the guiding principles?

Important principles to bear in mind include:

- **Process is as important as outcome**: project-affected communities need to feel that there has been a process where they have been actively involved, rather than having terms merely dictated to them
- **Perception is reality**: people will create their own reality/understanding of your project if you do not carefully engage with them
- **It is not just what you say, but how you say it**
- Stakeholder engagement is not just about words: **actions speak louder than words**
- Stakeholder engagement must be:
  - **Free of interference, manipulation, intimidation or coercion**
  - **Inclusive**: working with all stakeholders, not just those you like and who like you
  - Conducted on the basis of **relevant, understandable, appropriate and timely information**
  - Undertaken in a **culturally appropriate manner**
  - **Based on real two-way engagement and partnership** (listening as well as talking)
  - **Tailored** to the specific conditions and requirements of the project, the project phase and the stakeholder in question
  - Undertaken **based on a clear plan**
- Involve all project departments: **stakeholder engagement is not just the responsibility of the community relations department**

Levels of stakeholder engagement

The level of potential stakeholder engagement can range from limited information disclosure to the development of a close partnership approach.

Consultations and negotiations are different, but related, processes within the overall engagement spectrum. Consultation tends to be more open-ended, with the intent of exchanging views and information. Negotiation is focused on discussing and reaching agreement on specific issues. Consultations set the basis for negotiations, and continue around the negotiation process and afterwards.

A partnership approach takes engagement to a level beyond consultation and negotiation, although these aspects typically remain even where a partnership is developed. A partnership approach seeks to move relations between a project and, for example, local communities, government and NGOs beyond a situation where the project is seen as merely causing impacts and the purveyor of employment, procurement and community investment opportunities. Issues are seen as everybody's problem, with a move away from an adversarial approach to closer collaboration and solutions leading to win–win outcomes. This approach is based on a pooling of ideas and resources, and joint planning, implementation and monitoring.

> The level of engagement will depend on the project stage, the level of project impacts and risks, as well as the stakeholder in question and their concerns and importance

Characteristics of a successful partnership include:

- Common or sufficiently aligned objectives
- A pooling of resources (time, money, in kind), with a focus on complementarity, i.e. drawing on the core competences of the different partners
- Transparency, i.e. a sharing of information
- Joint fact-finding, planning and implementation
- Sharing risks and opportunities/benefits

What are the key components of stakeholder engagement?

One needs to adopt a comprehensive approach in order to manage stakeholder relations properly.

Depending on the specific project, elements of a comprehensive approach which may need to be considered include the following:

- Clear stakeholder engagement objectives
- Organisational structures and stakeholder capacity
- Stakeholder identification and analysis

- Impact, risk and opportunity assessment
- Development of a stakeholder engagement policy, strategy and plan
- Information disclosure
- Stakeholder consultation and participation
- Engagement methods and tools
- Reporting
- Stakeholder involvement in project monitoring
- Grievance management
- Language and cultural considerations
- Government-led consultations and negotiations
- Record-keeping and information management

Some of the key elements identified above are discussed briefly in turn below.

Organisational structures and stakeholder capacity

The exact make-up of the project stakeholder engagement team will depend on the project nature, stage, location and available resources. In broad terms, the project needs a team with the following characteristics:

- Representatives who have the position, authority and stature with stakeholders to play their designated roles
- People with the requisite skills and experience
- Good knowledge of the project stakeholders
- Good planning and organisational abilities
- Good interpersonal communication skills, including good listening skills, presentational skills, sensitivity to stakeholder concerns and interests (without being weak), ability to read moods and body language, etc.
- Ability to work well under pressure and ensure project objectives are met
- Patience
- A win–win orientation
- An appropriate balance of local people versus outsiders.

It may be necessary to capacity-build not only the project's personnel involved in stakeholder engagement, but also external stakeholders such as local community representatives and members, particularly so they can in turn effectively consult with their constituents.

Stakeholder identification and analysis

Undertaking stakeholder engagement without a clear understanding of project stakeholders will result in engagement that is not sufficiently targeted. All stakeholders must be engaged, with the nature, level and intensity of engagement tailored to the stakeholder in question. The extent to which a project focuses on different stakeholders largely depends on the nature and extent of project impacts on the stakeholder, the project stage and the level of influence of the stakeholder and whether they are a supporter or opponent of the project.

IFC PS1 provides that:

- Projects should identify the range of stakeholders that may be interested in their activities
- Where a project involves specifically identified physical elements that are likely to generate adverse environmental and social impacts, the project will identify affected communities

Stakeholder analysis is a two-stage process of identifying and analysing project stakeholders. The objective is to identify a comprehensive list of project stakeholders, fully understand and prioritise stakeholders, and thereby ensure a solid basis on which to prepare a comprehensive and targeted SEP (stakeholder engagement plan).

 Project example

A project in Eastern Europe proudly provided a copy of its SEP (stakeholder engagement plan) to an external reviewer. The plan was a detailed document and contained numerous planned steps for future engagement. However, when asked if the plan was based on a thorough process of identification, analysis and mapping of stakeholders, the project advised that no such process had been undertaken. A subsequently conducted process of stakeholder identification and analysis showed the need to modify the SEP in order to focus engagement activities on certain key stakeholders.

Dimensions for identifying stakeholders include by impact, proximity, interest, influence, responsibility, representation, dependence and project phase.

Key steps and tools include:

- Determine and map the project's geographic footprint and spheres of impact and influence using a multi-functional internal team.
- Brainstorm an initial list of stakeholders (using a multi-functional internal team) and then network (internally and externally) to:
  - Identify individuals, groups, organisations and local communities that may be affected by the project; in what way they will be affected; whether the impact will be positive or negative and direct or indirect; making special effort to identify those who are directly affected, including disadvantaged or vulnerable project-affected persons (taking into account possible cumulative impacts)
  - Identify broader stakeholders, including those who may be able to influence the outcome of the project, such as government and civil society

Figure 5.1: Identifying stakeholders.

STAKEHOLDER	VIEW OF PROJECT			LEVEL OF INFLUENCE			LEVEL OF PROJECT IMPACT		
	Pos	Neu	Neg	High	Medium	Low	High	Medium	Low
A									
B									
C									
D									

- Identify legitimate stakeholder representatives (including elected offi-cials, non-elected community leaders, leaders of informal or traditional community institutions), as well as key influencers.
- Analyse and assess the respective concerns and interests (overt and hidden) of the stakeholders identified, determine potential conflicts of interest, and the ways in which these interests could affect project riskiness and viability. Evaluate each stakeholder's view of the project (positive, neutral or negative), how influential that are (high, medium or low) and how greatly they will be impacted by the project (high, medium or low).
- Prioritise stakeholders into primary and secondary/high and low priority categories (as appropriate), in order to enable engagement efforts and resources to be targeted and optimally utilised.

Figure 5.2: Stakeholder mapping.

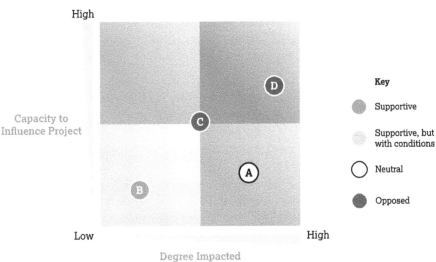

To carry out the above steps, it will be necessary to gather as much baseline data as practically possible and appropriate. Once these steps have initially been undertaken, one should determine what additional baseline data is required.

Remember to ask yourself two key questions at the end of the exercise:

- Have all primary and secondary stakeholders been listed? (Make sure you think beyond merely local communities and local government.)
- Have all potential supporters and opponents of the project been identified?

Impact, risk and opportunity assessment

This topic is dealt with in Chapter 7 in more detail. Key questions to ask that help to plan stakeholder engagement include:

- What environmental, social and other impacts will the project cause?
- Who will be impacted by these impacts, and to what extent?

It is important to emphasise here that stakeholder engagement needs to be focused on helping to address issues, risk and opportunities that are important to the long-term success of the project. Issues, risks and opportunities need to be considered not only from a project perspective, but also from that of communities and other stakeholders.

Developing a policy, strategy and plan

Undertaking stakeholder engagement without a clear policy, strategy or plan is no different from developing a project without a plan: it results in an unplanned, reactive, ad hoc and incomplete approach. When developing a policy, strategy and plan, key questions include:

- **For greenfield projects**: what policies, plans, systems, procedures, resources and other measures need to be put in place?
- **For brownfield projects**: how has stakeholder engagement been handled to date? What needs to change?

IFC PS1 provides that:

- The project will develop and implement an SEP that is scaled to the project risks and impacts and to the development stage, and is tailored to the characteristics and interests of the affected communities.
- Where applicable, the SEP will include differentiated measures to allow the effective participation of those identified as disadvantaged or vulnerable.
- In cases where the exact location of a project is not known, but it is reasonably expected to have significant impacts on local communities, the project will prepare an SEF (stakeholder engagement framework) outlining general principles and a strategy to identify affected communities and other relevant stakeholders, and plan for an engagement process compatible with PS1 that will be implemented once the physical location of the project is known.

Project example

A project in Eastern Europe undertook a process of stakeholder engagement for the initial phase of development of a mine. The processes of engagement—related to obtaining an environmental permit, acquiring land, resettlement and addressing other issues—were conducted by several project departments in an uncoordinated manner, resulting in gaps, delays and cost overruns. When planning the second phase of the project, the company reflected on the lessons from the initial phase, and developed a co-ordinated approach for all stakeholder engagement for the expansion.

Before developing a formal SEP, one must first determine what one's strategy is, as the strategy shapes the details of the plan.

A policy is a statement of intent, generally adopted by the board of directors or senior governance body within an organisation. The policy will, based on defined objectives, set out the parameters within which planning, implementation and other activities will take place. As with other corporate endeavours, it is important that the company has a clear stakeholder engagement policy to inform the actions of its personnel and contractors, as well as showing external parties that it is committed to acting in a certain way.

Probably the biggest issue in relation to corporate policies is whether actions on the ground, such as those of a Canadian mining company with a project in Africa, match commitments made in a Toronto office block.

The key parameters of a stakeholder engagement strategy and plan include:

- What stage is your project at? Clarify your purpose, i.e. what your strategic reasons are for consulting with stakeholders at this stage of the project.

- Who are your key stakeholders? Clarify this for each project stage based on key issues and risks, determine high-risk categories of stakeholders requiring special attention, and determine which steps and tools will be most effective for each category of stakeholder and project stage.

- What are your key issues, impacts, challenges, risks and opportunities?

- What are your key objectives?

- What are your guiding principles?

- What legal, corporate and lender requirements are there that stipulate stakeholder engagement?

> It is important that a company thinks carefully about what it will be publicly committing to: do not commit to what you cannot achieve on the ground

An example of an SEF structure is as follows:

- Introduction (including description of potential project and likely location, impacts and risks)
- Regulations, standards and policies
- Potential area of influence
- Possible stakeholders
- Guiding principles and objectives
- Strategy for engagement process
- Grievance mechanism
- Step-by-step process and responsibilities to prepare the SEP once exact project location is known

In developing or updating a stakeholder engagement policy, strategy, framework or plan, it is important to reflect on your project's past engagement, i.e. what worked and did not work, what needs to change and what should be retained. It is also useful to benchmark against other appropriate projects in order to see what issues peers are facing, what they are doing and what has worked/not worked, and draw useful lessons. Remember that each project is different so do not copy blindly as a 'cookie-cutter' approach does not work.

 Project example

While too many companies tend to rush into projects without spending time reflecting on their past experiences or those of their peers, some companies are realising the value of sharing their experiences to improve their own performance and the overall performance of their sector. A good example is a recent benchmarking exercise commissioned in three phases by Rio Tinto Alcan, Gold Fields and Glencore, which looked at, *inter alia*, stakeholder engagement related to land acquisition and resettlement on 40 extractive sector projects in over 20 countries.

An example of an SEP structure is set out below:
- Introduction, including project description
- Regulations, standards and policies
- Guiding principles and objectives
- Impacts, risks and opportunities
- Previous engagement activities
- Identification, characterisation and priority of stakeholders
- Engagement programme
- Grievance mechanism

- Schedule of responsibilities
- Monitoring and reporting

SEPs need to be developed in an iterative process with other project action plans. SEPs and other documents such as the SEF are typically not developed once, i.e. they go through a process of multiple drafts prepared by designated stakeholder engagement personnel (such as the community relations department) and reviewed by project management, external reviewers and other parties. A project SEP needs to be updated on an annual basis, or as appropriate.

Information disclosure

Failure to communicate accurate, timely and relevant information in an understandable manner can fatally compromise the engagement process, and hence stakeholder understanding, acceptance and support for the project.

IFC PS1 provides that the project will provide affected communities with access to relevant information on the purpose, nature and scale of the project; the duration of proposed project activities; any risks to and potential impacts on such communities and relevant mitigation measures; the envisaged stakeholder engagement process; and the grievance mechanism.

The purpose of information disclosure activities should be to make information available and accessible to stakeholders in order to provide them with what they need to engage fully with the project, and to disclose relevant project information to ensure the informed participation of project-affected communities. To achieve this, the project should aim to:

- Disclose information early
- Ensure the information is accessible to stakeholders
- Ensure that information disclosed is meaningful
- Tailor information for different audiences based on:
  - Level of technical detail
  - Language
  - Level of impact on or interest/concern of stakeholder
  - Cultural considerations
  - Roles of men and women
  - Vulnerability of people
  - Literacy levels
  - Leadership structures
  - Local methods of information dissemination
- Ensure accessibility of information through the use of methods that are most appropriate to the circumstances. Options include:
  - Public meetings
  - Smaller meetings
  - One-on-one household meetings
  - Radio, television, Internet and other media

- Notice boards
- Information centres
- Mobile phone and other similar tools
- Handouts and other project publications
- Project information offices (for example, in communities)

- Ask stakeholders what makes sense to them
- Carefully weigh the risks and benefits of situations in which disclosing certain types of information, for example at certain stages of a project, may be sensitive, such as how many local jobs will be generated by the project.
- Manage information on sensitive and controversial issues through the development of mini-communication plans (under the umbrella of the overall SEP).
- No matter how much information you disclose, always ensure that stakeholders know who to contact from the project if they have queries and require clarifications.

It is not enough simply to prepare an action plan such as an SEP: the policy, SEF and SEP should all be publicly disclosed.

Community consultation and participation

IFC PS1 provides that:

- When affected communities are subject to identified risks and adverse impacts from a project, the project will undertake a process of consultation in a manner that provides the affected communities with opportunities to express their views on project risks, impacts and mitigation measures, and allows the project to consider and respond to them.
- The degree of engagement should be commensurate with a project's risks and adverse impacts and with concerns raised by affected communities.
- For projects with potentially significant adverse impacts on affected communities, the project will conduct an ICP (informed consultation and participation) process that will result in the informed participation of affected communities.
- ICP involves a more in-depth exchange of views and information and an organised and iterative consultation process, leading to the project incorporating into its decision-making process the views of affected communities on matters that affect them directly, such as proposed mitigation measures, the sharing of development benefits and opportunities, and implementation issues.

Real participation in stakeholder engagement involves a two-way flow of information and ideas, and collaboration on joint planning for and addressing issues, risks and opportunities (to the level appropriate). Participatory tools, techniques and methods include:

- Participatory workshops
- Focus groups
- Role-play
- Historic time-lines and trends
- Participatory rural appraisal
- Seasonal calendar
- Daily schedules
- Semi-structured interviews
- Venn diagrams
- Local institutional analysis
- Resource mapping and village maps
- Poverty and vulnerability mapping
- Wealth ranking and other forms of ranking for decision-making
- Joint identification of issues and possible solutions

> Real participation in the stakeholder engagement process means much more than communities merely listening to what a project has to say

Engagement during an ESHIA (environmental, social and health impact assessment) process

The government-specified stakeholder engagement process related to obtaining an environmental permit sometimes does not stipulate a requirement for thorough engagement with affected communities. In such situations, it is dangerous for the project to assume that it can get away with less engagement merely in order to quickly obtain its environmental permit. Even where this is possible, bear in mind that your project also needs to obtain its social licence to operate.

 Project example

The legislative regime in an Eastern European country did not require extensive stakeholder engagement related to the ESHIA process, particularly in relation to affected communities. In order to comply with government requirements, but also ensure an internationally acceptable stakeholder engagement process, the project proponent prepared a locally compliant environmental impact assessment, and a more detailed ESHIA that was IFC compliant. Additional stakeholder engagement took place around and after the government-mandated public hearing, in order to ensure that communities were adequately engaged on all aspects of the project.

Engagement with different categories of stakeholders

Community leaders

IFC PS1 states that when the stakeholder engagement process depends substantially on community representatives, the project will make every reasonable effort to verify that such persons do in fact represent the views of affected communities and that they can be relied on to communicate faithfully the results of consultations to their constituents.

It is critical for projects to work closely with community representatives, but to bear in mind the following:

- Do not rely solely on engaging with community leaders
- Check how representative leaders are of all groups
- Do not rely solely on community leaders to communicate project messages to community members
- Ensure transparency to prevent and address community suspicions about the benefits that accrue to representatives working with the project.

 Project example

On a project in Africa, it was found that the local traditional chief and his elders were not accurately conveying the position of the company on a range of issues. It appeared that this was not due to malice, but that the leaders lacked the capacity to fully explain and discuss a variety of technical topics. On reflection, the company realised that it placed undue reliance on traditional leadership structures for engagement with the affected community, and that it needed to find ways to continue to respect and utilise engagement with the traditional leaders, while utilising other channels to reach the whole community. The company explained its desire to engage in a variety of capacity-building educational measures to help the community leadership in the engagement process. The chief understood that it was in his interest to ensure a good two-way process of communication between the whole community and the company. He therefore allowed other community representatives to join meetings with the company, provided his role as the chief was still recognised. All community representatives were then provided with capacity-building assistance to improve engagement between the parties.

Vulnerable people

IFC PS1 mentions that, where applicable, the SEP will include differentiated measures to allow the effective participation of those identified as disadvantaged or vulnerable.

It is natural for the project to focus large amounts of attention on community leaders and those stakeholders who most vociferously air their concerns. However, comprehensive engagement needs to include all community groups affected, including those who may be more vulnerable to project impacts, including women, the elderly, young people and people who are disabled. This may require specific measures to enable meaningful engagement to take place.

Gender considerations

IFC PS1 states that the consultation process should capture both men's and women's views, if necessary through separate forums or engagements, and reflect their different concerns and priorities about impacts, mitigation measures and benefits, where appropriate.

In order to get the full picture, projects need to properly engage with women as well, i.e. men and women often have different priorities and perspectives and are impacted in different ways.

Steps to take in this regard include:

- Disaggregate your data
- Pay attention to engagement team composition
- Get more women 'in the room'
- Use active facilitation to ensure adequate female involvement
- Hold separate meetings where necessary
- Raise and address priority issues for women.

However, remember that women are not one homogenous group.

Figure 5.3: Projects need to properly engage with women.

Project example

At a project in Eastern Europe community representatives were overwhelmingly male, and the project was concerned that these representatives were not adequately conveying the full spectrum of concerns and views of affected community members. Accordingly, the project put in place a series of small focus groups that were targeted to give women and other groups the chance to engage more fully with the project. Meetings were held with women, old people, physically disabled people, young people and other specific interest groups such as farmers and business owners.

Indigenous people

IFC PS1 provides that, for projects with adverse impacts on indigenous people, the project is required to engage them in a process of ICP and, in certain circumstances, obtain their free, prior and informed consent as discussed in more detail in PS7.

Countries are increasingly regulating how stakeholder engagement is undertaken with indigenous people.

Stakeholders defined as illegal by government

National legislation sometimes stipulates that unlicensed artisanal and small-scale mining is illegal. However, mining projects often have artisanal and small-scale

Figure 5.4: Artisanal mining activity in Africa.

miners on their concessions and therefore need to engage with these people, including situations where land access will require their displacement.

In such situations, projects can find themselves caught up in a situation where government (and the project) do not want to pay for loss of income from illegal activities, but where displaced communities are heavily reliant on these activities for their livelihoods and failure to mitigate the loss will preclude the viable resettlement of the community. This poses interesting challenges for the land access and resettlement stakeholder engagement process, where projects need to find a solution acceptable to all parties.

 Project example

A community affected by a project in Africa was highly dependent on artisanal gold-mining for its livelihood. As a result, a large and critical stakeholder group consisted of people engaged in an officially illegal activity. The government insisted that the company treat artisanal and small-scale mining as an illegal activity, and not formally recognise representatives of those miners in the community engagement forum it had established. Faced with the need not to ignore government stipulations, but anxious to ensure sufficiently broad stakeholder engagement, the company accepted membership on the community engagement forum of members who were officially church and mosque representatives, but who also doubled as representatives of artisanal and small-scale miners.

Government

Government is clearly a critical stakeholder for any project. This importance arises from a range of different roles and perspectives, including government as utility and service provider, project shareholder, regulator, tax collector, potential mediator, and receiver of project benefits (including increased employment, support with infrastructure provision and community development).

The project needs to fully map its range of government stakeholders, bearing in mind the different levels of government (i.e. local, regional and national) and the different and often competing functions of the different government departments and agencies. Stakeholder engagement needs to be tailored accordingly.

It is critical for projects to not get caught up in national politics and show favour to one particular political party, as this may reap short-term benefits but have costly long-term implications.

Engaging with civil society

Dictionary.com's *21st Century Lexicon* defines civil society as 'the aggregate of non-governmental organizations and institutions that manifest interests and will of citizens; individuals and organizations in a society which are independent of the government'.

The relationship of private-sector companies and projects to civil society has evolved significantly in recent times. In the extractive sector the relationship with NGOs was often hostile in the past. However, this is changing and forward-looking projects are, and should be, working with NGOs and CBOs to the extent possible. Even where an NGO opposes the extractive sector, projects should carefully consider ways to engage, as appropriate.

NGOs often have skills and experience that projects themselves lack, and can play a positive role in helping projects to adequately engage with stakeholders, including sometimes wary and suspicious communities. However, projects should be careful where NGOs claim to represent communities fully but may instead be trying to push their own specific agenda and replace or undermine local community representatives and structures that are, in fact, adequately representing local communities. Therefore, project proponents should consider each NGO on its merits, based on its relevance as a stakeholder of the project in question.

Engaging with banks and analysts

Many projects can only be developed if the proponent obtains financing from a lender, and the majority of banks that lend money to the mining sector are signatories to the Equator Principles. Adopting institutions undertake not to loan to projects in which the borrower will not, or is unable to, comply with the environmental and social policies and processes outlined in the principles. Therefore banks and their internal and external safeguard experts are critical project stakeholders.

Analysts that track and report on different sectors, such as the mining sector, are also an important stakeholder. Their word on the viability of a project can have important positive or negative consequences for the project proponent.

 Project example

A project in Africa needed commercial bank finance to fund its development. The consortium of banks therefore became a critical project stakeholder. Given the magnitude of project social issues, the consortium appointed an external expert to conduct quarterly reviews, including a review of project impact and risk assessments, as well as development of mitigation plans. In order to help ensure that it was ready for the external reviews, thereby trying to prevent delays caused by not being ready for the bank review, the project hired its own independent external reviewer. This person undertook quarterly reviews ahead of the bank reviewer in order to help the project prepare for the bank reviews.

Internal project stakeholder engagement

Internal stakeholder engagement is critical for the following reasons:

- Project technical personnel need to work with social personnel to determine the project footprint, how negative environmental and social impacts can be minimised, and external stakeholders convinced to support the project.

> Internal stakeholder engagement is as critical as external stakeholder engagement

- If internal stakeholders are not aligned then project planning, messages and actions in relation to stake-holder engagement and aspects of the business (such as local employment and procurement, community development, etc.), will not be consistent, leading to external stakeholder mistrust.

- Project actions and budgets for stakeholder engagement and all other business facets are approved by managers who need to be engaged with, and convinced that, what is requested by community relations and other departments is advancing the business as a whole by addressing key issues, impacts and risks, and is therefore worth doing and spending.

Therefore, it is critical that the social personnel of projects get better at explaining to and convincing company and project management (the accountants and engineers) of the merits and business case for undertaking stakeholder engagement better (and therefore, with adequate resources), in other words, speaking in a language that business decision-makers understand, i.e. time, money and risk to the business.

 Project example

Cognisant of the lessons learned from the initial project phase, and the need to align its social team and the rest of its project team and management, a project in Eastern Europe decided that the identification, analysis and mapping of its stakeholders for an expansion would not be undertaken solely by its community relations department. A workshop was arranged at which representatives from all relevant project departments worked together to brainstorm and identify project expansion phase stakeholders. One of the benefits of this exercise was that it allowed many of the project internal stakeholders to plan together and develop alignment.

Employees

Employees, who are often from local communities, are a critical stakeholder group. If they are positive about the project then they will help engagement positively on behalf of the project with other stakeholders. Many projects are lax about the types and levels of information that are accessible to employees (and hence become community knowledge): for example, plans showing where land acquisition is planned can lead to expensive building and crop speculation.

Engagement with employees is therefore not just the job of the human resources department. Engagement with employees needs to go beyond boiler-plate human resources issues, bearing in mind that if the project does not provide them with sufficient information they will form their own ideas and pass these on to other project-affected persons.

 Project example

A project in Australasia was deeply concerned about how it could manage community expectations about the likelihood and timing of its project go-ahead, as well as likely employment and other benefits accruing to local communities. However, at the same time, corporate security protocols were lax, resulting in local community members already employed by the project having access to documents detailing the project feasibility study, including estimated project impacts and benefits. This information was being circulated in the affected communities, even though the official corporate message was that its feasibility study was ongoing and that the company could say nothing further pending the completion of the study.

Contractors

Contractors who supply projects with goods and services are another external stakeholder, i.e. they often form a large part of the project where a company outsources key parts. For example, mining companies often outsource the process of transporting ore and waste to mining contractors who provide their own fleets of trucks and other vehicles (the companies thereby reduce the amount of capital they have to invest). In such situations, companies need to ensure that contractors act in accordance with overall project stakeholder engagement objectives, policies and plans, as local communities will regard the contractor as part of the overall project.

Engagement methods and tools

There are a number of different stakeholder engagement methods and tools, as outlined in Figure 5.5. Projects need to determine which of these methodologies are appropriate to various stakeholder groups, and at what points in the project cycle. In this regard, the various engagement methods need to be developed within a detailed engagement schedule, reflected in the SEP.

Figure 5.5: Stakeholder engagement methods and tools.

Types	Tools
Surveys	- Individual, small group and large group meetings e.g. with representatives, key informants, impacted individuals, households, small groups, individual communities, multiple communities, government agencies and other stakeholders - Focus groups, public hearings, seminars, conferences, meetings and negotiation committees
Public Information Sessions and Fora	- Qualitative and quantitative surveys - Household and community questionnaires - censuses, asset and social/economic surveys - Aerial and satellite imagery - Sample, preliminary rapid, and 100% surveys - Perception and attitude surveys and polls
Printed and Electronic Materials	- Reports, brochures, presentations, displays, exhibits, newsletters and direct mail - Scale models, 3D model simulators, videos
Media	- Newspapers, websites, twitter, blogs, news conferences, newspaper articles and advertisements, radio and televisions
Other	- Discussion on and disclosure of Management/Action Plans - Engagement register, meeting records (verbatim and summary) - Commitment register - Grievance mechanism - Lotteries e.g for resettlement site plot allocation - Stakeholder Fora - Community Investment Fund or Foundation

Figure 5.6: Focus group meeting.

Reporting

Whether in the realm of consultations, negotiations, grievance management, monitoring or any other aspect of stakeholder engagement, stakeholders will want feedback on progress and issues, in particular, asking the question: Is the project doing what it says it would?

IFC PS1 provides that:

- Projects should inform affected communities how their concerns have been considered
- Projects will provide periodic reports to affected communities that describe progress with implementation of project action plans on issues that involve ongoing risk to or impacts on them and on issues that the consultation process or grievance mechanism have identified as a concern of affected communities
- Communities will be updated on material changes or additions to mitigation measures or actions described in action plans on issues of concern to affected communities
- Projects are encouraged to make publicly available periodic reports on their environmental and social sustainability
- The frequency of reports will be proportionate to the concerns of affected communities but not less than annually.

Considerations when planning reporting back mechanisms include:

- Who is your audience?
- What is the issue or risk?
- What concerns have been raised?
- Is the party directly impacted or not?
- What is the stakeholder level of understanding?
- What is the project phase?
- What is the frequency of reporting?

Before sending out a report, ask yourself the following questions:

- Is the information provided relevant?
- Is the information provided accurate?
- Is the information provided understandable?
- Is the information provided complete?
- Is the information provided location and culturally appropriate?
- Is the information provided timely?
- Is the report too long or too short?

These criteria can be used to assess all documentation released by the project to stakeholders, and not just reports.

Stakeholder involvement in project monitoring

Involving external stakeholders in project monitoring can promote transparency and thereby build trust. However, this needs to be carefully considered: in particular, community members may require capacity-building to participate meaningfully. Participatory monitoring means more than sharing with communities the results of monitoring, i.e. it requires their physical involvement in the actual monitoring process, ideally including the joint development of monitoring indicators.

Where communities do not want to be directly involved in monitoring or adequate capacity-building is problematic, another way to address mistrust may be to involve the community in choosing mutually acceptable independent third-party monitors.

Involving government agencies in monitoring, even when not statutorily required, can help cement relationships and ensure effective handover of infrastructure to statutory authorities on completion.

Grievance management

IFC PS1 states that:

- Where there are affected communities, the project will establish a grievance mechanism to receive and facilitate the resolution of their concerns and grievances about project environmental and social performance.
- The grievance mechanism should be scaled to the risks and adverse impacts of the project and have affected communities as its primary user.
- The grievance mechanism should seek to resolve concerns promptly using an understandable and transparent consultative process that is culturally appropriate and readily accessible, and at no cost and without retribution to the party that originated the issue or concern.
- The grievance mechanism should not impede access to judicial or administrative remedies.
- The project will inform the affected communities about the mechanism in the course of the stakeholder engagement process.

No matter how a project addresses impacts and risks and engages with local communities, grievances will still arise. What is critical is how a project handles grievances: this is truly a case where **process is as important as outcome**.

Grievance mechanisms are a systematic method for recording, processing and resolving grievances between a project and local communities. It is worth distinguishing between the grievance mechanism used to address individual and small group grievances, and methods of dispute resolution that may be used to address disputes that arise in the sphere of negotiations, in particular related to land access and resettlement. In the latter situation third-party steering committees, mediators and other forms of third-party assistance are sometimes used to resolve outstanding issues (this is discussed further in Chapter 12).

Projects need to ensure that the grievance mechanism:

- Is understood by stakeholders
- Is easily accessible, including special measures for vulnerable persons
- Is culturally and locally appropriate
- Is considered fair by stakeholders
- Is cost free
- Is restitution free
- Is timely in addressing impacts and feeding back to complainants
- Is able to track and record grievances for immediate and future reference
- Takes account of and does not impede access to judicial or administrative remedies

 Project example

A project in Australasia put in place a formal grievance mechanism that included a contact mobile phone number. Community members were advised that the mobile phone number would allow them to contact a senior project person dealing with grievances during official working hours, when they had grievances. Although grievances could also be lodged in writing, the provision of a telephonic method to initiate the process was deemed a good innovation in a country where mobile phone usage was widespread. However, some months later, an external reviewer enquired how useful this innovation had been. Unfortunately, no one was able to locate the mobile phone, until it was discovered that the phone was locked in the accommodation of the designated person, who was away on leave for three weeks during their official leave rotation. No one had bothered to ensure that the phone was handed to an alternative person during the leave rotations.

Language and cultural considerations

Projects, in particular extractive sector and infrastructure projects, often take place in locations and with teams and stakeholders where different languages need to be used to interact with local and national stakeholders, as well as corporate offices and financial institutions. This necessitates ensuring that the project has personnel with adequate language skills; and/or that translators are available who can ensure that verbal and written communications and records accurately reflect what is being discussed, done and agreed in the relevant languages.

Taking into account cultural norms when undertaking stakeholder engagement is critical. Differences in regard to issues such as how to welcome people, making and keeping eye contact, making jokes, men and women shaking hands or being in the same room, can negatively or positively impact engagement, depending on how they are handled. Therefore, a project needs to take time to identify cultural norms and differences, train project personnel in how to deal with these, and take other measures to ensure that sensitivities are appropriately dealt with.

Government-led consultations and negotiations

Projects faced with this situation need to walk a delicate tightrope between making sure stakeholder engagement is done properly, while not negatively affecting the sensibilities of government agencies.

IFC PS1 states that where stakeholder engagement is the responsibility of the host government, the project will collaborate with the responsible government agency, to the extent permitted by the agency, to achieve outcomes that are consistent with the objectives of PS1. Where government capacity is limited, the project will play an active role during stakeholder engagement planning, implementation and monitoring. If the process conducted by the government does not meet the requirements of PS1, then the project will conduct a complementary process and, where appropriate, identify supplemental actions.

In practice, intensive consultation and negotiation with government will need to be undertaken to persuade them of the 'business case' of undertaking a project to international standards, while not setting unsustainable precedents for host governments.

Record-keeping and information management

It is all very well undertaking a comprehensive stakeholder engagement process, but you also need to be able to show that this has been done. For example:

- You may need to prove that a person sold the project land in a fair transaction if the person alleges in court that he received inadequate compensation and did not know what he was agreeing to
- An NGO or the media may allege that the project has not consulted people adequately
- A project monitor may ask to see records of engagement undertaken

Tools for keeping records include meeting records (verbatim and summary), engagement registers, commitment registers, grievance mechanisms, and databases/information management systems.

Tailoring engagement for different project stages

Depending on project requirements, stakeholder engagement can range across a spectrum of levels and detail. This could include the following steps: remaining passive, monitoring, informing, transacting, consulting, negotiating, involving, collaborating and empowering. Typically, projects will use a range of these steps, with the exact mix depending on the project stage and circumstances over time.

> Stakeholder engagement needs to be tailored to the different stages of a project

Project concept/scoping stage/exploration: identifying and beginning to understand stakeholders

- Engagement is about undertaking a preliminary identification and analysis of stakeholders, gauging potential local support for or opposition to the project, and identifying key issues and risks that could affect project viability.

- Where on-the-ground exploration needs to occur, then the project needs to develop and maintain the stakeholder relationships to enable it to access land as necessary (bearing in mind the critical need to establish the basis for a good longer-term relationship with communities, while not setting any unsustainable long-term precedents).

- Engagement will be selective and targeted, aimed at building a solid foundation for the future (without unduly heightening stakeholder expectations: do not exaggerate the possible future).

Pre-feasibility study/feasibility study/planning/permitting stage: detailed planning and engagement to obtain social licence to operate

- Engagement is progressively at its highest during the components of this stage, bearing in mind the need to:
  - Undertake detailed stakeholder analysis
  - Typically go through an ESHIA process and develop and engage on mitigation measures/action plans
  - Often undertake a land access and resettlement process.

- Failure to address stakeholder issues and concerns at this stage when project impacts start to occur, such as land take, will generally result in the project not progressing further.

- Most countries have specific requirements related to a formal process of stakeholder engagement: for example, a public hearing before a project is granted an environmental permit.

- Apart from formal permits and licences obtained for the project, failure to address key stakeholders' concerns, in particular those of affected local communities and government, can result in a project failing to obtain its informal but essential social licence to operate.

Construction stage: putting words into action

- Construction is a sensitive time as project impacts necessitate showing affected communities and other stakeholders that these are being addressed and that the project is starting to provide benefits as previously promised in discussions and action plans.
- Local employment and procurement is typically a very important issue for local communities, requiring careful engagement to manage expectations. Communities need to be shown that the project is doing all it can to maximise these opportunities to the practically possible extent, bearing in mind that process is as important as outcome, as it is often the case that project cannot address all requests for employment and therefore needs to show that the process of allocating positions is done fairly: be careful what you promise.
- This is also a time when project community investment and development initiatives start to intensify.
- Failure to do what it has promised and, critically, to satisfy key stakeholders adequately that this is the case, will result in a project losing its social licence to operate: perception = reality.

Operations stage: retaining the social licence to operate

- The operations stage continues to be a sensitive time, as projects will need to continue to show that they are addressing their impacts and sharing benefits.
- Local employment and procurement is often doubly challenging at this stage, particularly where levels are significantly lower than during the construction stage: this can create major tension with local communities.
- The danger at this stage is that the project assumes it has obtained its social licence to operate and becomes complacent. Remember that you are not granted your social licence to operate forever—only your actions and stakeholder perceptions will ensure it is retained.
- At the same time, operating income generally means the project has more wherewithal than ever to undertake stakeholder engagement.

Expansion stages: doing it all over again

- Many projects go through expansion phases, necessitating going through the stages mentioned above again.

Downsizing and closure stages: managing the end

- The downsizing and closure stages of a project are particularly challenging due to a reduction in project benefits.
- It is important that stakeholders, particularly local communities and government, are carefully prepared for and engaged during these stages.

- Local employment and procurement will inevitably reduce during these phases, as will a project's ability to invest in community development (unless it has had the foresight to build up a reserve pool in advance for this stage).

 Project example

During early project phases, a project proponent made a number of widely publicised statements about the level of local employment that would be generated by a new mine in Eastern Europe. All of the statements by different project personnel contained widely differing estimates of the number of jobs that would be generated. A local newspaper printed an article showing the various claims made and posed questions about which statement was correct and whether the company could really be trusted. The company was forced to clarify its position, informing people that the actual number of jobs would be significantly less than that promised in some of the statements. It learned the hard way that it was essential to co-ordinate all messaging to stakeholders from the outset, and that it is better to under-promise and then over-deliver, rather than vice versa.

Stakeholder engagement: key considerations

- **Engage early** and sustain this through all project stages
- Undertake a **thorough stakeholder mapping** exercise
- **Develop a formal SEP** to ensure a comprehensive and consistent approach
- Be strategic and **prioritise stakeholders** to ensure appropriate focus
- **Communicate directly with communities**: do not rely on just community representatives
- **Verify stakeholder representatives**
- **Do not just focus on the loudest stakeholders**
- Be as **transparent** as possible
- **Manage community expectations**:
  - Perception is reality: under-promise/over-deliver
  - Actions speak louder than words
  - Make sure all project messages and actions are consistent
  - Get credit for the good things you do
- **Assist/capacity-build community representatives**

- Put in place an **effective grievance procedure**
- **Engage with stakeholders in their own communities** unless there are good reasons to do otherwise:
  - This lends transparency to the process
  - It also increases accountability of community representatives
  - It emphasises that the project values community input
  - It contributes towards community feeling of involvement in and ownership of process
  - It tests the validity of people who claim to represent the community
- **Interaction with communities is one big negotiation**:
  - Listen/put yourself in their shoes
  - Differentiate between needs and wants
  - Get something in return for what you give
- **Internal stakeholder engagement is critical as well**:
  - Project employees are key stakeholders and information disseminators
  - Make sure contractors act in the same way
- **Manage stakeholder engagement as a business function**: it is no different from the rest of the business in needing to be well planned, structured and managed
- There is no one way of undertaking stakeholder engagement, i.e. **a 'cookie-cutter' approach does not work**, so you need to tailor the process to fit your project
- **Record processes and agreements properly**: prepare for unfavourable attention

6

Baseline data collection and analysis

The collection of baseline data is a critical step in project planning and underpins the effectiveness of the whole land access and resettlement process. This chapter outlines how to approach baseline data collection and analysis.

What are the objectives?

The main objectives of baseline data collection are:

- To help identify and evaluate environmental and social impacts, risks and opportunities of the project in order to develop mitigation measures. Baseline data provides critical information for examining project alternatives, including ways of improving project site selection, in order to avoid or minimise adverse impacts and enhance positive impacts.

- To identify the ownership of all resources which will be impacted by the project including loss of access to housing (physical displacement), land, crops, natural resources and cultural resources (economic displacement). This information must be recorded after an agreed cut-off date for eligibility for compensation and resettlement, agreed with local stakeholders and in compliance with national legislation.

- To inform the design of social management plans, particularly livelihood restoration.

- To provide a pre-project socioeconomic and community perception baseline with monitoring indicators in order to track project progress and to determine whether household wellbeing has been maintained and enhanced. International standards require companies

Poor baseline data means that resettlement planning is built on poor foundations

to demonstrate that the livelihoods of impacted people are re-established after a given period (commonly five years) and the IFC (International Finance Corporation) requires a RAP (resettlement action plan) close-out audit supported by monitoring data to demonstrate livelihood restoration.

What are the key challenges, issues and risks?

Key challenges, issues and risks that projects face include the following:

- Poor baseline data design and field supervision often leads to **poor quality data** which may be unusable.
- Baseline data is **often collected by a range of consultants, often in an unco-ordinated way**, and this can lead to **gaps in information** and the use of **different monitoring indicators** which often renders the data collected unusable later for monitoring and evaluation.
- Gaps in baseline data collection often lead to expensive resurveys or, after project implementation, efforts to recreate a project baseline which is generally inadequate.
- The impacted communities can suffer from **survey fatigue** when projects are delayed and repeated surveys are required over many years rendering communities less co-operative and the data collected less reliable.
- There is the risk of corruption related to survey results and potential additional compensation benefits.
- **Project delays** can lead to multiple cut-off dates and resurveys which create confusion in the communities and can lead to speculative building and cropping activities.

What are the key components?

Baseline data is required on all the key resources that impact on household's well-being. Focusing baseline data-collection efforts around these key resources will enable effective identification of associated project impacts. Utilising a **resources framework**, presented in Figure 6.1 and discussed in more detail in Chapter 7, can aid in these efforts.

Figure 6.1: A resources framework presenting the key resources contributing to household and community wellbeing.

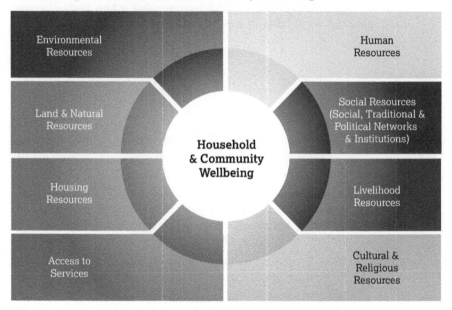

What are the guiding principles?

- **Detailed and comprehensive baseline information**, with co-operation between ESHIA (environmental, social and health impact assessment) and resettlement consultants, is crucial for proper resettlement planning and implementation.
- **Surveys need to be conducted early and in a timely fashion** to ensure that baseline information required for planning is relevant and available when needed.
- It is critical to have a **co-ordinated approach** to surveys, to ensure collection of appropriate data and to prevent survey fatigue in the impacted communities, as well as adequate quality control systems.
- Companies need to work closely with local authorities and communities early in the project cycle to **declare a cut-off date** in order to freeze development and limit speculation.
- **Monitoring indicators** should be defined early in the process to enable gathering of relevant baseline information against which to monitor living conditions after resettlement.

- **Ensure affected people and stakeholder representatives are present** at the time of the surveys and that they sign the survey forms, to ensure a transparent process.
- Ensure an **appropriate project database** is in place for effective storage and analysis of data.

 Project example

A project in Africa conducted surveys of the houses present on the mine area without mapping land ownership. This was done on the basis that compensation would be paid on presentation of a legal document from the government proving ownership. Unfortunately, the government documents certified an area of land which was owned by the claimant in the project area but did not provide a map. The area of land 'certified' by government documents was five times the actual project area. This led to thousands of conflicting claims and community unrest over a five-year period before all claims were settled at great expense. The lesson from this project is that mapping of land ownership is critical to determining eligibility for compensation and all data needs to be collected in a way which can later be defended in court.

 Project example

A project in Asia established a core group in the project including representatives from the client and key consultants to oversee the social management planning on the project. This led to the development of an integrated approach to social baseline data collection to support the ESHIA and resettlement action plan processes which avoided duplication, led to cost savings, and avoided project delays.

What are the key steps in developing a social baseline?

The key steps in developing a project social baseline are:

1. Establish a team
2. Research existing primary and secondary data available for the project area
3. Prepare a map of the project footprint
4. Conduct a scoping exercise

5. Develop a set of monitoring indicators

6. Identify data tools and develop a data matrix

7. Sampling

8. Develop data collection tools (quantitative and qualitative)

9. Declare a cut-off date

10. Survey implementation

11. Baseline data-recording and analysis

These key steps are outlined in more detail in the following sections.

Establish the team to plan the baseline data collection and development of the ESHIA and RAP processes

The main problem encountered with baseline data collection is the piecemeal collection of data by different experts in an uncoordinated manner. In many cases the socioeconomic data collected for the ESHIA process is not useful for RAP planning and the same surveys often have to be repeated a number of times. This results in delays in the project schedule and significant costs for the company, and creates confusion and often survey fatigue in the impacted communities. The team leader should be a general social expert with the ability to assess the overall data collection needs on the project and where specialist input is required. The project team should comprise social, environmental and project-planning specialists (company and consultants) to enable proper co-ordination of baseline data collection activities in line with the project design, schedule and budget. It is important for the project leader to have a level of empathy with the impacted communities to ensure that there is a genuine understanding of their position so they can participate in the development of mitigation measures.

Research existing primary and secondary data available for the project area

The next step is to review the key background documents generated by the project in the past (primary data) or by other agencies on the general project area (secondary data). Note that secondary data is someone else's primary data and, while useful for triangulation purposes, it may suffer from bias and errors.

Background documentation may include:

- Internal project design documents which inform the choices for the location of project infrastructure. The final project design is often not well defined at an early stage of the project but it is important for the company to present the project team with a project description, including infrastructure options, so that social and environmental factors can be considered at an early stage.

- Environmental baseline data reports with information on soils and water and outline impacts and proposed mitigation measures.
- Previous social baseline data reports collected by the project.
- Reports from other agencies, particularly NGOs (non-governmental organisations) and universities, who have conducted research and implemented development projects in the project area.
- Local, regional and national reports which describe the socioeconomic context including development plans, national census and health, education, planning, police and agriculture departments.

Prepare a map of the project footprint

With recent advances in satellite technology, maps can be procured for almost any project area at 40 cm or 50 cm colour resolution, relatively cheaply. The project will often have detailed aerial photography, including lidar (remote sensing) maps with topography, which can also be very useful in developing resettlement site options. The project should use this imagery to build up a master map with the following layers:

- **Project infrastructure**: liaise with the project design team and develop a map of the project infrastructure. The project design constantly changes in the early stages of the project but all options should be mapped to enable the social team to participate in decisions on the siting of key project infrastructure.
- **Environmental buffers**: the environmental consultants will advise on environmental buffers around each type of project infrastructure and a map should be prepared to show where residential and other land uses are not permitted or restricted.
- **Key features**: digitise roads, water sources (rivers, dams, lakes, etc.), crops, forests, artisanal mining and any other significant features.
- **Structures**: digitise individual houses and associated structures, as well as community infrastructure such as schools, churches, mosques and other cultural assets and government buildings.

There are a number of participatory methods to involve local people in mapping their own area, ranging from the most basic—using stones on the ground—to the most sophisticated, where impacted people are trained to use GPS equipment and record the key resources in their communities.

Figure 6.2: Example of a project map with roads, structures and rivers digitised.

Who should be surveyed?

The surveys will be undertaken on impacted households. The impacts will vary depending on the proximity of the community to the project area, although some significant impacts can be experienced by communities downwind or downstream of a project.

- **Physically displaced households** lose their homes and/or land and other assets inside the project area, which is the land required for project infrastructure plus the project's environmental buffers (physically and/or economically impacted). These include households resident in the project area, road/pipeline right of way, or port and resettlement sites, who will be resettled. A 100% census and socioeconomic baseline of physically displaced households is required. A rapid asset survey and full asset survey (outlined below) are normally undertaken for all buildings.

- **Economically displaced households**: households resident outside the project area who are not required to resettle but who lose access to land

Figure 6.3: Map depicting the main impact areas from a complex land access and resettlement project (or cumulative impacts from a number of projects).

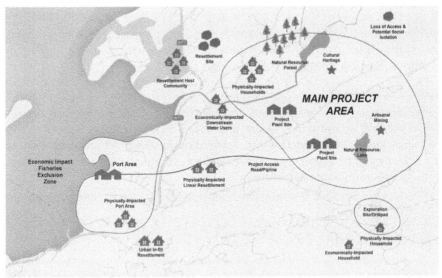

and other assets that leads to loss of income sources or other means of livelihood. A 100% census and socioeconomic baseline of economically displaced households is normally required. A field and crop survey will be undertaken on 100% of the households' fields to record all assets eligible for compensation.

- **Host community households**: households in communities hosting the resettlement sites face influx impacts from resettlers and other economic migrants. Host community households will also be impacted by land access and/or resettlement as the project will have to acquire land to accommodate the resettled households. A 100% census and socioeconomic survey is normally undertaken on all host community households which are physically and economically impacted by the project. Other households who are not directly impacted will be subject to a sample survey to develop a community profile.

- **Indirectly impacted households**: households living in the broader project area who will experience the general impacts, positive and negative, of the project on their lives. A (statistically representative) sample is normally sufficient to develop a profile of near-project communities for the RAP and environmental and social impact assessment.

Defining the project area of influence and buffer zones

An important step early in the baseline data collection and impact assessment phases is to demarcate the project's area of influence and buffer zone requirements.

The following key areas need to be identified:

Zones of direct impact:

- The project area: areas where the project activities and facilities are located, including access routes, water and power supply networks, supply chains, employee accommodation, etc. Areas used for livelihood practices such as hunting, fishing, grazing, gathering and agriculture, or religious or ceremonial purposes of a customary nature

- The watershed and airshed in which the project is located and which is impacted by dust, noise, etc.

Zones of indirect impact:

- The region where the project is located which will encounter the main economic impacts from the project, including the influx of economic migrants, employment and business opportunities.

Conduct a scoping exercise

The potential cost of mitigation for economic and displacement should be scoped early in the project design phase and integrated into the consideration of the project design and development. Mitigation and compensation for physical and economic displacement can be costly. Early assessment of this cost is important to assess the viability of alternative project designs, technologies, routes or sites (IFC 2012: Performance Standard 1, Guidance Note 21).

The project team should visit the project area but be careful to tailor the level of engagement with local stakeholders to the project stage so as to avoid creating expectations and encouraging speculative activities. Note how the communities are organised: the location of residences and farmsteads, the condition of community infrastructure, livelihood activities and the intensity of land use.

Speak with key project stakeholders, where appropriate, including local project staff/consultants, traditional and elected community representatives, government representatives and local development organisations and NGOs.

Develop a set of monitoring indicators

The development of a monitoring and evaluation plan is often an afterthought and a common complaint on projects is that the baseline is inadequate to enable proper monitoring to take place, often resulting in resurveys. The development of monitoring indicators should be a starting point for undertaking social research as this is how the performance of the project will be tracked. It is important that questions are aligned with how other agencies monitor data, such as national census or local health centre data. This will enable the project to compare the progress of impacted people with the general population. For example, asking whether there was an illness in the family in the past six months will not be useful if the regional health monitoring asks about illnesses in the past four weeks. The development of monitoring indicators is further discussed in Chapter 18 concerning monitoring and evaluation.

> Failure to develop monitoring indicators early on means that the ability to monitor post-resettlement conditions accurately against baseline conditions will not be possible

Identify data-collection tools and develop a data matrix

The **resources framework** presented in Figure 6.4 illustrates the key socioeconomic data-collection methods that are generally used to gather project data. This is not an exhaustive list as the baseline data requirements and tools used will be specific to the project context and must be assessed by social experts before implementation.

The requirements for baseline data collection are determined by the complexity of the project and the standards to which the project is adhering, and this can only be properly determined by the use of experienced ESHIA and RAP personnel. Figure 6.5 summarises the key social research methods which are utilised to collect the baseline data which are discussed below.

Data matrix

A data matrix is a simple tool which allows the project team and consultants to understand what data will be collected and what tools will be used. A common pitfall on projects is to take a questionnaire from another project, circulate this and start to add and remove questions depending on the project context. However, this generally leads to an endless list of questions as the team fails to understand that data can be collected using multiple tools and questionnaires are not suitable for the collection of all data.

Figure 6.4: An example of baseline data requirements and tools.

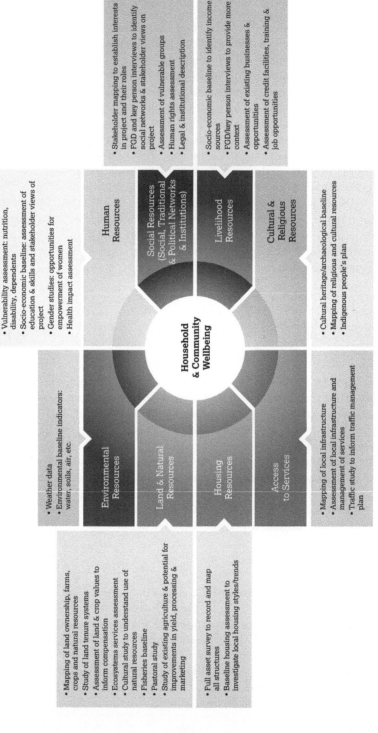

Figure 6.5: Summary of key research tools for collecting baseline data.

Social research method	Baseline data: resource category
Secondary data (primary data collected by others) (RAP/ESHIA)	All
Household census (RAP)	Physically and economically impacted households
Household socioeconomic survey (ESHIA sample and RAP 100%)	Livelihood resources, land and natural resources, access to services
Asset surveys (RAP): housing and buildings, infrastructure, commercial structures, crops and land	Land and natural resources, housing resources, cultural heritage resources
Mapping (RAP/ESHIA)	Human resources, land and natural resources, access to services, cultural and religious resources
Stakeholder mapping (RAP/ESHIA)	Social resources (social, traditional and political)
Focus group discussions (RAP/ESHIA)	All
Key person interviews (RAP/ESHIA)	All
Participatory research methods (RAP/ESHIA)	All
Specialist studies as required depending on the importance and complexity of key resources identified in the scoping study (RAP/ESHIA)	Health impact assessment, culture and archaeology, agriculture development and land tenure, pastoralism, artisanal mining, human rights assessment, business development, ecosystems services, etc.

Figure 6.6: An example of a how to start a data matrix.

Data Category/Research Tool	Census	Socio-economic Survey	FGDs	Secondary Data	Rapid Asset Survey	Full Asset Survey	Participatory Tools	Key Person Interviews	Direct Observation
Name of Household Head	x	x			x	x		x	
Religion	x	x							
Number of Residential Structures	x	x			x	x			
Type of Roof					x	x			
Source of Water	x	x	x	x			x	x	x
Community Conflict			x				x	x	
Perceptions of Project	x	x	x				x	x	

In a data matrix (Figure 6.6) the left-hand column lists the data categories and data to be collected, and the columns to the right indicate which research tool with be used to collect each data type. In many cases multiple research tools will be used to collect the same type of data in order to increase its accuracy. When the data matrix is completed all the project data requirements will be listed, together with the proposed tools for data collection.

The data matrix should be circulated to the project team, including the social and environmental staff and other consultants working on the project. The field survey team in particular should be allowed to give their feedback on the wording of questions and how these translate into the local language. All of this feedback should be incorporated into a revised document and a final data matrix produced. The survey instruments can then be developed from the data matrix by sorting all of the data to be collected using each tool. Once the draft data-collection tools have been developed, these must be circulated to the whole team again, particularly the database supervisor, to ensure the data can be easily coded for data entry.

Sampling

The collection of data from a representative sample is critical to be able to make generalisations about the population being studied. A 100% sample is appropriate as part of a census to record information on all physically and economically impacted households for land access and resettlement. However, for the purposes of an SIA (social impact assessment) of the wider population a survey sample will likely be more appropriate.

Many projects assume that a fixed sample of 10% is adequate to generate a statistically significant sample. However, this is not the case when it comes to a community affected by resettlement. A small village comprising 20 migrant households from a different ethnic group, living in a large population, would not be adequately researched with a general 10% sample. Depending on the level of statistical confidence required, it might be necessary to conduct a sample of 50% of the households in this village to be able to describe their socioeconomic status with confidence.

Another important issue is the definition of a household for the purposes of the research. There is no universal agreement of how a household is defined because there are considerable cultural differences around the world, such as multiple wives and/or married children continuing to live in some households. In most cases, households are generally considered to have the following characteristics:

- Sleeping in one house or compound
- A common source of livelihood or income
- A common source of food: 'eating from the same pot'

However, there are also issues around whether to include absent members as part of the household, or whether tenants or unmarried sons living with their partners in the house represent separate households. The advice is to include all members who are normally resident in the household, often taken to be resident for at least six months, and to agree on how to deal with exceptions depending on the project context.

Another issue is how to select households from the population on a random basis where there is no accurate list of all households to select from (the 'sampling frame'). Note that if a sample is not selected on a random basis the research can only describe the sample itself and cannot be said to represent the wider population, although it can be useful for describing a particular group in the population (for example, herders). Formal sampling methods such as simple random, systematic random or stratified random sampling can be appropriate depending on the project context.

Design data collection tools (quantitative and qualitative)

A variety of data collection tools are used to produce a record of the baseline conditions in the communities prior to project implementation. Social research methods are generally divided between quantitative and qualitative research.

Quantitative research

Quantitative data is data which is collected in a way that allows analysis using statistical methods with the results able to be displayed using charts, tables and graphs. Examples of quantitative data include:

- Secondary sources:
  - Previous surveys
  - Census data
  - Official statistics
  - Monitoring studies
  - Maps
- Primary sources:
  - Sample surveys
  - Observations

The key types of quantitative survey are outlined below:

Household census

This form is required to record all residents in the impacted area and can be combined with the socioeconomic baseline survey form depending on the stage of the project. This census gathers basic demographic data (age, sex, relationship to household head) on each household. Note that the design of the survey questions needs careful consideration on the survey forms so that the information can be easily coded for entry into a database and statistical analysis.

Reliability of data on household income and expenditure

Information on household income and expenditure is commonly used to track household wellbeing. However, it is difficult for households, who generally don't keep records, or have stable, regular sources of income, to recall this information. It is also common on resettlement projects for households to overstate income from assets in order to gain higher compensation while understating post-project income in order to seek additional benefits. Researchers should be careful to triangulate sources of information on income and expenditure using proxy values such as household commodities (ownership of cellphone, motorbike, tin roof, etc.).

Socioeconomic baseline survey

This can be applied to a sample of households to support the SIA or applied to the whole impacted community to support the development of the RAP packages. The socioeconomic data should include information on ethnicity, religion, health, education, and primary and secondary livelihood activities, including employment, agriculture, natural resource use and access to social services.

Impacted assets

The project must record the assets which the impacted households and communities own or use and will lose access to during project implementation. This information is required in order to develop RAP packages including compensation, resettlement housing and infrastructure and livelihood restoration packages. Projects need to collect data as if it will later need to be defended in court with the required local, government and expert sign-off, so that the veracity of the data meets national compensation and resettlement legislation. The key assets are land, crops, structures and natural resources, and there are often multiple ownership claims, including communal ownership, which need to be resolved prior to compensation and resettlement if the project schedule is to be achieved. The key asset surveys are as follows:

> All project data should be collected in a way that can later be defended in court as litigation is common on projects

- **Rapid asset survey**: in some cases a rapid asset survey will be conducted at the time of the declaration of the cut-off date, and this will mark each structure with a project code and include a short form to collect key data on structure location (GPS), structure ownership and a photo. This survey fixes the entitlement to compensation and resettlement only to those structures recorded at the time of the cut-off date and is undertaken rapidly to minimise the opportunity of people constructing speculative structures in anticipation of project benefits.

- **Full asset survey**: this survey records detailed information on each structure depending on national requirements including external size, number, size and use of rooms, construction materials and quality (including improvements such as tiling), GPS location, multiple photos of all buildings, a floor plan sketch, and ownership and tenancy information.

Project example

A project in Africa declared the cut-off date for the project and commenced the baseline asset surveys which, due to the size of the project, required four months to complete. However, during the survey process the communities engaged in speculative activities by constructing rudimentary structures in order to claim compensation and/or resettlement houses. At one point it was difficult for the surveyors to keep pace with the community speculation. When the surveys were completed the number of houses was twice the initial estimate, which led to delays to the project and a significantly increased cost of resettlement.

Project example

A project in Africa had been subjected to considerable speculation by communities over a rolling land access process. For a new phase the project consulted with the stakeholder representatives on the planned process, declared a cut-off date and commenced the baseline asset surveys. On the first day of the survey an aerial flyover was conducted in the presence of the communities, and on the same day aerial photographs were posted on notice boards in the communities to demonstrate that the company could identify all structures present and entitled to compensation/resettlement. The survey teams then conducted an RAS (rapid asset survey) of the project area over a three-day period, which quickly marked each building with an individual reference code and recorded the GPS location, photographs of the structure and ownership information (if the owner was present). A notice was placed on each structure and an independent witness signed each RAS form. At the end of the process a list of properties and owners was placed on community notice boards and the community were invited to register complaints if they believed their structure had not been recorded. These cases were then cross-referenced against the aerial photography to ensure they were not new structures, and then surveyed if eligible. Once the RAS was finished the detailed full asset survey was undertaken only on those structures identified in the RAS, over a period of two months. This process significantly reduced speculative activities and improved relations with the company as it was understood that the impacted households were genuine residents and not speculators.

Land and crop surveys

A cadastral map should be prepared for the project area outlining the ownership of each parcel of land both individually and communally. This land survey is normally combined with the crop survey which will demarcate both farm and internal field crop boundaries.

The land/crop survey should record the following information:

- Ownership, tenancy and sharecropping information to record all of the interests in the land and crops
- Differential GPS survey of the field boundary so that each field can be mapped to a ±1 m accuracy
- Crop type, size category (seedling/small/medium/mature depending on valuation method) and number/area (depending on whether it is an annual or tree crop)

The crop surveyors must be experienced and trained in the survey method which will reflect the proposed valuation process. The project must reach agreement with stakeholders on the technical definitions of crop maturity as different rates might be paid for seedlings, to discourage speculation, and small trees. The surveys will normally involve counting and marking individual trees, including recording tree girth and height where appropriate. The measurement of crop areas should also be done carefully, using differential GPS equipment which must be

Figure 6.7: Undertaking crop surveys utilising differential GPS equipment.

properly calibrated to ensure that margins of error are less than ±1 m, if possible. The survey maps can be overlaid on recent project imagery to verify that the field boundaries are being correctly measured. It is also possible for some satellite imagery to be processed to identify different crop types, indicated in different colours, and this is also useful for verifying that the crop surveys have been properly conducted.

Qualitative research

Qualitative methods and fieldwork are used to learn about life in the community or area and the potential impacts of a proposal, as perceived and spoken about by those living there (Vanclay and Becker 2003).

The key qualitative data sources are:

- Local histories/accounts and newspaper reports
- Previous studies/SIAs
- Focus groups and workshops
- Key person interviews
- Participatory rural appraisal

Focus groups

This is where a small group of stakeholders (6–10 people) are brought together to discuss key topics and questions to enable social researchers to understand the context and impacts of the project. A focus group guide should be prepared in advance so that the facilitator knows the information the researcher is interested in gathering. The facilitator can introduce these topics while also allowing the participants to discuss other issues which concern them. It is also important to prepare a template on which to record the key issues discussed in the focus group for later analysis. Separate focus groups should be held with the key socio-economic groups including older men, women, young people, farmers' groups, business groups, etc. Note that attendance registers should be used to demonstrate that the project is consulting with a wide sample of stakeholders.

Key person interviews

These are also called key informant interviews, although this term is not appropriate when projects are in conflict areas due to sensitivities around the local people being identified as 'informants'. A summary of the key issues discussed should be prepared so that the research team can pool responses around the main survey themes and triangulate responses.

Other qualitative data-gathering methods include community mapping, site observations, participatory rural appraisal methods including mapping, and seasonal calendars.

Stakeholder analysis

The analysis of stakeholders is dealt with in detail in Chapter 5. However, the baseline data-collection process does provide the first extensive engagement with stakeholders on many projects. Before the surveys take place, a proper community entry process must be undertaken to ensure that there is wide stakeholder support for the project. There also has to be a balance between the information given to communities about the location of project infrastructure in advance of the surveys, so as not to encourage speculative activities.

Consultation during the scoping process should ensure that no group within the community is excluded, and that the issues discussed and subsequently researched through baseline studies are posed in a culturally appropriate manner.

Declaration of an entitlement cut-off date

The legal framework in most countries requires that companies must secure permission from the government in order to proceed with the project, and record the assets (land, crops and structures) impacted by the project where resettlement and compensation is required. This process can range from a decree from the local or regional government to full approval of the permit for the project, which gives the project permission to freeze development on the project area and proceed with the survey, compensation and resettlement process. This section applies only to the RAP—a 'cut-off date' is not required for the SIA, although the approval and support of the authorities and community leaders will be required for both.

The IFC standards set the cut-off date (also often referred to as the moratorium date) as the date of completion of the census and assets inventory of persons affected by the project (IFC 2012). Persons occupying the project area after the cut-off date are not eligible for compensation and/or resettlement assistance. Similarly, fixed assets (for example, built structures, crops, fruit trees or wood-lots) established after the date of completion of the assets inventory, or an alternative mutually agreed date, will not be compensated.

It is important that the project has the legal right to undertake the asset surveys prior to proceeding, or the process could later be challenged in court by those who subsequently planted crops or built crops on the project area. Once permission is granted, a cut-off date for eligibility to compensation and resettlement is normally declared in partnership with local and/or national government. Although the cut-off date is often announced in advance to minimise speculation once the project has been declared, it is not fully valid until all the asset surveys are completed. This often leads to the community continuing to plant crops and construct houses while the surveys are under way in order to claim project benefits and the company must employ multiple methods to minimise speculative activities on the project as discussed in Chapter 7 on assessing impacts and minimising impacts. As outlined in the example above, with modern technology such as the use of satellite imagery and unmanned aerial vehicles it is possible to acquire imagery at the time of the cut-off date and agree with the authorities and communities that this map represents a valid record of all structures present and eligible for compensation/resettlement. It is then important to patrol the project area and inform any speculators that they will not be compensated and to have representatives from the local authorities and communities to support this process.

It should be noted that an entitlement cut-off date is not permanent. If a project is significantly delayed, survey information will be out of date and normal development will need to continue. In this case, a new cut-off date and baseline surveys would need to be agreed.

Survey implementation

The key to successful social research is to use experienced supervisors and enumerators and to conduct training on the specific survey tools well in advance of going into the field. There should be a testing phase where enumerators are monitored while interviewing a survey sample in the local language. This will give the survey enumerators an opportunity to seek clarification on the meaning of each question and how well this is understood by the person being surveyed.

The survey data can be collected either on handwritten paper forms or digitally on electronic devices. The project should comply with the national data protection code of practice, if one exists, to ensure that private data is only shared internally and that the household is aware of the purpose of the data collection and how this will be used. The choice of data collection tool will depend largely on the capacity of the survey enumerators. In many countries a digital document would not be accepted in a court process challenging the survey results being used for the determination of compensation. Therefore, it will be necessary to print out the asset survey forms and ensure the project-affected person fully understands what has been recorded and signs the form which will then represent the legal record. In most cases the form would also have to be signed by an independent witness or both a government and community representative in order to comply with national compensation legislation.

Survey work can require long periods in the field and can be tedious, so it is important that completed survey forms are checked each evening for quality control and errors. A major weakness in survey exercises is quality control, and it is often only during data entry that major issues are identified. It is important early in the process to identify enumerators who are not meeting quality standards, and resolve the issue or replace them. It is important that quality control is undertaken by someone from the social research team and that this is not just left to sub-consultants who might not understand the whole process.

It is important that a **communications plan** is prepared for the surveys in order to explain fully the process to local stakeholders and to ensure proper community entry. A sample table of contents for the communications plan is outlined below:

- **Introduction**: summary of the activity
- **Communication objectives**: the purpose of the communications plan
- **Target audience**: the primary (impacted households and local stakeholders, project team, government), secondary (regional stakeholders) and tertiary (national stakeholders, NGOs, IFC)
- **Action plan**: develop a table consisting of columns on the activity, target audience, why (justification), responsibility, and when the activity is scheduled
- Develop a **work plan** which outlines each key community activity by target audience
- **Key messages**: outline the high-level message about the activity that is about to take place
- **Sub-messages**: develop sub-messages with detail about the main activity broken down into bullet points
- **Speaking points**: develop speaking points for the project team to get their key messages across
- **Questions and answers**: develop a list of questions likely to be asked by project stakeholders and provide answers to each question. This will ensure that there is consistent messaging across the project.

The project team should produce a record of each communications activity as outlined and also make notes on which communications methods are the most effective and how the communications plan could be improved.

It is recommended that local political and traditional leaders endorse the process. It is also recommended that a community leader or technical expert, recognised by the government, signs off on the land, crop and building surveys to provide independent certification that the information is collected correctly, as this may have to be defended later in court. It is also important that the impacted households are given information on the purpose of the surveys: an information sheet can be prepared and presented to each household during the survey process, and also explained verbally for those who cannot read in the local language. Where owners are absent or cannot be identified at the time of the survey, notices can also be affixed to structures with information on the cut-off date and survey process.

The communications plan should outline the objective of each study being undertaken so that the communities understand the difference between ESHIA surveys and RAP surveys, i.e. that ESHIA surveys are just gathering information to generate a community profile whereas RAP households will be directly impacted by land access and resettlement. The enumerators and other project staff should be properly trained and fully conversant with the communications plan so that there are consistent messages coming from the project on the purpose of the data research activities.

The logistics for the survey are also very important as the surveyors will need adequate accommodation, meals, transport, communications, survey materials field materials (boots and raincoats; sunhats; pens, forms, etc.) and space to work in the evenings.

The timing of the survey process is also critical as surveys undertaken outside the cropping season might miss critical crops which could need to be compensated, while surveys can be very difficult to undertake in the cropping season when crops such as millet are very tall. It is also important to consider wet/dry access to villages and fields, as well as harvest periods when households are usually busy. The time of the day is also important to ensure that both the male and female senior household members are present. Survey teams should also be sensitive to times which may be culturally or religiously inappropriate for visiting farms, as well as important religious and national holidays when households might not be available for interview.

It is important that all impacted households are properly identified and recorded. The project should ensure that each asset owner can be individually identified by a form of ID such as a voter's card, national identity card or driving licence. However, in some countries not all households will have identity cards and the project may have to develop an internal identity card system where all impacted households are issued with a photo ID in order to relate to the project. Each structure should be given a unique identification number so that it can be tracked through the RAP process and linked to the household ID. This number can either be painted on the structure or else a small durable card can be printed with the number which is then fixed onto a door or structure frame. The surveyors should consult with the household on the placing of the ID number on the house and ensure that it is not defaced with gaudy paintwork.

Once the data is collected, the forms should be reviewed by the survey supervisors before being passed onto the data-recording teams. Any errors should be noted and discussed with the enumerators in order to ensure the accuracy of data.

Data-recording and analysis

How should data be recorded?

The entry of data into a database is a key step in the research process and errors can occur at this stage. Once the survey forms are reviewed and presented to the data-management team the first step should be to log the forms using the household, form and surveyor identification numbers. With electronic forms the data is automatically entered into the project database but must be carefully screened for errors before being fully validated. With paper forms the originals should be scanned into the database. The forms must be carefully filed as it is these files that would be required as evidence in any future court case which might challenge the survey results. The data-entry staff should be supervised to ensure that they are entering the data as per the coding on the survey forms.

The capturing of data can be time-consuming and requires a qualified team with requisite quality controls and random checks in place. Database systems may either allow multiple users on one server (with results automatically collated) or require separate input, which then needs to be combined manually. Online access is often required for the former option, creating restrictions in some locations, while manual compilation of data allows additional potential for error.

It is worth remembering that the baseline data collected will be referenced for the life of the project. Getting an effective and reliable system set up at the beginning of the project will enable this data to be used in future for effective monitoring purposes. Although data management is often the responsibility of a consultant during initial baseline assessments, there needs to be a handover to the client for future use.

What sort of project database is required?

There a number of options available to manage data on projects depending on the size of the project and the resources available.

Any database should be assessed based on the following key criteria:

- **User friendliness**: Does the software have a user-friendly interface that non-technical people can understand? Can the software be managed by national IT staff? What number of users does the system support? What is the flexibility of the system for future expansion?

- **Data security**: Will the data be secure or can a third party who has access to the database change data fields? A key risk is that the original data can be manipulated on the project, such as the number of trees for compensation, creating opportunities for fraud.

- **Cost**: Can the project afford the initial database package and also the recurring costs in terms of licences and further training and support?

- **Needs**: Does the software meet your needs for social and environmental data-recording, analysis and reporting, together with integrated mapping?

- **Support**: Is support available if there are issues with the system and what is the cost of this support?

- **Security**: Does the system provide secure levels of access to protect against fraud?

- **Reporting**: Does the system enable users to configure their own reports and present these in an easily understood format?

The advantages and disadvantages of the different database options are outlined in Figure 6.8.

Figure 6.8: Advantages and disadvantages of different database options.

Database type	Advantages	Disadvantages
Spreadsheet	• Can be designed and developed in house with basic spreadsheet skills • Simple to enter data into and is understood by the maximum number of users • Cheap as most projects will have spreadsheets on their existing computers • Useful to manage the data for a small number of users (<10)	• Difficult to integrate mapping information • More difficult to integrate with reporting and monitoring systems • Data security is very limited leaving the project open to potential fraud • Not suitable for medium to large projects with large amounts of data to record and process
Access database	• Can be designed by a mid-level IT technician in house • Simple to enter data into and users can easily be trained in its use • Cheap as most projects will have an Access database on existing computers • Useful to manage data for a medium number of users (<20)	• Difficult to integrate mapping information • Data security is limited leaving the project open to potential fraud • Not suitable for medium to large projects with large amounts of data to record and process • Access can only deal with a limited number of users
Integrated GIS/ SQL server database	• Specialist software solutions are available to manage social, resettlement and environmental processes on projects • Specialist software integrates mapping data and presents customised reports • These packages offer high levels of data security with different levels of data access to users in the company • The packages can deal with a large number of users	• Software can be costly in terms of upfront and recurring costs depending on the package required • The level of technician required to manage the software is higher than Excel or Access

Commercial software packages

There are a number of tailored software solutions designed to manage social and environmental systems on projects which specifically address land access and resettlement data requirements including:

- Isometrix Software (www.isometrix.com): Metrix Software Solutions in partnership with Intersocial Consulting
- BoréalisIMS Software Suite (www.boreal-is.com): Boréalis

What analysis of baseline data is required?

The environmental and social researchers and project staff need to liaise closely with the database manager so that reports are designed which meet their needs. Land access and resettlement projects generate huge amounts of data, including survey forms, reports of qualitative data, maps, photographs, GPS locations, etc. It is important that the database can store and analyse the data in a way that is quickly accessible to the project team in a format that they can design themselves in consultation with the database team.

Projects typically generate a lot of data and reports need to be prioritised. As outlined above, it is key to develop a set of monitoring indicators before the data-capture tools are finalised, and the database reports generated must facilitate this monitoring process.

Figure 6.9: Example of a database report on crop surveys.

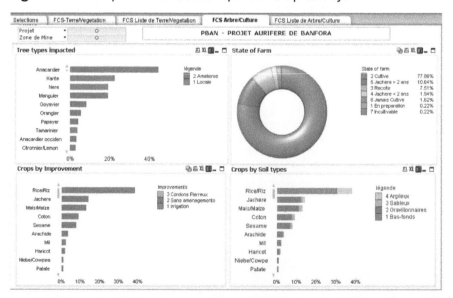

It is useful to present only a summary of key data in key documents such as the RAP or SIA, leaving the full data-analysis report as an appendix so as not to overwhelm users with information.

Note that the data is only as good as the process used to collect it. The researchers should be careful not to extrapolate based on small samples without a statistical basis: data from small samples can only be used to describe the specific respondents surveyed.

Analysis needs to be useful for the determination of appropriate resettlement and livelihood packages, and for the accurate determination of compensation, according to agreed values. The project database should be able to collate this data and produce reports which can be readily audited for the purposes of compensation payments.

Baseline data collection and analysis: key considerations

- **Detailed and comprehensive baseline information**, with co-operation between ESHIA and resettlement consultants, is crucial for proper resettlement planning and implementation.

- **Surveys need to be conducted early and in a timely fashion** to ensure that baseline information required for planning is relevant and available when needed.

- It is critical to have a **co-ordinated approach** to surveys, to ensure collection of appropriate data and to prevent survey fatigue in the impacted communities, as well as adequate quality control systems.

- Ensure that the data collected is **comprehensive and is uniformly collected**.

- **Involvement of numerous consultancies** for different components (for example, census, valuation, resettlement planning) **can cause problems** with alignment of data.

- Companies need to work closely with local authorities early in the project cycle to **declare a cut-off date** in order to freeze development and limit speculation.

- It is important to **minimise lag time between the cut-off date, the census and socioeconomic and asset surveys**, and the actual physical resettlement, because if the project is delayed there will be pressure on the community for further development which may require resurveys.

- **Significant project delays requiring multiple cut-off dates confuse communities** and companies need to improve both planning and communications with communities.

- **Use of early satellite/aerial imagery and mapping can help** to plan prior to on-the-ground data-collection activities.

- **Use of a rapid asset survey can reduce speculation**.

- **Monitoring indicators** should be defined early in the process to enable gathering of relevant baseline information against which to monitor post-resettlement living conditions.
- Risks of disputes related to documenting/recording traditional land ownership/ land users to determine compensation eligibility can be minimised through a **participatory approach to surveys**.
- **Involve traditional chiefs, local authorities and government agencies in the survey process** to ensure that national regulations are complied with.
- **Ensure affected people and community representatives are present** at the time of the surveys and that they sign the survey forms, to ensure a transparent process.
- **Engage all relevant government institutions in a timely manner**, involving them in the resettlement process including the census and surveys.
- **Use of an independent expert** to conduct surveys can help to ensure impartiality.
- **Surveyed houses should be clearly marked** to avoid the possibility of double-counting, and reduce the potential for speculative claims.
- Where there is a high percentage of **absentee landowners**, ensure that socio-economic surveys incorporate approaches for canvassing their views.
- A **secure and flexible database** is essential to manage data on complex projects.

7

Assessing project impacts and risks, and minimising displacement

The land access and resettlement process is really a 'project within a project' in terms of the sheer complexity of social and environmental impacts generated on communities living within and around the project area. The requirement to get a specialist resettlement team to manage the land access and resettlement process as a subproject can result in a separation between the ESHIA (environmental, social and health impact assessment) and RAP (resettlement action plan) teams leading to poor co-ordination. The ESHIA is normally prepared early in the project cycle to satisfy permitting requirements, while the RAP is a much longer process of consultations and negotiations with impacted households and implementing compensation, resettlement and livelihood restoration. The RAP is a sub-plan of the overall SIMP (social impact management plan), but the linkages are often not properly established between the two plans.

The objective of this chapter is to set out a practical process of planning the SIA (social impact assessment) and RAP in a co-ordinated way to ensure that the linkages between the SIMP and RAP mitigation measures are complementary and aligned. A resources framework is introduced as both an analytical tool and practical framework to understand the key community resources which need to be focused on separately in the land access and resettlement process to ensure integrated project planning.

The chapter is divided into three main sections:

- Outline of the SIA process
- Using the resources framework as a tool to identify impacts
- Assessment of impacts in land access and resettlement projects

Outline of the SIA process

The impacts of projects are generally determined by a social and environmental analysis of the proposed design and delivery of project activities, building on the baseline assessment process described in the previous chapter. A **social impact assessment (SIA)** determines the key social impacts and related mitigation measures required, particularly where projects will require significant land access

> A comprehensive set of resources can be found at the SIA hub for SIA practitioners (www.socialimpactassessment. com/resources.asp)

and resettlement. This chapter provides a brief introduction to SIA.

The definition of an SIA is:

> The process of analysing (predicting, evaluating and reflecting) and managing the intended and unintended consequences on the human environment of planned interventions (policies, programmes, plans and projects) and any social change processes invoked by those interventions so as to bring about a more sustainable and equitable biophysical and human environment. (Vanclay 2002: 388)

What are the objectives of an SIA?

The purpose of an SIA as defined by the IFC (International Finance Corporation) is (IFC 2012):

- To identify and evaluate environmental and social risks and impacts of the project
- To adopt a mitigation hierarchy to anticipate and avoid, or where avoidance is not possible, minimise, and, where residual impacts remain, compensate/offset for risks and impacts to workers, affected communities and the environment
- To promote improved environmental and social performance of clients through the effective use of management systems
- To ensure that grievances from affected communities and external communications from other stakeholders are responded to and managed appropriately
- To promote and provide means for adequate engagement with affected communities throughout the project cycle on issues that could potentially affect them, and to ensure that relevant environmental and social information is disclosed and disseminated

What are the key challenges, issues and risks?

Key challenges, issues and risks that projects face include the following:

- Project-permitting **legislation in many countries does not require that a comprehensive SIA is prepared**, leading to the importance of social impacts being downplayed on projects.

- **ESHIAs are often fast-tracked** to support rapid project development and this can lead to a substandard impacts analysis and the development of social management plans with limited community consultations which fail to meet community expectations.

- **SIA practitioners generally do not implement the plans that they develop** so there is limited learning from experience and a tendency to churn out generic SIAs with unrealistic social management plans that are often not implemented.

- SIA practitioners **often raise the expectations of communities during ESHIA public consultations** as their goal is to get the document passed with minimal objections by local permitting agencies. This can lead to conflict with the company at a later stage when the resources are not there to meet community expectations.

- There is often **limited engagement between the SIA and RAP planning teams** resulting in the duplication of data collection and conflicting messages on the project.

What are the guiding principles in SIA?

The IFC has broadened the definition of SIA in the context of ESHIAs to include a sustainable development component. This ensures that the assessment includes the identification of positive impacts and opportunities for enhancing the socio-economic wellbeing of the people who live and work in the project's area of influence, leading to the development of an SIMP.

The SIA process should therefore:

- Include local knowledge and values in the design of the project and help decision-makers identify the most socially beneficial course of action for local, regional, and national interests.

- Help affected communities and agencies plan for social change resulting from a proposed action.

- Bring about a more ecologically, socioculturally and economically sustainable and equitable environment, and promote community development and empowerment, build capacity and develop social capital.

- Ensure that development maximises its benefits and minimises its costs, especially those costs borne by people. A good assessment and management system enables continuous improvement of environmental and social performance, and can lead to better economic, financial, social and environmental outcomes.

- Comply with both national legislation and international guidelines, including lender requirements in order to gain access to funding.
- Enable the project proponent to be recognised as a socially responsible organisation and achieve a social licence to operate for all project developments.

What are the key components?

The SIA should be undertaken by professionally qualified, competent persons.

The type, scale and location of the project will guide the scope and level of effort devoted to the risks and impacts identification process. Following initial screening, appropriate and relevant methods and assessment tools can then be selected for the project.

It is critical that social and resettlement experts are involved at an early stage of the project development so that they can make a contribution to the project design and planning process with the purpose of minimising the project footprint, as discussed further later in this chapter. Such experts can provide inputs into the selection of the location of key project infrastructure to avoid displacement, which can be both costly and present delays for the project. This approach allows for key risks to be identified and avoided, reducing the need for costly mitigation measures to reduce or compensate for impacts.

The key components in the SIA process are outlined in Figure 7.1.

The approach to scoping and baseline data collection and analysis has been described in Chapter 6. This chapter focuses on the assessment of impacts and development of proposed mitigation, particularly minimising displacement.

What is the key legislation governing SIA?

International guidelines

IFC PS (Performance Standard) 1 on the assessment and management of environmental and social risks and impacts states that the aim of the assessment is to identify and evaluate environmental and social risks and impacts of the project and to adopt a mitigation hierarchy to anticipate and avoid, or where avoidance is not possible, minimise, and, where residual impacts remain, compensate/offset for risks and impacts to workers, affected communities and the environment.

World Bank Operational Policy 4.01 on environmental assessment (World Bank 1999) notes that environmental assessment evaluates a project's potential risks and impacts in the area of influence; examines project alternatives; identifies ways of improving project selection, siting, planning, design and implementation by preventing, minimising, mitigating or compensating for adverse environmental impacts and enhancing positive impacts; and includes the process

Figure 7.1: The key components in the SIA process.

Scoping
- Develop an integrated team with client, social and environment consultants
- Confirm legislation and study requirements
- Identify area of influence
- Identify and engage communities
- Identify key project risks and impacts

Baseline studies
- Collect regional and local baseline data
- Engage with project-affected communities

Impact assessment
- Analyse, describe and assess impacts
- Integrate with other specialists

Mitigation
- Suggest mitigation measures: practical, implementable, affordable

Management
- Develop a social management and monitoring plan
- Integrate with client and environmental impact assessment team

Monitoring and engagement
- Implement a monitoring plan, engage with community on impacts and mitigation measures and adapt as required

of mitigating and managing adverse environmental impacts throughout project implementation.

National legislation

National legislation on environmental permitting of projects often contains limited references or requirements to SIA. National legislation commonly specifies 'social' within the context of environment, often with a focus on consultation but without any specific requirements. It is important to engage with the regulator to ensure all the requirements are fulfilled and any new or future legislation is taken into account. The SIA team must ensure that the gap between national and international legislation is filled. In some cases two SIAs will be prepared; one to meet national permitting requirements and a more comprehensive SIA to international standards to address any gaps in national standards.

What impacts need to be considered?

In determining what impacts need to be considered a project needs to undertake the following:

- **Consider key questions**: what are the potential displacement effects related to key infrastructure? What are the impacts relating to proposed work methods to be employed?
- **Identify impacts in relation to key project activities**: consider all project phases including planning, construction, operations, decommissioning and closure, and post-closure. Impacts need to be considered in relation to project phases and in relation to key project infrastructure.
- **Consider the distribution of impacts** (whether social, economic, air quality, noise or potential health effects) to different social groups. Social impacts are also dependent on the environmental impacts identified.
- **Need to specifically consider impacts to women, children and vulnerable groups**, which is why baseline data is disaggregated as such.
- Consider types of impact:
  - **Direct**: occurring as a direct result of project activities in the same time and space, such as displacement or employment with the mine.
  - **Indirect**: caused by primary impacts, often occurring later both in time and geographic distance, such as the establishment of businesses as a result of demand from a project.
  - **Cumulative**: impacts arising from the combination of existing and future impacts (discussed below).
  - **Transboundary**: impacts which cross international boundaries, such as water bodies, customary land ownership, or as a result of labour.

Cumulative impacts

The IFC advises that multiple environmental and social impacts from existing projects, combined with the potential incremental impacts resulting from proposed and/or anticipated future projects, may result in significant cumulative impacts that would not be expected in the case of a stand-alone project or business activity. These cumulative impacts must be assessed in the ESHIA process.

Cumulative impacts are those resulting from the incremental impacts of an action added to other past, present and reasonably foreseeable future actions regardless of which agency or person undertakes them. For example, air quality impacts in an environment already affected by mining operations and poor air quality, or agricultural land take in an area subjected to numerous developments, reducing the availability of agricultural land in general in the region.

Using the resources framework as a tool to identify impacts

The complexity of land access and resettlement projects arising from the collective impacts on households often leads project planners to focus on what are perceived as the major issues, ignoring what are seen as less important impacts. Project planners have struggled to present a framework that captures this complexity in everyday project language that can be understood by all stakeholders while ensuring that all scenarios and impacts are identified. This section seeks to take the best from existing frameworks and present a **new resources framework** to assist project planners in capturing all the main impacts and risks and present a practical approach to developing management plans.

Existing frameworks

The early understanding of the social impacts of projects on communities stemmed from work by social researchers such as Amartya Sen, who had witnessed at first hand the terrible Bengal famine of 1943. He published an influential book, *An Essay on Entitlement and Deprivation* (1981), in which he argued that famine occurs not only from a lack of food, but from inequalities built into mechanisms for distributing food. He also pointed to a number of social and economic factors, such as declining wages, unemployment, rising food prices and poor food distribution systems, as causes of famine. Sen's 'entitlement theory' focuses on economic inequalities that limit the purchasing power of the most vulnerable in society and prevent them from accessing certain resources over time. While Sen's theories have been challenged, the idea that communities can adapt to the impacts of disasters and projects has led to the development of a number of analytical frameworks, briefly described below, to help practitioners to plan for these events.

The access model

The **access model** (Wisner *et al.* 1994, 2003) was developed to present the complex and varied sets of social and environmental events and longer-term processes associated with natural disasters, for example earthquakes, and man-made disasters such as wars. The model was developed from rejection of the idea that disasters were caused by natural events only, and suggested instead that social systems operated to generate or exacerbate disasters by making people vulnerable. The access model is based on the ability of an individual, family, group, class or community to use resources which are directly required to secure a livelihood, and their ability to adapt to new situations. A livelihood is defined as 'the command an individual, family or other social group has over an income and/or bundles of resources that can be used or exchanged to satisfy its needs. This may involve information, cultural knowledge, social networks and legal rights as well as tools, land and other physical resources' (Wisner *et al.* 2003: 12).

'Resources' in the access model are defined as the physical and social means of gaining a livelihood. Resources include labour, land, tools, seed for crops, livestock, draught animals, cash and jewellery, as well as skills. In order for tangible resources to be mobilised people must be able to use social resources to access markets and exercise rights through relationships with family, kin and friends. The availability of resources creates an 'access profile' for each household, and a good access profile is where households possess a large number of income opportunities. Access to such resources is always based on social and economic relations, termed 'access qualifications', including the social relations of production, gender, ethnicity, status and age, meaning that rights and obligations are not distributed equally among all people. Power relations between people at different levels determines access to resources, and this 'political economy' includes wider family and kinship ties of reciprocity and obligation, as well as those between employees and workers, members of different ethnic groups and between individual citizens and the state.

Impoverishment risks and reconstruction framework

The best-known model for highlighting the impacts of land access and resettlement is the **impoverishment risks and reconstruction framework**, which was developed by Michael Cernea (1997) and built on earlier ideas on the underlying causes of vulnerability to impoverishment. IFC PS5 on land acquisition and

Figure 7.2: DFID sustainable livelihoods framework.

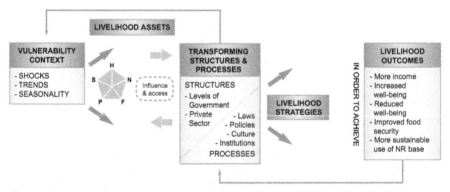

H represents **human capital:** the skills, knowledge, ability to labour and good health important to the ability to pursue different livelihood strategies;

P represents **physical capital:** the basic infastructure (transport, shelter, water, energy and communications) and the production equipment and means that enable people to pursue livelihoods;

S represents **social capital:** the social resources (networks, membership of groups, relationships of trust, access to wider institutions of society) upon which people draw in pursuit of livelihoods;

F represents **financial capital:** the financial resources which are available to people (whether savings, supplies of credit or regular remittances or pensions) and which provide them with different livelihood options; and

N represents **natural capital:** the natural resource stocks from which resource flows useful for livelihoods are derived (e.g. land, water, wildlife, biodiversity, environmental resources).

Source: Carney *et al.* (1999: 9).

involuntary resettlement uses this framework to identify the main land access and resettlement risks.

The key risks and mitigations outlined in the impoverishment risks and reconstruction framework are:

- From landlessness to land-based resettlement
- From joblessness to re-employment
- From homelessness to house reconstruction
- From marginalisation to social inclusion
- From increased morbidity to improved healthcare
- From food insecurity to adequate nutrition
- From loss of access to restoration of community assets and services
- From social disarticulation to networks and community rebuilding

The risks outlined in the impoverishment risks and reconstruction model are incorporated into the resources framework.

Sustainable livelihoods approach

The **sustainable livelihoods approach** was promoted in the late 1990s by DFID (Department for International Development) in the UK and is presented in the sustainable livelihoods framework (Figure 7.2). This approach represented a shift towards a more poverty-focused approach with the active participation of the impacted population in the process, based on different forms of capital. The basic livelihoods framework is presented in Figure 7.3:

The key positive of the sustainable livelihoods framework is that it introduces a new focus in the development on the livelihoods of marginal groups, and it has mainly been adapted by development agencies for poverty eradication

Figure 7.3: The basic livelihoods framework.

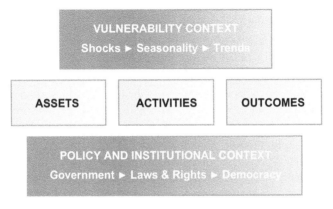

Source: Ellis and Allison (2004: 3).

programmes. A number of mining companies have also used the approach as a framework for livelihood restoration in their resettlement projects.

DFID discontinued promotion of the sustainable livelihoods approach in the early 2000s and development agencies reported a number of difficulties in using the approach as a planning tool. The key problem is that this approach has often proved too abstract for field staff. The use of the term 'capital' to describe livelihood resources introduces a practitioner language which is not easily grasped by communities and project staff. The sustainable livelihoods approach is very useful for conceptualising all the complexity that can exist within any given community. However, this often leads to projects trying to address too many issues simultaneously, resulting in a scatter-gun approach with little real impact. In reality, households have a limited number of livelihood choices which should be the focus of targeted restoration measures.

The resources framework

The **resources framework** incorporates elements of the access model, impoverishment risks and reconstruction framework and the sustainable livelihoods approach to be used as a practical tool on development projects to plan and manage the ESIA (environmental and social impact assessment) and RAP processes.

At the centre of the resources framework is the concept of household and community wellbeing. There is no single definition of wellbeing, but the OECD argues that 'most experts and ordinary people around the world would agree that it requires meeting various human needs, some of which are essential (e.g. being in good health), and includes the ability to pursue one's goals, to thrive and feel satisfied with their life' (OECD 2013: 27).

Reflecting this multi-dimensional approach, the OECD's Better Life Initiative identifies three pillars for understanding and measuring people's wellbeing (OECD 2013: 27):

- Material living conditions (or economic wellbeing), which determine people's consumption possibilities and their command over resources.

- Quality of life, which is defined as the set of nonmonetary attributes of individuals that shapes their opportunities and life chances, and has intrinsic value under different cultures and contexts.

- The sustainability of the socioeconomic and natural systems where people live and work, which is important for wellbeing to last over time.

The resources framework therefore embraces the idea that household and community wellbeing is dependent on a range of tangible and intangible resources.

The key tenets of the resources framework are as follows:

- **Keep it simple**: present the complexity of social impacts on development projects using language that is readily accessible to project engineers, community development staff, community members and nonsocial practitioners. The resources framework can therefore be a tool for all stakeholders to participate in the planning and implementation of projects. The resources framework uses language and concepts which can be more easily translated into the main international languages and also into local languages.

- **Use categories that are aligned with practical ESIA and RAP development**: the resources framework has eight resource categories which require project managers to focus separately on the most important elements of the resettlement process as set out in a standard ESIA and RAP.

- **Move from complexity to practical steps**: the resources framework presents the complexity of social impacts and recommends practical measures based on experience for mitigating impacts on the eight key resource categories. All of the eight resources should be included in the impact assessment; however, an experienced social practitioner must ensure that the mitigation measures are focused on the priority impacts.

- Presents the **overlap between SIMPs**: there is considerable overlap between SIMPs on resource projects which can result in the duplication of work and the development of elaborate plans which are never implemented in full. The resources framework seeks to simplify the development of SIMPs by streamlining impact analysis and baseline data collection and ensuring co-ordinated planning.

- **Compliance with international standards**: the resources framework assumes compliance with the World Bank and the IFC Performance Standards.

- **Identify where specialist expertise is required**: the resources framework's eight resource categories require an initial interpretation from a social specialist with practical experience in developing and implementing SIMPs to assess the depth of baseline studies required for the project. This initial review will determine which social specialists should be engaged and what SIMPs are required for the projects.

The eight resource categories introduced by the resources framework identify the factors that contribute to household wellbeing which should be considered individually in order to come to develop a complete picture of how to plan and manage complex social projects.

The term 'resource' is used as it is sufficiently well known and broad; it is defined in the access framework as 'the physical and social means of gaining a livelihood' (Wisner *et al.* 2003: 113). The resources framework's eight resource categories require separate treatment in the ESIA, RAP and livelihood restoration process:

1. **Human resources**: these are the people that make up the household and their ability to contribute to its management and economy. The availability of labour, education and skills will determine how the household can exploit the livelihood resources available to it. The health and nutrition of the family are the basic needs required to ensure that the household can achieve a minimum level of wellbeing. The role of women in the household will be determined largely by cultural and economic factors and is an important consideration when seeking to provide equal opportunities for women on a project. The

aspirations of the household and community are also important contributors to wellbeing and are strongly influenced by project communications, or lack thereof. Households with limited labour availability, comprised of children, the elderly and the infirm, will be more vulnerable to project impacts and will require special support.

2. **Social resources (social, traditional and political networks and institutions):** the household is generally part of a community in a particular traditional and political setting. The household is generally dependent on a combination of family, community, traditional and political networks to gain access to land, housing and livelihood resources. Local community, traditional and political institutions can provide safety and security for households and support in times of natural and political crisis. The media provides the household with access to information which influences decision-making. Changes to local networks and institutions due to processes such as decentralisation and globalisation impact on the household's access to support structures in positive and negative ways.

3. **Livelihood resources:** these are the resources that contribute to the household's income and assets including livelihood activities (land-, wage- and enterprise-based), remittances, bartering, labour exchanges, etc. The household's access to these livelihood resources is dependent on the social, traditional and political networks and institutions available. Livelihood activities include cropping, herding, hunting, fishing, gathering, etc. Note that even in rural areas, up to 50% of household income can come from nonagricultural sources.

4. **Cultural and religious resources:** many societies have a common belief system that frames their existence and provides psychological security to the household. Religion and culture are important to the identity of a community and provide a structure through which households engage and support each other.

5. **Access to services:** the household's access to basic services such as health, education and water resources is critical in determining the ability of its human resources to exploit livelihood opportunities.

6. **Housing resources:** structures to live in and conduct livelihood activities are the most basic requirement of any household. The quality of buildings can have a big impact on the health of a family. The housing plot and the household's security of tenure on this land is critical to the long-term ability of the family to guarantee shelter and livelihoods.

7. **Land and natural resources:** access to land, water bodies, forests and other natural resource areas is critical for the livelihoods of the world's population. Access to land and natural resources is governed by community, traditional and political institutions and secure tenure is critical for fighting poverty. Ecosystems services such as medicines, genetic resources, timber

Figure 7.4: The resources framework.

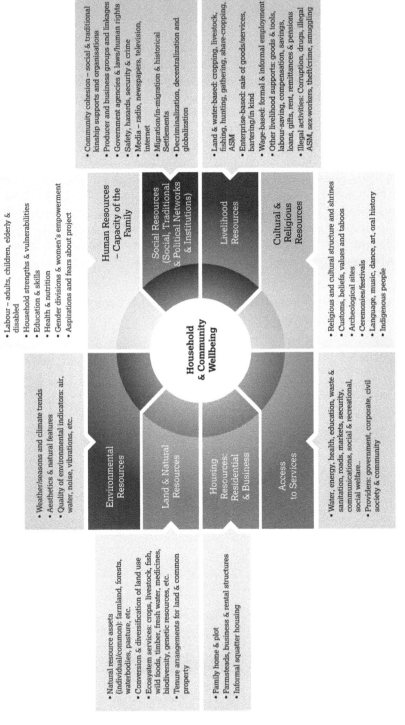

- Labour – adults, children, elderly & disabled
- Household strengths & vulnerabilities
- Education & skills
- Health & nutrition
- Gender divisions & women's empowerment
- Aspirations and fears about project

Human Resources – Capacity of the Family

- Community cohesion – social & traditional kinship supports and organisations
- Producer and business groups and linkages
- Government agencies & laws/human rights
- Safety, hazards, security & crime
- Media – radio, newspapers, television, internet
- Migration/in-migration & historical Settlements
- Decriminalization, decentralization and globalization

Social Resources (Social, Traditional & Political Networks & Institutions)

Household & Community Wellbeing

- Land & water-based: cropping, livestock, fishing, hunting, gathering, share-cropping, ASM
- Enterprise-based: sale of goods/services, bartering/in kind
- Wage-based: formal & informal employment
- Other livelihood supports: goods & tools, labour-saving, compensation, savings, loans, gifts, rent, remittances & pensions
- Illegal activities: Corruption, drugs, illegal ASM, sex-workers, theft/crime, smuggling

Livelihood Resources

- Weather/seasons and climate trends
- Aesthetics & natural features
- Quality of environmental indicators: air, water, noise, vibrations, etc.

Environmental Resources

Cultural & Religious Resources

- Religious and cultural structure and shrines
- Customs, beliefs, values and taboos
- Archeological sites
- Ceremonies/festivals
- Language, music, dance, art, oral history
- Indigenous people

Land & Natural Resources

Housing Resources: Residential & Business

Access to Services

- Water, energy, health, education, waste & sanitation, roads, markets, security, communications, social & recreational, social welfare.
- Providers: government, corporate, civil society & community

- Natural resource assets (individual/common): farmland, forests, waterbodies, pasture, etc.
- Conversion & diversification of land use
- Ecosystem services: crops, livestock, fish, wild foods, timber, fresh water, medicines, biodiversity, genetic resources, etc.
- Tenure arrangements for land & common property

- Family home & plot
- Farmsteads, business & rental structures
- Informal squatter housing

and trees in watersheds to prevent flooding are all critical resources for many communities.

8. **Environmental resources**: households and communities need a stable and clean environment in order to maintain their health and safety. Stable and predictable weather is also important to farmers, herders and fishermen in order to maintain seasonal exploitation patterns. The disruption to the quality of air, water, noise, odour, aesthetics, etc. can impact negatively on the health and stability of the household. There is increasing evidence that the climate is changing and this will have serious consequences for many poor communities with limited resources to adapt.

The resource categories include not only assets, such as land and housing, but also services and knowledge provided by government agencies or traditional leaders which can contribute to household wellbeing. It is important to note that the resources listed in the framework can have both positive and negative impacts on household wellbeing depending on their nature and availability. The factors that contribute to changes in wellbeing can be social impacts on resources or social change processes (Van Schooten *et al.* 2003: 77).

Figure 7.5: Resources framework presented in comparison to the livelihoods framework.

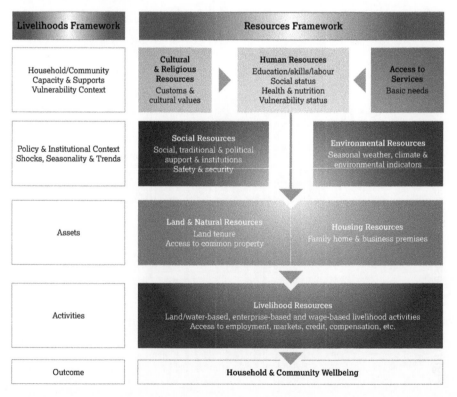

The resources framework follows the same logic as the sustainable livelihoods framework: a household/community uses its human resources (labour) to exploit land and natural resources and housing resources (business premises) to develop livelihood resources to meet the family needs for food, cash and other goods. The household is dependent on the psychological wellbeing (reduced stress) of its members, provided by its cultural and religious base, and physiological wellbeing (health and nutrition), provided by access to services, to maximise family labour. Access to land and natural resources, and housing resources, is dependent on social resources—the social, traditional and political support and institutions the household can rely on. This access can be disrupted by political problems such as conflict, and also environmental problems such as extreme weather events (storms, droughts) and social conflict.

Identifying project impacts

As presented in the resources framework, the key impacts requiring separate baseline research, impact assessment, stakeholder engagement and mitigation planning are as follows:

1. **Impacts on human resources**:
   a. **Impacts on health and wellbeing**: these are linked to morbidity, nutrition, actual and perceived health, mental health, fertility, etc.
   b. **Impacts on people's way of life**: it is important to consider people's fears and aspirations about the project, perceptions about the future of their community and of their children.
   c. **Impacts on gender relations**: these include impacts on women's physical integrity and the ability to make decisions about their own bodies, impacts on the personal autonomy of women, the gendered division of labour and access to resources and facilities and the political emancipation of women.

2. **Impacts on social resources** (social, traditional and political networks):
   a. **Family and community**: these impacts are linked to alterations in family structure, loss of community networks and support structures, obligations to family/ancestors, family violence, changes to community connectivity and sense of belonging, changes in community cohesion, social differentiation and inequity, social tension and violence, etc.
   b. **Traditional networks**: these are the shared kinship ties that bind groups together and which usually follow a chief or leader who guides them on the traditional rules governing access to land and common resources and who maintains their traditional belief system. In certain communities land access is only available to members of a traditional group, and in times of need the group also support each other so these ties are particularly important. A key goal in resettlement planning is to maintain the

Figure 7.6: Resources framework identifying potential positive project impacts.

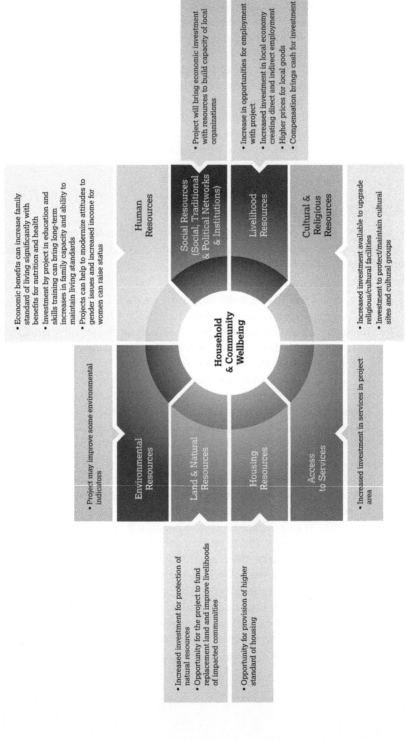

Figure 7.7: Resources framework outlining potential negative project impacts.

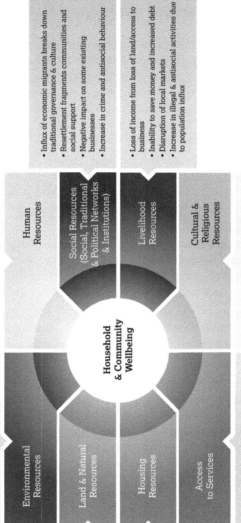

resettled household in their traditional area but this is sometimes impossible and can result in the household becoming part of a marginalised group.

c. **Political-institutional, legal, political and equity impacts**: these relate to the capacity of government agencies to handle workload generated by a project, the impact on the integrity of government agencies and absence of corruption and competence of the agency, impact on legal and human rights and social justice, the impact on participation in decision-making and access to legal advice and impact on fairness of distribution of impacts across the community.

3. **Impacts on livelihood resources (economic displacement)**: impacts on economic and material wellbeing are linked to changes in workload, standards of living, economic prosperity and resilience, income, property values, employment, replacement cost of environmental functions and economic dependence, etc.

4. **Impacts on cultural and religious resources**: these impacts relate to changes in cultural values, violation of culture, the experience of being culturally marginalised, commercial exploitation of culture, loss or marginalisation of local language and loss of natural and cultural heritage, etc.

5. **Impacts on access to services**: physical and social infrastructure (such as health clinics, schools, public transport, etc.), personal safety and exposure to risk and hazards, levels of crime and violence, etc.

6. **Impacts on housing resources (physical displacement)**: changes in the availability and quality of housing, associated buildings and business structures.

7. **Impacts on land and natural resources**: impacts include loss of access to farmland for cropping and livestock, to natural resources such as waterways for fishing and forests for hunting and gathering, medicinal plants, genetic resources and timber, to ecosystem services such as trees in watersheds to prevent flooding, and to access routes.

8. **Impacts on quality of environmental resources with social consequences**: impacts on the quality of the living environment are linked to changes in physical quality, water, exposure to increased noise, dust, vibrations, odour, etc., safety hazards, leisure and recreation opportunities, changes in aesthetic quality and sense of place.

The key positive and negative impacts from a typical project are outlined in Figures 7.6 and 7.7. Note that this is not an exhaustive list and that the process outlined in this chapter should be followed to identify risks specific to every project.

Trends and shocks

Projects are significant drivers for positive and negative changes in the community, but there are many other drivers of change which are impacting on communities and which should be considered when assessing project impacts. In developing countries the pace of change has been huge in the past 50 years due to the following trends:

- The population of developing countries, particularly in Africa, has increased tremendously, increasing poverty in those countries where food, water and farmland are already in short supply. There are greater numbers of dependent children on smaller land-holdings which puts further stress on health and education services. The competition for scarce land resources means that projects are being developed in areas where there are existing conflicts which can be exacerbated by the project.

- There has been a massive shift of populations from rural to urban areas and this has led to huge squatter populations living in shantytowns in most developing countries. These urban migrants often occupy land earmarked for development and governments have limited resources to resettle these squatters into proper settlement areas. There is also a considerable amount of seasonal migration from rural to urban areas.

- There has been a shift from ecological farming towards mechanisation and the use of chemicals. However, while the green revolution was critical in feeding the growing population of the world, in many areas the cost of inputs is increasing, the land is infertile and the net income is often lower with a dependence on world market commodity prices.

- There has been a huge increase in the number of people engaged in artisanal mining worldwide and increased conflict as commercial and artisanal miners seek to access the same resource.

- Information technology has spread rapidly to all corners of the world enabling migrants to keep in contact with families back home and also informing young people of the opportunities beyond the village boundary, fuelling migration.

- There is increasing consensus that climate change is occurring and that this is likely to lead to more extreme weather events and also flooding of coastal populations.

There is debate about whether extreme weather events are on the increase due to global warming but flooding, storms, heatwaves and droughts are still the norm for many countries, causing considerable loss of life, destruction to property and disruption to agricultural activities. In addition, there are numerous conflicts, some localised and some on a national scale, in many countries which are creating millions of refugees and an insecure environment for investment to

It is important to identify impacts based on specific baseline information rather than using a check-box exercise and blanket approach

develop these countries. The cumulative impact of longer-term trends and shocks must be considered when assessing project impacts to understand how households can be assisted to cope.

 Project example

A social impact assessment for a project in Asia failed to properly identify the impacts on downstream users from the construction of a dam for a mining project. It later materialised that these downstream water users were indigenous people with a right of consent to the project, and the failure to identify impacts adequately resulted in them not being properly engaged, leading project opponents to claim that the project was not meeting international standards.

 Project example

A project in Africa brought together environmental impact assessment, social impact assessment and resettlement action plan consultants early in the pre-feasibility stage for a major project in order to design a team approach to baseline data collection and stakeholder engagement. This ensured that all impacts were identified at an early stage and fed into the project design. The collection of baseline data was streamlined to avoid the duplication of resources and the project proceeded smoothly through the permitting phase.

Assessment of impacts in land access and resettlement projects

The analysis of the project description, determination of areas of influence and analysis of baseline data will determine all potential impacts arising from the project.

For each impact, the project needs to consider:

- **Nature of impact**: what is affected and how
- **Extent/scale of impact**: site only, local, regional, national or international
- **Duration of impact**: short-term, medium-term, long-term or permanent
- **Intensity of the impact**: low, medium or high
- **Probability of the impact**: improbable, probable, highly probable or definite
- **Significance of the impact**: negligible, low, medium or high

Figure 7.8: Options in the development of appropriate mitigation measures.

AVOID	What design techniques can be used to avoid the impact?
REDUCE	What methods will be used to minimize the impact?
RESTORE	What methods will be used to rehabilitate/repair an impact?
COMPENSATE	What will be undertaken to compensate for impacts?
ENHANCE	What will be done to enhance positive impacts?

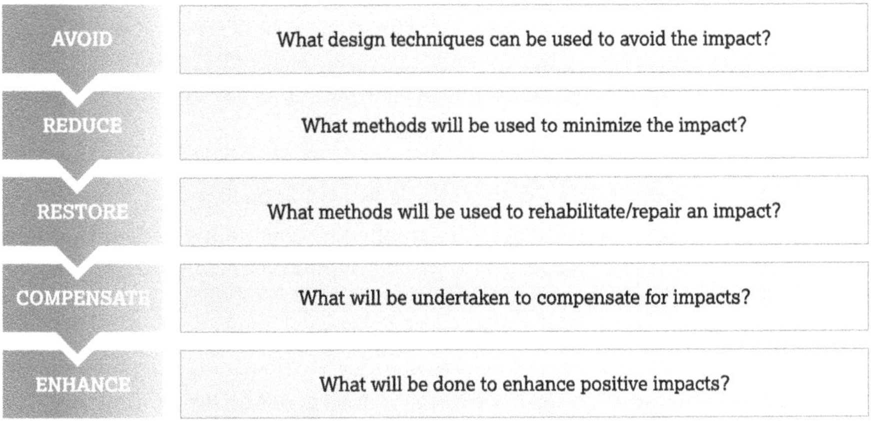

In practice, there can be difficulties with applying such assessment criteria to social impacts, and projects need to be careful that they consider how impacts affect different sectors of society, including vulnerable groups.

There may often be no measurable or objective indicator for impacts, and assessment needs to be guided by comments and opinions from communities; as a result, impacts can be highly personal and subjective. Assessment therefore needs an experienced practitioner and professional judgement when determining the significance of such impacts.

Once impacts have been assessed, a number of options can be considered in the development of appropriate mitigation measures, as illustrated in Figure 7.8. In practice, a land access and resettlement package will consist of a range of these mitigation measures to address impacts, including avoiding (such as avoiding displacement), reducing (such as minimising displacement), restoring (such as restoration of farms), compensating (such as cash compensation for loss of crops), and enhancing (such as improved housing, additional community facilities, etc.).

The remainder of the book is largely concerned with the determination of these mitigation measures in respect of land access and resettlement projects. However, a key goal in land access and resettlement is to avoid or minimise displacement in the first instance, as emphasised by the IFC Performance Standards. This is discussed more fully below.

How to avoid or minimise displacement?

It makes good business sense to minimise the scale of land access and resettlement on projects given the cost of providing replacement houses, compensation and livelihood restoration.

The IFC standards require the project proponent to demonstrate that it has considered 'feasible alternative project designs to avoid or minimize physical and/or economic displacement, while balancing environmental, social, and financial costs and benefits, paying particular attention to impacts on the poor and vulnerable' (IFC 2012: PS5, §8).

There are a number of strategies that can be used to avoid or minimise the need for physical resettlement and economic displacement:

- Change the project design to reduce the area of land required, for example by using underground mining methods instead of open pit
- Change the location of project infrastructure by conducting trade-off studies on alternative sites and routes for infrastructure, for example by changing road or pipeline routes to avoid houses
- Change the technology used by the project, for example by mining oxide-only deposits which do not require blasting, thereby reducing the environmental buffer area required, or through directional drilling for oil and gas projects
- Manage the impact of the project's activities to reduce environmental impacts, for example by operating only during the day near communities, which would remove the need for night-time noise buffers and the need to resettle these communities
- Negotiate temporary relocation with impacted communities for short-term project activities which would avoid the need for permanent resettlement

As discussed in Chapter 6, the scoping phase prior to baseline data collection is important in understanding the initial project design and developing strategies in order to minimise impacts. The stakeholder engagement during the process of baseline data collection and impacts assessment will also lead to an in-depth understanding of the scale of resettlement and economic displacement and how this can be minimised.

The need to minimise land access and resettlement must also be balanced with the potential impacts on communities left living close to the project and providing flexibility for the project to expand in the longer term. A common mistake on resource projects has been only to acquire land sufficient for project start-up and not to plan for project expansion. Given that most projects become the subject of considerable influx of economic migrants resulting in significant development on the project boundaries, acquiring land later for project expansion can be very costly, time-consuming and complex. There have been many examples where impacted households have had to be moved twice on projects.

The project planners therefore need to be realistic about the likely land needs over the life of the mine and balance the need to minimise short-term impacts with the long-term cost of acquiring land and the risks of an increased level of impacts into the future.

Figure 7.9 highlights the advantages and disadvantages of minimising land access versus acquiring larger project areas for the projected life of the project upfront.

Figure 7.9: Advantages and disadvantages of limiting initial land access.

Advantages	Disadvantages
Lower cost of purchasing land upfront as less area required.	Buying less land at the start can limit project expansion. Once the project commences, the area around the mine often becomes urbanised, making it very expensive and difficult to acquire more land later.
Less livelihood impact as lower number of farmers impacted.	Project seeks to minimise buffers around infrastructure and allow farming close to infrastructure, but this can lead to complaints about dust impact on crops, complaints that the project is causing flooding, animal health problems attributed to the project, etc.
Less resettlement costs as lower number of residences impacted.	Residents left living close to the project often complain about damage to their houses from blasting, requiring companies to put expensive monitoring and repair programmes in place. Local residents must be moved a minimum distance from project infrastructure in line with international environmental standards.
Less disruption of social networks as more local residents left living in existing communities.	The greatest influx of economic migrants will be in communities close to the project and these communities can suffer significant disruption and conflict. Moving impacted communities to planned resettlement sites can lower the influx impacts on local communities.
Where the project is short term, for example utilising the land for just one year, it can make sense to negotiate a deal with residents to remain *in situ* with management systems in place to deal with environmental impacts, rather than pay the cost of permanent resettlement. This also allows communities to retain their ancestral lands.	Projects often seek to minimise resettlement as a way of cutting costs without assessing properly the longer-term impacts on local communities.

 Project example

In Africa a local community chose to stay living close to the project, which required the company to redesign the infrastructure at a greater cost than resettlement. The community wanted to stay close to the project to ensure that they achieved maximum employment and economic benefits.

Figure 7.10: Google Earth imagery showing a pit boundary in Africa close to local communities.

 Project example

In Africa a project which started in a rural area minimised land take to reduce impacts and costs. However, once the project was operational the local city expanded around the mine resulting in the mine being located in a suburb. The mine is now expanding and land access and resettlement cost has seriously escalated, and there are considerable complaints from the local community for resettlement due to noise, blast, air and dust emissions from the project.

What about the need for appropriate environmental buffers?

There is considerable debate on projects internationally concerning the issue of appropriate environmental buffers to mitigate for impacts. For example, a complete exclusion zone of 500 metres from the edge of the pit is recommended as a blast buffer on many mining projects. However, in practice many projects use smaller buffers or start with 500 metres but the pit gradually expands and erodes this buffer distance to the nearest communities. There is a growing trend for increased government regulation concerning environmental impacts, but in many cases there is limited guidance on what the buffers should be.

In the absence of clear government regulation there is a tendency for environmental consultants to recommend the absolute minimum buffer area in order to lower costs, but this can result in community impacts and considerable grievances. Impacts from project vehicles, including noise, damage to roads, dust and safety concerns, can cause a considerable number of grievances.

Common problems with buffers are listed in Figure 7.12.

Figure 7.11: Project truck creating a dust problem on a project in Africa.

Figure 7.12: Impacts and solutions to environmental buffer issues.

Impact	Solution
• Night-time noise buffers are inadequate, resulting in complaints from residents particularly about 24 hour loading and hauling of ore around waste rock dumps and haul roads. • Projects often fail to mitigate for short-term impacts from noise impacts such as from drill rigs leading to considerable community complaints.	• Specify adequate noise buffers to ensure that there are no residences in the area where night-time noise thresholds will be exceeded. • Build berms between communities and waste rock dumps to reduce the noise reaching residences. • Design waste rock dumps so that ore is deposited closer to residences during the day and behind this berm during the night. • It is important that noise buffers are modelled on the topography of the project area as this can determine the range of the impact.
• Buffers from dust impacts from unsealed project roads, waste rock dumps, pits and tailings storage facilities are often inadequate. This can lead to complaints about damage to crops and respiratory problems in local communities. • Projects often fail to implement adequate dust suppression measures to mitigate for impacts, particularly during the dry season. • Projects are reluctant to invest in sealing project roads through residential areas due to cost factors.	• Buffers for dust must be related to resources that the project is prepared to invest in mitigation, such as frequency of watering of roads and other dust-suppression measures. • Projects should consider sealing roads through residential areas for long-term projects as the cost of dust-suppression measures and dealing with community complaints can also be high.
• Many projects implement inadequate buffers to deal with the impacts of blast vibration and pressure impacts resulting in considerable grievances. In some countries the national environmental protection agency has required companies to repair cracks in houses up to 2 km away from the project due to the absence of a pre-project baseline to identify existing structure problems.	• Buffers from blasting should be based on studies from experienced consultants, and at a minimum avoid the potential for fly-rock injuries. • Projects should conduct a pre-blast baseline on residences near the project to establish what existing faults exist in structures in order to prove that blasting did not cause these issues. • A proper communication system must be implemented to ensure communities are aware of blasting time and educated on the real impacts of blasting. • Projects should only allow agriculture in buffer areas in limited circumstances when the local community are fully supportive and areas can be cleared prior to blasting.

What about minimising impacts of resettlement site acquisition?

The process for selecting and assessing resettlement sites is outlined in Chapter 9, including the need to consider host communities.

In terms of minimisation efforts, in many cases the impacts on existing landowners/users of the land selected for the resettlement site are ignored. It is often assumed that paying cash at negotiated rates to acquire the land for the resettlement site is adequate to meet the company's responsibilities. However, these landowners/users are impacted just the same as those losing access to land in the project area, and they may also face similar impoverishment risks.

It is therefore in the interest of the company to minimise the impact of land access and resettlement on these households. In some cases landowners of large tracts of land are prepared to sell this for cash, but there may be a significant number of local households employed to work this land and the sale might result in them losing their livelihood.

 Project example

On a project in Africa, impacted farmers complained that they had no access to replacement land. The company responded by providing a choice from two solutions:

1. The company purchased a large block of land from the local chiefs and farmers were invited to enter into a traditional agreement with local chiefs to farm this land. Farmers were reluctant to take up this option as they did not want to lock into an agreement with the chiefs.

2. The company provided a fixed per-area price for farmers to source their own replacement land on a land-for-land basis up to a minimum threshold. Once the farmer located the land, the company surveyed the field and provided funds for the farmer to clear the land and also for seedlings and inputs for the farmer to replace his crops. The replacement land which was sourced was generally undeveloped and did not impact the livelihoods of the vendors. This approach also resulted in cost savings as the company used the market to supply land directly to farmers and this resulted in a cheaper price than if the company had to buy the land directly.

The outcome was that over 3,000 farmers chose to source their own land and successfully re-established their farms.

Project example

On a project in Asia the company negotiated with large local landowners to provide large resettlement sites. However, it was later discovered that the proposed sites were already intensively farmed and the acquisition of this land would lead to economic displacement. The approach to land acquisition was therefore changed to focus on multiple smaller sites. Local landowners were invited to propose land for sale to the company which met a number of criteria, including not impacting local farming families. The assessment of farmers selling land is that the family must have retained a minimum amount of land to support their own livelihood based on the dependence of each family on the land area. This enabled the company to target smaller residential sites and a patchwork of farmland in the vicinity of these resettlement sites.

Minimising speculation

The irony of minimising resettlement impacts on many projects is that some community members often seek to place themselves in the project zone in order to maximise their entitlement to compensation, resettlement housing and other project supports.

Figure 7.13: A speculative structure in Africa.

Speculative activities include building structures to claim eligibility for resettlement housing and planting perennial crops, such as trees, to benefit from crop compensation. Speculators also seek to become eligible for livelihood support packages offered by the project. These speculative activities can result in considerable costs, time delays, and grievances and litigation from community members. Speculative activities also result in a deterioration in relations between the company and the community as companies find it harder to differentiate between genuine and speculative households and tend to treat the whole community with suspicion. This can result in the company trying to reduce compensation and resettlement benefits which may penalise the majority of the community who are genuinely impacted.

The trigger for speculation is often the release of information about the project investment or the discovery of a major resource. In many cases, company staff with access to information about critical project infrastructure collaborate with speculators to make money from the project. Many of the speculative structures are often rudimentary and uninhabitable.

 Project example

On a project in Africa, the local community built 1,100 structures on the project area during a three-month period in order to secure resettlement benefits from the project. The structures were built before a legal cut-off date could be declared according to national law, and the company was required to compensate these houses. In response, the company renegotiated the resettlement entitlement to include proof of residence to qualify for resettlement. This resulted in only 55 genuine households receiving resettlement houses while the speculators were paid compensation for their structures at replacement rates. This policy, combined with greater security of project information, greatly reduced the amount of speculation taking place on subsequent projects undertaken by the company.

Companies can take the following steps to minimise speculation on a project:

- The company must ensure that all sensitive project information is kept as confidential as possible while balancing this with the need to disclose information to project stakeholders.

- The company should work closely with local and national government to declare cut-off dates for development on the project area and to freeze the building of structures and planting of crops. A cut-off date is normally set under national law as the date the area is surveyed and assets recorded which will be compensated.

- The company should secure aerial or satellite imagery concurrent with the declaration of the cut-off date to demonstrate to the community that a record exists of all structures eligible for resettlement benefits. The company should post these images in the communities in order to discourage speculation.

- Following the cut-off date the company should ensure that all information on structures and crops which help to determine eligibility should be carefully recorded. For example, the age of the structure, whether it is complete and habitable and whether the structure is inhabited at the time of the survey can help differentiate between households genuinely entitled to resettlement and those entitled to cash compensation. Structures which were never occupied as residences or are incomplete could be compensated with cash at replacement values in order not to incentivise speculative activities. The company should also seek to negotiate a seedling rate for crops at replacement value so there is no big incentive to speculate by planting young crops.

- The company should undertake a rapid asset survey immediately after the declaration of the cut-off date and quickly mark and record all structures present to minimise the opportunity for speculation.

- During the RAP negotiations, the company should negotiate packages, including eligibility criteria, to ensure that only households which are genuinely impacted are entitled to RAP benefits.

Figure 7.14: Aerial photograph of a project in Africa where the community built over a thousand speculative structures.

Risk and opportunity assessments

The ESHIA process identifies the project impacts on communities and identifies actions and plans to mitigate these impacts by enhancing positive impacts and minimising negative impacts. The purpose of the environmental and social management system is to manage these mitigation activities, monitor their performance and make changes where required. The risks from environmental hazards and social conflict on projects can threaten the project's social licence to operate and result in schedule delays, budget overruns and serious reputational damage. The environmental and social management system also identifies positive impacts and opportunities to maximise benefits for local communities.

While the focus of resettlement planners is primarily on community impacts, the focus of the project management will be firmly on the overall project risks. The project's goals, while including provision of development benefits to local communities, will be primarily focused on construction and operational activities to ensure that the budget and schedule are on track. It is important for all stakeholders, and particularly social experts, to understand that the project's success depends on the efficient management of project finances and timetable and that too many demands or disruption can make the project unfeasible.

Figure 7.15 shows how the resources framework can be used to set out the key resources required by management to ensure project success.

'Risk management is the systematic application of management policies, processes and procedures to the tasks of identifying, analysing, assessing, treating and monitoring risk' (Bowden *et al.* 2001: 15). Projects usually have an overall business risk management process to manage the key risks:

- Strategic risk: the risk of planning failure

- Financial risk: the risk of failure of financial control

- Operational risk: the risk of human actions, including unsafe practices and conflict

- Commercial risk: the risk of business interruption, including legal and compliance issues

- Technical risk: the risk of failure of physical assets, including infrastructure breakdown, sabotage, pollution and natural events

The risks are quantified by multiplying the likelihood of the risk occurring and the consequences of that risk. Most projects put in place a risk management system to identify potential risks and manage these over the life of the project. The leading international risk standard is the joint Australian/New Zealand Risk Standard (AS/NZS ISO 31000:2009).

This standard sets out a risk management process which is presented in Figure 7.16. The steps for implementing a risk management system are outlined below:

Figure 7.15: Project's key resource requirements outlined using the resources framework.

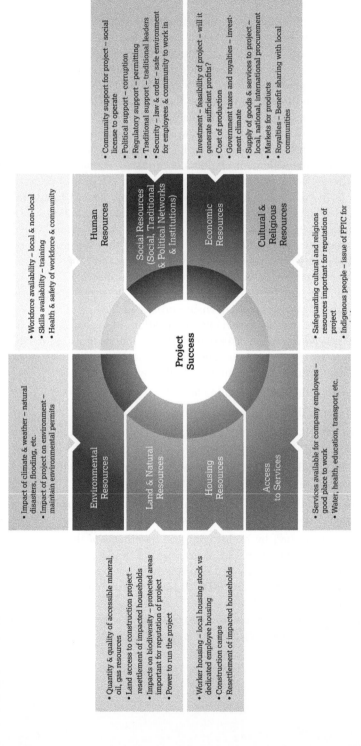

Figure 7.16: The Australian/New Zealand risk management process.

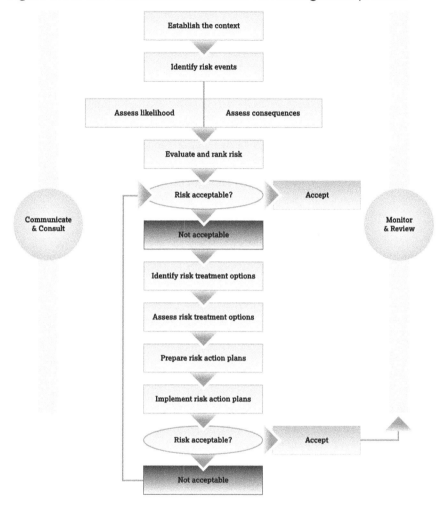

Source: Adapted from Bowden *et al.* (2001: 9).

Step 1. Define the context and risk management criteria

This step will need to consider:

- The company's operational footprint and impacts
- The company's policies and procedures and the standards to which it is adhering
- The company's level of control over risks: legal requirements, political risks, community expectations and demands and financial opportunities and penalties

This step should define the stakeholders who may be impacted by any of the risk areas (as outlined in Chapter 5):

- Company staff and shareholders
- Local community who will be impacted by the project
- Wider public who use the company's products
- Government regulatory and permitting authorities
- Traditional and political leaders who may be affected by project activities
- Businesses providing goods and services to the project
- Special interest groups such as indigenous landowners and NGOs (non-governmental organisations)

Risk criteria should be developed: for example, control of hazards such as traffic accidents.

Step 2. Identify the risks and opportunities

The multidisciplinary project team, including management, technical, environment and social staff and consultants, should be involved in the identification of risks. The risks can be identified through experience from similar projects, benchmarking, specialist studies, industry best practice and expert judgement. The team should develop a register of risks and their key characteristics.

Examples of key risks on land access and resettlement projects include:

- Community expectations for compensation will be too high and impact on the project feasibility
- Political interference in the RAP negotiation process results in unrealistic community expectations, protests and conflict
- Increased traffic leads to accidents injuring and killing community members, leading to outrage and protests against the project
- Speculative activities by community members and migrants who seek to capture additional compensation and resettlement benefits from the project, leading to increased costs, schedule delays and community conflict
- Changing laws and regulations on land access and resettlement by national governments leads to uncertainty around permitting and land access and resettlement processes

Examples of opportunities on land access and resettlement projects include:

- Skills training for local people to participate in the construction of the resettlement houses

Step 3. Assess the significance of risks and opportunities

The team should now evaluate the likelihood of the risk occurring and give this a score as presented in Figure 7.17, assess the consequence of the risk (Figures 7.18 and 7.19), compile an opportunity assessment table (Figure 7.20) and draw up a risk assessment (Figure 7.21).

Figure 7.17: Example of a likelihood table.

Level	Description	Criteria (read as either/or)
5	Certain	The event will occur
		The event occurs daily
4	Likely	The event is expected to occur
		The event occurs weekly/monthly
3	Possible	The event will occur under some cirucmstances
		The event occurs annually
2	Unlikely	The event will occur under some cirucmstances
		The event occurs annually
1	Rare	The event may occur in exceptional circumstances
		The event has rarely occured in the industry

Figure 7.18: Example of a negative consequences matrix.

Level	Project Design	Health & Safety	Environmental	Community	Legal Compliance	Estimated Cost
1 Insignificant	Schedule slips one day	- First Aid Injury - Nuisance value	- No or very low environmental impact - Impact confined to small area	- Isolated complaint - No media enquiry	- Minor technical/legal compliance issue unlikely to attract a regulatory response	> $5,000
2 Minor	Schedule slips one week	- Medical Treatment Injury - Restricted Work Injury	- Low environmental impact - Rapid cleanup by site staff and/or contractors - Impact contained to area currently impacted by operations	- Small numbers of sporadic complaints - Local media enquiries	- Possible fraud implications - Technical/legal compliance issue which may attract a low level administrative response from regulator - Incident requires reporting in routine reports (e.g. monthly)	> $50,000
3 Moderate	Schedule slips one month	Single Lost Time Injury	- Moderate environmental impact - Cleanup by site staff and/or contractors - Impact confined within lease boundary	- Serious rate of complaints, repeated complaints from the same area (clustering) - Increased local media interest	- Breach of regulation with possible prosecution and penalties - Continuing occurrences of minor breaches - Incident requires immediate (≤ 48 hours) notification	> $500,000
4 Major	Schedule slips 3 months	- Multiple Lost Time Injuries - Admission to intensive care unit or equivalent - Serious, chronic, long term effects	- Major environmental impact - Considerable cleanup effort required using site and external resources - Impact may extend beyond the lease boundary	- Increasing rate of complaints, repeated complaints from the same area (clustering) - Increased local/national media interest	- May involve fraud - Major breach of regulation resulting in investigation by regulator - Prosecution, penalties or other action likely	> $5,000,000
5 Catastrophic	Schedule slips one year	Fatalities or permanent disability	- Severe environmental impact - Local species destruction and likely long recovery period - Extensive cleanup involving external resources - Impact on regional scale	- High level of concern or interest from local community - National and/or international media interest	- Serious breach of regulation resulting in investigation by regulator - Operation suspended, licenses revoked	> $50,000,000

Figure 7.19: Example of a positive consequences matrix.

	Noticeable 1	Useful 2	Valuable 3	Significant 4	Exceptional 5
OH&S	Safety performance trending positive.	Measurable consistent improvement in safety. Positive health impacts on some people or systems improvements.	Major positive impacts on healthy lifestyle behaviours. Significant improvements in system ratings.	Single life saving action. Significant permanent health impacts on a group of people. Significant achievements in H&S Lag indicators. (Zero Level 4 & 5 H&S for 1 year.	Multiple life saving impacts. Life changing long term positive health impacts on entire workforce or community.
Environment	Positive effect or trend in specific areas. Improving trend in water, waste or emissions management.	Noticeable improvement in specific areas, Meaningful improvements in water, waste or emissions management. Some improvements in land impacts or biodiversity issues.	Land impacts improved or reduced by < 10% from plan. Positive improvements on flora & fauna. Positive improvements in community environmental awareness & education.	Significant long term improvements in ecosystem function that gains national recognition. 10% - 40% reduction in emissions and waste stream. Land impacts improved or reduced by 10% - 40% from plan. Significant leadership in developing positive community environmental performance that gains national recognition.	Positive and sustainable impact on highly valued species, habitat or ecosystem that gains international recognition. Elimination of significant damaging emission or > 40% reduction in general emission & waste stream. Land impacts improved or reduced > 40% against plan.
Social / Cultural Heritage	Relations with community improving. Improvement in workplace culture.	Written recognition from community or national body. Noticeable improvement in workplace culture.	Major improvements in or resolution of significant social issues. Establishment of significant capacity building initiatives effective for LOM. Workplace culture improves long term through initiative.	Significant positive impacts on highly valued items of cultural significance. Significant sustainable improvements to community social capital. Significant positive sustainable improvements in workplace culture.	Exceptional contribution to community's future that is sustainable beyond closure and gains international recognition. Permanent project saving positive changes in social order. Dramatic reversal in workplace culture, positively impacts mine life.
Reputation	Public acknowledgement by local or district communities or governments.	Provincial, positive public or media attention and acknowledgement. Positive response from regulator.	Positive attention from national media and/or very public support by local community. Support and recognition by NGOs. Ease in gaining approvals. Environmental credentials moderately improved.	Significant positive national media / public/ NGO attention. Project approval significantly enhanced. Environment / management credentials are significantly recognised. National or regional sustainability award.	Significant positive international media / public/ NGO attention. Project approval guaranteed by positive performance. International sustainability award.
Financial	< $500k reduction in capital costs or increase in NPV. Up to 1% improvement in reserves or 2% improvement in resources.	$500k - $5m reduction in capital costs or improvement in NPV. Up to 2% improvement in reserves or 4% improvement in resources.	$5m - $50m reduction in capital costs or improvement in NPV. Up to 7.5% improvement in reserves or 15% improvement in resources.	$50m - $100m reduction in capital costs or improvement in NPV. Up to 15% improvement in reserves or 30% improvement in resources.	>$100m reduction in capital costs or improvement in NPV. >15% improvement in reserves or >30% resources.

Figure 7.20: Example of an opportunity assessment table.

Opportunity Description	Consequence	Likelihood	Level of opportunity	Potential Benefits if Opportunity is realised	Additional Measures required to Realise opportunity	Responsibility
Phased resettlement and housing construction, combined with new approaches to construction management - potentially positively impacting the time & money	4 Significant	3 Possible	18 Excellent	Resettlement housing will be completed ahead of schedule saving money enabling earlier access to land to accelerate mine construction schedule	Recruit additional experienced construction supervisors	John Smith
Sharing best practice among sites/regions	3 Valuable	3 Possible	13 High	Reduction in additional staffing cost, faster implementation of new systems	Best Practices must be documented and implemented on Project	Mary Jones
Maximise local employment early on for senior staff	2 Useful	3 Possible	8 Medium	Use the skills and experience from open pit at Project A other regional properties. Improved relations with National regulators	Continue people development	James Ryan
Developing trade skills within local community could be seen as beneficial and provide higher community acceptance of company activities	2 Useful	3 Possible	8 Medium	Implementation of established internship for trades will accelerate learning relations with National regulators	Continue people development	James Ryan

Figure 7.21: Example of a risk assessment table.

Risk/Event Description	Existing Controls	Consequence	Likelihood	Risk Level	Responsibility	Rev Likelihood	Remedial Risk Level	Responsibility
Onsite potential for light vehicle or haul truck accident causing fatality, personal injury, property damage or process loss	1. Pre-operational checks 2. Roll over protection 3. Education	5 Catastrophic	3 Possible	22 Extreme	1. Road design standard 2. GPS trackers on company vehicles and major contractor's vehicle 3. Overpass/Underpass consideration	1 Rare	15 High	John Smith
Land access process extended resulting in scheduling delays to the resettlement program	1. Compensation negotiations started and ongoing 2. Use of community valuer 3. Sub-commitees in place to focus negotiations 5. Ongoing Engagement sessions 6. Involving local community reps to identify farmers as part of the crop surveys	4 Major	3 Possible	22 Extreme	1. Increase the number of field terms 2. Intensify engagements with key stakeholders 3. Undertake surveys in all zones simultaneously to increase momentum (started) 4. Understand Permitting including zoning requirements for current site to reduce delays	2 Unlikely	14 High	Mary Jones

Step 4. Identify, select, and implement risk treatment options

The team should now identify mitigation measures to eliminate the risk or reduce it to an acceptable level. Alternatively, the project may decide to accept the risk even if it occurs. A list of actions is then prepared to mitigate the risks and these actions are incorporated into the various business areas of the project to define the detail of when, how and for whom the measures are implemented.

Step 5. Perform monitoring, review and corrective actions

The last step is to monitor the mitigation measures through internal and external monitoring and evaluation, with regular reporting to management, so that the status of the risk can be reassessed periodically. Where there is a residual risk, this needs to be monitored after the mitigation measures have been applied, and if it is not acceptable then additional mitigation measures need to be implemented.

This chapter has outlined a practical process for identifying all the important impacts found on projects. The development of mitigation measures to address these impacts is outlined in Chapter 16 on social impact management and livelihood restoration planning.

Assessing impacts and minimising displacement: key considerations

- **Define the project area for the life of the project**: plan for project expansion as land access is costly in terms of time and cost during project operations.
- Ensure that the **social and resettlement teams are fully engaged in the process of defining the project area** so that social impacts are fully considered and minimised.

- **Engage with project stakeholders** to ensure that they provide input into the project design while being careful not to disclose details too early which can result in speculative activities.
- Ensure that the **environmental impacts of the project are fully understood** and adequate buffers put in place to balance the impacts of land access against community grievances during the life of the project.
- Develop **a land management plan** to ensure that there is ongoing input into project development from environmental and social consultants and project stakeholders (see Chapter 19).
- Ensure that any land selected for resettlement sites or livelihood projects is fully explored through **sterilisation drilling**.
- **Continue to monitor the land requirements of the project**, consulting with the environmental and social monitoring teams to ensure that any further expansion is planned in advance and all efforts made to minimise impacts.
- Engage with the project team and communities to explore ways **to minimise land take** but ensure that the project has planned for expansion before project influx takes place.
- Work with local authorities to develop ways to **limit speculative development** on the project area and keep project information as confidential as possible.
- Ensure that resettlement planners are part of the project risk and opportunity assessment process in order to maximise their input and reduce risks associated with resettlement.

8
Compensation frameworks

The determination of compensation is a critical step on land access and resettlement projects, and although experience has shown that in-kind replacement of assets such as land is preferable, cash is often the predominant or a significant form of compensation on most projects. An important principle of compensation is that this money is

> not a net benefit to those displaced: this is only a restitution of what was taken away (very often, an incomplete restitution). Neither is it correct to interpret the financing of compensation as an investment for expanding resettlers' former productive potential: it is only a refund for replacing equal value assets that already had existed and are destroyed through condemnation. (Cernea and Mohan Mathur 2008: 8)

The payment of large sums of cash compensation often distorts prices, leading to high local inflation and, in rural areas, the transition from a subsistence to a cash economy. The impacted communities are always focused on maximising the immediate cash compensation offered and it is tempting for the project to pay cash for land and houses in order to access the land quickly. However, experience has shown that poor communities are ill-equipped to deal with large cash inflows which often results in short-term spending on consumer goods, leading to longer-term impoverishment without an asset base to support the household's basic needs.

There are risks with cash compensation, but finding adequate replacement land is often difficult

The objective of this chapter is to outline the compensation process and provide guidance on how to manage the risks around cash payments on projects.

What are the objectives of a compensation framework?

The objectives of a compensation framework are as follows:

- Set out the legal requirements for compensation payments and resettlement packages by the host government and how any gaps with international standards will be addressed
- In the absence of national guidelines which meet international standards, set out the methodology that the project will use to compensate for losses
- Set out the proposed types and levels of compensation to be paid
- Set out the eligibility for the various forms of assistance and compensation in an entitlement matrix
- Outline where and when compensation will be paid

What are the key issues, challenges and risks?

- The **provision of cash for houses and land** is still the primary compensation method on many projects despite ample evidence that poor households focus on short-term spending leading to longer-term impoverishment.
- Cash compensation can lead to the abandonment of traditional livelihoods, an increase in antisocial behaviour and more negative impacts for women as payments are generally paid to male household heads.
- The payment of cash compensation causes significant **inflation** in many project areas which undermines the value of the payments and causes stress for families dependent on buying food.
- **National compensation guidelines often set rates far below the replacement value of assets** and national governments are reluctant to approve higher payments which will set precedents for their own projects.
- The determination of a **compensation process for common property is difficult** in the absence of replacement land. The provision of cash or community investment in services is unlikely to support the restoration of livelihoods for the poor and marginalised who are dependent on these areas.
- Where the compensation is individually negotiated with households, instead of group negotiations, this often leads to different rates for similar assets which can lead to conflict in the community and hold-outs.
- The **provision of replacement land in kind is very difficult** on many projects given the pressure on land. Paying cash compensation for land often results in longer-term impoverishment as these households are left without their traditional resource base.

What international guidance is there?

PS (Performance Standard) 5 of the IFC (International Finance Corporation) states that:

> When displacement cannot be avoided, the client will offer displaced communities and persons compensation for loss of assets at full replacement cost and other assistance to help them improve or restore their standards of living or livelihoods … Compensation standards will be transparent and applied consistently to all communities and persons affected by the displacement. (IFC 2012: PS5, §9)

What are the key steps in developing a compensation framework?

1. Conduct **detailed baseline studies** to record and measure the assets that are owned by the impacted communities. As outlined in Chapter 6, this will include asset surveys to record ownership of land, annual and perennial crops, residences and associated immovable structures, business structures and community structures and infrastructures. The baseline data collection must map the location of all assets and provide measurements of the size of each asset category and the nature of the asset, such as the materials used to build a house.

2. As outlined in Chapter 7, investigate ways to **minimise the land access requirements** and assess the impacts on the owners and users of the land and natural resources. It is important to assess the impacts not just on assets but also on livelihoods and cultural practices, as mitigation measures will have to be put in place. It is important to understand not just the ownership of assets but also who has an interest in the asset: this is particularly important in the case of tenancy arrangements. In the case of land, there may be lease or share-cropping arrangements in place which may be recorded in formal agreements or by traditional agreements which are not documented.

3. Establish what, if any, **compensation rates have been used to date on the project**. Often during preliminary project phases, including exploration on mining projects, land is acquired for preliminary infrastructure, including worker camps and exploration camps. The compensation rates are sometimes negotiated by project development staff with little knowledge on the true value of assets. These compensation rates are often higher than replacement rates that the project cannot meet at subsequent project stages. It is important to understand the basis for these rates as this will set expectations for local communities.

    On many projects there are different rates used for land access required for different types of infrastructure including the port, access roads and project

Project example

On a project in Africa, the local landowners had complex traditional sharecropping arrangements with economic migrants where the migrants agreed to clear the land and establish a cocoa plantation. After five years the land was divided and the migrants acquired ownership of 50% of the land. The project recorded the status of all these sharecropping arrangements and divided the compensation between both the landowner and sharecropper based on these agreements. Where there were disagreements, these were lodged in the project grievance mechanism to try to negotiate a resolution between the parties. Where agreement could not be reached the compensation was placed in an escrow account until a court determined the division of compensation, but the company was allowed to move forward and acquire the land and proceed with the project.

area. The basis for offering different rates on the same project must be well understood as project-affected households will try to cherry-pick the highest rates, although land on other parts of the project may be of a higher market value. Project-affected households often assume that the highest rate that the company is willing to pay for any piece of land is the rate that they should be paid.

International standards are clear that paying cash compensation to impacted households presents considerable risks for the project. The general result is that poor families are not used to handling large sums of money and this gets spent quickly on consumable items, leaving them with little to live on after a relatively short period of time. Once the money is spent, the impacted households are often semi-destitute and return to put pressure on the project to improve their situation, which can cause considerable tension and sometimes conflict. It is therefore a risk mitigation strategy to provide compensation in kind as replacement land, housing and agricultural inputs, rather than in cash. Where cash has to be paid under national legislation, the project should provide some financial training to the impacted households, including investment advice and assistance to establish bank accounts. However, it should also be clear that providing a few short classes to project-affected households who are poor and illiterate will likely not have a significant impact on their spending behaviour.

4. Undertake a **benchmarking of government rates and other projects** in the region or country to establish a range that may be acceptable to the community. Note that government rates are often only reviewed every five or ten years and can seriously underestimate the value of crops, for example, and may not meet international standards to provide replacement rates. Other projects may use a negotiated rate which does not have a scientific basis and may be well above replacement value. For example, the project may have

been close to an urban area or the community refused to accept anything lower, forcing the company to pay a high rate to proceed with the project.

5. **Engage an experienced independent valuer** to determine the replacement value of each asset. The replacement value is defined as the market value of the assets plus transaction costs. It is important to use an independent valuer who is properly certified in the host country in order to give some independence to the valuation process. In many countries the government has mandated valuation rates which are often below the replacement value for assets. In these cases it is important to negotiate a process where the impacted households receive a top-up of government rates in a form acceptable to the government. In some cases the ownership of all land is vested in the state, although the land is still allocated according to traditional practice and passed on through inheritance. In this case the government may not allow the payment of compensation for land acquisition and land-for-land replacement is the best solution, if possible.

The IFC provides the following guidance on compensating for key assets and determining replacement values:

> Agricultural or pasture land: land of equal productive use or potential, located in the vicinity of the affected land or the new housing site, plus the cost of preparation to levels similar to or better than those of the affected land, and transaction costs such as registration and transfer taxes or customary fees. In situations where blocks of replacement land are identified by the client in areas not immediately adjacent to affected land, the client should establish the difference between present and potential land use to ensure that replacement land is of equivalent potential. Typically this requires an independent assessment of land capacity and/or carrying capacity (e.g. soils surveys, agronomic capability mapping). Compensation for affected land with land of less productive potential may prevent the restoration of livelihoods and require a higher cost of inputs than prior to displacement. Land-based compensation strategies are the preferred form of compensation for agriculturally based households. (IFC 2012: PS5, Guidance Note 22)

Where compensation in cash is required, this should be based on the market value of the cost to the project-affected person of acquiring land of similar characteristics locally plus any transaction costs.

> Fallow land: market value of land of equal productive value in the vicinity of the affected land. Where value cannot be determined or land for land compensation is not feasible, in-kind communal compensation is recommended. (IFC 2012: PS5, GN22)

It is preferable to provide replacement fallow land in kind as a priority if this can be sourced locally.

> Land in urban areas: the market value of land of equivalent area and use, with similar or improved infrastructure and services preferably located

in the vicinity of the affected land, plus transaction costs such as registration and transfer taxes. (IFC 2012: PS5, GN22)

It is recommended that the company provides replacement residential plots in sites where the project-affected households can re-establish their livelihoods to prevent them from wasting the compensation and ending up in inferior accommodation or homeless. It is important that a proper title is secured for the household.

> Houses and other structures (including public structures such as schools, clinics and religious buildings): the cost of purchasing or building a replacement structure, with an area and quality similar to or better than those of the affected structure, or of repairing a partially affected structure, including labor, contractors' fees and transaction costs such as registration, transfer taxes, and moving costs. (IFC 2012: PS5, GN22)

Note that the international best practices recommend the replacement of residential housing and associated structures and community infrastructure in kind to prevent the problems of poor communities wasting cash compensation in the shorter term. However, cash compensation is often paid for secondary structures such as grain stores, kitchens, fences, chicken pens, etc.

> Loss of access to natural resources: the market value of the natural resources which may include wild medicinal plants, firewood, and other non-timber forest products, meat or fish. However, cash compensation is seldom an effective way of compensating for lost access to natural resource ... and every effort should be made to provide or facilitate access to similar resources elsewhere, thereby avoiding or minimising the need for cash compensation. (IFC 2012: PS5, GN22)

Women are generally affected most by the loss of natural resources, particularly concerning the collection of fuelwood and natural food resources. However, this loss is often not compensated for in kind or, if compensated in cash, this is paid to the male household head. It is therefore essential to prioritise compensation in kind, particularly as replacement land, as cash compensation is generally directed at the male household head.

> Crops: many countries have legally defined rates of compensation for crops and/or land. It is recommended that clients assess the government-established compensation rates and adjust as necessary to meet the replacement rate criterion. The assessment of these rates is best achieved via the commissioning of an experienced agronomist or similarly qualified professional with a working knowledge of the host country's compensation and agricultural pricing systems. (IFC 2012: PS5, GN10)

Note that crop compensation must take into account the loss of income from the crop during the time taken to re-establish the crop. In different countries there are various practices for payment of compensation on crops, including the payment of compensation for annual crops even when these can be harvested, so it is important to conduct thorough benchmarking as outlined above.

6. **Negotiate resettlement packages in kind and cash, as appropriate**, for the range of assets impacted with representatives of the impacted communities as outlined in Chapter 12. It is critical that the community representatives feed back to the impacted households to ensure that they support the packages being agreed with the company. Otherwise, there is a risk that some households will not agree with the final package resulting in hold-outs and delays to the project.

It can be useful to pay also for the community to engage their own valuer so that their position has an informed scientific or market basis, rather than being founded just on wild expectations of what they can force the project to pay. The final rate the project is required to pay is often based on the time available to negotiate the rates: the faster the project needs the land, the more likely a higher rate will be negotiated by the communities. The advantage of allowing the community to have their own valuer is that this requires them to adopt a professional approach to determining valuation and engage with the project's valuer to reach agreement in a shorter time-frame. However, there are risks as the community valuer may try to deliberately negotiate higher rates in order to claim a share for themselves, resulting in a longer negotiations period and disputes in the community. It is recommended that the community produce a list of proposed valuers that must be approved by the project. This allows the project to conduct the necessary checks to ensure that the proposed valuer has the required experience to undertake the exercise and will behave in a professional manner.

In many cases the compensation rates for crops are established early in the project development process, for example by exploration teams on mining projects, and it may be difficult to try to reduce these rates later when they

 Project example

A project in Africa was facing demands from impacted communities for levels of compensation up to 50 times that being paid on other projects. The project facilitated the community to engage an independent valuer to advise them on the compensation process for land and buildings. The independent valuer conducted a market analysis and developed a compensation table on behalf of the community. The project and community independent valuers then worked together and presented a range of compensation values for all assets which were discussed in the consultations committee. This process allowed the project and community to quickly establish a realistic basis for compensation, and an agreement was reached to pay a replacement value with a top-up required to finalise the negotiations to the satisfaction of all community groups.

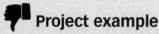

Project example

A project in Africa engaged an independent valuer to survey crops and advise on compensation rates. The valuer colluded with the community to propose a very high compensation rate based on him receiving 25% of the compensation personally. The project rejected the compensation rates and had to engage an alternative valuer, which delayed the project and led to protracted discussions with the community representatives until an agreement was finally reached.

need to be scaled up for the whole project. Ultimately, the rates that are negotiated are what the company is willing to pay and what the community and government are willing to approve. It is common to establish a 'scientific' rate based on market valuation and then to negotiate a top-up of this rate to seal a deal with the community.

Sign a final agreement with the community representatives for each asset type impacted by the project and record this in a formal agreement, including a ceremony where appropriate. A compensation table is prepared for the project which summarises all the key asset compensation categories. Note that the compensation rates are normally renegotiated annually to take account of inflation in the value of goods and services. Outline the formulas for calculating compensation rates so that rates can be easily adjusted to inflation in subsequent phases of the project.

7. **Develop a sign-off and payments strategy** for the project. While the overall rates have been agreed with the community representatives, it is important that each individual household is given the opportunity to review the RAP (resettlement action plan) packages and options which have been negotiated as they apply to their assets for sign-off. It is recommended that, after the baseline data is collected, a report is prepared for each individual household summarising their key assets. Each household should be given an opportunity to review the report with a community representative and verify that it is correct. Usually this process generates grievances. The carefully registered data on each household can be checked in the field and the project can agree on a final determination of assets. Once the final rates are agreed, the project can issue the compensation payments confident that the majority of grievances have been resolved. This pre-sign-off process can significantly speed up the payments process. The sign-off process is outlined in more detail in Chapter 13.

Determining eligibility

The baseline data research and consultations and negotiations with the project stakeholders will determine the project impacts and identify the owners of all impacted assets, whether individually or communally held.

As explained in Chapter 6 concerning the baseline data collection, the asset surveys are normally conducted after the declaration of a cut-off date. The cut-off date is defined as the date designated by the project sponsor that serves as cut-off period for its obligation to compensate affected, eligible assets, and is based on proper disclosure. This date is normally agreed with the government and traditional authorities and must conform to the laws of the host country.

Persons occupying the project area after the cut-off date are not eligible for compensation and/or resettlement assistance. Similarly, fixed assets such as built structures, crops, fruit trees and wood-lots established after the cut-off date and completion of the assets inventory and proper disclosure, or an alternative mutually agreed date, will not be compensated.

Note that, according to international standards, displaced people fall into the following categories (IFC 2012):

- Category 1: those who have formal legal rights to the land or assets they occupy or use

- Category 2: those who do not have formal legal rights to land or assets, but have a claim to land that is recognised or recognisable under national law

- Category 3: those who have no recognisable legal right or claim to the land or assets they occupy or use

Project-affected households are eligible for compensation and other assistance if they have a 'legitimate interest' in respect of 'immovable assets' in the project area that are in place (i.e. established, in the case of crops or constructed, in the case of buildings) at the time of the cut-off date.

'Legitimate interest' in immovable assets at the household level is usually held by a single member: the household head. Through traditional and family practice, the household head is typically the most senior male member of the household. In some instances the legitimate interest may be held jointly, i.e. by the household head and his/her spouse, or with other members of the extended family. When the household head dies, the company requires that other household members identify the inheritor through a court order or other appropriate resolution measure before compensation will be paid.

Note that 'legitimate interest' is not synonymous with ownership. Even those project-affected persons/households/communities with no recognisable legal right or claim to the assets they are occupying are considered eligible for resettlement assistance.

Developing an entitlement matrix

The IFC recommends projects to prepare an entitlement matrix to identify affected people (entitled persons), all types of loss (impacts) and the types of compensation and assistance provided (entitlements). There has been some discussion in practitioner circles on the use of the term 'entitlement matrix' and alternatives have been proposed such as 'impacts and packages matrix' (as discussed in Chapter 4).

The entitlement matrix should set out the following categories:

- All categories of affected people, including property owners and land-right holders, tenants, squatters, sharecroppers, grazers, nomadic pastoralists and other natural resource users, shopkeepers, vendors and other service providers, communities and vulnerable groups
- All types of loss associated with each category, including loss of physical assets; loss of access to physical assets; loss of wages, rent or sales earnings; loss of public infrastructure and elements of cultural significance (as identified in the inventory of losses)
- All types of compensation and assistance to which each category is entitled

An example of an abbreviated entitlement matrix, showing the key impacts, eligibility and entitlements which may be considered on a project, is shown in Figure 8.1.

Other allowances

In addition to compensation for loss of assets and income, the project should also support the households during their move to their resettlement house and until they are food secure. Projects normally provide the following support to households during the resettlement process:

- **Transport assistance**: a truck to transport their belongings to their resettlement house. This is discussed further in Chapter 14 on physical resettlement implementation.
- **Moving allowance**: projects generally provide households with a moving allowance to allow them to make small purchases to smooth the move process to their new house. This is separate from any compensation payments for income lost until they restore their business or livelihood.
- **Food rations**: where the impacted households miss a harvest then the project should provide food rations or an allowance to enable the family to meet its basic needs until the new crop can be planted and harvested. The rations should take into account the size of the households, their calorific and nutritional needs and be comprised of mainly local food products.

Figure 8.1: An abbreviated entitlement matrix.

Category of loss	Impact	Category of Project Affected Person (PAP)	Basis of approach	Packages
Loss of Structures				
Residential structures or houses				
Complete structures				
General	Loss of structure or access to structure	Immovable house owner	Square meter for square meter replacement in form of resettlement of existing immovable houses	Standard size house, latrine and kitchen depending on the negotiated house design, cash compensation for annexes
Incomplete structures		Owner	Cash compensation	Cash compensation at agreed square meter rate for % completed and provision of replacement plot.
Tenants				
Tenant accommodation	Loss of accommodation	Immovable accommodation/ tenant		Livelihood restoration programs Re-establishment allowance Transport assistance Assistance in finding accommodation
Residential annexes (structures separate from house, e.g. granaries, storage bins, animal pens etc.)	Loss of structure or access to structure	Immovable building owner	Cash compensation for all annexes, depending on resettlement house design	**Resettlement**: For people who currently have, cash compensation at applicable valuation rate for total existing square meters based on existing materials. All resettled households will be provided with a kitchen and latrine depending on negotiated house design.
Worship buildings (public / private)	Loss of structure or access to structure	Immovable building owner	Replace at resettlement sites	Private and public buildings of worship will be replaced
Small/Medium Enterprises (SMEs)	Cost of moving	Business owners	Transport assistance will be provided to move business materials as part of half a truckload allocated per household	Transport assistance to new resettlement site **Non-resident in Project Footprint**: Transport assistance to move business to resettlement site or nearby home town
	Re-establishment costs	Business owners	Salvaging will be facilitated	No resettlement nor relocation package because covered under other package
	Livelihood improvement	Current business owners	Access to credit and/or training depending on assessment of credit/training providers in area	Access to micro-credit (subject to rules) and other elements as set out in Livelihood Restoration Plan **Non-resident in Project Footprint**: Access to micro-credit if they move their business to a resettlement site or to where they live nearby (subject to review of specific cases)
Loss of rental income	Lost business location	Landlord (owner of Eligible Structure)	IFC standards – maintain livelihoods	New business structure and commercial plot provided
	Cost of moving	Landlord and tenant	General transport assistance	Transport assistance in kind to new resettlement site
	Loss of income	Landlord	Livelihood restoration	**Resettlement, Non-resident in Project Footprint**: Access to Livelihood Restoration Program
	Re-establishment costs	Landlord	Benefit from worker influx	Covered by other elements of packages set out in this table
	Livelihood improvement	Landlord	Better quality buildings to attract clients	No compensation

Landless households

The treatment of landless households, including squatters and transient herders, causes particular problems on projects. They often live on public or common property, without any legal rights and limited community and political support, and are generally not entitled to land compensation. The project must consult with these landless households and project stakeholders and endeavour to find them alternative sites to live on with tenure rights if possible. The new sites should ensure that access is maintained to their sources of livelihood, natural resource areas, markets or businesses for employment. Where possible the project should encourage landlords to retain commitments to tenants and tenant farmers at the new resettlement sites, although in many cases this is difficult to achieve.

Figure 8.2: Migrant herders in Africa.

Where tenants will be left without accommodation, the project should provide them with an allowance to cover rent for a period of up to six months to enable them to re-establish themselves.

Compensation frameworks: key considerations

- **Minimise cash compensation**: general experience demonstrates that poorer households don't have the skills to invest cash compensation wisely. Projects should therefore construct replacement housing and provide replacement land to impacted households to ensure that they have the minimum safety net required to provide shelter and food for themselves.
- **Implement measures to support households to manage cash compensation**: provide households receiving significant sums of cash compensation with financial management training, investment advice and assist them to open bank accounts. However, be realistic about the impact that training courses can have on the investment behaviour of poor households with low levels of education.
- **Use staged payments**: projects should try to stage cash payments over a number of years to limit the risk of households spending one large payment unwisely.

- **Provide methods for compensating for common property and cultural resources**: it is difficult to compensate for the loss of common property and cultural resources in cash. The project should investigate the potential to provide alternative sites and also to support wider community projects to compensate for this loss.
- **Investigate alternative models of cost–benefit sharing** which give impacted communities a long-term stake in the project benefits.

9
Physical resettlement planning

Physical resettlement (physical displacement), namely when households living in the project area are required to move, requires effective identification, design, planning and construction of alternative communities, housing and related facilities, in order to mitigate effectively for physical losses, but also to ensure the future cohesion and success of the communities affected.

This chapter details the planning of resettlement sites, infrastructure and housing in a way which should maximise the success of physical resettlement, including through the effective participation of affected households and communities and due consideration of their real needs and wants. Attention is also given to instances of physical resettlement in post-conflict or disaster-related situations, or in connection with the protection of ecosystems, and what special considerations are required in these cases.

What are the key components of the physical resettlement planning process?

Depending on the circumstances of a project, the issue of physical resettlement may be dealt with in one, or a combination of, the following ways:

- The project develops alternative resettlement sites (new or infill into existing communities) and housing for affected households
- The project provides cash for households to purchase plots and/or housing and/or build their own housing

Where cash is provided to households to purchase or build their own housing, safeguards need to be put in place to ensure that cash is utilised effectively and there is no increased risk of homelessness or settlement in unsustainable areas for households.

Where the project intends to deliver physical resettlement through the planning and development of sites and housing, the following steps or components need to be addressed:

- **Assessment** of the existing situation: a great deal of information on the current living conditions and social organisation and networks of impacted communities and households will come from the stakeholder engagement process and various surveys undertaken, particularly surveys of existing structures and assets. However, in addition to this a detailed analysis of community- and household-level organisation, housing and asset utilisation, and housing layouts, is required to be undertaken by resettlement planners in order to understand how people live and use their assets, particularly housing, house plots, community facilities and communal areas.

- **Analysis** of all data and studies of living conditions will aid in determining what will be the required characteristics of any replacement resettlement site, associated community facilities and infrastructure, and housing.

- **Preliminary identification and evaluation** of potential replacement resettlement sites, according to key criteria that respond to identified community needs (e.g. surrounding quality agricultural land, close to markets, etc.).

- **Preliminary design, engineering and costing** of resettlement site layouts, infrastructure, plot sizes, replacement housing and community facilities.

- **Extensive consultation and negotiation** on preliminary designs culminating in consensus and agreement on resettlement site locations, standards of provision, and ultimately agreement on detailed design, and other related issues such as handover and maintenance. Consultation needs to be undertaken with all statutory authorities throughout the process, as well as affected communities and households.

> Physical resettlement planning is not just concerned with engineering and design, but how to ensure the preservation of the existing social fabric in a new location

- **Detailed evaluation, design, engineering and costing**, which should occur iteratively in parallel with ongoing community and key stakeholder consultations and agreements.

- **Approvals** of all designs and layouts by the relevant statutory authorities.

- Development of a **handover and maintenance plan**, to ensure all stakeholders are aware of statutory and personal responsibilities in respect of the completed site and that handover to households and authorities takes place in a timely fashion.

- Ensuring grant of **security of tenure** for resettlers through registration of property rights by regulatory authorities.

- Development of a **construction management plan** and **tender documentation** to allow for timely and effective implementation (discussed further in Chapter 14).

Each of these key components are discussed further below.

What is the key objective of the physical resettlement process?

Physical resettlement is one of the major impacts of land access projects on individuals, households and communities as a whole. The process of physical relocation and the demolition of existing hamlets, villages or towns is not just a physical disturbance, it can be emotionally disturbing for people. The process can particularly affect vulnerable and potentially vulnerable people, including the elderly, who may have a deep attachment to their existing locality. The planning process itself can create tensions within a community as underlying issues may be brought to the fore, such as long-running local leadership disputes, issues of property ownership and rights being unclear, or differing levels of wealth and assets becoming more starkly felt. The issue of physical resettlement therefore requires sensitive planning that goes way beyond physical planning and design considerations.

The objective of physical resettlement is to enable the relocation of individuals, households and communities to new locations in a way that:

- **Reflects the way people** live in their current location and **meets their key requirements** in terms of living space, functionality and access to resources
- **Respects current social networks** and maintains community and household cohesion
- **Maintains links with existing assets and resources** not affected by resettlement, or replaces them
- Creates an **enabling environment** that allows the livelihoods and standard of living of project-affected persons to be improved, or at least restored
- Enables resettled people to appropriately **share in project benefits**, e.g. project-related employment
- Offers **fair, equitable and adequate replacement housing** and house plots that is at least at the same standard as existing housing and ideally better
- Ensures the **replacement of all existing community facilities** and related infrastructure, and provision of additional facilities and infrastructure as required by local planning regulations
- Offers improved **security of tenure**

> The objective of the physical resettlement process is to preserve social networks and livelihoods, but also create the basis for new opportunities and improved standards of living

- Is **affordable** for the project proponent
- **Avoids** the need for **large-scale resettlement or compensation of host lands**
- **Provides security of tenure**
- Allows for **ongoing development and expansion** of the new community

In what circumstances does physical resettlement occur?

The following are the main circumstances where physical resettlement usually occurs:

- **Natural resource projects** (e.g. mining) where significant areas of land are often required for project development, including areas where people are currently living
- **Infrastructure projects** (e.g. dams) where the area of the construction itself, and related affected areas (e.g. inundated areas) or safety buffers can require the relocation of settlements
- **Disaster-related resettlement** (e.g. tsunamis) when communities affected by a natural disaster need to be resettled either because the existing area becomes unbuildable, or it is necessary to relocate to safer locations
- **Transitional or post-conflict resettlement** (e.g. internally displaced people) where people affected by conflict or persecution in one location have migrated to safer locations and require permanent shelter solutions there
- **Environmental protection measures**, where populations living in protected environments may be moved to relieve pressure on endangered ecosystems

> No matter the cause of physical resettlement, the same objectives apply of maintaining social cohesion in an improved environment with increased livelihood opportunities

What are the key issues, challenges and risks?

As referred to above, physical resettlement is a major impact of a land access project and projects will inevitably be faced with a range of difficult issues, challenges and risks, including:

- **High community and individual expectations**
- **Precedents created elsewhere** which may not be appropriate to project circumstances or sustainable once handed over to communities

- Community leaders who may not be fully representative, and the **potential for community disputes**
- **Failing to fully understand** community and household structures
- **Differing needs and wants** among the community (e.g. elderly vs. young people, farmers vs. traders)
- **Lack of available suitable replacement land**
- **Lack of appreciation of the cost and time** required to ensure adequate physical resettlement
- **Lack of government capacity** to sometimes be meaningful development partners
- **Length of time it sometimes takes to put in place legally binding security of tenure**

The purpose of this chapter is to help you identify and deal with the issues, challenges, risks and opportunities that will arise.

Is there one definitive standard that provides all the answers?

The IFC (International Finance Corporation) recommends that project proponents undertake the following actions on behalf of project-affected persons:

If people living in the project area are required to move to another location, the client will (i) offer displaced persons choices among feasible resettlement options, including adequate replacement housing or cash compensation where appropriate; and (ii) provide relocation assistance suited to the needs of each group of displaced persons. New resettlement sites built for displaced persons must offer improved living conditions. The displaced persons' preferences with respect to relocating in pre-existing communities and groups will be taken into consideration. Existing social and cultural institutions of the displaced persons and any host communities will be respected.

The client will offer them a choice of options for adequate housing with security of tenure so that they can resettle legally without having to face the risk of forced eviction. Based on consultation with such displaced persons, the client will provide relocation assistance sufficient for them to restore their standard of living at an adequate alternative site. (IFC 2012: Performance Standard 5)

> While laws and standards provide useful guidance to projects, much of this guidance is of a general nature. This chapter provides more detailed and practical assistance in planning for physical resettlement

The IFC *Handbook for Preparing a Resettlement Action Plan* (2002) also provides some useful general guidance on physical resettlement, noting that:

The two most critical concerns in selection of a resettlement site are **location and community preservation** [IFC's emphasis]. The selection of resettlement sites that provide people with reliable access to productive resources (arable and grazing land, water, and woodlands), employment, and business opportunities is key to the restoration of livelihoods. Resettlement options should avoid breaking up communities, because the maintenance of the social networks linking members of the affected communities may be critical to the successful adaptation of those communities to their new circumstances. (IFC 2002: 36)

What are the guiding principles for physical resettlement?

Key principles apply regardless of the impetus for physical resettlement or where a project is located.

In terms of the overall process:

- **Informed participation**: all households and communities physically affected need to participate in the physical resettlement planning process, not just community leaders or statutory authorities
- **Compliance with laws and standards**: all aspects of the design and engineering process, and applications for security of tenure, must comply with applicable laws and be guided by agreed best practice standards
- **Local context**: the approach needs to be firmly rooted in the local socio-economic context, i.e. ordinary, practical and sustainable, and meeting the needs of resettlers in terms of shelter and livelihood solutions (e.g. available farmland)
- **Choice**: offer choice in terms of resettlement solutions (to the extent that they are practically possible)
- **Do not promise what you cannot deliver**

In terms of resettlement site identification and design:

- That **land identified is available**
- **Sufficient agricultural land of quality** which can be accessed from resettlement housing
- Access to **natural resources** (e.g. water sources)
- **Not prone to natural disasters** (e.g. flooding)
- Consistent with the **existing settlement pattern**
- **Largely unoccupied**, to minimise impact on other inhabitants and maximise flexibility in the design of the resettlement community

- **Enough area** to accommodate the number of households likely to be resettled
- Located as **close as possible to the project area**, to maximise home area continuity and economic opportunities for resettlers
- **Good soil** for construction and relatively flat topography
- **Close to existing settlements** and transport networks where possible to benefit from existing facilities and infrastructure (including educational, health, religious, roads)
- **Availability of adjoining land** for future village growth and expansion
- Close to other **livelihood opportunities**

In terms of plot design:
- Plots should conform to **planning standards**
- Plots should be **large enough** to provide for ancillary activities undertaken by resettling families (e.g. backyard farming, drying of crops, rearing livestock)
- Plots should **provide space** for future expansion of the house
- Plots should conform to the **typical size** of homes and compounds
- Plots should be **sufficiently close to farm lands or other sources of livelihood** where applicable

In terms of housing and community facilities design:
- **Affordability**: construction costs are affordable for the project, and maintenance costs are affordable for residents and statutory authorities
- **Familiarity and simplicity**: materials, technology and design are familiar to local contractors and residents, meet sociocultural requirements and are easy to maintain
- **Availability**: building materials and appropriate construction competence are available locally
- **High performance**: materials are carefully selected in terms of sustainability and performance, together with good design, providing for a good quality of life
- **Flexibility**: designs provide for residents to change uses over time (e.g. change in function of rooms)
- **Potential for expansion**: designs and plot layout provide the potential to add new rooms, as residents' needs and economic situation change

What assessments and analysis are required before preliminary planning and design can commence?

In order to inform preliminary planning and design, the following activities first need to be undertaken:

- As part of the stakeholder engagement planning described in Chapter 5, the project should have undertaken a **stakeholder identification and analysis**. This involves assessing community organisation, power relations and divisions; conflict within and between the communities; and community issues and concerns.

- As part of the **stakeholder engagement** process, households and communities need to be consulted on their physical environment, including what assets and facilities they value and would like to see in any resettlement community. This can be done through focus groups and household interviews, but must be careful not to raise expectations.

- **Asset surveys** will be undertaken as part of the baseline surveys, as discussed in Chapter 6, which will record, as an average and per household, existing standards of construction, house size, room number and room use, and other information such as use of communal facilities, household organisation within compounds, and livelihood activities. This information will inform replacement requirements for communities as a whole and at a household level.

- **Other baseline surveys** need to be analysed on a community and household level to understand current livelihood activities, which will inform the required characteristics of any replacement site.

- Resettlement planners should supplement the asset surveys with detailed **architectural analysis** of existing houses and homesteads, including design, orientation, ancillary structures, plot demarcation and use, etc. This should include **observational studies** to see how people are living in their current environment and how they make use of existing built assets and the natural environment.

- **Other participatory studies** can be undertaken with communities to understand their use of existing sites, facilities and resources, such as developing a **community calendar** or undertaking a **transect walk**.

- **Statutory plans** need to be thoroughly reviewed, to understand any government plans, zoning and other development plans or building regulations which may impinge on resettlement planning.

Analysis of all baseline data and studies of living conditions will aid in determining what should be the required characteristics of any replacement resettlement site, associated community facilities and infrastructure, and housing.

Figure 9.1: Example analysis of an existing homestead.

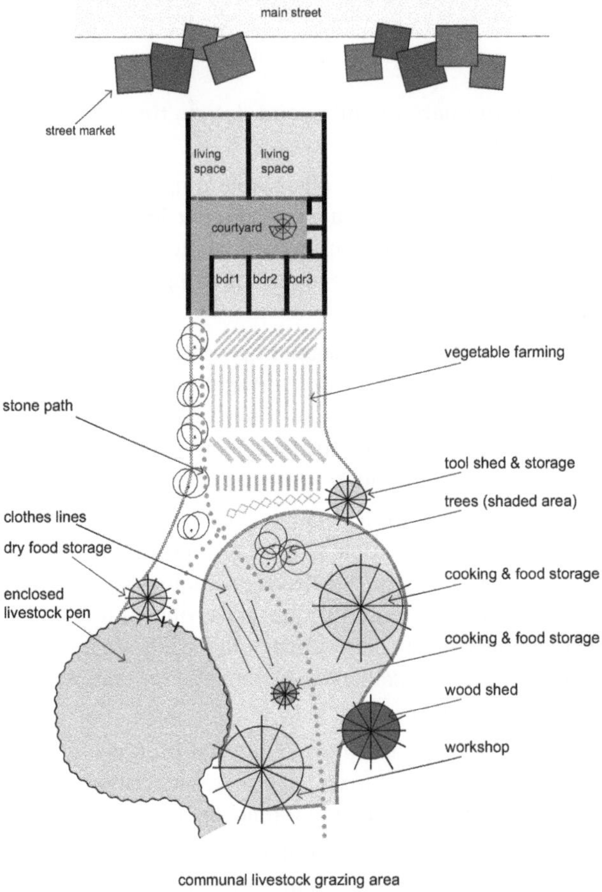

main street

street market

living space

living space

courtyard

bdr1 bdr2 bdr3

vegetable farming

stone path

tool shed & storage

trees (shaded area)

clothes lines

dry food storage

cooking & food storage

enclosed livestock pen

cooking & food storage

wood shed

workshop

communal livestock grazing area

👎 Project example

A project in Africa selected a resettlement site with a primary focus of replacement land for agriculture based on consultations with the key leaders who were predominantly older men and farmers. However, in order to find sufficient land the site was 25 km from the original village and remote from the project and employment opportunities. Ultimately, it was found that the soils were not fertile and the resettlement site selection had to be revisited. The key lesson was that the views of women and young men who wanted to be close to the project and economic opportunities were not considered. Also, soil sampling should be conducted early in the process to inform the selection of sites before these are presented to the community for approval.

Project example

A project in Africa required the resettlement of one major village, one smaller village and a number of hamlets. In addition to the usual baseline surveys, analysis was done on the use of assets, land and resources in each locality, as well as an analysis of compound use and lifestyles, through observations of daily life. The findings were reflected in the initial house and plot designs put to the communities, while the resettlement site layout was also zoned to reflect the differing identities and needs of the villages and hamlets.

How does a project identify potential resettlement solutions?

The project needs to undertake a **preliminary identification and analysis** of resettlement sites that accords to key criteria. Initial identification of sites can be desk based, making use of satellite imagery and topographic maps, with minimal ground-truthing, so as to not raise expectations or concerns in the community before a preliminary proposal has been sufficiently developed.

An initial identification of sites may therefore involve the following steps:

- **Identification with the project proponent** (both social and technical teams) of areas where the company would not wish to develop resettlement sites, based on issues such as project expansion potential, the need for safety buffers or other project-related concerns.

- **Review of any statutory development plans and legislation**, to understand areas where resettlement site development may be possible, or preferable, and to understand other potential developments in the area which may impact on future resettlement sites. Plans and guidance may also include information on plot sizes, population thresholds for various infrastructure provision, etc.

- A **table on replacement land and housing requirements** related to each community should be developed from the baseline data, taking into account likely plot sizes, in order to determine approximate areas of land required, taking into account need for roads, open space, etc., and in accordance with national standards.

- **Exploration of a mix of resettlement/housing solutions** will often be necessary, especially where large areas of replacement land are not easily available, or impacted households have a variety of requirements and wishes. Projects may have a preference for one or more sites depending on baseline findings and consultations regarding the size and characteristics of the various communities to be moved, and related social, cultural and political considerations. It is usually preferable to have as few sites as possible from a cost perspective, especially if these are stand-alone sites, but opportunities for **infill development and extensions** to existing villages also need to be considered at this stage, especially given the benefits of shared infrastructure and potential for maintaining social cohesion in certain circumstances. Projects need to consider the full mix of physical resettlement solutions, including building on stand-alone plots associated with farms, or plots acquired by impacted persons in nearby towns and villages. The costs/benefits of a number and mix of approaches will need to be considered by the project, as well as the most appropriate solution for the resettlers and the host communities.

- **Desk-based assessment** of the area utilising digitised satellite imagery, to identify sufficient areas of land capable of resettling the required number of households and associated infrastructure (based on the baseline data).

- **Initial prioritisation** of sites for further investigation, based on **criteria that respond to initial identified community needs**, such as likely agricultural potential, proximity to existing settlements and services, proximity to the project, proximity to home area and existing farms for continuity, good topography and drainage potential, etc.

Figure 9.2: Preliminary resettlement site location plans.

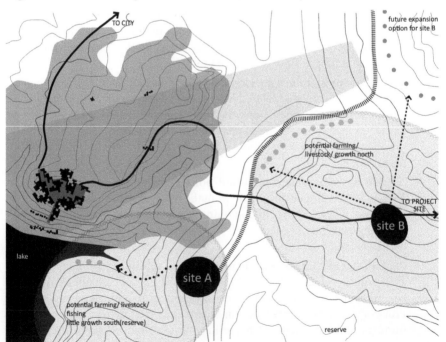

- **Confirmation from the project proponent** in writing that any initial proposed sites are of 'no interest' to the project. In some cases this may not be finally agreed until further investigations, such as sterilisation drilling in the case of a mining project, are undertaken.
- **Initial discreet site visits** to undertake an initial visual assessment of identified potential sites, and allow for further prioritisation of preferred sites.
- **Preferred sites should be mapped**, and details of area and carrying capacity estimates included, as the basis for further investigation and consultations.

From this initial identification of sites, the project proponent can develop a **shortlist of potential preferred sites**. At this point the **views of stakeholders** can be sourced, in addition to additional work on the shortlisted sites.

 Project example

A project in Eastern Europe choose a single resettlement site based on the recommendations of the community to be resettled. This seemed like a very participatory approach to resettlement site identification. However, the cost of development of the site, particularly earthworks, was very high, and there was a lack of farmland nearby for restoration of livelihoods, particularly because of cumulative impacts from nearby developments. It later transpired that a key reason for the community identifying the site was that key community leaders owned the land.

 Project example

A project in Africa required the relocation of 500 households with farmland of over 1,000 hectares. There were no large areas of replacement land available in the area. Working with the local authorities, the project identified 150 separate land parcels which were then developed into 'clusters' capable of incorporating houses surrounded by farming plots, linked together by tracks, with each 'cluster' serviced by the road network. The shortlisted clusters were those closest to existing infrastructure and the main town which would benefit economically from the project. Preliminary designs illustrated this concept to stakeholders, who could then be consulted on their preferred 'clusters' for further development.

Figure 9.3: Resettlement site selection criteria.

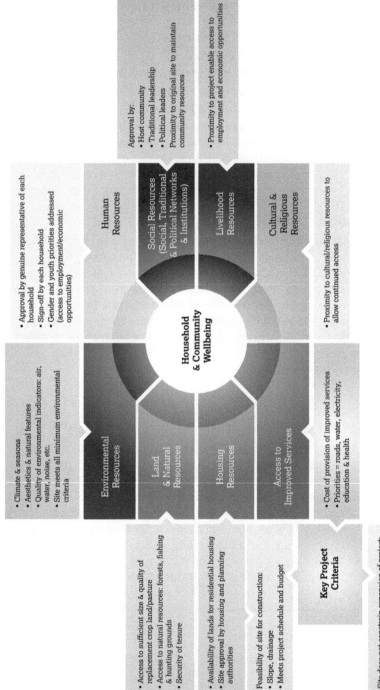

What criteria should be selected in prioritising potential sites?

As referred to above, criteria for initial site assessment should respond to initial identified community needs based on the baseline data collection and analysis, and additional housing and participatory community-specific analyses (e.g. observational studies, transect walks, etc.).

Key criteria are likely to include agricultural potential, proximity to existing settlements and services, proximity to the project, proximity to home area and existing farms for continuity, good topography and drainage potential, etc.

The resources framework discussed in Chapter 7 in the context of identification of impacts can also be used to ensure all aspects of household and community wellbeing, such as livelihoods, community facilities and social networks, are fully considered in determining the specific criteria for resettlement site location, and subsequent detailed site and housing design (Figure 9.3).

Who should be consulted on preliminary resettlement sites?

Note that up to this point the resettlement site identification exercise should be largely confidential and internal, and not discussed with external stakeholders, in order not to raise expectations or concern, or risk disputes in the communities.

Initially identified sites should be discussed in the first instance with:

- The regional and local authorities
- Relevant village authorities (both impacted and host communities as required)
- Community representative forums (such as a consultation committee)
- Key informants

Discussions should be framed as preliminary to investigate the suitability of certain sites or otherwise in principle, and to obtain feedback.

The purpose of initial consultations is to:

- Get initial feedback
- Determine in principle the acceptance of sites for further investigation and discussion
- Ensure as much as possible that sites are protected from development in the short term

> It is important to stress the preliminary nature of site investigations with communities at all times, and that multiple sites are being considered, to reduce the possibility of speculation on resettlement sites

Figure 9.4: Initial resettlement site consultations.

- Obtain suggestions from authorities and project-affected persons on any other proposed sites and their reasons for this; these sites can then also be investigated

No decision or agreement should be made at this stage, since the ultimate suitability of each site will not be known, and costs will not be confirmed. It should be emphasised in consultations that all sites are subject to further investigation and may be excluded if found to be unsuitable or not to have project potential (these caveats are important as it essentially provides a veto over unsuitable sites that may sometimes be pushed for purely political or other reasons).

How can preliminary designs be developed?

Following preliminary investigations and initial consultations, preferred sites can then be progressed to **preliminary design, engineering and costing**. This should include **further investigations** together with detailed design and costing which will determine the ultimate suitability of sites, preferred sites from the point of view of the project proponent, and **sufficient detail on costs** for initial negotiations to commence.

The following steps need to be considered in the ongoing investigation and design of shortlisted sites. **Detailed assessments** of shortlisted sites, depending on complexity, may include, but are not limited to:

- **Livelihoods assessment**: a comprehensive livelihoods assessment should be undertaken of shortlisted sites, in collaboration with a project's livelihoods specialists. Historically site selection in resettlement projects, while taking some account of livelihoods, has been lead more by engineering considerations. While the costs of development are crucial to determining viability of sites, the long-term livelihood potential is much more critical, and particularly in cases where the engineering differences between sites are more marginal. The livelihoods assessment should review each site according to established criteria, such as prevailing activities and the sustainable livelihoods approach, to determine the sites most amenable to livelihood restoration and long-term development.
- **Sterilisation drilling**: natural resource projects may need to undertake exploration on identified sites to confirm that they are not of interest to the project. This is often referred to as sterilisation drilling. The decision as and when to undertake this work will be dependent on a number of factors, including availability of equipment, and the cost of undertaking the drilling against the likelihood of the site being developed.
- **Hydrogeological studies**: it will be important to identify the possibility of available water sources early, and a hydrogeological investigation may be required in order to identify suitable areas for borehole drilling.
- **Geotechnical studies**: a geotechnical analysis of potential sites can include detailed soil assessments to identify suitability for both construction and farming.

Further **detailed design** of shortlisted sites will be informed by the following:

- **Planning and infrastructure design standards**: these need to be established as a norm for planning of all the potential sites, and will usually be developed with consideration for the following:
  - Existing levels of service/facilities in host communities
  - Standards and guidelines of relevant government agencies
  - Applicable international standards and guidelines
  - Estimated number of resettlers

  Regardless of existing provision and national standards, plans should ensure adequate physical space for non-residential land uses, including community, institutional, commercial and industrial areas, reflective of the communities to be resettled. Specifically, plans should consider:
  - Space for residential plots for resettling households, and additional plots for future allocation
  - Mixed plots for both residential and commercial purposes
  - Sites for worship
  - Plots for commercial, retail, light industrial use and markets, as appropriate
  - Public open spaces
  - Sanitary areas for solid waste collection and management

- Space for community facilities, including schools, clinics, etc. (dependent on availability nearby, statutory regulations, population size, etc.)
- Green belts and development buffers
- Pedestrian and vehicular networks and the relationships between these
- Access from sites to surrounding facilities and farmlands
- The need to maintain social networks and identities in the new site
- Opportunities for shared infrastructure improvements and provision with nearby and host communities

- **Topographical survey data**: depending on the complexity of sites, survey data should be obtained which can form the basis for physical planning and layout of sites.

- **Development of physical plans**: sites need to be planned to a level of detail sufficient for accurate cost estimates and articulation of proposals to stakeholders, including directly impacted households and the statutory authorities who will ultimately approve the plans. Physical plans can also be used in determining the scope of work for contractors and civil sub-consultants.

- **Development of detailed budget estimates**: shortlisted sites need to incorporate detailed budget estimates, including all aspects of development from earthworks and approvals to handover.

- **Development of supporting visual materials**: to support consultations and negotiations with stakeholders and clearly articulate designs to non-technical stakeholders.

How should resettlement sites be considered in negotiations and consultations?

- The final decision on preferred locations will be agreed with government, the communities and potential host communities
- Ideally, multiple resettlement sites will be considered and made available for communities to select their preference
- The basis of negotiations, in terms of site design and layout, should be agreed with permitting authorities in advance, so as not to result in abortive discussions on designs and locations
- Any traditional village authorities should be consulted in tandem with negotiations to ensure no potential disputes regarding authority over the land or other unforeseen issues

If resettlement designs are only agreed with community leaders and statutory authorities, there is a risk that final resettlement designs will be rejected by resettlers, leading to costly delays

- Preliminary agreements on a preferred site or sites in negotiations should be the basis for final detailed engineering and design, which should form part of a continued participative consultation with stakeholders

Since resettlement sites and housing provision is an emotive subject in land access and resettlement projects, and is a very clear physical manifestation of the process, it tends to draw the attention and interest of a wide range of stakeholders, both internal and external to the process, such as NGOs (non-governmental organisations).

Intensive consultations with communities and particularly resettling households must continue throughout the design and implementation process. This is important in ensuring broad agreement with approach and designs by resettling families in addition to community representatives and statutory authorities, as well as getting important inputs and feedback from communities on what will work for them in terms of design solutions.

 Project example

On a project in Eastern Europe, key aspects of resettlement site and housing design were agreed with community leaders in an informal setting, without formal agreements or consultation with all affected households. Not surprisingly, aspects of the housing design were later considered inappropriate by resettling households and, in the absence of agreements, costly amendments to house designs and site layouts had to be made after construction had commenced.

 Project example

A project in Africa found that the issue of resettlement site location was particularly contentious, due to a combination of chieftaincy disputes and rivalries, and disagreements between young people and elders on an appropriate location that would best serve the population's needs, even though one site was largely considered superior in terms of proximity to facilities, the project, and farmlands. Therefore, in addition to ongoing project consultations and negotiations with the community negotiation committee, the project undertook a large-scale and intensive consultation including (i) separate meetings with local chiefs to resolve disputes and ensure alignment for the benefit of the population; (ii) presentations to all statutory authorities and local politicians culminating in approvals in principle; and (iii) a series of public consultation meetings and presentations with over 300 households to outline the pros and cons of each site and the rationale for a preferred site. The final resettlement site chosen was approved by the resettling population, traditional leaders and statutory authorities.

What further detailed design work should be undertaken post-negotiations?

Following agreements in principle on a preferred site or sites, **detailed engineering and design** should be completed in order to produce final tender drawings, specifications and costed bills of quantities for all aspects of the development, which may include, but not be limited to:

- Roads, drainage and earthworks
- Water supply and distribution
- Electrical supply and distribution
- Solid waste collection
- Housing and community facilities
- Landscaping

Figure 9.5: Preliminary resettlement site layout.

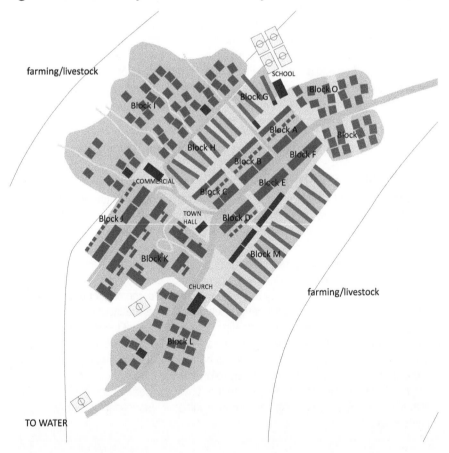

The physical plan will need to be updated and finalised to incorporate any changes based on the negotiations and details of design in respect of infrastructure and services, such as road layouts, location of water storage tanks, etc.

Finally, the development of a **construction management plan** and **tender documentation** will allow for timely and effective tendering and construction implementation (discussed at Chapter 14).

In practice, much of this work will progress iteratively in tandem with negotiations and consultations, and will be developed in consultation with statutory authorities.

What about replacement housing?

As referred to above in terms of resettlement sites, preliminary house designs must be based on the same initial activities and assessments outlined, including:

- Stakeholder identification and analysis
- Stakeholder engagement
- Asset surveys
- Other baseline surveys
- Architectural analysis and observational studies
- Other participatory methods
- Statutory plans review

As referred to above, objectives that should guide house design include:

- **Affordability**: construction costs are affordable for the project, and maintenance costs are affordable for residents
- **Familiarity and simplicity**: materials, technology and design are familiar to local contractors and residents, meet sociocultural requirements and are easy to maintain
- **Availability**: building materials and appropriate construction competence are available locally
- **High performance**: materials are carefully selected in terms of sustainability and performance, together with good design, providing for a good quality of life
- **Flexibility**: designs provide for residents to change uses over time (e.g. change in function of rooms)
- **Potential for expansion**: designs and plot layout provide the potential to add new rooms, as residents' needs and economic situation change

Based on an analysis of the baseline situation, architectural and observational studies, statutory regulations and consultations with stakeholders, it will be critical to get early agreement on the **following key aspects of house design**:

- **Basis of replacement**: the establishment of principles including like-for-like replacement, where people will get differing offers based on what they have now. This might derive from the size of house, number of rooms, or a combination of criteria.
- **Community priorities**: the most important elements for communities that need to be reflected in designs. For example, whether increased floor area is valued over the number of rooms and what this might mean for final house designs.
- **Size of houses and rooms**: the size of replacement houses and rooms, whether this be a standard size, or a set of standard sizes depending on existing room sizes or room use.
- **Facilities**: consideration needs to be given to room uses and facilities, standards of sanitary provision, water supply, electrical provision, etc.
- **Plot sizes**: this needs to take account of traditional household use of the areas around their house and what is considered adequate.

All the above aspects have cost implications and therefore need to be **considered holistically** when negotiating with stakeholders. The types of housing solution will be very much dependent on the resettlement solutions developed, such as large stand-alone sites or infill development, as discussed above.

Figure 9.6: Resettlement house design options.

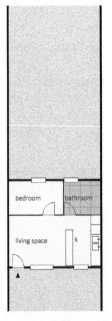

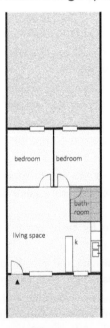

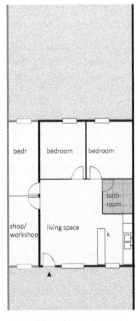

ground floor house
option A

ground floor house
option B

ground floor house
option C

Project example

Initial house designs developed by a project in Africa proposed a standard room size based on existing room size in the communities, but also taking into account building standards and the need to offer improvements. However, introducing a larger standard room size and basing replacement on existing house area would have meant a loss of rooms for some resettlers, albeit that their new houses would be bigger overall. It became clear in consultations with resettlers and statutory authorities that the issue of room number was important: as a result, the project guaranteed that no resettler would lose rooms in replacement housing.

Ultimately **a range of house designs and sizes should be developed** to reflect current house and family sizes, and offer resettlers a choice that reflects living arrangements and can also introduce diversity and character into the resettlement site.

House design will need to take careful account of **cultural considerations** in certain circumstances. For example, in areas where polygamy is common, special arrangements for separate living quarters in one house or compound may need to be taken into account.

The presentation to households of various options developed, **sign-off of households** on individual house choices, and their move to the resettlement site is considered further at Chapter 13 on compensation and resettlement sign-off and Chapter 14 on physical resettlement implementation.

What about community facilities and infrastructure?

Similar to considerations of housing above, the provision of community facilities needs to take into account a detailed assessment of the existing situation, including the following specific considerations:

- **Existing provision**: both in terms of facilities and infrastructure which will be directly impacted, or to which the affected population may lose access
- **Carrying capacity**: allowing for the size of the resettled communities and future population growth
- **Statutory requirements**: for example, population thresholds for certain infrastructure provision such as clinics, standard government designs for schools, road standards, etc.
- **Separating community needs from wants**: communities may request certain infrastructure for 'status' or other reasons, whereas if real needs

are investigated with as wide a range of stakeholders as possible it can be agreed that limited funds are better spent elsewhere

- **Potential for shared infrastructure provision**: for example, a larger clinic shared between resettlers and a host community may maximise social spend and business benefits
- **Ultimate end-user**: consideration of who will ultimately run the facility, such as a school or clinic (end-users need to be intimately involved in the design to ensure adoption later)

 Project example

A project in Africa was required to build a clinic to serve the new resettlement community, due to the population size which would result from the resettlement of several smaller communities at one site. The nearby host community also lacked medical facilities. It was agreed to build a larger clinic equidistant between the two communities which could serve both, thereby maximising the mine's social spend, demonstrating benefit to the host community and resulting in a higher standard of facilities for the communities than a stand-alone clinic in either community could provide.

What about resettlement of businesses?

Baseline surveys and engagements must identify all businesses eligible for moves to the resettlement site. In developing an appropriate strategy and offer for business moves, the project will need to consider the type of business property (e.g. immovable or movable):

- **Movable businesses** (such as small kiosks or 'table-top' businesses) can be moved to the resettlement site by the project, with appropriate allowances for loss of income during transition.
- **Immovable businesses** will need to be analysed through the asset survey. A number of **standard designs** can be developed for the replacement of these business premises at the resettlement site, or an alternative of cash compensation and a plot at the resettlement site may be offered. In the case where a plot plus cash compensation is offered, it will be important to ensure that any subsequent development is in accordance with planning and

> There is an opportunity to link the resettlement of businesses with livelihood programmes. Both resettling and new businesses will help drive the success of resettled communities

building regulations at the new site. Immovable businesses will also require compensation for loss of income during transition.

The determination of the appropriate amount of compensation for **loss of income in transition** will depend on the type and size of business. Where multiple businesses are affected a **small business survey** should be utilised to identify the level of business activity. This survey should be done at the time of the baseline surveys so that responses are not explicitly linked to the anticipation of compensation. It will be useful to group compensation for businesses into bands for the purposes of transparency, equity, agreement and administration.

 Project example

A project in Africa had several businesses of various sizes to be resettled, ranging from table-top businesses and kiosks to substantial restaurants/bars, shops and small industrial units. Based on the asset and business surveys, separate consultations were held with business owners on (i) proposed relocation of movable businesses, and basis for replacement; and (ii) compensation for loss of income, which was based on grouping similar businesses based on turnover. Commercial areas within the resettlement site to relocate businesses, including space for a market area, were also agreed. This was then presented to all stakeholders to ensure broad agreement.

How should religious buildings and shrines be treated?

The approach to dealing with religious buildings and shrines will vary from project to project. In some case it may be possible to cover this as part of the group negotiation process with community representatives. In most cases, while the issue can be covered broadly in consultations and negotiations, specific consultation and negotiation will be required with key community and religious leaders. National religious bodies may also need to be consulted, and it will be important to determine through stakeholder identification all those who may have a stake in decisions, and where ultimate ownership of any structure resides.

As referred to in Chapter 17 on cultural heritage, traditional sites that are identified need to have been utilised in living memory as part of a long cultural tradition, to prevent the proposal of spurious sites in the anticipation of compensation. Information received regarding potential traditional sites needs to be triangulated in order to confirm as much as possible the genuine nature of sites.

How should cemeteries and graves be treated?

The issue of cemeteries and graves is a necessarily emotive one. There are two key factors to be considered in relation to cemeteries and graves:

- How to treat cemeteries and graves located within the land area requiring resettlement and development
- How to ensure provision for cemeteries at any new resettlement site

The issue of dealing with graves, cemeteries and sacred sites is dealt with in detail in Chapter 17 on cultural heritage. However, a number of issues are worth highlighting in respect of physical resettlement.

- **The provision of cemeteries at a new resettlement site** can be relatively straightforward, provided the space requirements are taken into account in early planning and all cultural requirements are considered in advance and incorporated in project planning. Specific stakeholders such as religious and traditional leaders should be consulted. Where households have graves close to their homes, consultations will need to conclude if this should be integrated into the design and layout of plots, or whether these can be transferred to a communal cemetery.

> Understand the local context and show appropriate respect and sensitivity when dealing with religious issues

- **Where graves or cemeteries are located in the area to be resettled**, the issue of **how to consult and negotiate** on the treatment of these is important. Depending on the specific community characteristics, it may be preferable either to deal with this in the usual negotiation forum, or to deal with the issue 'offline' with a core group of stakeholders such as community elders, religious leaders and statutory authorities. However, whether the issue is considered in a small group or through the negotiation forum of community representatives, consultations must also be undertaken with the wider community to ensure broad support. Such emotive issues can sometimes be used to express deep frustrations with other aspects of the process, or even frustration with community leadership or government, if not handled appropriately.

- **Investigations** should be undertaken to determine whether cemeteries and grave locations will be directly affected by project infrastructure. If not directly affected, the potential to leave the graves and cemeteries *in situ* should be considered and discussed with stakeholders. In some cases it may be acceptable to communities to leave graves *in situ*, especially if access to the area can be secured on a regular basis. In other cases, even where graves are directly affected by project infrastructure, a symbolic ceremony may suffice to 'move souls' from the area to the new sites. In other cases, exhumation and relocation of the bodies may be required. This is a process that will require specialist assistance and close liaison with national and local authorities.

Project example

Two cemeteries and a number of graves were affected by a project in Africa. The project considered it preferable to consult on such a sensitive issue offline with a number of community elders and religious leaders. It was agreed that a traditional ceremony would suffice to relocate the souls of the departed, after which the headstones would be removed and the bodies left *in situ*. However, the consultations and proposed agreements were not sufficiently disclosed to the wider community by either the village leaders or the project. As a result the community protested against the moves, even though the anger behind the protests really stemmed from a leadership dispute within the community. The project needed to spend extra time consulting with the community before the plan could go ahead, alongside acting as a mediator to resolve the leadership dispute.

How should host communities be treated?

A **host community** can be any one, or a combination of, the following:

- Landowners of a potential resettlement site
- Farmers using a potential resettlement site
- Other users of the potential site (e.g. for gathering of wild plants, traditional ceremonies, etc.)
- Households living on a potential site
- Nearby communities with traditional, informal or formal rights over the site (e.g. rights of way, grazing), or who will be impacted by the resettlement (e.g. increased traffic)
- In the case of infill development or urban extensions, the existing community who will accommodate the resettlement

As discussed above, it is preferable to identify resettlement sites which are largely unencumbered. However, in many situations this is not possible.

Stakeholder analysis should identify all stakeholders with an interest in potential resettlement sites. Early engagement with host communities is essential in order to ensure their views are taken into account and to prevent development on potential sites.

> Host communities must be integrated into resettlement planning from day one

Seeing the benefits accruing to resettlers, host communities will naturally also want to gain benefit from the project. The project needs to ensure that host communities receive adequate benefits in order to enable resettlement implementation to go ahead smoothly.

Depending on the circumstances of host sites, any, or a combination of, the following actions may be appropriate:

- **Purchase** of a vacant site (on a willing buyer/willing seller basis)
- Identification of the site within the project area and **payment of compensation** to landowners and/or farmers (on the same basis as the project-affected populations)
- Extension of **livelihood programmes** to host communities
- **Integration** of households in the resettlement master plan
- Delivery of **shared or stand-alone benefits** such as community facilities for nearby host populations, in order to share in project benefits and help ensure good relations with resettlers and host communities
- **Procurement and contracting of services** from host communities
- Promoting formal and informal **engagements** between resettlers and host communities

As discussed in Chapter 12 in respect of the negotiation process, the **extent and timing of discussions** with host communities can be challenging. The replacement land cannot be acquired before being evaluated and discussed with the displaced people, but it also cannot be put forward as an option, evaluated or acquired without the involvement of the potential host community. Careful scheduling of the various negotiations is essential.

 Project example

A project in Africa undertook extensive negotiations on resettlement sites. In order to ensure shortlisted sites were not developed during the period of negotiations they entered into an agreement with identified host communities, which included preventing speculative building on the sites. When the final site was chosen, the project included shared community facilities for both resettlers and the host community, maximising the mine's social spend, and demonstrating benefit to the host community, helping to ensure their buy-in to the project.

How can formal approvals be assured?

What formal approvals are required will vary depending on jurisdiction, and a comprehensive understanding of all national and local legislation related to urban planning, building regulations and property registration is essential.

Any project is likely to require approvals from authorities in relation to:

- Design of resettlement sites
- Design of housing and community facilities
- Specific approvals from education, health, power authorities, etc., in respect of specific infrastructure
- Approval of plot allocations
- Property and ownership registration, with the aim of maximising security of tenure
- Approvals for demolition of existing settlements and structures

All regulatory and approving authorities need to be engaged and consulted throughout the process. In many cases local government capacity is likely to be limited and **ongoing engagement will reduce time-scales for approval**, which can otherwise delay resettlement projects considerably. Officials who have been properly engaged and given due recognition throughout the process are also more likely to be willing to facilitate speedy approval as a willing development partner.

Distinct engagements need to be undertaken with approving authorities, ideally with all key authorities together. Often this meeting can be facilitated by one of the leading authorities rather than the project proponent being seen to drive the process. Appropriate efforts should be made to include quality visuals and presentation aids to ensure all stakeholders can visualise the development.

At the same time, efforts should be made to have the project and any resettlement sites recognised in the relevant statutory development plans.

The approvals process and related deadlines need to be tracked in detail as part of the project schedule.

 Project example

A project in Africa undertook early consultations with the relevant statutory authorities, and even shared baseline information on the wider project area to assist the local authority with their planning of the area. A series of presentations and consultations were made to the various heads of departments at national, regional and local level, as well as one-on-one meetings with approving officers. Quality presentation materials and visuals were developed to explain the scheme. The key authorities, including town planning, were included in the negotiation forum as advisers and observers to the entire process. The statutory bodies were also included in a handover committee that oversaw construction of the resettlement site with community representatives, helping to ensure a smooth approvals and handover process.

How can a project ensure security of tenure for resettlers?

A valuable outcome of a resettlement process should be improved security of tenure for resettlers, within the limits of the relevant national legislation.

Applications for registration of ownership can take a long period in many juris-dictions, and the project needs to ensure that it has researched this early in the process, and fast-tracks applications where appropriate. It also needs to be agreed with key stakeholders that moves to the resettlement site can be undertaken before property registration is completed, so as not to unduly delay land access.

What other packages are required for resettlers?

In order to ensure resettlers can move to the resettlement site and settle success-fully into their new homes, a project needs to consider the following:

- Agreement with resettlers on an appropriate allowance to compensate for **cost of moving, loss of income while moving, and general disturbance**
- A **'welcome pack'** can be developed which will be used to introduce reset-tlers to their new environment, outlining any special arrangements in terms of management of the property and communal areas, including rights and responsibilities: for example, resettlers may be moving from a rural to a peri-urban environment which will require adjustments in ways of living, such as management of lots and communal areas, and control of livestock
- **Follow-up visits** to ensure the physical and psychological welfare of resettlers

The **moves of resettlers** to the resettlement site is considered further in Chapter 14 concerning resettlement implementation.

How should a project plan for handover of resettlement sites?

Project proponents need to ensure that sites can be ultimately handed over to resettlers and adopted by the relevant statutory authorities, in order to avoid ongoing costs of managing infrastructure.

As with the securing of formal approvals, key to this is the need to **engage with relevant stakeholders early**. In many cases local government capacity is likely to be limited, and ongoing engagement will reduce time-scales for agreeing on handover modalities. These should ultimately be agreed in writing, if not explicitly included as a condition of approval. As said, officials who have been properly engaged and given due recognition throughout the process are also more likely to be willing to facilitate speedy approval and handovers as a willing development partner.

A project should develop a **handover committee** to ensure all stakeholders are aware of statutory and personal responsibilities in respect of the completed site and that handover to households and authorities takes place in a timely fashion. This should include representatives from the key approving authorities and those who will ultimately adopt the various infrastructures (such as roads authority, electrical authority, etc.). Resettler representatives should also be on the committee.

The handover committee can ensure an ongoing participatory process in the monitoring and evaluation of both the design and construction process. The committee can also play a role in ensuring the integration of resettlers into their new environment.

The role of the handover committee is considered further in Chapter 14 concerning physical resettlement implementation.

 Project example

A project in Africa did not consider handover modalities until a resettlement project was nearing completion. Although a handover committee was then established, statutory authorities were reluctant to adopt key infrastructure (such as water supply) particularly as they had not monitored the construction and were unsure of the specifications. The project ultimately had to agree to maintain the system for a period of years, including the replacement of key equipment, before adoption could be agreed.

 Project example

A project in Africa set up a handover and maintenance committee very early in the planning process, consisting of resettler representatives and statutory authorities. The committee could then lead the participatory approach to site selection, design review, and monitoring of resettlement sites construction and moves of resettlers, while there was also sufficient time to agree on detailed handover agreements with each authority.

Are there any special considerations for transitional and post-conflict resettlement?

Many of the issues discussed above can be applied to resettlement occurring in transitional and post-conflict situations. Resettlement of large populations is often required where there are large numbers of internally displaced people and/ or refugees living in dangerous or unsanitary conditions.

A number of additional key considerations can be highlighted in such circumstances:

- The population to be resettled is much more likely to be **ethnically or culturally different** from any host population and there may be discrimination or stigmatisation towards the resettling population. This may be reflected in the attitudes of authorities as well as the general population. The issue of where replacement land should be sourced and the need to bring host populations on board needs particular attention in this regard. Resettlement of vulnerable households from the host population may need to be included in any scheme, together with shared infrastructure, to demonstrate significant benefit for the host population and encourage integration.

- **Governing authorities may be unclear**, and there may be a number of competing leaderships claiming jurisdiction in certain areas. Detailed stakeholder analysis is critical in this regard to make sure that all authorities and stakeholders are engaged in the process.

- **Budgets are likely to be extremely limited** and projects will be largely funded by international organisations. Various methods to maximise budget potential need to be explored, including participatory design and construction by beneficiaries, which can be combined with skills training.

- **Land ownerships may be unclear**, arising from lack of records, movement of populations or land-grabbing occurring in the wake of political instability. In sourcing land for resettlement, practitioners should consider the

 Project example

A project in a transitional conflict situation in Africa needed to find land for resettlement of internally displaced populations currently living in temporary camps in the city. Land was identified on the outskirts and, through negotiations with local authorities and 'land-grabbers' (who had grabbed land during the conflict), plots of land were donated to the project. The first resettlers included a mix of internally displaced and host community beneficiaries to ensure the host community saw benefits were not exclusively for 'outsiders', while the project included an expansion of city infrastructure to the outskirts to demonstrate benefit to the population as a whole.

need to develop agreements on use of public land or donations of land from individuals.

- **Numbers in need of resettlement** may be very high, and an early assessment of the most vulnerable families will be required. However, a diverse range of families in terms of economic abilities is required in order to ensure vibrant settlements and avoid ghettoisation. As referred to above, host population families in need of housing may be integrated in resettlements.

Are there any special considerations for disaster-related resettlement?

As with post-conflict resettlement, many of the issues discussed in this chapter can be applied to varying degrees to resettlement arising from natural disasters. Resettlement of populations is often required where they have been made homeless by disaster and cannot return to their homes, or the potential for natural disasters makes the existing area unsafe for the foreseeable future.

A number of additional key considerations can be highlighted in such circumstances:

- **Budgets are likely to be extremely limited** and projects will be largely funded by international organisations. Various methods to maximise budget potential need to be explored, including participatory design and construction by beneficiaries.

- Related to this, **co-ordination** of various agencies and government is critical to ensure comprehensive planning, avoidance of duplication, and to ensure that resettlement solutions are integrated with long-term master planning.

- While shelter solutions are required rapidly, **initial temporary solutions** may be preferable to costly mistakes in hurried implementation of permanent solutions.

- **Numbers in need of resettlement** may be very high, and an early assessment of the most vulnerable families will be required. However, resettlement plans should ultimately aim to recreate existing social networks, even if this needs to occur on a phased basis.

- **Resettlement sites** need to be located as close as possible to original areas for home area continuity, but outside danger areas, such as on higher land away from coastlines in the case of tsunami-prone areas. The opportunities to **continue livelihood activities** in original home areas and the need for links with these areas should be carefully considered (for example, linking new living areas with port and fishing facilities on the coast).

- **Special design and construction considerations** need to be included in the context for potential natural disasters to reoccur, such as appropriate building materials, site design, and housing layout and orientation.

Are there any special considerations for resettlement from environmentally protected areas?

Resettlement of populations is often required where they are living in, or have increasingly encroached on, environmentally sensitive and protected areas such as national parks.

The key issue to bear in mind in such situations is that, just as with resettlement in the natural resource sector, outcomes must be **win–win**, where the affected communities are left no worse off than before, and ideally better off, otherwise the project will fail. Indeed, unlike a mining project, the area from which populations are removed remains undeveloped, so there is a real risk that encroachment will occur again unless affected populations see real benefit in the relocation.

Obviously environmental protection efforts will not have the same revenues accruing from any project development, so innovative methodologies have to be considered to ensure all affected populations can benefit sustainably for the project. This may include employment as environmental stewards or within the tourist industry, or permitting of limited sustainable agricultural activities in certain areas.

Physical resettlement planning: key considerations

- Physical resettlement is **not just concerned with physical engineering and design**, but the preservation of the existing social fabric in a new location.
- The objective of the physical resettlement process is to relocate households and communities in a way that **preserves existing social networks and livelihoods**, but also creates the **basis for new opportunities and improved standards of living**.
- **Detailed assessments must be done** to fully understand communities, households, livelihoods and social networks before planning commences.
- Any resettlement solution needs to be **rooted in the local context, with the informed participation of affected people** and statutory authorities, and **offer choices** to resettlers.
- Resettlement sites, housing and community facilities need to **meet the real needs of resettlers**, now and in the future, not just in terms of physical structures, but also livelihoods opportunities and social networks.
- Ensure resettlement sites and designs are **developed and agreed with all stakeholders**, not just community leaders or statutory authorities.

- Take into account specific **cultural considerations** in the design process.
- **Consider businesses early** in the process, as potential drivers of resettlement communities.
- **Host communities** must be considered in planning from day one, and must see benefits in the resettlement process.
- **Involve statutory authorities from day one**, in order to ensure timely approvals and adoption of infrastructure.
- The process of **security of tenure** may be lengthy, and needs to be planned accordingly.

10
Livelihood restoration planning

Up until relatively recently, the resettlement process was considered to be final-ised when the impacted households were paid cash for their assets or provided with resettlement houses and cash. However, it has been established that, in the majority of cases, resettled households struggle to attain their former standard of living. There has been increasing recognition that livelihood restoration requires a focus beyond just income and that other social factors such as education, health and social cohesion serve to sustain living standards over time. However, despite this recognition and the development of social performance standards, livelihood restoration is not being properly planned on many projects and the majority of resettlement households continue to struggle to re-establish their former standard of living. The role of women in contributing to the livelihood of the household is not being given sufficient consideration and is resulting in women losing access to land and common property resources with a resulting lowering in income and status.

A key problem is that the LRP (livelihood restoration plan) is seen as a component of the RAP (resettlement action plan) and often prepared in isolation from the overall SIMP (social impact management plan). The SIMP is meant to address the wider social impacts of the project on local communities into which the resettled households are moved. However, the SIMP is often prepared early in the planning process, as part of the permitting requirements, based on little real commu-nity engagement and with high-level commitments. The key to good livelihood restoration planning is therefore to make a clear connection between all the key social plans and ensure that these are prepared to a practical level early in the project development cycle.

> Livelihood restoration is one of the most challenging aspects of resettlement

The key elements of livelihood restoration are the location of resettlement sites to the project area, replacement of quality agricultural land/natural resource areas, and training and support to access employment and business opportuni-ties. However, on many projects a distinction is being made between these key planning elements resulting in a disjointed approach with missed opportunities for the project-affected households to benefit from training, employment and business opportunities.

The objective of this chapter is to set out a framework for planning livelihood restoration by focusing on how the SIMP and RAP processes can be integrated. The resources framework, as described in Chapter 7, is used to show how the impacts on all the collective household resources of the impacted communities can be mitigated according to IFC (International Finance Corporation) standards. Chapter 15 focuses on community investment and development while Chapter 16 focuses on livelihood restoration and community development implementation.

What are the key issues, challenges and risks?

- **Livelihood restoration is not being planned in a holistic manner on projects** and opportunities are being missed to provide households with a combination of replacement assets, training for employment and a location close to employment and business opportunities.

- Many projects rely on cash compensation to mitigate for the loss of land and natural resources. However, experience shows that **compensation is often poorly invested** leaving impacted households without resources to maintain their livelihoods.

- Many projects are failing to engage properly with women and young people resulting in their priorities being ignored in development of LRPs. Women often lose access to land and natural resources essential for their livelihoods.

- Projects are often managed by engineers focused on construction with a limited understanding of the complexity of local livelihoods, a tendency to focus on short-term solutions, including cash compensation, and a lack of appreciation that livelihood restoration and implementation of alternative livelihoods is a long-term process. This often means that **livelihood restoration is seen as a luxury the project cannot afford**.

- The SIMP is often prepared early in the project life-cycle to satisfy permit conditions, independently of the RAP, which results in the wider support for social factors for livelihood restoration not being provided.

- Projects generally change the whole economic context of an area resulting in the influx of economic migrants and inflation, so even if the same resources are available, the households' standard of living can still drop significantly.

- Many projects, particularly for large dams and mining projects, require considerable areas for land acquisition which puts pressure on the remaining land resources. **It is often impossible to find enough replacement land** to replace agricultural livelihoods.

- Many of the lessons in livelihood restoration come from the development sector which has had limited success in improving the standards of living of the poor. Projects need to have a realistic understanding of what can be achieved so that expectations from stakeholders can be checked.
- On an increasing number of projects, previously resettled communities who have suffered from impoverishment are making demands for restitution, resulting in increased conflict and the risk of disruption to the project.
- Projects often focus solely on resettlement households and ignore the needs of host communities, which leads to tension between the two groups.

What are the guiding principles?

The IFC guidance requires companies to 'improve, or restore, the livelihoods and standards of living of displaced persons' (IFC 2012: Performance Standard 5, Guidance Note 5) and notes that:

> compensation alone does not guarantee the restoration or improvement of the livelihoods and social welfare of displaced persons and communities. Restoration and improvement of livelihoods often includes many interconnected assets that may include access to land (productive, fallow, and pasture), marine and aquatic resources (fish stocks), access to social networks, access to natural resources such as timber and non-timber forest products, medicinal plants, hunting and gathering grounds, grazing and cropping areas, fresh water, as well as employment, and capital. Major challenges associated with rural resettlement include restoring livelihoods based on land or natural resource use and the need to avoid compromising the social or cultural continuity of affected communities, including the host communities to which the displaced population may be resettled. (IFC 2012: PS5, GN11)

The IFC believes that while the effects of resettlement may be common to women and men, women are often more adversely affected by, or vulnerable to, resettlement. Affected people, and particularly women, can experience a loss of livelihood, the breakdown of social networks and a loss of access to services, among other consequences. There is increasingly a recognition that livelihood restoration requires a focus beyond household incomes to other social factors including education, health and social cohesion, which serve to sustain standards of living over time. The challenge is therefore to capture the complexity of all the livelihoods impacted in a particular community while at the same time implementing practical programmes focusing on a limited number of interventions in order to have a manageable and effective livelihood restoration approach.

Livelihood restoration, replacement or re-establishment?

There has been some discussion claiming the term 'restoration' inadequate, interpreting this as requiring the recreation of the original livelihood which is often unachievable or not desired by the impacted household. For the purposes of this discussion, livelihood restoration is taken to mean the restoration of 'a livelihood' which can provide for the wellbeing of the family. This can include elements from the original livelihood and/or new livelihood strategies.

Livelihood restoration planning

Livelihood restoration requires the project to consider the collective resources that the community depends on to maintain household wellbeing as outlined in the resources framework presented in Chapter 7. The project must consider impacts on all communities living in the project area but also in the project's primary zone of influence, which is generally defined by the main villages and towns close to the project and varies from country to country. It is important that the SIMP focuses on reintegrating the resettled households back into the local

Figure 10.1: Social impact management plans and RAP/LRP coverage of impacted communities.

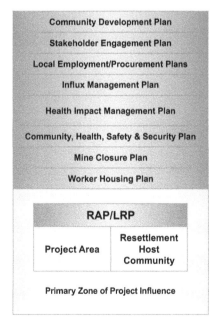

Figure 10.2: Resources framework outlining social impact management plan.

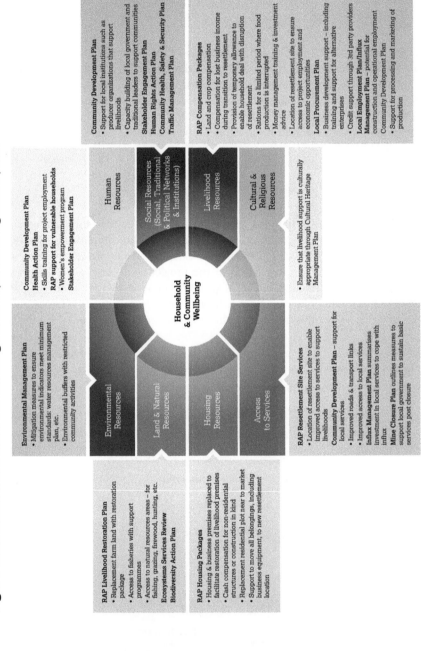

Figure 10.3: Summary of key social impact management plans to support livelihood restoration.

Social impact management plan	Livelihood restoration mitigation
RAP (livelihood restoration plan)	• The RAP will provide cash compensation for some assets. The LRP should provide for financial management training and advice to project-affected households so that they invest their compensation to support their families' future.
	• The RAP LRP is focused primarily on physically replacing the land as land-for-land where possible and relocating/re-establishing the business premises.
	• The LRP also provides direct support to re-establish production and sales of goods.
RAP (resettlement site selection)	• The location of the resettlement site is critical in accessing replacement land, maintaining community cohesion and providing access to project employment and economic opportunities.
CDP (capacity-building support for wider community groups)	• The CDP provides capacity-building support to local producer, processing and marketing groups to improve their business productivity.
	• The CDP can also provide improvements to local services including roads, markets, schools/training centres, health clinics, etc., which are important in capacity-building of project-affected persons and supporting livelihood restoration through improved service support and market access.
Local employment/ skills training plan (skills training and employment targeting local people)	• The Local Employment Plan should provide for training and targeted employment based on existing/developed skills to avail of direct and indirect employment opportunities with the project. The project-affected households must be included in the local employment target zone to give them an equal opportunity within the wider community to secure project employment.
Local procurement/ business development plan (business capacity-building and procurement from local businesses)	• The local procurement plan should provide capacity-building support to project-affected businesses to provide them with opportunities to provide goods and services directly or indirectly to the project.
Other SIMPs (community health, safety and security)	
Vulnerable support plan	• The vulnerable support plan should provide additional support to project-affected households at risk of impoverishment from the project impacts.

communities, and experience has shown that this works best when host communities share in the additional support offered by the project. This support can be enhanced infrastructure and services, preferential access for local people to training and employment with the project, support to increase production, and/ or processing and sales of local goods. A failure to properly integrate resettled households into host communities can result in jealousy, isolation and an ongoing dependence on the company.

The SIMP is therefore the framework for livelihood restoration with the following elements:

- The RAP or LRP, where there is only economic displacement, is a transitional plan to restore the livelihood base of the impacted households.

- The CDP (community development plan) is a life-of-project plan to support the development of the project area, including the integration of the RAP households into host communities and ensuring that they share the wider project benefits.

- Other plans, such as local employment and procurement plans, which help local communities to benefit from the employment and business opportunities offered directly and indirectly by the project.

Figure 10.1 illustrates how SIMPs support all the project-impacted communities while the RAP/LRP focuses just on project area and host communities experiencing economic and physical impacts.

The key supports for livelihood restoration can be understood by analysing each of the key resources to which households require access in the resources framework. Figure 10.2 presents an example of how the social management plans can support livelihood restoration by addressing impacts to a households' key resource categories.

The key plans concerning livelihood restoration are summarised in Figure 10.3.

Key planning components

The livelihood restoration planning process therefore follows from the ESIA (environmental and social impact assessment) and development of the social management plans, including the RAP, by a multidisciplinary team of experts depending on the complexity of the project and the scale of predicted impacts. Given the linkages between these plans and the importance of a combination of multiple aspects and plans in restoring livelihoods of project-affected households, it is essential that effective planning and integration is undertaken.

Further to the baseline data collection planning discussed in Chapter 4, the key steps related to livelihood restoration include the following:

1. **Establish a multidisciplinary team** comprised of company and consultants to plan the baseline data collection and development of the ESIA and RAP processes.

2. **Research existing primary and secondary data** available for the project area.

3. **Prepare detailed maps** of the project area and surrounding communities. In addition to mapping the data from the baseline surveys (field boundaries, crops, houses, natural features, etc.) it is also useful to map the livelihood zones in the project area. The HEA (Household Economy Approach; www. heawebsite.org/hea-framework-overview) outlines how to map livelihood zones as areas where people share the same patterns of access to food and have the same access to markets and employment. Livelihood zones are useful in the context of land access and resettlement projects which cover large geographic or linear distances. It is important not to categorise all impacted households as farmers or businessmen but to understand that, based on where they live, households will adopt different livelihood strategies which need to be considered when developing livelihood restoration support.

4. **Conduct a scoping exercise**.

5. **Develop a set of monitoring** indicators using a data matrix which should be circulated to all the project team, and a monitoring and evaluation plan for all social investments.

6. **Develop a stakeholder engagement plan** and engage with the project stake-holders. Ensure that there is an equal focus on men, women and young people in the development of livelihood restoration programmes.

7. **Develop a baseline data collection plan**.

8. **Conduct the baseline data research**, including focus group discussions with men, women and young people in order to understand their livelihood choices. Prepare a report on the existing livelihoods and their importance to different groups in the communities. Collect information on the stakeholders' preferred livelihoods and gain an understanding of what local services require support. Be careful not to ask the community for list of development needs as this can also lead to unrealistic expectations: many communities believe that if you request their needs and they tell you then you have agreed to fund these.

9. **Conduct specialist studies** on areas identified as requiring detailed management plans.

10. **Livelihood restoration project planning**: the development of a livelihood restoration programme should follow a professional project cycle which has five key steps—identification, preparation, appraisal, implementation, and monitoring and evaluation—as presented in Figure 10.4.

Figure 10.4: The project cycle.

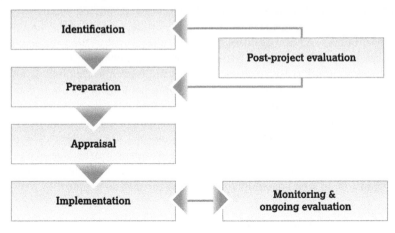

Project identification

The identification of which projects to implement involves engaging with project stake-holders and identifying their development problems and opportunities. There are a number of tools available for designing and planning development programmes as outlined in the ICMM *Community Development Toolkit* (2012). The key is to engage with the community using participatory techniques to identify their development priorities and also to review government and civil society local and regional development plans.

While participation of the impacted communities is important, the project should also exercise caution in using this approach. Communities can often be very unequal with some groups, particularly migrants, lower caste members, women and ethnic minorities being subject to exclusion and discrimination. Minority groups may be afraid to voice their views on the project and participatory methods can strengthen powerful voices in the communities. The project needs to conduct a thorough stake-holder identification process to identify and consult with minority groups to ensure that they have a voice in the project and that their specific needs are addressed.

Projects should be wary of bringing in specialist experts prom-ising guaranteed results in their sector. There is often a profes-sional bias in project identification as experts seek to twist the solution to the problem to suit their own agendas and skills. Projects should take a critical approach to any solutions proposed and undertake due diligence to understand whether the proposed activity has proved successful in a similar context and whether the success continued when project funding ended.

> Beware of gurus: the project should maintain a healthy scepticism towards novel solutions. The development field is littered with failed projects and field benchmarking is critical to verifying whether an activity can work

Project example

On a project in Africa, the community refused to allow 'newcomers' to participate in the resettlement negotiation forum. The 'newcomers' had in fact been living in the community for over 40 years but there was jealousy that they had gained control over community land and would now benefit from compensation and resettlement. The project was forced to negotiate separately with the migrants to ensure that their viewpoints were heard.

---

11. **Benchmark the livelihood and community development interventions** that government, development agencies and other mining companies have implemented, and build the lessons learned into SIMP planning.

    When benchmarking projects this should include field visits and not just depend on desktop exercises. Field visits are also useful for assessing the capacity of potential implementation partners. There are a number of issues that must be considered when benchmarking projects implemented by other projects/agencies:

    • **Embracing error**: a key problem with benchmarking existing projects is the tendency for implementing agencies to overstate short-term success and under-report failure. This is because agencies are constantly searching for funding and donor partners are unlikely to support organisations that report significant failures on projects.

    • **Expected outcomes**: when planning social programmes the team needs to consider what the expected outcomes of the programmes will be based on benchmarking of programmes in similar contexts. For example, if a women's training programme on another mine only resulted in 10% of the women starting their own business after the project support finished, then the expected outcome is a 10% success rate. Too often social programmes are designed with expectations of a 100% success rate which is completely unrealistic and creates unnecessary expectations in the community.

    • **Differences between commercial and civil society projects**: planners should also recognise the difference between social planning on resource projects compared to donor-sponsored development projects. On NGO (non-governmental organisation) development projects the support is generally targeted at vulnerable groups in society often based on national antipoverty planning. The community is not in a strong negotiating position to dictate where this 'charity' is targeted. However, on commercial projects the social support is part of a larger package that the company must offer the community in order to get access to land. This puts the community in a strong negotiating position and often community investment will reflect the aims of strong local groups or individuals. It is important for social planners to recognise that a balance will have to be achieved between anti-poverty measures and infrastructure investments often favoured by local leaders and politicians.

- **Carefully evaluate novel approaches and 'appropriate' technologies**: while all appropriate technologies, such as fuel-efficient stoves, seem to make sense on paper, the rate of update can be patchy on projects and the project should be careful before recommending a new technology without proof that it has been widely adopted and in continuous use in a similar context.

12. **Select resettlement sites** with a primary focus on livelihood restoration.

The selection of a resettlement site(s) is the most critical step in the livelihood restoration process. There are clearly many criteria which must be considered and this can be difficult to communicate to the project team who are focused primarily on shorter-term considerations of budget and schedule. Although there is a long list of criteria, these can be prioritised.

A key issue is that even within a household there may be different livelihood priorities:

- In rural areas older male household heads may favour agriculture over other livelihood options. Given that older men are normally the community leaders and dominate the community consultation forums, they can often select a more remote resettlement site based on its agricultural potential without considering other criteria fully, such as proximity to the project.

- In rural areas there is a trend for young people to want to leave the land. Their priority is normally to be resettled close to the project so that they can avail themselves of training and employment with the project. Young people also generally want to be close to urban areas where they have access to businesses, shops, bars, etc.

- In rural areas women may gain some income from petty trade. Their priority for a resettlement site might also be close to the project area so that they could benefit from trading opportunities and also to urban areas for access to better schools and health facilities.

The resettlement site selection process is outlined in detail in Chapter 9 on physical resettlement planning. The key criteria for livelihood restoration planning are:

- **Proximity to the existing community**:
  - Important to maintain links to family and friends who will not be resettled and who provide support to the project-affected households. Note the alternative is to move the whole community together.
  - Many project-affected households who will be physically impacted will have land or access to other natural resources (fishing, hunting, etc.) outside the project area and it is important that they can maintain access to this for their livelihood.
  - Important to maintain access to existing cultural and religious sites.

- **Availability of quantity and quality of replacement land for farming and natural resource areas for other livelihood activities** (fishing, hunting, gathering, etc.): the primary consideration in resettlement site planning is to restore the existing livelihood activities of the project-affected households and this requires the project to enable access to equivalent resources.

Additional guidance on implementing livelihood restoration programmes on replacement land is presented in Chapter 15.

- Note that sites should be subject to an evaluation by an agricultural expert before being deemed suitable for agricultural development. Note that in some countries a separate environmental impact assessment will also be required for the resettlement site as part of the permitting process to construct the resettlement housing.

  There are two main options for replacing land lost to the project in a resettlement site:

  - **Blanket option**: acquire a large site which will accommodate both houses and replacement land. It is often difficult to get a site close to the project area given pressure on land and this often forces the project to select a more remote resettlement site.
  - **Patchwork approach**: acquire a smaller site just for residential resettlement and source smaller areas of land among the local farms. This solution can enable to the project to find a resettlement site close to the project area, thereby maintaining community cohesion. However, it can be challenging to replace the land area-for-area and project-affected households may have to travel a distance to source replacement land.

- **Proximity to the project to allow access to employment and economic opportunities**: although the restoration of existing livelihood activities is critical, the project will also offer employment and economic opportunities which will be the priority of young men and women from the impacted communities. Another important consideration for project-affected households is that resettlement houses located close to the project area will be more valuable and there may be opportunities to rent rooms to local employees for additional income.

- **Proximity to services**: the project should improve access to services and this can be done by building resettlement sites close to existing services and investing in upgrading and expansion or by providing new services which is more costly. The following services are particularly important:
  - Access to potable water and water for livestock/irrigation
  - Access to markets to sell goods and services
  - Access to roads
  - Access to electricity (where this exists or there is an agreement for the project to support electricity transmission)
  - Access to schools
  - Access to health services
  - Access to security services
  - Access to communications (cellphone network coverage)

13. **Identify implementation partners**: conduct research to identify specialist partners who have experience in implementing the proposed social packages and visit their projects to assess their capacity and the performance of their projects on the ground. Look for independent monitoring reports and ensure that claims of success are not based only on pilot projects or ongoing projects where funding is propping up the initiatives. The real test of the success of a development intervention is whether the communities can continue to implement the projects independent of the partner agency when the funding support has finished.

14. **Develop draft social management plans**: ensure that social experts with significant practical experience of implementing development projects are engaged to develop the SIMP management plans. Develop draft plans and workshop these internally with the company so that the plans are properly appraised and to ensure that there are adequate resources to support the implementation of the plans. The draft social management plans should be developed using professional project management tools such as a logical framework. Planning approaches should consider individual measures to address differences in livelihood dependence, including those based on land, wages and enterprises.

The Logical Framework

While a full description of all the planning tools available to manage livelihood restoration activities and community investment is beyond the scope of this book there are a considerable number of resources available. The logical framework is a standard project planning tool in the development sector and there takes the form of a 4x4 project table (Figure 10.5).

There are extensive resources available on the Internet to demonstrate the use of the tool (http://en.wikipedia.org/wiki/Logical_framework_approach). The four rows are used to describe four different types of event that take place as a project is implemented: 'Goal', 'Purpose', 'Outputs' and 'Activities'. The four columns provide different types of information about the events in each row. The first column is used to provide a **narrative** description of the event. The second column lists one or more objectively verifiable indicators of these events taking place. The third column describes the means of verification, where information will be available on the objectively verifiable indicators, and the fourth column lists the **assumptions**. Assumptions are external factors that it is believed could influence (positively or negatively) the events described in the narrative column. The list of assumptions should include those factors that potentially impact on the success of the project, but which cannot be directly controlled by the project or programme managers. In some cases these may include what could be **killer assumptions**, which if proved wrong will have major negative consequences for the project. A good project design should be able to substantiate its assumptions, especially those with a high potential to have a negative impact.

Figure 10.5: Typical logical framework matrix.

Project Description		Objectively verifiable indicators of achievement	Sources and means of verification	Assumptions
Goal	What is the overall broader impact to which the action will contribute?	What are the key indicators related to the overall goal?	What are the sources of information for these indicators?	What are the external factors necessary to sustain objectives in the long term?
Purpose	What is the immediate development outcome at the end of the project?	Which indicators clearly show that the objective of the action has been achieved?	What are the sources of information that exist or can be collected? What are the methods required to get this information?	Which factors and conditions are necessary to achieve that objective? (external conditions)
Outputs	What are the specifically deliverable results envisaged to achieve the specific objectives?	What are the indicators to measure whether and to what extent the action achieves the expected results?	What are the sources of information for these indicators?	What external conditions must be met to obtain the expected results on schedule?
Activities	What are the key activities to be carried out and in what sequence in order to produce the expected results?	**Means** What are the means required to implement these activities? (e.g. personnel, equipment, supplies, etc.)	What are the sources of information about action progress? **Costs** What are the action costs?	What pre-conditions are required before the action starts?

Source: www.sswm.info/category/planning-process-tools/implementation/implementation-support-tools/project-design/logical-f (accessed 23 November 2014).

The next step is for the implementation agency to produce a work plan for each project so that the activities can be scheduled to avoid any problems with scheduling such as:

- Too many activities being run at the same time and competing for labour resources and project management resources, such as support from the community relations teams.
- Activities not being aligned with the project construction schedule when labour resources may be tied up.
- Activities not being aligned with the seasons.
- Delays in the delivery of training or other inputs required for other activities such as construction employment.
- Overoptimistic assumptions about what can be achieved within a short time-frame.

15. **Develop budgets** for each proposed livelihood restoration and community development initiative. The budgets should include all the costs involved and a budget-reporting mechanism should be prepared so that the implementation partners can account for project expenditure for project monitoring.

16. **Develop a schedule** for the implementation of SIMPs. The scheduling of livelihood restoration is critical as many of these activities are seasonal. It is critical that farmers do not miss a season's harvest, if possible, and it may be necessary to transport project-affected households to the new site to ensure that they can prepare fields before the final move. Where an agricultural

season will be missed it will be necessary to provide food rations to the project-affected households in order to sustain them through this period.

Another important scheduling consideration is the timing of livelihood restoration activities in relation to the project cycle. If there are significant project construction employment opportunities available for the first few years of the project it might make sense to allow households to delay agricultural support until construction is completed. This is because the end of construction is a difficult time on projects as the project-affected households transition out of salaried employment into other livelihoods where they need support. Support for women's agricultural activities could continue if jobs for women were limited on the project.

17. **Present the draft plans to the community consultations forum** which is in place for the project and ensure that the representatives provide feedback to the communities. Following community feedback, finalise the community development and livelihood restoration packages and sign an agreement with the community.

18. **Pilot proposed livelihood programmes**: if livelihood restoration planning is conducted early in the project cycle there will be an opportunity to pilot some of the proposed programmes in the impacted communities, particularly for improved agricultural techniques. The skills training and apprenticeship programmes should be launched as early in the planning cycle as possible. It is important to verify that the implementing agency has the capacity to manage the activity and is achieving the intended outcomes before expanding this to all impacted households.

19. **Develop a management mechanism for the SIMP**: there are a number of programme structure options depending on how much control the company wants to exercise over their spend on community development: company-managed, independent or hybrid. The choice of programme will depend on the regulatory framework, the capacity of the community to participate and manage the programme, and the availability of management and funding partners. Independent foundations are being promoted but it may be wise to start with a company management programme in the early phases of a project and move to a more independent foundation when the capacity of the community to manage the programme has reached a sufficient level.

20. **Implement the SIMP plans**: see Chapter 16 for advice on implementing livelihood restoration and community development activities. The main livelihood restoration support will include the key support areas outlined below.

21. **Conduct ongoing monitoring and evaluation** using both internal and external experts of the performance of social investments against targets and make revisions where required. The development of a monitoring and evaluation plan is outlined in Chapter 18.

Designing livelihood support programmes

Rural livelihoods

There are two key elements to livelihood restoration on projects in rural areas:

- Access to replacement land to ensure a livelihood safety net for households, to guarantee food security and to permit households who want to focus on farming to maximise the potential of their land for production and opportunities for processing and marketing their produce.

- Diversification: it is estimated that roughly 50% of rural household incomes in low-income countries is generated from non-farm activities (including remittances and pensions) (Reardon 1997). Better-off households tend to diversify into non-farm business activities (trade, transport, etc.) while the poor tend to focus on casual labour, especially on other farms.

Figure 10.6: Water provision as part of an agricultural livelihood restoration project.

Within a given household there can be a diversification in livelihoods where the men will work on the farm but also off-farm for periods of the year in order to make additional income. Women can also work on the home farm but also be engaged in off-farm labour and trading activities. Migration can also be very important with some household members moving to urban areas, temporarily or permanently, in order to earn wages to support the family.

Social planners therefore need to ensure that households have access to a mixture of land-based, wage-based and enterprise-based opportunities, although there will always be trade-offs depending on where replacement land is available in proximity to the project and local urban centres.

Urban livelihoods

The majority of urban households are dependent on wage and enterprise-based livelihoods, including retail, manufacturing, construction, services and transport. The informal sector is also very important to urban households and includes a wide range of services, often run from home, including:

- Food processing and selling: e.g. bread baking, food sellers
- Retail: e.g. kiosks selling food and drink
- Repairs: e.g. motorcycle and car repairs, shoe repairs
- Manufacturing: e.g. metal and wood products
- Construction: e.g. kiosks, houses
- Services: e.g. kiosks, hairdressing
- Transport: e.g. taxi drivers

Informal sector jobs are usually low-skilled, labour-intensive micro-enterprises employing small numbers of people who are often family members as presented below. The key to urban livelihoods is to maintain access to employment and markets. This means finding resettlement sites close the original household location or near transport networks.

Land-based livelihoods

Chapter 16 on livelihoods implementation provides further guidance on restoring agricultural and natural resource livelihoods.

For households who are predominantly dependent on land and access to natural resources, the following measures should be proposed:

Land and natural resources:

- Select a resettlement site location which provides project-affected households with access to replacement land and/or natural resources as outlined in Chapter 9 on physical resettlement planning.

- Provide the project-affected households with secure access to land for crops, grazing land, fallow, forest and water resources. Security of tenure should be provided (where possible): there are a number of strategies including outright purchase by the project and providing funds to the project-affected households to acquire the land themselves through formal or traditional processes.

Livelihood resources:

- Provide support to the project-affected households to prepare the land for production through clearing trees, levelling, access routes, soil stabilisation and fencing.
- Provide support to the project-affected households to enable them to quickly achieve production through the provision of agricultural inputs (such as seeds, seedlings, fertiliser, irrigation), veterinary care, and agricultural extension advice. Provide support to other livelihood activities, including fishing, hunting and gathering.
- Through the CDP enable farmers, particularly women, to establish producer groups and provide training and materials to enable them to process crops into higher value crops.
- Through the CDP and local procurement plan, support producer groups with microcredit through third-party providers and also with storage and marketing to enable them to get better prices for their products.

Wage-based livelihoods

Livelihood resources:

- It is key that the resettlement site provides the opportunity for employees to continue to access their original workplaces or these re-established businesses close to or at the resettlement sites. If this is not possible then compensation should be paid to business owners for the loss of business and a resettlement allowance paid to employees to allow them to transition into new economic activities.
- It is also key that the resettlement sites provide the resettlement households access to employment and economic opportunities at the project sites.
- As outlined above, the project SIMP should include a local employment plan which should contain the following measures:
  - Define the zone within which local people will be prioritised for project employment. It is essential that the resettlement sites are within the local employment zone in order to give project-affected households an equal opportunity to gain employment with the project. There are a number of processes for identifying who is a legitimate local, including a census of all households in the zone or a verification process by community, traditional and political leaders. As there are normally many more applicants

than available jobs, the employment plan can outline processes, such as balloting, where eligible applicants take it in turns to benefit from short-term contracts with the project.

- Skills training should be provided for people living in the local employment zone, including economically impacted households. This is generally best done by supporting existing vocational training institutes or partnering with experienced training agencies. The skills training should be matched to the opportunities created by the project, including direct and indirect employment, and should be targeted particularly towards young men and women. Young men in particular are generally the most volatile stakeholders and the most likely to protest and disrupt the project if the maximum number of jobs are not given to local people.

Enterprise-based livelihoods

Livelihood resources:

- Where business premises are impacted by the project, the company must provide support to re-establish the business outside the project zone or at the resettlement site at a location of their choice. This will include reconstructing the business premises or providing compensation to allow the business owner to construct the business premises themselves.

- As outlined above, a local procurement plan should be prepared as part of the SIMP and the company should provide support to local businesses to benefit from the project. This will include an assessment of local businesses and opportunities for them to provide goods and services to the project by implementing the following measures:
  - Develop a register of local businesses who will be favoured to supply goods and services to the project.
  - The company should provide training on credit planning, business planning, marketing, inventory and quality control to enable them to expand their businesses to meet the demands of the project.
  - The company could also support the development of a local business forum in order to provide a focus for the local procurement plan and a committee of local businesses to engage with.

Livelihood restoration planning: key considerations

- The development of LRPs must include engagement with men, women and young people on their development priorities so that they have ownership of the process.
- The livelihood restoration strategy should adopt a broad concept of both income replacement (cash and in kind) and social development processes (health, education and social cohesion) which enable project-affected households to maintain their standard of living in the context of a changing social and economic environment.
- Planning livelihood restoration requires a partnership between the project, communities, government and civil society who all contribute to the wellbeing of each household.
- The LRP in the RAP should focus on the basic restoration of land, natural resources and business premises, and direct aid to re-establish production and sales. The CDP should focus on capacity-building of processing and marketing groups to add value to local production and take advantage of improved economic conditions and the creation of new market opportunities by the project.
- The support provided in the CDP for improvements in physical infrastructure such as roads and markets is important to ensure investments in processing and marketing are effective.
- A major missed opportunity on many projects is to **start skills training of local people during the early stages of the project** to prepare them for construction and operation employment opportunities.
- The **resettlement site selection process needs to balance** pressure from young people and women to be near urban centres and the project for jobs, economic benefits and access to services, and from older men, who are more powerful in the community, to be located where more traditional livelihoods can be practised. **Ultimately it is a question of providing options** and ensuring a free and informed negotiation process which is not dominated by any one interest group.
- Projects should **not fear maximising short-term construction employment opportunities** for project-affected households as this provides a welcome injection of cash into the community at a critical time following resettlement. What is important is that the project times the main livelihood restoration activities so that they provide a safety net to project-affected households who lose their jobs post-construction, which is often a period when community conflict is high as young men adjust to life without a regular salary. Ongoing engagement is also required to communicate opportunities, limit expectations and potentially avoid conflict.

- The livelihood restoration strategy needs to ensure a **partnership with government** and its responsibility for ensuring access to health and education services and the maintenance of infrastructure in resettlement areas.

- The livelihood restoration strategy needs to ensure the **integration of resettlement communities** and reach agreement on access to resources and any improved services prior to resettlement. There is often conflict post-resettlement over resources as assumptions were made on shared use of natural resources such as forests and water resources without negotiating a firm agreement.

- It is important that the project focuses not only on resettled households but also on **project-affected households whose homes are not impacted, but whose livelihoods are impacted** though the reduction in the size of their farms or loss of a place of business.

- The livelihood restoration needs to include **support for vulnerable households**. However, it is important to have good baseline data to demonstrate the pre-project socioeconomic situation of these houses and to track their post-resettlement livelihoods to ensure that the programme does not result in dependence on the project.

- Livelihoods planning should be based on an understanding that **successful restoration and alternative livelihoods requires long-term planning**.

11

Vulnerable persons

The main objective of a land access and resettlement process is to ensure that the impacted households' standard of living is maintained or enhanced. However, it is widely recognised that some households are more vulnerable to impoverishment risks, as a result of their initial vulnerability and being unable to take full advantage of the opportunities offered by the project. Households that are particularly vulnerable include landless, squatters, tenants and those with limited labour resources, such as households headed by women, the elderly and those in poor health. The objective of this chapter is to identify the key measures required to support vulnerable households through the land access and resettlement process.

What are the key challenges, issues and risks?

Projects seeking to support vulnerable households face a number of challenges:

- **There is limited experience among social and resettlement experts in implementing vulnerable support programmes**: this can lead to the use of overly wide criteria and low thresholds in determining eligibility, resulting in longer-term commitments and dependence on the project.

- **The needs of women are often ignored on resettlement projects** with cash compensation, employment and farming opportunities targeted mainly at men, leaving women vulnerable to impoverishment.

- **In poorer areas it is difficult to differentiate between pre-project and project-induced vulnerability**: in areas where poverty is endemic, a large proportion of impacted households are already vulnerable to impoverishment and it can be difficult to differentiate between pre-project poverty-induced vulnerability and project-induced vulnerability, resulting in the project being held responsible for general poverty impacts.

- **Many projects fail to identify or support vulnerable households**: this can result in some households becoming destitute as a result of the land access and resettlement process.

- **There is stigmatisation of minority groups on some projects**: providing additional support, above that received by the majority of households, can lead to considerable jealousy and conflict in the community.

- **Many projects fail to develop exit strategies for vulnerable support**, making it difficult to wean poor families off the programme and creating longer-term dependence.

- **Vulnerable support programmes can cause considerable community jealousy**: on land access and resettlement projects it is preferable to offer households a consistent package to avoid conflict. The opportunity to gain additional benefits by becoming classified as 'vulnerable' can result in households misrepresenting their socioeconomic status and this can create tension in the community.

- **Households who are destitute and living in severe poverty in the project area may find themselves in a similar situation post-RAP (resettlement action plan) implementation** as they had limited assets, which were fairly replaced, and a limited livelihood to restore. The poverty situation of these households is not caused by the project and not the project's responsibility, although the project can choose to help these households as part of its contribution to improving community welfare. The challenge is working with government services to get them to take responsibility for destitute households whose situation is not caused by project impacts.

Guiding principles

The IFC (International Finance Corporation) defines vulnerable or 'at risk' groups as 'people who, by virtue of gender, ethnicity, age, physical or mental disability, economic disadvantage or social status may be more diversely affected by displacement than others and who may be limited in their ability to claim or take advantage of resettlement assistance and related development benefits' (IFC 2012: PS (Performance Standard) 5, Guidance Note 29).

IFC PS1 requires projects to identify vulnerable groups during the ESIA (environmental and social impact assessment) or through the social baseline studies component of resettlement planning. This requires special measures to engage with vulnerable groups, including focus groups and ensuring that project staff has representatives from these groups (such as the elderly, disabled, etc.). Most ESIA baseline studies are not thorough enough to identify vulnerable households and therefore vulnerability to impoverishment should be identified in the RAP baseline studies.

There are two types of vulnerability:

- Pre-existing vulnerability: vulnerability that exists regardless of the project development as a result of impoverishment factors in the project area. These households are vulnerable by virtue of the challenges they face to sustain their household and the project will bring additional pressure. Examples of vulnerable people are:
  - The destitute/homeless, street children, child labourers, child survivors of families living with HIV/Aids, single mothers and persons with severe disabilities or disabling disease
  - Households with handicapped, chronically ill and socially stigmatised persons
  - Caretakers/sharecroppers/farm labours with no lands/fields or buildings of their own
- Project-induced vulnerability is caused by project-related physical and economic displacement. These households are coping on their own but the changes brought about by the project may cause impoverishment which can be temporary or permanent. The impoverishment risks, developed by Michael Cernea, are outlined in Chapter 7.

It is important to note that a household does not qualify as a vulnerable just because a household member has a disability or illness, as the remaining household members could compensate for this vulnerability. The capacity of the household to cope with the project impacts should be assessed based on the composition of the whole household and its relative wealth.

There are a number of sound business reasons for providing additional support to households vulnerable to project-induced impoverishment:

- IFC standards require that support is provided to households who are at risk of impoverishment by the project. Compliance with standards is often critical for project funding.
- If the company does not offer support to vulnerable households and they become destitute because of the project, third parties can use this against the project, causing reputational damage.
- Supporting vulnerable households is generally well received by the community, and if the programme is developed properly this can add to the reputation of the company and its social licence to operate.

Who is vulnerable?

The concept of a vulnerable household can be difficult to explain to a project-impacted community. However, most communities will have language to describe extremely poor households and it is these households that need to be identified and supported. Practical implementation of vulnerable persons support programmes has demonstrated that the communities must be made to understand that the project is not responsible for pre-existing poverty in the project area. In some communities the poorest members can be stigmatised and it can be hard to win community backing for providing these households with additional benefits not available to all impacted households. The vulnerable household support programme can lead to considerable jealousy within the community and requests for all households to receive the same benefits.

The poorest households tend to be those with the fewest assets, such as landless farmers or households with holdings less than 0.5 ha, with no livestock, low levels of educational attainment of household members, no savings and limited social support (Ellis and Allison 2004: 8). The most vulnerable are often dependent on subsistence agriculture and labour on other farms. Poorer households have often a high dependence on natural resources found in common property areas to engage in activities such as gathering fuelwood, wild foods (fruit, insects), making charcoal, etc. Some of the poorest communities are hunter-gatherers, nomadic pastoralists, shifting cultivators, migrant fishermen and forest-dwelling poor who are all heavily dependent on common property resources. Households headed by single, widowed or divorced women are often the poorest as in many countries women are not permitted to own or inherit land. In countries with HIV/Aids infections the loss of household members and associated health issues can result in extreme vulnerability which can also be accompanied by social exclusion.

The focus on vulnerable households has stemmed largely from work in the emergency sector and the HEA (Household Economy Approach; www.heawebsite. org/hea-framework-overview) provides a useful framework and tools to identify vulnerable households and predict the impact of hazards (environmental and social). The HEA is concerned with how people get by from year to year and with the connections with other people and places that enable them to do so. This is called the baseline and has three components: livelihood zoning, a wealth breakdown and an analysis of livelihood strategies for each of the identified wealth groups. While designed for emergency situations, the tools can also be useful in the context of land access and resettlement to identify the most vulnerable households.

The HEA emphasises that while geography tends to define a household's options for obtaining food and income, the ability to exploit those options and to survive in a crisis is determined largely by wealth. In other words, what people have by way of land, capital and livestock, together with their educational status and access to political and social networks, determines the ways in which they will be able to get food and cash, or how they will respond to sudden or long-term change. The HEA seeks to quantify food, income and expenditure in order to be able to predict how a poor household will cope with the loss of employment or poor rains and the likely impact on the household livelihood. The HEA helps to determine the level of poverty by comparing income levels for different groups with the cost of a 'minimum nonfood basket', together with the cost of food purchase, to see whether households can access basic needs.

Developing a programme to support vulnerable households

It is important to note that without the correct mitigation programmes, including compensation, provision of resettlement housing and livelihood restoration, any individual household impacted by the project can be considered vulnerable to impoverishment. However, the purpose of the RAP mitigation measures is to ensure that the vast majority of households can cope and are not considered vulnerable. The support recommended in this chapter should only be required for the most vulnerable households based on locally acceptable criteria for households under severe stress. The support should also be targeted at households who will be losing access to resources which cannot be easily replaced, for example where landless households have to move from land where they are squatting. Where a project is predicting that more than 20% of the households require additional support for vulnerability then this is an indication that the RAP is not properly designed to mitigate general project impacts and needs to be revised.

In some communities vulnerable households can develop a type of 'learned helplessness' where exclusion from community discussions and decisions has resulted in an attitude of hopelessness and passivity. This concept is related to dependence where households can become dependent on project support over a long time, losing the incentive to provide for themselves. It is important that livelihood restoration and vulnerable support programmes emphasise the responsibility of the household for their own wellbeing so that dependence is not encouraged. A difficulty with vulnerability programmes is determining when households exit from this support so that it is not seen as long-term welfare support.

The term 'transitional hardship programme' can be used to emphasise that the company is responsible for supporting households who are experiencing or vulnerable to impoverishment through the land access and resettlement process, but that this support is only for a limited period of time. There must be an exit strategy and it is the responsibility of the project to provide the resources to vulnerable households so that they can meet their basic needs but also so that they understand that they must avail themselves of the opportunity to help themselves as this support is only temporary. This chapter therefore focuses on the development of a support strategy for vulnerable households, termed the transitional hardship programme, which requires the following steps:

1. **Establish a team to identify and work with vulnerable households in the project area**

    The initial project scoping by social experts should identify the scale of poverty in the project area and an indication of the number of households at risk from impoverishment from the project. The team required depends on the threat and scale of impoverishment due to the project. The team should have a lead social expert and one or more community liaison officers who have some experience of social work, or dedicated social workers. Local CBOs (community-based organisations) and/or NGOs (non-governmental

Project example

On a project in Africa, the company developed a comprehensive programme to support vulnerable households which included food packages and support for health and education as required. The vulnerable persons team reviewed the socioeconomic baseline and, using indicators, identified potentially vulnerable households who were visited by caseworkers for assessment. A subcommittee, comprised of community and company representatives, of the main consultations forum was established to review applications for vulnerable programme support.

organisations) who are partnering in the implementing of support to vulnerable households can also be invited to participate in the planning team.

The team needs to engage with government social welfare services, if these exist in the area, to develop a programme jointly so that responsibility can be handed over for ongoing support to the targeted households.

2. **Develop a comprehensive socioeconomic baseline** which enables the project to identify households that are currently impoverished and those that are vulnerable to impoverishment due to the land access and resettlement process. The vulnerability criteria must be developed using a participatory approach with the local community to ensure that they understand the project's responsibilities regarding vulnerable households and that they accept the criteria being used to assess households. The process for developing a baseline for the project is outlined in Chapter 6. The key is to develop a set of vulnerability indicators which enables the project to identify the vulnerable households. While every project context is different, the key vulnerability indicators may include the following:

   • Households headed by a single woman or widow: women are particularly vulnerable on many projects as they are often afforded a lower social status and may have no rights to property in their name

   • Households headed by a juvenile or an elderly person

   • Households which are landless or who will be rendered landless by the project

   • Households currently suffering from malnutrition and who are unable to produce enough food or sufficient income to purchase enough food: obtain statistics on malnutrition from health centres

   • Indigenous people and ethnic minorities who might suffer from discrimination and marginalisation and who might be more dependent on natural resources and face greater hardship from the loss of access to these areas

   • Destitute households with no visible sign of income

   • Households whose children do not attend school regularly

   • Impoverished households with limited income or assets

It is particularly important to disaggregate baseline data and information on women so that their particular circumstances can be understood.

3. **Identification of vulnerable households**

The project's overall approach to land access and resettlement should ensure that most households will receive the support they require in order to make a successful transition. The definition of which households require additional support should focus on those who might suffer extreme hardship. If the identification process throws up more than 20% of the households then the whole RAP approach should be revisited to ensure that the majority of households are receiving the support they require. During data analysis, prepare a report on households that are currently vulnerable or who are at risk of impoverishment during the resettlement process.

It is advised that the households are identified from the baseline data-collection process, which will involve both quantitative and qualitative information, including focus groups and interviews with key people on which households are most at risk. It is not recommended that the households are given the option to self-select as vulnerable. This is because the majority of households will see themselves as vulnerable in some way and it needs to be

Process for the identification of vulnerable households at risk from transitional hardship

- Using the indicators developed for the socioeconomic baseline data collection, identify vulnerable households and also use information provided by the community liaison officers to create a list of potentially vulnerable households.

- Develop criteria for the assessment of whether a household is vulnerable. The caseworkers should visit the potentially vulnerable households and undertake an assessment of whether they should be included in the programme. The caseworkers will monitor the households through the land access and resettlement process and take referrals from the community liaison officers if they feel that certain at-risk households should be included in the programme. The caseworkers will also assess when the households should be exited from the programme.

- Some projects allow project-affected households to self-refer to the vulnerables support programme but this is very difficult to manage as each household seeks to position itself for additional assistance. Vulnerable households should be identified using community-based criteria for extremely poor households and the project should work with a local committee to support these households. The project-affected households will have recourse to the grievance mechanism if they consider they have been overlooked by the vulnerables support and these claims can be dealt with through the normal grievance process and ultimately assessed by the caseworkers.

Project example

A vulnerable person's support programme on a project in Africa caused considerable community jealousy as the initial criteria for participation were too wide. Some community members claimed that those receiving support were being rewarded for being lazy. Powerful community members tried to pressurise the project to include them in the programme. The project also found it difficult to phase households off the programme as they became accustomed to the support.

explained that the transitional hardship support is targeted at the destitute and most extreme cases.

4. **Develop the transitional hardship programme**

    It is critical that the transitional hardship programme is developed as part of overall project social planning, i.e. that it is conceptualised and has linkages to other initiatives such as livelihood restoration planning.

    Develop a plan to provide additional support for these households during the resettlement process. The approach should include the following elements:

    *   Dedicate a community liaison officer or social caseworker to work closely with the identified vulnerable households.

    *   For more complex projects, initiate a subcommittee of the main resettlement consultations committee—a transitional hardship support subcommittee—to assist in the development of an appropriate vulnerable households support programme in order to ensure a participatory approach. The subcommittee should have representatives from the company, impacted communities and the local social welfare services, if appropriate. The company can agree the criteria for eligibility for project support and the subcommittee can help to explain these to the impacted communities so only deserving cases qualify. The subcommittee can also help the company deal with grievances and the process for phasing out support when the households are re-established.

    *   An assessment should be made of what government and traditional support programmes are available to support vulnerable households. The transitional hardship support team can work with the local authorities to ensure that families that are already in extreme poverty can be supported by government services so that they do not become dependent on the project.

Figure 11.1: Vulnerability of engaging in roadside trading in Papua New Guinea.

Vulnerable households and livelihood restoration

The key focus of the transitional hardship support programme should be to ensure that vulnerable households are provided with additional support to access the main livelihood restoration and social management plan benefits. Vulnerable households must be given specific attention in relation to the project's main livelihood restoration programmes as outlined in Chapter 10:

- Land- and natural-resource-based livelihoods: support to re-establish their farming/fishing/hunting/gathering activities at the resettlement site so that they don't miss a cropping season and can feed their families. This might require additional support to clear and plant the new land.
- Wage-based livelihoods: support to maintain their jobs from the resettlement site. The local employment plan should include additional support to ensure that women and disabled people can avail themselves of skills training and job opportunities with the project.
- Business-based livelihoods: the company will already be providing support to business owners to relocate and compensate them for transitional losses. For vulnerable households who own businesses may need additional

mentoring and support to take advantage of the opportunities being offered by the project. The local procurement plan should ensure that vulnerable households with businesses are specially targeted.

- Resettlement support package: the project generally gives the resettlement households a resettlement support package which can include a cash allowance or rations to help them feed their family until their livelihoods are re-established. The duration of this support depends on when they can re-establish their livelihoods.

Special supports

The caseworkers will make an assessment of each vulnerable household and develop a tailored package to ensure that they can cope with the land access and resettlement process. The key areas of support are:

- Emergency healthcare for pregnant women, the elderly and disabled people as required.
- Support for children to attend school.
- Additional support with transport to their new house which might include providing a team to salvage their belongings, including house material.
- Counselling to the households so that they can understand the short-term support the project can offer and also to make them aware of government services and longer-term options. Vulnerable households with mobility issues should be assisted to attend project consultation events and they should also receive home visits in order to have the project impact and mitigation events explained to them.
- Support should be given to vulnerable households to ensure that they maintain their social networks of family and friends. This will include ensuring that they are resettled close to family and friends and that they have access to social services.
- International standards require that the resettlement household be given tenure over their resettlement plots and replacement land. However, in most cases the tenure is given in the name of the male household head only. In addition, many countries do not recognise the ownership of a house by women. IFC guidance (IFC 2012: PS5) requires that:

> under circumstances in which national law and local customary tenure systems do not give women equal opportunities or rights with regard to property, provision should be made to ensure that the access of women to security of tenure is equivalent to that of men and does not further disadvantage women.

The IFC guidance states that:

clients are not expected to become involved in law-making but are encouraged to raise the profile of gender related matters in discussions with government agencies and other relevant groups in the course of resettlement planning, and in so doing encourage more equitable treatment of affected women.

Providing women with equal access to the right over tenure of land may be difficult, but the company must be able to demonstrate that they have made every effort to achieve this.

- IFC guidance is that 'compensation and restoration packages for vulnerable people should include additional forms of support, and should favor the lowest risk mitigation options wherever possible, e.g., in-kind compensation over cash compensation'. Vulnerable households should therefore be encouraged to participate in financial management training offered by the project. Additional financial advice should be given to vulnerable households on how to invest compensation so that this is not wasted in the short term.

- As outlined in Chapter 10, on livelihood restoration planning, the support measures need to be benchmarked, piloted, costed and scheduled utilising professional project management support before the transitional hardship support plan is finalised.

Communications planning

The company must develop a communications plan (see Chapter 5) for the transitional hardship support programme so that all stakeholders, company, community, government and non-governmental agencies understand the objectives of the programme and where the company's responsibilities start and finish. It is critical that the programme is presented to the community consultations forum and agreed to by the community representatives.

Grievance procedure

The community liaison officers must be able to communicate to the project-affected households how the transitional hardship support is targeted in order to minimise grievances. However, project-affected households who feel they have been excluded from the programme will be able to submit a grievance under the normal grievance process. The grievance will first be vetted by the transitional hardship support team and a response given following an assessment of their situation. If they do not accept this assessment, the project-affected person's grievance can then be heard by a subcommittee of the main community consultations forum, which can make a recommendation to the company which will normally be accepted.

Monitoring and evaluation

The company's monitoring and evaluation team should support the transitional support team to put in place indicators to monitor performance and criteria for when households are ready to exit the programme.

Exit strategy

The project team needs to develop an exit strategy for the programme to emphasise that the hardship support is transitional and will, therefore, be phased out over time. This can be difficult where local government social welfare services are limited or non-existent. In this case the company needs to make it clear to the community that the support is to ensure that the project-affected person is restored to a pre-project situation, but that it is not the responsibility of the company to take care of the vulnerable household permanently. This is the most difficult part of providing vulnerable support, where families are already destitute or suffering from debilitating illnesses and there is no clear solution for the household. The community development and livelihood restoration programmes should focus on trying to increase the resilience of all affected households, from which the vulnerable households will benefit also.

The exit strategy should have the following elements:

- The support to vulnerable households should be termed a transitional hardship support programme to emphasise that the support will end at a point in time and that the household will have to focus on becoming self-supporting from the outset.

- The transitional hardship support programme needs to be developed in partnership with government services and the limit of the company's responsibility needs to be agreed with them.

- The transitional hardship support subcommittee needs to assist in the development of the programme and to increase the understanding of the communities of the responsibilities of the company and that the support will be short term. The subcommittee will assist in the vetting of cases and helping the community to understand the process. Furthermore, the subcommittee can assist in reviewing grievances and explain to households the process for exiting the programme.

- Each participating household should be presented with a time-limited plan which outlines the support they will receive and what is expected of them in terms of using the support to improve their wellbeing. The support plan

> Vulnerable assistance programmes must have an exit strategy and be linked to livelihoods programmes and other broader project social initiatives

should be clearly explained to the household by the caseworker in the presence of a community member and signed off by the household so that it is clear when the support will be phased out and what milestones should be met along the way.

- The programme must have a handover process to the government or other agencies so that vulnerable households do not develop a long-term dependence on the project. The programme team will develop indicators as discussed above which will be agreed with the subcommittee and government services to measure when the project-affected households will exit the programme.

Supporting vulnerable households: key considerations

- **Ensure that roles and responsibilities are clear regarding vulnerable households**: the role of the project is to support vulnerable households to deal with project-induced impacts for a transitional period until their pre-project livelihoods are restored. It is the role of the government and communities to deal with general poverty issues and the project can support this through the project's community investment initiatives.

- **Use a participatory approach to define what vulnerability means in the context of the project communities**: engage with government and the communities to understand how vulnerability is defined locally so that the community understands that only those households in danger of impoverishment will be supported by the programme. On projects with significant impacts, a committee should be formed with membership from government agencies and community and project representatives to support the project to develop criteria to identify vulnerable households and to review grievances.

- **Focus on ensuring vulnerable households' access to main RAP and social impact management plan support**: the main focus of the transitional hardship support should be to ensure that the vulnerable households access the main RAP livelihood support programmes and the social management plan support for the wider communities. The focus should be on ensuring the household can produce sufficient food and income to provide for food security and basic household needs.

12
The negotiation process

The negotiation process is the critical central component of the land access and resettlement process. It can be seen as the centrepoint around which the whole land access and resettlement process turns. All planning and field activities up to this point have been in preparation for the negotiation process. The outcome of the negotiations will inform all subsequent activities, including resettlement construction, compensation, moves and livelihood restoration. How effectively the negotiation process is managed will in large part determine the success or failure of a land access and resettlement process.

The land access and resettlement process is one big negotiation

Regardless of whether resettlement is involuntary or voluntary, the negotiation objectives, guiding principles, approach and desired outcome should not be different

What are the key components of the negotiation process?

One can broadly split the negotiation process into the following elements or components (typically with some overlap and iteration):

- **Preparations**, including developing a clear strategy, proposed offer packages, negotiating positions and tactics, undertaking necessary capacity-building, and other measures to prepare and set the scene

Undertaking detailed planning is not a luxury that will overcomplicate negotiations: as with planning for the rest of a mining, oil and gas or infrastructure project, it is a basic necessity

Figure 12.1: The land access and resettlement process.

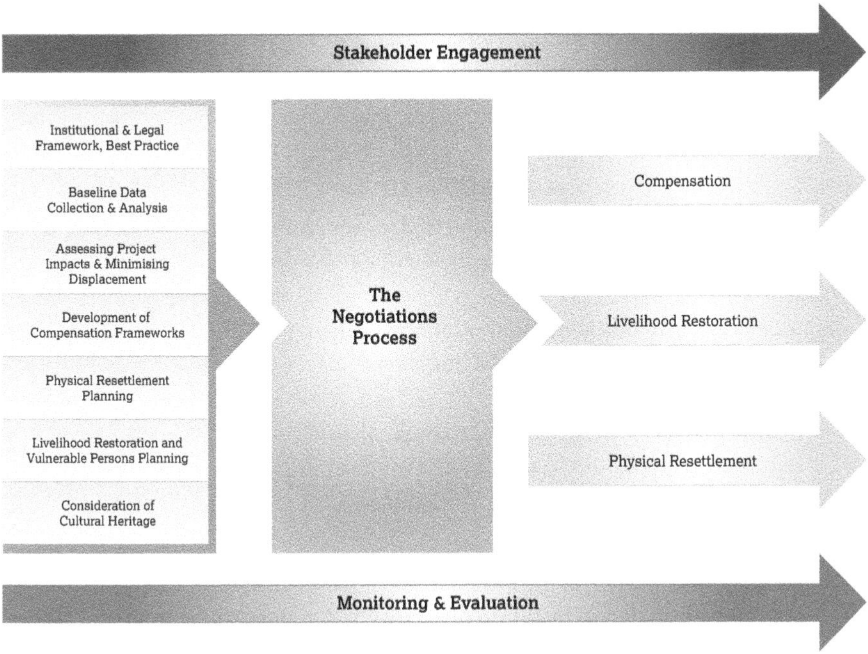

- **Information sharing** with participants and other key stakeholders
- **Discussions** on relevant topics and the arrival at a consensus
- **Obtaining mandates and ensuring consensus**: the steps to ensure that constituencies are aware of and on board with proposed positions taken and agreements reached by their representatives
- **Recording** of the negotiation process and agreements reached

What is the objective of the negotiation process?

Mining, oil and gas and infrastructure projects cannot take place without securing access to land. However, this objective cannot be met unless land is accessed in a manner that adequately engages affected people to hear their concerns and include their thoughts in the development of mitigation measures and other planning aspects.

Therefore the objective of negotiations is to enable the conclusion of **suitable agreements** with project-affected persons that:

- Are based on all participants having **adequate information and a range of choices** (to the extent possible) to enable them to make informed decisions
- Are concluded with **all relevant owners and affected people**
- **Cover all relevant issues**
- **Are fair and equitable**, thereby helping to ensure that they are implementable
- Enable **timely project access to required land**
- Ensure that **displacement impacts are addressed** in a manner that meets **legal requirements and relevant standards**
- Enable the **livelihoods and standard of living of project-affected persons to be improved, or at least restored**
- Enable project-affected persons to **appropriately share in project benefits**, such as project-related employment
- Are **affordable** for the project proponent
- **Avoid the need for expropriation**
- Help to ensure that the project will **have peaceful undisturbed possession of land acquired**, and the **ability to develop and operate without disruption**

> The objective of the negotiation process is to create a win–win–win outcome for communities, governments and the project proponent

What types of negotiation are there?

There are two broad types of negotiation related to land access and resettlement:

- **External discussions** with project-affected persons (and government where necessary)
- **Internal discussions** between project personnel directly responsible for land access and resettlement, senior management and other disciplines/departments within the organisation, such as in relation to what form compensation packages, resettlement budgets and negotiating mandates for discussions with project-affected persons should take

> A properly planned and implemented resettlement project is not possible without the informed and active involvement of affected communities and other relevant stakeholders

What are the key issues, challenges and risks?

Land access and resettlement negotiations are not easy to undertake, and projects will inevitably be faced with a range of difficult issues, challenges and risks, including:

- **High community and individual expectations**
- Concluding agreements with **community leaders who are not fully representative**
- **Failure to engage with all relevant stakeholders**
- **Lack of informed agreement** by affected communities
- Undertaking negotiations with an **inadequate strategy, tactics, budget or time-line** to engage communities
- Being **unrealistic about the time and resources required** to undertake negotiations properly and successfully
- **Getting project and corporate management to fully appreciate** the challenges of and the business case for doing land access and resettlement properly

> Each issue, challenge or risk constitutes a potential opportunity for improved performance

The purpose of this chapter is to help you identify and deal with the issues, challenges, risks and opportunities that will arise.

Is there one definitive standard that provides all the answers?

Countries are increasingly legislating on how resettlement should be undertaken. However, in many jurisdictions these requirements are often not comprehensive and sometimes fall below best practice requirements.

A range of best practice standards have been developed by different institutions, but there continues to be healthy debate, particularly between civil society and the natural resources sector, about the level at which the bar should be set.

Within the private sector, the Performance Standards of the IFC (International Finance Corporation) are widely used. In the context of land access and resettlement, IFC PS (Performance Standard) 5 provides a useful best practice standard. In the context of stakeholder engagement and the negotiation process, PS5 provides that:

- Projects are encouraged to use negotiated settlement to meet the requirements of PS5, even if they have the legal means to acquire land without the seller's consent, such as expropriation.

- There should be appropriate disclosure of information, consultation and the informed participation of those affected.
- Decision-making processes related to resettlement and livelihood restoration should include options and alternatives, where applicable.
- The consultation process should ensure that women's perspectives are obtained.

Other best practice standards include those of the European Bank for Reconstruction and Development as well as other banks. Of particular importance to private-sector projects are the Equator Principles, which stipulate that commercial banks who are signatories should not provide finance to projects that do not commit to complying with IFC standards. Most of the banks that provide finance to mining projects are Equator Principle signatories.

All the various standards are either aligned with the IFC standards or include very similar criteria. Therefore the IFC standards are a useful checklist for a project.

> While laws and standards provide useful guidance to projects undertaking negotiations, much of this guidance is of a general nature. The rest of this chapter provides more detailed and practical assistance in undertaking negotiations

What are the guiding principles for a negotiation process?

Key principles apply regardless of where a project is located:

- **Informed participation**: all participants in the negotiations and the communities they represent will participate in the land access and resettlement process on an informed basis.
- **Openness**: all participants in the land access and resettlement negotiations will undertake their activities in an open and transparent manner.
- **Mutual respect**: all participants in the land access and resettlement negotiations will treat each other with respect.
- **Mutual benefit**: the outcome of the negotiation process should be beneficial both to affected communities and to the project, i.e. a win–win scenario.
- **Compliance with laws and standards**: all participants in the land access and resettlement negotiations will comply with applicable laws and be guided by agreed best practice standards.
- **Local context**: the approach needs to be firmly rooted in the local socioeconomic context, i.e. ordinary, practical and sustainable.
- **Choice**: offer choice (to extent practically possible).

- **Affordability**: the compensation rates and other mitigation measures negotiated must be affordable to the project.
- **Do not promise what you cannot deliver.**

What preparations are required before starting negotiations?

During the period prior to the commencement of negotiations, the project negotiation team will need to undertake extensive preparations. These need to include the following:

- Undertake **stakeholder identification and analysis**, taking into account the results of a displacement impact assessment. This involves assessing community organisation, power relations and divisions; conflict within and between the communities; the potential effects of external stakeholder groups; project displacement and other impacts; community issues and concerns, posturing, and strengths and weaknesses.
- Develop and analyse potential **negotiation scenarios**.
- Undertake a **risk and opportunity assessment**, i.e. identify key risks for all parties and potential common ground.
- Consider **objectives**, i.e. determine your objectives, anticipate the objectives of the other parties, prioritise your objectives and determine which are critical versus noncritical, and make sure you distinguish between wants and needs.
- **Assess community interests, expectations and likely responses** to the proposed negotiation process, and mitigation and assistance measures.
- Develop an internal **negotiation plan**.
- Put in place a negotiation **work plan and schedule**.
- Determine the **project negotiation team** (roles and responsibilities).
- **Create the right atmosphere**, i.e. set the scene for formal negotiations.
- **Ensure people are truly representative** of communities and other stakeholders.
- Put in place a **grievance mechanism**.
- Determine a suitable **dispute resolution procedure** should negotiations deadlock.
- Determine suitable mechanisms to **record engagement and agreements**.

> No matter how well you plan, communities will have their own views, agendas and approach, and a variety of issues may arise that require a modification of the project's approach

- Determine required **capacity-building**.
- Prepare **presentation materials**.
- Prepare a list of **anticipated key questions and answers**.
- Undertake internal **'strategic planning and dry run' workshops** to ensure the project negotiating team is ready and that there is internal alignment (including on initial mandates).
- Make necessary **administrative arrangements**, such as transport, refreshments and audio-visual equipment. Put in place a **secretariat** to do this.
- Prepare **files for each household**, including asset survey records; a summary of project displacement impacts on the household; a list of anticipated key questions and answers; a record of past discussions with household members and any grievances lodged; an explanation of the project offer to the household; and an explanation of the choices they need to make.
- Put in place clear **feedback loops** internally and for affected communities and other relevant stakeholders.

 Project example

A project in Eastern Europe commenced negotiations without adequate planning. A comprehensive agenda was not prepared, and there was no work plan, schedule or negotiation strategy. As a result, negotiations took place in an uncoordinated manner and lasted much longer than originally anticipated.

 Project example

A project in Latin America undertook extensive prenegotiation planning, including preparation of a detailed negotiation plan, work plan and schedule. A number of planning workshops were held to inform the planning process. As a result, the project was able to conduct negotiations in a structured and well co-ordinated manner.

What is the need for a negotiation plan and what should it include?

All projects dealing with land access and resettlement need an appropriate management plan, e.g. a RAP (resettlement action plan). However, **to plan and manage the negotiation process, the project should also prepare a negotiation plan**. The negotiation plan should have linkages to the overall project SEP (stakeholder engagement plan), while the public RAP should also have a chapter setting out the resettlement-related engagement process.

> A negotiation plan is a crucial tool for helping to plan for negotiations and ensure internal alignment

The critical difference between a negotiation plan and the SEP and RAP is that **the negotiation plan would be a confidential internal project document**, providing a place for the project to develop its negotiation strategy and tactics, and ensure any offer will be fair as well as being affordable for the project. Elements of the negotiation plan would include:

- Determining the **nature of resettlement negotiations**, i.e. group and/or individual
- Determining the **negotiation agenda**: objectives, principles, rules and procedures, substantive resettlement topics, etc.
- Determining the make-up, roles and participants of the **negotiation forum(s)**
- Considering the possibility of **facilitation and mediation mechanisms**
- Developing the **negotiating strategy: opening, fallback and final positions, and tactics**
- Determining **procedural measures** to ensure orderly proceedings

Figure 12.2: Example negotiation plan outline.

1. Introduction
2. Negotiation Participants
3. Negotiation Phases and Topics
4. Lessons Learned, Important Points to Remember and Guiding Principles
5. Key Considerations and Questions
6. Critical and Non-Critical Issues
7. Approach to Negotiations
8. Proposed Negotiations Agenda
9. Project Negotiating Team
10. Project Opening, Fallback and Final Positions
11. Preparations and Steps for Setting the Scene
12. Procedural Issues
13. Information Sharing and Capacity Building Measures
14. Negotiating Style
15. Scenarios
16. Negotiation Work Plan and Schedule
17. Conclusion

Project example

On a project in Eastern Europe, management stated that they were ready for negotiations to be undertaken. However, after being convinced of the need for a formal negotiation plan, the process of developing the plan soon identified significant differences of opinion among senior management and within the negotiation team in relation to key elements of the proposed mitigation packages and the best approach towards negotiations.

Is it really possible to develop a work plan and schedule for a negotiation process?

A detailed work plan and schedule is a necessary tool to manage the negotiation process. Estimating the duration of negotiations is not easy, but doing this early on is useful in order to ensure that the project is being realistic and that the resettlement time-line and overall project schedule are aligned. The duration of negotiations can be partly based on assumptions about:

- The list of topics to be discussed, how long it will take to discuss each topic and reach agreement
- The number of meetings required at group, household and community level
- How often meetings can be held, taking into account factors such as the need to prepare for each meeting, regularly consult with constituents and obtain necessary mandates, taking into account other activities participants are involved in

> Projects often underestimate the time required for negotiations, and are then forced to either delay the overall project or attempt risky and dangerous short cuts during negotiations

 Project example

A project in Africa developed an overall project schedule during the feasibility study stage, but did not develop a detailed work plan and schedule for the resettlement process until later on. At that point, it was realised that resettlement negotiations would take longer than originally anticipated. The detailed resettlement work plan and schedule enabled project management to closely monitor the negotiation process and ensure that other project activities were aligned.

Project example

The resettlement negotiation team at a mining project in Eastern Europe estimated how long was necessary to thoroughly undertake negotiations. However, corporate management informed them that the company was solely reliant on this project and that they had already promised the board of directors, shareholders and the market that land access would be completed and mine construction started by a certain date. Therefore the negotiation team was told to ignore its original negotiations schedule and fast-track the process. The project was unable to conclude negotiations successfully.

What needs to be discussed in the negotiation process?

It is critical that the project is clear about the topics that need to be discussed during negotiations and the manner in which this occurs.

Assuming that the project involves physical and economic displacement, **core substantive negotiation topics** would, depending on the asset types affected, need to include in-kind and monetary compensation and other packages and assistance in relation to:

- **Loss of land**: e.g. urban, agricultural and grazing
- **Loss of livelihoods**: e.g. farming (crops and trees), fishing, commercial enterprises and rental income
- **Loss of structures/buildings**: e.g. houses (primary and secondary residences), residential annexes/other structures, religious, commercial, fishponds, public/institutional
- **Loss of infrastructure**: e.g. water, electrical, roads and drainage, sanitation
- **Loss of access**: e.g. watercourses and sources, forests, roads, pathways
- **Loss of cultural heritage**: e.g. graves/cemeteries, shrines
- **Other components**: e.g. vulnerable persons, tenants, allowances (re-establishment), assistance (transport, loading and unloading), social disarticulation, security of tenure and broader community development
- This would also include discussion on **eligibility criteria and rules**: which people and assets are eligible for what

In addition, the following **other topics and aspects** need to be covered to help ensure a well-structured, informed and smooth negotiation process:

- **Initial overview of topics** that need to be discussed
- Determine the **negotiation forum(s)** and their purpose, structure and membership
- Agree on **negotiation agenda and time-line**
- Required negotiation **capacity-building** for participants
- Overview of the **pre-displacement community baseline and nature and extent of anticipated displacement**
- Key **terms and definitions**
- **Negotiation objectives and guiding principles**
- **Negotiation rules and procedures**
- Overview of **applicable laws and standards**
- Discuss **concept of project having a limited budget** (including what it takes to build a project)
- Agree on **what constitutes success**
- **Implementation process**: procedures for signing off on choices, payment of compensation and transfer and vacation/occupation of land, resettlement site handover and maintenance
- **Monitoring and evaluation**

> Determine which topics are critical for you versus those that are not and undertake a similar assessment for the community: this will help to focus on a win–win outcome

 Project example

A project in Eastern Europe was reviewed by a resettlement expert, who was advised that negotiations with communities were almost complete. After reviewing project displacement impacts and the resettlement action plan, the expert identified a number of outstanding issues and prepared a list of topics still to be discussed. Some months later, on another review trip, the expert was advised that all necessary topics had been discussed and that negotiations were complete. However, once the resettlement site had been constructed and the project announced that it was ready for occupation, the affected community stated that it would not move until a list of outstanding topics were resolved to its satisfaction. This resulted in the move of people being delayed and the project exceeding its resettlement budget to meet remaining community demands at this late stage.

What is the best way to negotiate with people who will be affected by displacement?

Stakeholders can come from the following broad categories:

- **Displaced communities**, including: impacted individuals and households, impacted businesses and institutions, and community representatives
- **Project representatives**
- **Government**, e.g. local representatives
- **Civil society**, including NGOs (non-governmental organisations) and CBOs (community-based organisations)

Exactly who should be involved, and their level of involvement, will depend on the circumstances of each project. In addition to the above negotiations, it will also be necessary to engage with **host communities**, i.e. communities where displaced people will move to.

With respect to displaced people, the basic options are:

- Only individual negotiations with each affected household

or

- Group-level negotiations on certain topics, followed by individual household negotiations on other topics (within the limited parameters of the group-level agreement)

or

- Group-level negotiations on all packages, followed by individual household sign-off (not negotiation, but recording of choices from the range of group-level pre-agreed packages), in accordance with the group-level agreement

---

 Project example

Two projects in Latin America chose to pursue a strategy of undertaking individual household-level negotiations focused on paying monetary compensation for required land. Initially good progress was made in concluding land purchase agreements. However, in both instances, a significant number of landowners refused to sign deals. At the same time, many people started to ask about how other impacts on them would be addressed, in particular long-term livelihood issues. The situation took a turn for the worse when some landowners found out that some people had been paid higher unit rates of compensation for the same types of asset. They therefore demanded to receive top-up payments to ensure equality, and refused to move in the interim, despite having already been paid their agreed compensation.

Figure 12.3: Challenges, risks and benefits of different approaches to negotiation (individual vs. group).

Issue	Solely individual household approach	Group negotiations and household sign-off/limited negotiations
Logistics involved in doing negotiations for large number of households	Even though the number of displaced households related to a project may be relatively small, the team may still find the process challenging = **Result**: lengthy process with a co-ordination challenge.	**Result**: could result in the need for fewer one-on-one meetings with each household.
Framework of transparent and consistent principles and packages	There is no such framework = **Result**: a free-for-all, with people all trying to get the best deal for themselves resulting in different compensation being paid for the same types of affected asset, leading to dissension once people inevitably find out about this.	Such a framework is created before household-level discussions take place further = **Result**: people are treated fairly and consistently.
Compensation rates	Different compensation rates for the same assets = **Result**: lack of fairness and transparency.	Standard compensation rates for same assets = **Result**: fairness and transparency.
Coverage of all aspects of mitigation packages	Certain elements of required mitigation and assistance packages not covered in discussions = **Result**: certain impacts are not discussed and, for example, tenants and vulnerable people are ignored or impacts are not fully addressed.	All elements of impacts and mitigation measures/packages are covered = **Result**: tenants and vulnerable people are dealt with and impacts fully addressed.
Perception of fairness	Each individual thinks they got the best deal = **Result**: when they find out and compare what they got people could be jealous. Could lead to inter- and intra-community distrust as well as distrust towards the project. Could also lead to people reneging on agreements and refusing to move.	Everyone knows they got a fair and good deal = **Result**: when they compare with each other, people and communities are less likely to be jealous, and there will be more community and project trust.
Compliance with good practice	Non-compliance with good practice = **Result**: applicable best practice standards not complied with/corporate commitments not met.	Compliance with good practice = **Result**: best practice standards are complied with/corporate commitments are met.

Issue	Solely individual household approach	Group negotiations and household sign-off/limited negotiations
Differential treatment	People are treated differently where this cannot be justified = **Result**: when they find out and compare what they got people could be jealous. Could lead to inter- and intra-community distrust as well as distrust towards the project. Could also lead to people reneging on agreements and refusing to move.	People are treated the same where they have the same affected assets/impacts, but different packages are agreed where differences exist = **Result**: when compared, people can see that packages are the same or different as appropriate. Nothing is hidden.
Retroactivity	Risk of demands for retroactive adjustments to packages = **Result**: project delays and increased costs.	Demands for retroactive adjustments to packages can be avoided/defended = **Result**: project delays are avoided, and the community supports the project and applies peer pressure to recalcitrant households.
Length of negotiations	Process will be lengthy = **Result**: project delays.	Process will be thorough, but ultimately shorter than solely individual negotiations = **Result**: project can plan with more confidence that agreements reached are sustainable.
Being held to ransom	Project is held to ransom by toughest households = **Result**: project delays and increased costs.	People may still try to hold the project to ransom = **Result**: the project can more easily defend its position and will have a broader/group forum to discuss issues.
Allegations of unfairness and exploitation	Risk of civil society/media allegations of unfairness and exploitation = **Result**: people hold project to ransom.	Less risk of civil society/media allegations of unfairness and exploitation = **Result**: project will be better able to defend its position.
Grievances	Danger of multiple grievances and claims that cloud relationships with communities = **Result**: atmosphere of distrust.	Limit grievances and claims that would cloud relationships with communities = **Result**: the majority of people will have no basis to make claims, and any individuals who do make claims can be dealt with within a clear framework of principles and packages.

Project example

A project in Africa established that its land take requirement would affect thousands of households living in multiple communities. The project determined that the best way to undertake negotiations was through an initial process of joint group-level discussions, followed by each affected household making their choices from a set of defined mitigation measures agreed at group level. The project successfully concluded negotiations and implemented resettlement on time and on budget.

In the authors' experience, there should, based on the issues discussed above, be good reasons not to have only individual household-level discussions. The proposed structure for typically conducting land acquisition and resettlement negotiations is, unless there are good reasons to the contrary, a dual-level structure as follows:

- **Group-level discussions**: at this level there would be discussions aimed at negotiating an agreed framework of, *inter alia*, objectives, guiding principles, standard compensation rates, livelihoods programmes and other assistance measures, as well as implementation and monitoring and evaluation provisions. In broad terms, the purpose of group-level discussions would be to agree on those topics that need to be uniformly applied to all households and people. Group-level discussions will save time and enable a fair and consistent approach across all households, which would be much more difficult to achieve if the same topics have to be discussed with each household.

> Each project must consider its own circumstances carefully and tailor the negotiation process to its requirements

- **Individual household-level discussions and sign-off**: there would be discussions with each household, based on the types of displacement impact suffered by the household in question. However, any discussions and negotiations at this level would take place within the framework of what has been agreed at group level. For example, a household that owns land will not be able to negotiate a different rate per hectare for the same type/quality of land as compared with their neighbour, i.e. they would both get the same compensation rate. Obviously, if their respective land-holdings differ in size then they will get different overall amounts of compensation (based on standard rates for standard asset types). In relation to some topics there would be no negotiations *per se* at household level, but merely households choosing from a range of options that had been developed and agreed at group level. For example, people with land required by the project could elect to receive cash compensation (at fixed rates for each land type) or in-kind physical replacement of some or all of their affected land (this example assumes suitable replacement land can be found).

- **Other meetings**: in addition to the above, there would be community-level meetings and smaller focus group meetings as necessary to ensure that all community members are kept adequately informed.

What about when multiple communities are affected?

Where project land access requirements are extensive, it is often the case that multiple communities will need to be displaced. In these situations, the project needs to consider whether or not to engage with all the communities together or separately.

Factors to consider include:

- The number of communities involved
- The locality and characteristics of each community
- The nature and timing of displacement impacts on each community
- The challenges of holding multiple community-level negotiations
- The risks and opportunities of putting all communities in one forum

What happens if one community opts to boycott a negotiation meeting?

Each situation needs to be individually evaluated. While it is generally preferable to have all communities at each resettlement committee meeting, there may be circumstances where a meeting would be held with representatives of only one community being present.

Each project needs to decide which approach best suits its particular circumstances

Project example

A project in Africa needed to conclude an agreement with more than ten communities, which were dominated by three larger towns. The representatives of each of the major communities made it clear that they had specific issues that concerned them, and that they did not want to negotiate jointly. The project analysed their concerns and established that one large community primarily wanted cash compensation for affected houses. The second community was more interested in in-kind replacement of houses by the project, while the third major community was mainly concerned about land and crops. The project got the communities to agree that it would negotiate building compensation with the first community, in-kind building replacement with the second community, land and crop compensation with the third community, and that all affected people would be bound by what was negotiated. After running all three negotiation processes in parallel, the company was able to conclude group-level negotiations, after which individual households in all affected communities signed off on their choices from a defined set of mitigation measures.

 Project example

Another project in Africa also needed to conclude agreements with multiple communities and thousands of households. However, most affected people lived in the main community. Representatives from the different communities agreed to negotiations in one group forum, with each community's number of representatives being proportional to their number of affected people. Group-level negotiations were successfully undertaken in a resettlement committee, followed by individual household-level sign-off from a set of defined mitigation packages and options.

What is the best way to structure group negotiations?

There are a range of different options, each with a multitude of potential permutations. These include the following:

- **Resettlement committee**: a forum consisting of representatives of the project, affected communities, relevant government agencies and other relevant stakeholders, as appropriate. This is where agreements are negotiated.

- **Subcommittees**: if the scope of the negotiating agenda and project circumstances warrant it, one can make use of subcommittees of the main committee to investigate and discuss certain specific issues, before bringing them back to the main committee for final deliberations. This would consist of smaller groups of resettlement committee representatives to whom authority is delegated to help expedite negotiations, while ensuring they are thorough and fully participatory. **One can use two types of subcommittee**:
  - Limited duration type: review, provide input and achieve preliminary consensus before presenting to the main committee
  - Continuous type: for the duration of the negotiation and implementation phases

Subcommittees would often work in parallel with each other and the main committee. Individual subcommittees could be formed to deal with issues such as replacement land and resettlement sites; resettlement site layouts, public facilities and infrastructure; residential plots, housing and other structures; compensation rates and eligibility criteria; livelihoods and community development; and cultural heritage, vulnerable persons and other issues.

Figure 12.4: Example structure for negotiations.

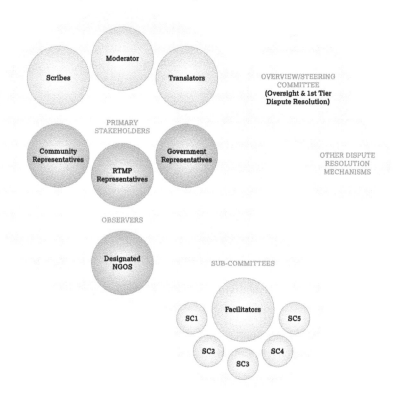

- **Resettlement steering committee or advisory group**: depending on the scale of resettlement, it may be useful to establish, in addition to a resettlement committee, a steering or oversight committee to help facilitate the process and broker deadlocks; and/or an advisory group to help with discussions by providing expertise:
  - **Steering committee**. Members would be chosen because of their experience and reputation. A key requirement would be that the members are perceived by communities and the project as being neutral and unbiased. Members would commit to work together jointly to help facilitate the process and broker deadlocks on topics referred to them by, for example, the chairperson of the main resettlement committee. The steering or oversight committee would provide broad oversight of the resettlement process, and would be briefed regularly on the progress of resettlement negotiations.
  - **Advisory committee**. Such a committee could be formed in addition to a steering committee. One example is an expert panel consisting of independent experts formed by a project to ensure that the people responsible for planning resettlement do this properly and in accordance with the appropriate standards and requirements. Members would be chosen because of their experience and reputation (typically people who have successfully planned, negotiated and implemented resettlement on other projects). The advisory committee would not have a direct role in the negotiation process, but would be there to advise the project on how to undertake negotiations.

> Each project needs to consider its particular circumstances and choose the negotiation structure that is best suited for its requirements

- Important positions to support these structures could, as appropriate, include the following:
  - A neutral **chairperson/moderator**: to chair all meetings of the resettlement committee and ensure they are conducted smoothly and in a manner conducive to enabling an agreement to be reached.
  - An independent **facilitator**: to facilitate on issues by providing the parties with a structure and process for solving their issues and reaching consensus, including finding ways to enable the parties to listen more to each other, consider each other's points of view, and ways to find common ground.
  - An independent **mediator**: to help the parties deal with the particular conflict that they have been unable to resolve, such as by considering the issue from all angles, explaining issues to the parties, helping the parties to create their own solutions, suggesting their own solutions where appropriate and necessary.

Project example

Realising the magnitude of its land take requirement and the extent of resettlement involved, a project in Africa determined that there was a high chance of the need for outside support, no matter how well it conducted negotiations. To address this, the project suggested putting in place a number of supporting structures and roles, and got the affected communities to agree to this. All resettlement committee meetings were chaired by a respected ex-FIFA football referee. In addition, a steering committee was formed, chaired by a senior regional government official who was also respected by all parties. When negotiations with one community could not be concluded in the resettlement committee, outstanding matters were referred to the steering committee which managed to broker a mutually acceptable agreement.

 Project example

A project in Latin America established a well-staffed and resourced resettlement team. However, it was felt that the scope of the resettlement challenge warranted additional expertise and support. Accordingly, the project put in place two additional structures, namely an internal panel of experts (consisting of people from elsewhere in the company with relevant experience) and an external panel of experts (made up of three independent internationally recognised resettlement experts) to provide oversight and advice. In addition, the project brought in a locally acceptable facilitator.

What should be the make-up of the project negotiation team?

The project needs a negotiation team that includes following characteristics:

- Representatives who have the **authority** and will be recognised by the communities as capable of discussing and reaching agreements
- People with the requisite **skills and experience** (resettlement technical expertise and negotiation expertise)
- People **capable of playing the necessary roles** during the negotiating process
- Good **knowledge** of the communities; the project's proposed land access and resettlement plan and packages; and the project's negotiation plan (strategy and tactics)

- Good **planning and organisational abilities**
- **Credibility** with community counterparts
- Good **interpersonal communication skills**, including good listening skills, presentational skills, sensitivity to counterparts' concerns and interests, and the ability to read moods and body language
- Hard **negotiating skills** coupled with flexibility and willingness to explore new ideas and alternative solutions (and the ability to know when to be firm or flexible)
- Ability to **work well under pressure** and ensure project objectives are met
- **Patience**
- A **win–win orientation**, enabling all parties to walk away feeling satisfied that they have achieved a good deal

There will need to be a 'front room' team and a 'back room' team:

- A **'front room' team** consisting of a core group of company personnel made up of:
  - Resettlement committee representatives who will negotiate on behalf of the project
  - Household-level community relations personnel
  - Other senior project management who will attend meetings periodically, depending on the topics under discussion
  - Technical experts who will periodically attend meetings to present and advise on specialist topics
- A **'back room' team** consisting of:
  - Senior management who will be responsible for giving mandates to the negotiation team
  - Specialist land access and resettlement consultants

There will necessarily be overlaps between the front and back room teams.

For face to face negotiations, **a well-structured project negotiation team requires a mix of positions** (with some of these overlapping), for example:

- **Team leader/lead negotiator**: leads and orchestrates the team
- **Good guy**: expresses sympathy and understanding for the other side and puts them at ease; suggests ways to resolve issues
- **Bad guy**: counters and undermines the other side's arguments and says the tough things that have to be said
- **Observer**: watches the other side during deliberations, such as to see whether they are listening, what their responses are, who is being convinced and who not, what points are hitting home and what tactics are working
- **Sweeper**: ensures that all agenda items are covered and that the necessary detail is not forgotten on each core topic; makes sure the negotiations do not go off-track

The exact make-up of the team will depend on project circumstances and resources, and it is sometimes possible for one person to cover more than one role/position. It is also tactically possible and sometimes useful for people to change positions and evolve over time.

Factors that require careful consideration when deciding on the make-up of the negotiation team is the balance between:

- **National and expatriate personnel**: there is sometimes the perception that expatriates are softer during negotiations. There is also sometimes the perception that expatriates are less understanding and perceptive, but this is not always that case when it comes to a comparison between expatriates and nationals from 'the big city'. Expatriates are typically less attuned to local conditions, but they may also be better able to be objective and more strategic about the negotiation process. Sometimes local people may also be more comfortable negotiating with an 'outsider', who they may see as more impartial.

> A properly structured and carefully chosen project negotiation team is a prerequisite for successful negotiations

- **Local staff and other nationals from elsewhere in the country**: there is sometimes the fear that if local staff form part of the main project negotiating team there will be a risk of the project's negotiation plan being divulged, due to their links to impacted people. It is also sometimes the case that nationals from elsewhere, for example 'the big city', are perceived as being arrogant and insensitive to local customs and requirements.

 Project example

A project in Africa was faced with a situation where it wanted to put in place a core negotiation team of no more than four people. A larger team was considered to be potentially intimidating for the affected communities. The project was acutely aware of national sensitivities about the use of local staff, but also wanted to ensure that issues such as confidentiality were addressed. There was also a lack of significant in-country resettlement experience. Accordingly, the project formed a four-person team consisting of a company expatriate employee with negotiation experience (who led the team), an ex-local government official who had held senior positions in the local administration and was well respected by all parties (they played the role of a senior negotiator who would take firm but fair stances), another national from the region with an impeccable reputation for honesty and hard work (who played the role of observer and kept records of proceedings), and an expatriate with urban planning experience necessary for the resettlement exercise. Other personnel with suitable expertise were brought in on an ad hoc basis as required.

Each project will have different circumstances and considerations, but it is the authors' experience that the project negotiation team should have a careful mix of national and expatriate personnel. The more important issue is whether people have the requisite negotiations skills and experience.

 Project example

A project in Latin America was at the exploration stage, but decided to start acquiring land because it was felt that this would take a long time and an early start would help to complete the exercise in a timely manner. The only people available to undertake land acquisition at this stage was the site geology department. Hence, the expatriate chief geologist and two national geologists, who had no relevant experience, commenced land acquisition without a detailed social baseline and impact assessment being undertaken. People were paid cash compensation, with rates and amounts being determined on an ad hoc basis, largely dependent on how hard landowners chose to negotiate and the location and importance of their land relative to planned project infrastructure. Despite making significant initial progress in acquiring land, the process ran into problems once 'low hanging fruit' had been picked. The project then decided to bring in additional experienced resources and establish a community relations team to take over the process. However, by then the manner in which people had been engaged and compensated had created an environment of mistrust between communities and the project.

Language and cultural considerations

Land access and resettlement is often undertaken by foreign companies. This poses the risk of language and cultural misunderstandings, which can negatively impact on the negotiation and broader stakeholder engagement process. Measures to take to address this include:

- Determining the language preferences and cultural norms and sensitivities of communities and other stakeholders (and capacity-building of all the parties at the outset of negotiations)
- Ensuring the negotiation team has the necessary mix of language skills
- Ensuring expert translators are available
- Ensuring the mode of recording discussions and agreements is appropriate

How does a project ensure that community representatives are truly representative?

It is obviously up to communities to decide who they wish to have representing them. However, if the project is concerned about the adequacy of this representation and its potentially negative impact on the outcome of negotiations, then the following steps may be helpful:

- Provision of a list of unbiased suggested key criteria that the community negotiation team should contain/meet in order to ensure it can fully represent its constituents
- Suggest the addition of representatives who have skills or experience on specific topics, such as a suitable vulnerable person
- Provision of capacity-building measures to develop the capacity of existing representatives
- The project should make every possible effort to ensure that women and vulnerable households are represented
- Agree that the project can observe elections or nominations for community representatives
- Verify as much as possible that the communities agree on the chosen representatives

Given the difficulty in getting some communities to record who represents them in writing, this will need to be discussed with the communities to find an acceptable way of doing so, such as a community meeting.

 Project example

A project in Africa required the resettlement of thousands of people who lived in a number of communities of different sizes and demographic make-ups. The communities were characterised by differing mixes of long-time local inhabitants, newcomers (who had lived in the area for differing periods, with some as long as 20 years but who were still considered as outsiders), people from neighbouring countries, and nomadic people who spent part of the year in the area. As a result of these factors, the project wanted to be certain that each community, and the elements therein, were adequately represented in the resettlement committee. In order to determine this, the project considered the viability of holding secret ballots in each community, but this was deemed to be unsuitable in the circumstances. The project therefore engaged with the different elements of the communities, and consulted with key informants and knowledgeable government officials to obtain their views on the existing make-up of the resettlement committee. General meetings were then held with the inhabitants of each community where they were asked to confirm the suitability of their representatives. Each representative was confirmed by public acclaim.

Figure 12.5: A negotiation forum in Africa.

Should issues be discussed as part of one comprehensive package, or separately?

Some projects conduct land access and resettlement negotiations in a piecemeal fashion, using lawyers first to try to purchase land as a purely compensation-oriented commercial transaction, and then using their community relations staff to subsequently discuss other resettlement issues such as livelihood restoration.

Compensation rates for land, trees, crops and other affected assets are very important issues to be discussed with project-affected persons. However, these topics are only part of the broader set of topics that must be discussed in order to ensure that all impacts and issues related to land access and resettlement are addressed in a manner that meets best practice standards and enables comprehensive and effective agreement(s) to be concluded.

> There needs to be very good reasons for conducting negotiations on a piecemeal basis

For the above reasons, the authors typically recommend that all topics are discussed as part of a comprehensive package, i.e. offering people a **total value proposition** (Figure 12.6), instead of undertaking piecemeal discussions where compensation rates are first agreed before other topics such as livelihoods programmes are discussed. One advantage of this is that people are aware of the project offer before they judge whether compensation rates are adequate. However, each project will need to consider what makes sense in its circumstances.

Figure 12.6: A total value proposition.

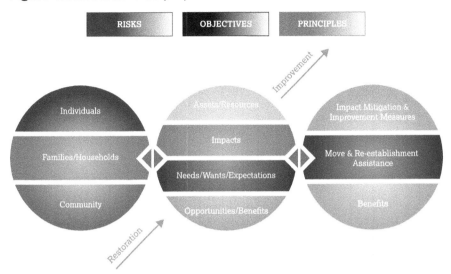

 Project example

In Latin America, a project chose to purchase land using a law firm on what it thought was a willing buyer/willing seller basis, with owners being paid cash for their land and immovable assets. However, it transpired that there were a number of tenants who were impacted and nothing had been done about them. In addition, having signed deals to sell their land and after receiving cash payments, many landowners started to raise questions about the impact of moving on their future livelihoods. The project also determined that it needed to undertake any land acquisition in compliance with IFC standards. At this point, despite having no resettlement action plan, the project instructed its community relations department to discuss livelihoods measures with affected people. It became painfully clear to the project that it should have undertaken more comprehensive and co-ordinated planning for land access and resettlement, that negotiations should have occurred in a more co-ordinated manner, with people being offered packages that addressed all displacement impacts, and that cash compensation offered was too high in some instances (with some people receiving more than others and this causing a lot of dissension within communities).

Figure 12.7: Example of a negotiations agenda (where there is only economic displacement).

Topics	Resettlement committee	Household level	Community level
Setting the Scene			
Overview of topics that need to be discussed	Present, discuss and agree	X	Explain
Determine negotiation forum(s) and their purpose, structure and membership	Present, discuss and agree (but explain group level is essential)	Explain	Explain
Agree on negotiation agenda and time-line	Present, discuss and agree	Explain	Explain
Required negotiation capacity-building	Present, discuss and agree	X	X
Overview of the pre-displacement community baseline and extent of anticipated displacement	Present	Explain (only as applies to each household)	X
Key terms and definitions	Present and explain	Explain as necessary	X
Negotiation objectives and guiding principles	Present, discuss and agree	Explain	Explain
Negotiation rules and procedures	Present, discuss and agree	Explain	Explain
Overview of applicable laws and standards	Present and explain	Explain as necessary	Explain
Discuss concept of limited budget	Explain	Explain	Explain
Agree on what constitutes success	Discuss and agree	Explain	Explain

Negotiating the packages

Compensation rates for land (including valuation methodology)/replacement land programmes	Present, discuss and agree (all at same time)	Explain, then household to accept or refuse offer based on resettlement committee rates x their assets	Explain
Livelihoods programmes	Present, discuss and agree	Explain, then household to choose from options	Explain
Other displacement impacts, e.g. loss of access to roads and pathways, cultural heritage, etc.	Present and explain	Explain	Explain
Community development programmes	Present, discuss and agree	Explain	Explain
Assistance for vulnerable persons/households	Present, discuss and agree	Explain	Explain
Other assistance measures/project benefits	Present, discuss and agree	Explain	Explain
Which people and assets are eligible for compensation/ programmes/assistance	Present and explain	Explain	Explain

Implementation issues

Procedures for signing off on choices, payment of compensation, transfer and vacation	Present, discuss and agree	Explain	Explain
Monitoring and evaluation	Present, discuss and agree	Explain	Explain
Recording agreements	Either in stages or agreement at end	Sign-off by household representatives	

Which topics should be negotiated (agreed) versus merely consulted on (information and discussion), and in what sequence?

Comments and suggestions in this regard are:

- Structure the agenda to ensure a logical sequence that enables all necessary topics to be discussed in an order that builds goodwill, trust and confidence in the process
- First discuss topics that will set the scene before immediately getting into discussions on substantive/compensation/mitigation-related issues
- Start with uncontroversial general points
- Stress the need for agreement from the outset
- Get agreement on certain topics early on can help to achieve this, i.e. 'quick wins'
- Bear in mind that each project setting is different, and hence no fixed sequence is necessarily best for each project

It is critical to carefully structure the negotiation process to maximise the chances of reaching implementable agreements

An example of a negotiations agenda is set out in Figure 12.7.

 Project example

At a project in Latin America, investigations showed that past interactions with mining companies had made communities in the concession area nervous about the intentions of the project proponent. It was clear that people who would need to be resettled were deeply attached to their land and were not simply interested in compensation issues. The project therefore started the negotiations with an extensive period of initial discussions that did not talk about compensation and other mitigation measures. Community representatives were asked to explain their concerns in detail and the project made it clear that it was sensitive to these concerns. Thereafter, discussions on mitigation measures took place in a holistic manner, with all impacts being considered and the communities being offered a total value proposition.

How to get the process started?

It is critical to set the right scene for negotiations, by ensuring the following:

Ensuring core knowledge

At the outset, and during the negotiation process, the project needs to help ensure that project, community, government and other relevant stakeholders have sufficient knowledge about key topics that form part of setting the scene for discussions on compensation rates and other mitigation measures. Topics could include:

- Overview of the pre-displacement community baseline and extent of anticipated displacement
- Key terms and definitions
- Negotiation objectives and guiding principles
- Negotiation rules and procedures
- Overview of applicable laws and standards
- Concept of project having a limited budget (including what it takes to build a project)
- What constitutes success?

Capacity-building will also be required to help ensure that people have the skills to participate fully in proceedings. Depending on the project, elements of capacity-building could include:

- Ensuring the project land access department has the necessary resources to properly prepare for and undertake the negotiation process
- Ensuring communities understand the importance of selecting suitable representatives and what sorts of attribute are desirable
- Providing an explanation of the key tasks of a representative during the negotiation process, and ensuring representatives understand their respective roles and the attributes required, including:
  - Handling the unexpected
  - Dealing with disagreements
  - How to find common ground
  - The importance of attending all designated meetings
  - The importance of proper comportment (including cultural sensitivity)
  - How community representatives should feed back to their communities/ constituents

Relationship building

The project negotiation team should focus not simply on achieving agreement on mitigation measures, but also on establishing the basis for successful implementation of the land access and resettlement process and for positive long-term relationships with affected communities: **signing a resettlement agreement is only the beginning of the process of creating value for the project and communities.** The focus on agreements that can be successfully implemented will require that the project negotiators ensure that negotiations are conducted in a manner which will maintain goodwill and collaboration throughout the land acquisition and resettlement process. Success will depend on the extent to which the project team:

> The ultimate product of negotiations will not be a formal resettlement agreement—it will be community confidence in project willingness to meet commitments and the strength of relationships developed through the negotiation process

- Shows respect for its community counterparts
- Shares information
- Is open to exploring a range of measures which address community interests, needs and concerns
- Works to achieve outcomes which deliver mutual benefits to the project and the displaced people

Obviously, success will not be possible if community and government representatives do not play their parts in the process. However, it is necessary that the company negotiation team takes a lead in the process.

Ensuring an appropriate atmosphere

It is important to ensure that an atmosphere is in place that is open and transparent, friendly and trusting, focused on the agenda, designed to ensure attendance, aimed at creating common ground, and designed to conclude negotiations to meet the overall project schedule and budget.

There are numerous possible ways to help ensure the right atmosphere, for example:

> Even if they sign formal agreements, communities are unlikely to fully support implementation if they feel negotiations were flawed, their interests were inadequately addressed or the outcomes were inequitable

- Creating an appropriately structured negotiation process and forum
- Locating resettlement committee and other meetings at appropriate venues, such as in the community; at an independent venue, such as, if there are multiple communities, alternating meetings between the communities; or at company facilities

- Ensuring appropriate and clear role delineation
- Optimising the meeting venue, such as table layout, seating arrangements, caucus facilities (a place where people can confidentially discuss issues before rejoining the main meeting), and lighting and ventilation
- Ensuring people are aware of and follow the correct protocols
- Ensuring there is a clear and agreed negotiations agenda and schedule
- Ensuring there are clear negotiating objectives, guiding principles, rules and procedures
- Ensuring communications are optimised, such as clear and simple project presentations use of appropriate presentation tools (e.g. models), appropriate recording of proceedings, use of appropriate language(s), clear recording of agreements reached, joint public communications, minimisation of nuisance factors (e.g. ban use of mobile phones during meetings), and ensuring meeting session and overall times are not too long

> It is essential to create an atmosphere conducive for negotiations instead of immediately rushing into substantive discussions

- Provision of refreshments
- Provision of transport assistance, where necessary and appropriate
- Ensuring adequate and timely dispute resolution mechanisms are in place

 Project example

A project in Africa developed a work plan and schedule for its resettlement negotiations and realised that the process was likely to take as long as a year or more. This would entail significant time, effort and cost on the part of community and government representatives. Despite initial reluctance due to concerns about collusion and bribery, the project agreed to pay community and government representatives a daily sitting allowance for each meeting they attended. Community members and senior government officials were made aware of this and the reasons were carefully explained. In addition, meetings were structured so that they were punctuated by a lunch break during which food was served in a separate room and the representatives of the various parties were able to circulate in an informal manner. The project also helped to arrange, or pay for, transport and accommodation, as necessary. This resulted in a high regular turnout for meetings of the resettlement committee.

How does a project ensure negotiation meetings are properly run?

Rules and procedures cannot be bureaucratic, so they should be limited to simple and essential rules and procedures necessary to ensure the smooth operation of the process. Issues that require clear rules and procedures include the quorum for meetings, speaking at meetings, how decisions will be made, recording proceedings and decisions, dispute resolution and public statements.

Meetings of the resettlement forum need to be conducted in accordance with a set of agreed rules and procedures

 Project example

A project in Africa had previously conducted successful resettlement negotiations but, after reflecting on lessons learned from its initial land take process, had concluded that negotiations for a second land take needed to be improved and undertaken in a more structured manner. Accordingly, the project developed a formal set of rules and procedures to govern resettlement committee discussions. These included issues such as the quorum for meetings, when people could speak at meetings, how decisions would be made, how proceedings and decisions would be made, and dispute resolution mechanisms. Community and government representatives reviewed the draft rules and proposed some changes. The final version was agreed on and formed the basis for resettlement negotiations related to land takes for the next two project expansion phases.

Once negotiations have commenced, what is the process?

Undertaking negotiations involves a process of setting the scene, proposal, counterproposal, establishing positions and reaching agreement. During this, the parties will share information, pursue their respective strategies, and employ a variety of tactics and ploys.

Is there a one-size-fits-all negotiating style?

The negotiation style adopted by the project negotiation team will influence the attitudes of community and government representatives and help shape both the outcome of negotiations and the project's longer-term community relations.

The project needs to define its preferred negotiations style, to recognise the style adopted by community representatives, and to be aware of any changes that occur or need to occur during the course of negotiations. In general terms, we may identify **five styles**:

- **Competitive**: a win–lose approach which views negotiations as a zero-sum game, unlikely to achieve equitable outcomes which promote communities' future wellbeing and can be potentially destructive of longer-term relationships.

- **Accommodative**: characterised by a desire to please others at the expense of one's own interests, and unlikely to achieve equitable outcomes. An accommodative approach is likely to create a false impression of the company's position and unrealistic community expectations of benefits and concessions.

- **Avoidance**: defined by avoidance of difficult or sensitive issues, agreements may be based on incomplete understanding of parties' interests and positions, thereby creating problems for future implementation.

- **Compromise**: splitting the difference, likely to mean that both sides achieve suboptimal outcomes and neither is committed to implementing the agreements reached.

- **Collaborative**: characterised by seeking to achieve win–win outcomes, a desire to satisfy all interests and a willingness to explore openly the full range of opportunities and possible solutions. The collaborative approach may be more, or may appear to be more, time-consuming and demand input from a number of participants, but it is most likely to produce sustainable agreements and positive long-term relationships.

The collaborative approach will, in general, be most appropriate for resettlement negotiations (bearing in mind that elements of other approaches may need to be used from time to time as part of the overall negotiating strategy and tactics).

To be a good negotiator, bear in mind the following:

- **Keep calm** at all times
- **Be organised**
- **Put yourself in their shoes**
- **Aim for a win–win outcome**: if the agreement is not reasonable for all parties then it runs the risk of not being implementable
- Remember that **there are alternatives in every situation**

It is important to explicitly define a preferred negotiations style

- **Be strategic**: avoid piecemeal negotiations and remember the big picture and what is critical for the project
- **Be tactical**
- **Be realistic** about the relative bargaining strengths of the parties
- **Do not take things personally**
- **Never be arrogant**
- **Never be a push over**
- Understand the **difference between being assertive and aggressive**
- Be **polite but persistent**
- Be **magnanimous** when appropriate
- **Teamwork**

 Project example

A project in Eastern Europe was characterised by uncoordinated planning for resettlement negotiations, including inadequate preparation for resettlement committee meetings. Even though the project resettlement team leader was designated as the chairperson for each meeting, he allowed community representatives to dominate proceedings, raise issues that were not part of the agreed agenda, and conclude agreements on issues of importance to the community while failing to obtain reciprocal agreement on issues important to the project. This approach constituted an extreme form of the accommodative approach mentioned above. It resulted in the negotiation process taking significantly longer than originally envisaged, particularly as the community felt that the project would accede to new demands if they just pushed hard enough, and the cost of mitigation measures being much higher than had been originally budgeted for.

How does a project create a good atmosphere?

In this context, the project negotiation team should **consider the following**:

- **Listen** to what people say, how they say it and observe non-verbal signals (body language)
- Bear in mind **cultural differences**
- In order to help create the right mood at the outset, the project needs to **think carefully about how it starts and conducts negotiations**

- Begin with **general points that are not controversial**
- **Set the scene** with necessary 'foundation' information
- **Stress the need and desire for agreement** from the outset
- **Think carefully about your own way of speaking and acting** (including body language)

> Negotiating is not just about talking: it is about listening, observing and judging the mood

Who should make the first proposal?

As the project is seeking to obtain land access, it is typical for the project to open negotiations with a proposal (after first setting the scene). However, it is important to consider whether it may rather be better first to ask the community to tell the project about their issues, concerns, needs and wants, and even to ask them to make their proposal first.

There may be risks and advantages to asking the community to make a proposal first, so each situation needs to be considered on its merits.

A critical issue to decide on is the extent to which the project wishes to batch or link substantive topics which are related, such as mitigation packages.

Three generic options are, in principle, available:

1. Each substantive topic, such as crop compensation, is discussed and agreed on separately
2. Substantive topics are batched into related or key issues and discussed as a package, i.e. agreement is reached on them together
3. All substantive topics are discussed as one package, with agreements on individual topics being made on a conditional basis, pending final agreement on the whole package

Each project will need to carefully consider its situation and what makes the most sense for it. However, there are typically risks associated with the first and second options, such as the first leading to a piecemeal approach where the project may give on one topic without getting something in return, while the second runs the risk of effectively leaving all the issues on the table until the very end.

Factors to take into account when making proposals and counterproposals include:

- **Do not make statements indicating your position is immovable**, unless you are sure it is, i.e. keep your options open initially to leave room for manoeuvre
- **Do not make your opening offer so extreme that you will lose face when you compromise later on**: at the same time, consider if it makes sense to make your initial offer unrealistic so that the community feels it got you to compromise later on

- **Get something in return**: link your offer to something the community must give/agree to in return
- **Give the community a range of options** where possible and appropriate
- **Do not use the word 'never'**
- **Do not give too much away too early**
- Think carefully about how your proposal will sound, taking into account **language/translation and cultural considerations/differences**
- **Explain underlying assumptions** on which any proposal/counterproposal is based

 Project example

A project in Africa looked at all the topics that needed to be discussed with affected communities. Based on detailed data about the existing assets of affected people and the project's estimate of what mitigation measures would be necessary, a budget estimate of the cost of resettlement was prepared. Analysis showed which mitigation measures were the most costly 'big ticket' items. The project then developed a negotiation agenda that, after setting the scene with preparatory topics, initially focused on the big ticket items. The logic was that the project needed to know first whether agreement could be reached on these significant items, and what the cost would be, before discussing other elements of the mitigation packages. The project negotiation team was careful to link certain issues to each other, thereby enabling agreement on certain topics to be conditional on agreement on other critical topics.

Factors to consider in relation to community proposals and counterproposals:

- **Listen/listen/listen**
- **Wait for the other party to finish** before you respond
- Give proposals and counterproposals from the community (and government suggestions) **due consideration** and be seen to do so (even if your immediate desired reaction is to reject them)
- **Do not feel pressured to respond immediately**: buy time if necessary
- **The community will carefully watch your response**: be neutral until you are sure what reaction you want to show
- **Ask for clarifications** when necessary
- **Summarise the community proposal/counterproposal as you understand it,** in order to confirm the community is clear what it means and be clear you understand the proposal/counterproposal

Other factors to consider:

- **Do not try to pin the community down to a fixed position too early**, i.e. they may need some room to manoeuvre initially
- **Do not try to be too clever**, i.e. 'a smart Alec'
- **Be willing to modify your strategy and proposals** if necessary, for example if you can see a viable compromise
- **Communities typically want to know that they have 'made the project jump through some hoops'**, i.e. that there has been a true negotiation with real give and take
- **Think carefully about the timing of all your actions**
- **Look for common ground** instead of just differences in positions
- **Analyse differences** to see where there is scope for compromise based on critical and noncritical issues
- **Do not just give things away**: when making concessions, make it clear this is costly to you and get something in return

How to determine a project's opening, fallback and final positions?

Opening positions

Gauging what an appropriate opening offer is, in relation to each mitigation measure and other elements of proposed packages, will depend on a number of factors:

- The resources available to the project
- The time available for negotiations
- The level of trust between the parties
- The relative strength of the negotiating positions of the parties
- How many topics/elements of the package are bundled together for the opening offer
- To what extent the communities are likely to haggle and want to feel they have squeezed a good deal from the project

Consider your opening, fallback and final positions before negotiations commence, but be willing to adjust them during discussions, if necessary

Fallback positions

The nature and number of fallbacks required will depend on the individual circumstances of the project. A process of give and take is generally desirable and the project will therefore need to be seen to be willing to take into account community feedback to initial offers. Moreover, no matter how well project prepares, it is typically difficult to anticipate all issues and angles communities will raise. Fallbacks will need to be carefully considered and based on the initial feedback on the different elements of the packages.

Final positions

The factors discussed above will come into play again. Be sure you mean it when you say your offer is final: having to backtrack will make you look vulnerable. When considering the cost of a final position, bear in mind the hidden costs of a delay in concluding negotiations, such as equipment standby time.

What tactics and ploys are utilised in negotiations?

Tactics and ploys are typically designed to shift the emphasis, distract or manipulate, and are an inevitable and generally useful part of the negotiation process. There are a wide variety of potential tactics and ploys. Things to bear in mind include:

> An overuse of tactics that constantly 'score points off the opposition' will undermine the formation of a longer-term bond with your development partners

- Not all tactics have to be short-term/immediate actions or responses, e.g. a good long-term tactic (or rather measure) may be to develop good relations between, for example, lead negotiators or other members of the respective negotiating teams, so that these provide 'back channels' through which discussions can be held in support of the overall formal negotiating process
- **Tactics can be positive or negative**
- **Think carefully about the appropriateness and timing of all your actions**: never undermine the dignity of another party
- **Typically wait for the other party to finish before you respond**: think carefully before choosing to interrupt
- **Do not make community and government representatives look foolish**: losing face can be particularly problematic in some cultures
- **Use humour carefully and only when you are certain it is appropriate**
- **Be wary of short-term gains from the use of tactics, but long-term damage** to the overall negotiation process

Project example

A project in Africa had two separate ore-bodies which could be accessed to expand the existing mine. One ore-body was the preferred first expansion target due to its higher grade and lower strip ratio (although accessing both ore-bodies would require the displacement of a community). However, the project was not certain whether it could reach agreement with the community located on the preferred ore-body. Therefore, it commenced separate but parallel negotiations with both communities, and made it clear that it would start resettling the first community that it could reach agreement with, and that this community could then have priority preference for employment and procurement opportunities related to the initial mine expansion. While negotiations with the community located on the preferred ore-body took a long time, negotiations with the second community were successfully concluded in a quicker time-frame, thereby enabling mine expansion to go ahead, albeit in a less attractive area, while also taking the pressure off negotiations with the other community. Negotiations with the remaining community were eventually concluded successfully, thereby enabling a seamless transition from the first to the second expansion phase.

Think carefully before you respond to tactics and ploys:

- Is the other party using tactics or do their actions show underlying vulnerability, confusion, indecision or a genuine feeling of unhappiness?
- Is the other party unified or are there differences among their negotiating team or constituents?
- What tactics are appropriate and when?
- Only engage in arguments that will be constructive.
- The appropriate response will depend on the situation and circumstances at the time.

 Project example

During negotiations on a project in Australasia, community representatives demanded that the project fire one of its representatives. On investigation, the project found that there were no good grounds for the firing of its representative, and that the real reason was that the community representatives considered him to be a good and firm negotiator with whom they could not just get their way as they wished. The project therefore refused to fire its negotiator. After a short impasse when the community representatives threatened to boycott the negotiations, they relented once they saw the project would not budge, and the negotiation process was able to continue.

How to ensure community representatives are really feeding back to communities?

A key issue in negotiations is the need to ensure that community representatives are feeding back information to their constituents, that the information is an accurate record of what has transpired in negotiations, and that they also ensure the communities' opinions and concerns are reflected in the negotiation process.

In reality, community representatives are often very reluctant to feed back to their communities, as they will often feel that their representative should have won more concessions from the company, no matter what package is being offered. Representing the community can therefore be a thankless task. In some cases, representatives may be accused of collusion or corruption.

Projects need to consider ways in which they can meaningfully assist community representatives in feeding back on negotiations, and ensuring they have received inputs from the community. These may include:

- Capacity-building of community representatives
- Agreeing on joint statements and how information will be disclosed when agreeing guiding principles for the negotiations
- Undertaking joint public meetings and other briefings in the community, to support representatives in providing feedback, supporting them with technical information and ensuring consistent messages from both community representatives and the project

 Project example

A project in Africa undertook extensive capacity-building of community representatives, including university seminars on valuation methods, to ensure they could both negotiate effectively and discuss technical issues with their constituents with confidence. A technical expert was also employed by the project on the community's behalf to advise them and represent their interests. The company also arranged a series of joint feedback sessions in the communities during the negotiations, attended by both project and community representatives.

How do the negotiations move towards agreement?

After initial proposals and counterproposals have been made and the parties have provided each other with a good understanding of their basic positions, i.e. where they are coming from, their key issues and what they want, **the negotiation process will need to move towards reaching agreement on topics**. To do this, **the following steps and actions are/may be necessary**:

- **Extensive discussion** about the underlying facts and assumptions, as well as the merits and demerits of each other's positions
- As intensive debate takes place, it is easy for parties to become tired, frustrated, angry and pressured, leading to emotional outbursts and the risk of deadlock or breakup: this requires **calmness and efforts to defuse situations that may arise**
- **Continually analyse the other party**, for example disaggregating their negation team and endeavouring to distinguish between real positions, hidden agendas and posturing
- **Regularly summarise the topics and issues on which there is already agreement**
- Seek to **re-characterise and rephrase areas of disagreement** so that deadlock does not arise
- **Use breaks, facilitators or mediators, as appropriate** (but remember that both parties need to agree)

 Project example

On a project in Africa, the negotiation venue was carefully chosen to ensure that there were places where refreshments and meals could be provided, informal discussions could take place, and the respective negotiation teams could separately and confidentially meet to deliberate on issues. A particular room was designated as the caucus room, and the chairperson (an ex-FIFA referee) would, to the amusement of all, signal a 'yellow card' when he felt one of the parties needed time to cool down or reflect on issues raised or offers made by the other party. The project negotiation team sometimes asked for a 'yellow card' so that it could use the caucus room to deliberate before responding to community proposals or making its counterproposals.

How to close out the negotiation process?

As one gets towards the end of the process, parties will be feeling fatigued and there is likely to be pressure on both the project and the community to conclude matters, for example:

- Community representatives may be accused by some of their constituents of being too soft and having sold out to the project.
- Project management, faced with longer than anticipated negotiations, may be under pressure from directors, corporate management and shareholders and may, in turn, put pressure on their negotiation team and accuse them of lack of firmness.

In the run-in to concluding negotiations, the project negotiation team therefore needs to take the following steps:

- Carefully review the status of negotiations, i.e.:
  - What topics have been agreed?
  - What topics have not been agreed?
  - What topics still need to be raised and discussed?
  - For outstanding topics: what the positions of the parties are, how close or far apart the parties are, which issues are critical to each party, what scope there is for common ground and compromise (bearing in mind the project's key objectives, time-line, budget and hidden costs)
  - How willing and intent are the project and the community/ies on reaching agreement?
  - What is the relative strength of each party?
  - Is there a real risk of the negotiation process not being successfully concluded, and how this would be handled?
- Determine the best possible strategy and tactics to conclude negotiations (with identified fallback and final positions).
- Ensure that there is clear internal project and corporate understanding of the status of negotiations; the key issues, risks and opportunities; the proposed strategy and tactics; and the time and cost implications of the proposed approach.

When endeavouring to reach final agreement consider the following:

- **Reiterate the overall objectives and guiding principles** that the parties agreed to at the outset, as well as key facts and baseline information.
- Make sure you **discuss outstanding issues for discussion in a sequence that makes the most sense**.
- **How big are the concessions you need to make?** Large concessions may not always be necessary.
- **Consider whether or not it is time to make one comprehensive closing offer** covering all outstanding issues.

- **Make sure you explain the basis of a concession**/climb down from a past position
- **Consider the use of hypothetical proposals/concessions**
- **Get something in return** for concessions made
- Before making any concessions, **make sure the parties are agreed on what has already been agreed**
- All offers and concessions should be linked **to clear conditions and reciprocal actions** by the other party
- **Make sure the other party understands you have limited room to manoeuvre/that this is your genuine final offer**
- **Do not ignore topics/necessary details in order to conclude negotiations**: the devil is in the detail and leaving issues unclear will always come back to haunt you
- **Highlight the risks and consequences of a failure** to reach agreement
- Put in place necessary **measures to create an enabling environment**: for example, change the venue?
- **Carefully consider when to make your final offer**: an offer rejected at one moment may be accepted at another
- **Be careful when calling a proposal 'final'**: are you sure it will be?
- **If a proposal/offer is 'final' use clear, unequivocal language** (verbal and non-verbal from the whole project negotiation team) and make sure you explain why it is final
- **Insist that the other party does not immediately respond**, but takes time to consider your proposals
- **Make sure the community representatives have full authority** to conclude an agreement

Methods for closing negotiations include the following:

- Introducing new facts or ideas even at this late stage
- Making concessions on some points but asking for concessions on others
- Giving the community a choice of two or three alternatives
- Splitting the difference between the parties, such as on a compensation rate
- Introducing new incentives or sanctions
- Emphasising the benefits of the deal
- Showing empathy and sympathy for community negotiators who get jittery at the last moment, while continuing to push for final agreement, such as emphasising

It is critical to remember that a negotiation can only be brought to a successful conclusion when both parties have made concessions that are mutually acceptable

that you have also been under pressure and insisting that they must act honourably

- Letting the other party take the credit for reaching final consensus

Which of these approaches are suitable will need to be considered on a project-by-project basis.

How should agreements be recorded?

Each project is different and the manner in which agreements are recorded will need to be discussed in the resettlement committee, and a culturally and project appropriate but accurate approach adopted.

> Failure to record agreements adequately can lead to disagreements later on about what was agreed

What about when negotiations break down?

Factors and options to consider when negotiations break down include:

- A **cooling-off period** between the parties may be necessary; however, immediate or early steps need to be taken to ensure that the situation does not deteriorate further and become irretrievable
- The project needs to carefully evaluate the **nature and extent of the breakdown**, for example:
  - Is a walkout, for example, proof of a real breakdown or merely a tactic on the part of a community?
  - Do the community representatives really represent the views of the community?
  - Are all community representatives intent on a breakdown?
  - Is the project in any way to blame for the breakdown?
- **Communication between the parties should be restored as soon as possible**, so agree, for example, a cooling-off period and when the parties will next meet
- One needs to consider **how the agreed dispute resolution mechanism is activated**

> Honestly consider if the project is to blame for a breakdown

- A **steering committee, government representative or a respected third party** may be able to play a role
- Make sure that government and other key **stakeholders (including community members) are adequately informed of the project's position**, what its final offer was, what has been agreed and not agreed, and how breakdown occurred

- Do not necessarily allow the community representatives to be the sole mode of communication to the community members
- Do not always insist on an apology for the breakdown if you feel the community representatives caused this: this may be counterproductive in the bigger picture

 Project example

After lengthy negotiations on a project in Africa, agreement was apparently reached on all issues, and a date was set for a formal signing ceremony of the overall resettlement agreement. However, on the designated day, a key community representative suddenly refused to sign the agreement and walked out of the proceedings. The project was unclear on whether this was merely a tactic to extract further concessions, or whether there was an underlying issue of real significance that was preventing the representative signing the agreement. The project referred the matter to the steering committee that was overseeing the negotiations. After a series of meetings at the steering committee, it was ascertained that the representative was willing to sign the agreement, but had wanted to be seen by his constituents to have taken a hard line and to have got the best possible deal from the project. However, he now faced the prospect of losing face if he went ahead and signed an unchanged agreement. In return for a clear commitment that no other demands would be made by the community, the project agreed to small face-saving concessions and the overall agreement was signed by all the representatives.

What about when the project does not have sole responsibility for the project, such as government-managed resettlement?

Where land acquisition and resettlement are the responsibility of government, private-sector projects will need to collaborate with the responsible government agency, to the extent permitted by the agency, to achieve outcomes that are consistent with IFC PS5. However, government agencies can often be sensitive about private-sector involvement, particularly where they are used to utilising expropriation mechanisms.

Projects sometimes therefore face the often challenging task of pushing a reluctant government to undertake a more rigorous stakeholder engagement process while trying to ensure that corporate and lender best practice requirements are met. This often needs careful capacity-building of government, including showing the clear reasons for and benefits of a more open and rigorous approach, as well as satisfying government why this will not create unacceptable precedents for public-sector projects.

 Project example

A project in Africa was taking place in a country with no history of private-sector mine development, and all aspects of land access and resettlement were traditionally undertaken by government. In order to ensure that the land access and resettlement process could be undertaken to international standards and to the project proponent's satisfaction, an intense strategy of government engagement was required. This included workshops with all levels of government to agree on the benefit of following IFC standards on each aspect of the process, including agreements on where the company would undertake activities to supplement limited government capacities, including house design and resettlement site identification, and development of livelihood programmes. In addition, training for local government officials was agreed.

What about when indigenous peoples are involved?

Projects where land access and resettlement will impact indigenous people typically bring another layer of complexity to already challenging negotiation processes, particularly when projects will require the displacement of both indigenous and nonindigenous people.

Where indigenous people will be displaced, the project needs to take care to, as applicable, comply with a plethora of evolving best practice standards (including IFC PS7) and the legislation that more and more countries are putting in place. From a stakeholder engagement perspective, projects need to, in addition to other requirements discussed in this chapter, consider the following:

- In cases where IFC standards are applicable, PS7 needs to be complied with.
- Where indigenous people will be displaced, their free prior informed consent is required: in essence, this means that a good faith negotiation needs to take place culminating in an agreement between the parties.
- Free, prior and informed consent does not necessarily require unanimity, and may be achieved even when individuals or groups within an indigenous community do not explicitly agree. However, it must be clear that there is a clear and significant majority consensus among members of the indigenous community in favour of displacement.

How about linear projects, where affected communities cover a wide area?

Projects that involve infrastructure, such as roads, railways, pipelines, power lines and other **linear land access requirements, pose some particular challenges** when it comes to negotiations. For example:

- The logistics of conducting negotiations (and broader stakeholder engagement) over the length of the required land-take can impose significant logistical challenges and require careful timing and scheduling if there are resource constraints (and in order to take account of the risks of speculation).
- While they often only involve economic displacement, the challenge is to conduct negotiations with individual households and communities that are often far apart, sometimes in geographically distinct areas and even in different countries.
- While striving for a consistent and fair set of mitigation measures, the project will also need to take account of differences in types and levels of impact and regional and country differences, including cultural differences.
- People will be anxious to be treated fairly but may be suspicious of some people getting more in other areas.

Taking into account the above, the biggest challenge will be to end up with mitigation measures that, while different or appearing different on the surface, are fair and equitable, in the sense that they treat people with the same types and amounts of assets in a consistent manner (after factoring in, for example, different replacement values and currencies). To address these issues and challenges, the project will **need to think carefully about how to structure the negotiation process and the packages offered**:

- **Information disclosure**: there will be an added onus to ensure that communities and other stakeholders fully understand the project, its impacts, regional and national differences, and the project's approach to land access and resettlement negotiations, mitigation measures and project benefits.
- **Negotiation process**: it may not be appropriate or practical to adopt the same approach, depending on the nature of displacement impacts and land take requirements across regions and countries. The project will need to ensure a suitable process is put in place that takes account of unavoidable differences but is still seen as fair and transparent, and adheres to national legislation and corporate and lender standards and commitments.

Project example

On a project in Latin America, land access was required for a range of different facilities, including pipelines, roads and power lines. These facilities would extend over hundreds of kilometres, through different regions, provinces and geographical areas, from mountainous areas to the coast. The project therefore structured its negotiation team to consist of a central management core and teams located along the linear routes across the regions. Because some communities and areas would only be economically displaced, and crops and yields differed across regions, the leitmotif of the project became fairness and equity for similar asset types, while taking account of differences where these existed. It was also realised that the magnitude of the land take meant that it was better to focus first on land take in areas where this was critical for the development of initial facilities as determined by the overall project development schedule, rather than trying to secure access to all land at once.

How should a project negotiate with host communities?

Displaced people will need to be resettled in host communities, i.e. in existing host communities or on land acquired from people living nearby. Seeing the benefits accruing to resettlers, host communities will naturally also want to gain benefit from the project. The project needs to ensure that host communities receive adequate benefits in order to enable resettlement implementation to go ahead smoothly.

The extent and timing of discussions with host communities can be challenging: for example, potential land for resettlement sites may be identified and require discussions with both displaced people and host communities. The replacement land cannot be acquired before being evaluated and discussed with the displaced people, but it also cannot be put forward as an option, evaluated or acquired without the involvement of the potential host community. Careful scheduling of the various negotiations is essential.

How to negotiate with stakeholders defined as illegal by government?

National legislation often stipulates that certain stakeholders are illegal. For example, mining projects often have artisanal and small-scale miners on their concessions and situations where land access will require their displacement. This raises two potential scenarios:

- Activities are undertaken by people who are living outside the project area, but whose livelihood, although illegal, will be impacted (economic displacement)
- Activities are undertaken by people who are living within the project area (physical and economic displacement)

In such situations, projects can find themselves caught up in a situation where government (and the project) does not want to pay for loss of income from illegal activities but where displaced communities are heavily reliant on these activities for their livelihoods, and failure to mitigate the loss will preclude the viable resettlement of the community.

This poses interesting challenges for the land access and resettlement stakeholder engagement process, where **projects need to find a solution acceptable to all parties involved**.

 Project example

Communities that needed to be moved on a project in Africa were overwhelmingly dependent on artisanal gold-mining for their livelihoods. Taking these livelihoods away, without adequate provision for alternatives, posed a real risk of famine for some people, but government insisted that these activities were illegal and not eligible for compensation. The project was also wary of encouraging an influx of people if it became apparent that people engaged in these activities could benefit from compensation on offer. At the same time, the project was anxious to address the livelihoods impacts it would cause. Taking into account the various considerations required a delicate balance on the part of the project. It did not formally recognise or discuss artisanal and small-scale mining issues, but turned a blind eye to people moving elsewhere on its concession to undertake replacement artisanal and small-scale mining activities, while offering alternative livelihood programmes for people who wanted these. People with houses were offered replacement houses or cash compensation, and everyone was offered transport assistance and re-establishment allowances.

How to ensure gender considerations and vulnerable people are fully taken into account

Men and women often have different priorities, perspectives and are impacted in different ways and to different extents when displacement occurs. However, it is still often the case that women are inadequately involved in land access and resettlement-related consultation and negotiation. The project needs to ensure that the engagement process adequately captures both men's and women's views, and reflects their different concerns and priorities about impacts, mitigation measures and benefits.

This can often be challenging given cultural norms and traditions that limit the involvement of women in some societies. In such situations, the project needs to evaluate its particular circumstances and find the appropriate balance to respect cultural norms, but still evolve practice to ensure women are adequately involved. Options may include:

- Separate or supplementary forums or engagements with women
- Ensuring the project negotiation team and land access department/ community relations department have a suitable gender balance
- Ensure the negotiation agenda includes priority issues for women

Similar issues and points as those raised in respect of women also pertain to vulnerable people.

 Project example

At a project in Eastern Europe, community representatives were overwhelmingly male, and the project was concerned that these representatives were not adequately conveying the full spectrum of concerns and views of affected community members. Accordingly, the project put in place a series of small focus groups that were targeted to give women and other groups the chance to engage more fully with the project. Meetings were held with women, old people, physically disabled people, young people and other specific interest groups such as farmers and business owners.

The negotiation process: key considerations

- **Start early**: you will need the time. Be realistic about how long negotiations will take.
- Before you commence planning, **reflect on lessons learned** on other projects and during your earlier project phases.
- **Make sure you have right team**: land access and resettlement negotiations are not for the faint hearted, inexperienced or unprepared.
- No land acquisition and resettlement negotiations should be undertaken without first developing explicit overall **objectives and guiding principles**, as well as a comprehensive **negotiation strategy and plan** (including opening, fallback and final positions) and agenda. Plan thoroughly but be flexible when necessary.

- Each project has different circumstances and the process needs to be **tailored accordingly**, but that is not an excuse to cut corners.
- **Help communities prepare** before negotiations commence, i.e. assist with capacity-building.
- **Go where you have to** in order to engage people.
- **Ensure leaders/representatives are truly representative** of communities.
- Offer nothing during land acquisition and resettlement negotiations without it first being **fully costed and approved** by management.
- **Avoid setting unaffordable precedents**.
- **Do not negotiate in a piecemeal manner**.
- **Listen** (put yourself in the shoes of project-affected persons).
- Rather than focusing on wants and positions, the negotiations should **focus on key interests and issues**; on addressing communities' underlying values, needs and concerns; and project objectives.
- **Manage expectations**.
- **Do not just give**, be seen to negotiate: get something in return.
- Project negotiators should **remain open to counteroffers and alternative solutions**: it is impossible to build communities' confidence and support if they believe that outcomes are predetermined.
- The negotiation process must result in **a win–win situation** in order to ensure implementable agreements and a long-term environment in which a project can be developed and operated peacefully, i.e. one-sided agreements are typically not sustainable.
- Negotiated packages must be **fair and transparent**.
- **Prepare for unfavourable attention**: act as if your approach may need to be defended in court. Record discussions, agreements and transactions properly.
- **The objective is not the conclusion of the agreement, but its implementation**: reaching agreements that are not comprehensive and fair will mean that there is a real risk that they cannot be fully implemented in a timely manner.
- **Process is as important as outcome**: project-affected communities need to feel that there has been a process where they have been actively involved, rather than having terms merely dictated to them.
- **Do not be scared to acknowledge mistakes**—then rectify them.
- Whatever the project initially offers, **communities will always feel that it has more to offer**.

13
Compensation and resettlement sign-off

Once the final negotiated agreements have been signed, as discussed in the previous chapter, and the RAP (resettlement action plan) has been disclosed to project stakeholders for the required period, normally 60 days under international standards, the implementation process can occur, including construction of resettlement sites (discussed in Chapter 14), payment of compensation (discussed in this chapter), full-blown roll-out of livelihoods programmes (dealt with in Chapter 16) and other measures (see Chapter 17 and other subsequent chapters).

The project will be under considerable pressure to begin payments and resettlement and it is important to have a sign-off process so that each household is satisfied that they have been fairly treated, and that agreements are properly recorded in case there are grievances later which could end up in court. While the sign-off process is at the end of the project, the planning should begin much earlier as there is always a risk that some households will reject compensation and resettlement, potentially delaying the project. The objective of this chapter is to outline a process to ensure that the impacted households verify their ownership and interest in assets early in the project cycle so that the sign-off process at the end runs smoothly with limited grievances.

What are the key issues, challenges and risks?

- There is a risk with group negotiations conducted by community representatives that there will be individual households, called hold-outs, that reject the group agreement and refuse to be resettled or accept cash compensation rates.

- There is also a risk with individual negotiations conducted over different phases of the project that some households paid less in earlier rounds will come back later and demand additional compensation.
- It is common on projects for claimants to come forward once the compensation and resettlement process is being implemented to make new or additional claims, causing project delays and inflated budgets.
- It is also common for some impacted households to challenge the project's record of assets in order to claim additional benefits. This can result in court action which can be costly and difficult to defend.

What are the key components of a compensation and resettlement sign-off process?

The basis for an effective sign-off process stems from a **robust baseline data-collection process** as outlined in Chapter 6. The impacted household and community and government witnesses, where appropriate, must sign the survey forms to verify that the information was collected properly and is a correct representation of the assets present on that date. Where the household representative cannot read or write, the information must be explained to them in their own language and they should mark the form with their thumbprint.

The **cut-off date** which set an entitlement to compensation and resettlement must be robust, follow national laws and must be individually communicated to impacted households.

There must be a **comprehensive communications plan** around the cut-off date and baseline surveys so that all community members, including those absent, can come forward with claims.

Once the survey forms are completed, the forms must be directly scanned and filed securely, and the data entered into a project **database to ensure data security**.

Ensure the **project grievance mechanism** is designed to record all disputes over ownership of assets such as land, crops and buildings. Where there are numerous disputes it makes business sense for the company to invest in resources to support the resolution of these grievances. The company must have a legal process which will enable land access to continue and compensation funds to be put in escrow until the dispute resolution process has been completed.

When should households sign off on entitlements and individual choices?

There are normally two key stages of household sign-off:

- **Verification** by the household that the assets have been properly surveyed and that the records fully reflect their interests in the asset.
- **Sign-off**, where households confirm that the compensation and resettlement packages as applied to their assets are acceptable to the household and they agree to allow the company to take ownership of their assets based on the overall agreement, and confirmation of household choices in relation to house type, livelihood programmes, etc. as may be applicable.

On large complex projects, the verification and sign-off process can be phased so that the issues around land disputes are being resolved before the RAP agreements are finalised. Once the RAP agreements are finalised it should then be a straightforward process to run the sign-off process. On smaller, less complex projects it can be possible to run the verification and sign-off process simultaneously and deal with any grievances that arise.

The verification process

It is recommended that, following the baseline surveys, the impacted households are given an opportunity to verity that all their assets have been recorded properly and that they agree to use this record as the basis for their RAP entitlements. This will allow the project to identify all households where there are conflicting claims for assets.

The verification requires that the project develop a report from the database that sets out the following information for each impacted household:

- Demographic information including name, ID type and number, address, main residence GPS location, contact information and photo
- Table for each main asset type (land, crops and structures), outlining the survey date, survey code, location (GPS) with map, and interest of household in asset (full ownership, joint ownership, sharecropper, etc.)
- Record of grievances lodged: this will help the team to assess any outstanding issues so that these can be resolved with the household
- Photos of crops and structures taken at the time of the survey
- A statement that the household accepts the information on the form or wants to lodge a grievance, with a space to lodge the details of the grievance. The form should be witnessed by a community and government representative who should state that the household understood the information and agreed to what was proposed.

It is recommended that the verification process is undertaken by the household head together with his spouse so that they both fully agree to the survey findings and assessment of assets. The project team undertaking the verification process should ideally be the same team which will later undertake the household sign-off process, supported by community representatives.

The sign-off process

For the sign-off process the same information listed in the verification form is presented, with the following additional information in the form of a household dossier:

- Table of land and crop areas, location (GPS) with map, type, maturity, compensation rate and total compensation due
- Table of residential house areas qualifying for resettlement and the type of resettlement house that the household is entitled to
- Table of non-residential house size, types of material, compensation rate and total compensation due
- Photos of crops and structures taken at the time of the survey
- Choices/options may be presented regarding various housing designs or livelihood packages
- A statement that the household accepts all the information on assets in the form and the proposed compensation and resettlement entitlements. If the household does not agree then there should be space for the household to lodge a grievance.

The sign-off process should be witnessed by a community and government representative who should state that the household understood the information and agreed to what was proposed. This is discussed further below.

Note that all verified agreements for sign-off should be recorded in the database and the original copies filed should the agreement need to be defended in court at a later stage.

What needs to be in place for a successful sign-off process?

The process of sign-off will vary from project to project, but needs to consider the following key elements:

- **Individual household dossiers**: as referred to above, individual dossiers should be prepared for each resettling household, outlining their current assets in brief and, based on the negotiated agreements, their available

Figure 13.1: Example of a combined verification/sign-off form.

STAKEHOLDER PROFILE REPORT

Forename **: Adama**		Location **: Tambi**	
Surname **: Ouedraogo**		Address **: No 4, Wusiwusi**	
Gender **: Male**		Identity type **: National card**	
Contact # **: 025-XXXXXXXX**		Identity No **: XXX-XXXXXX-XXX**	

FIELD SURVEY AND COMPENSATION STATUS

Date surveyed	Plot code	Chit no	Cropping type	Location	Ownership type	Amount (LC)	Status
06.11.2012	P4-04036	10045	Intercrop	Tambi	Share cropper	28,582.27	*Paid*
16.08.2012	P4-04336	10034	Cocoa	Tambi	Farmer	16,626.24	*Paid*
22.06.2011	P5-02955	10028	Oil palm	Kangbe Creole	Farmer	21,255.54	*Verification*
					Total:	66,465.05	

STRUCTURE ASSESSMENT AND ENTITLEMENT STATUS

Date surveyed	Structure ID	Asset usage	Construction Status	Ownership type	Amount (LC)	Entitlement
06.03.2013	P5-013/ST/001	Annex	Complete	Owner	529.66	*Compensation*
16.02.2011	P5-013/ST/002	Residential	Complete	Landlord		*Relocation*
				Total:	529.66	

GRIEVANCES REPORTED

Date received	Grievance type	Submission	Complainant	Brief description of complaint
08.11.2012	Property Litigation	Unresolved	Adama Ouedraogo	Two family members are claiming ownership to farms that belongs to their late father. One indicate...

AGRICULTURE RESTORATION AND FOOD SECURITY

Date	Land location	Crops cultivated	Administrative note	State
06.03.2013	Akyiawa	Oil palm(Agric)	Land to be checked and verified. Some assistance to be provided in documenting the land with the local council and lands commission.	Approved

VULNERABILITY ASSESSMENT AND MITIGATION

Date	Committee recommendation	Supply HH Food	Monthly Supplies	Supplies duration	HH qualify for health insurance	Insurance Termination date
14.08.2013	Approved	Yes	Gari, Dry hearings,Maize	1 year	Yes	19.08.2014

choices for resettlement, together with any cash compensation and related entitlements such as transport assistance and/or mobilisation allowances. Depending on project timing, the dossiers may also include options concerning available livelihood programmes.

- **Appropriate locations**: the sign-off process needs to take place as close to the resettling households as possible, ideally in the existing settlements. Requiring resettlers to go to the project site office, for example, may be extremely inconvenient considering other responsibilities of the household, and may be intimidating for households who feel they are not making choices in their home environment.

- **Appropriate facilities**: the sign-off needs to take place in a comfortable and weather-tight building as appropriate, where households have time to sit, review and discuss their choices as appropriate. This may be, for example, a public building, a school meeting room or a purpose-built information centre related to the project.

- **Representative**: as much as possible, the project needs to ensure that decisions made at the sign-off meetings are representative of the wishes of all household members. In certain cultures it may be usual for the male household head to make such decisions. However, efforts should be made to include the views of the spouse where possible.

- **Peer oversight and advice**: the sign-off process must be overseen by a peer group in addition to project personnel. A **'sign-off committee'** can be drawn from the community representatives who were party to negotiations, together with any third-party observers, facilitators and statutory authority representatives as may be appropriate.

> While the sign-off process may vary from project to project, there are certain key elements and steps that need to occur to ensure a structured and efficient process

Depending on the numbers of communities to be resettled, a number of sign-off committees may be in operation, with the make-up of these committees reflecting the various community characteristics.

The sign-off committee plays an important role in not just overseeing and witnessing that the process is free, fair and informed, but may also counsel their peers on pertinent choices, with the aim of protecting them against vulnerability. For example, it may be unwise for a household to take cash compensation if they have nowhere else to live.

- **Staged process**: the sign-off process needs to allow sufficient time for households to consider any available resettlement or livelihood choices. This will usually require at least two meetings with each household: one to explain choices, and a second to confirm and witness choices after a period of review and reflection by the resettling household.

- **Recording and documentation**: as with all aspects of the resettlement process, final choices need to be carefully documented and witnessed, and entered into the project database.

 Project example

A project in Africa developed detailed dossiers on each resettling household and established three separate sign-off committees, reflecting the different communities to be resettled. A series of meetings were held with each household (household head and spouse) to ensure all choices and entitlements were clearly understood. All agreements were scanned and entered into the project database.

What elements are included in household sign-off?

The various options on which households may need to make choices will vary from project to project, and depend on the outcome of negotiations.

A typical sign-off process may include the following elements:

- **Verification of existing assets**: this should be based on information from surveys as recorded in the project database, and may have been through a verification process already, as discussed above
- **Verification of cash compensation entitlement**, based on negotiated rates for assets (e.g. crops, land, structures) and additional assistances (e.g. loss of income, transport allowances)
- **Verification of housing entitlement**: an explanation of the size of house (e.g. area and/or number of rooms) based on existing floor space and other factors which may have been taken into account
- **House type choice**, based on a range of standard designs
- **Other design choices**, which may include positioning of certain elements, such as doors, choice of paint colours, etc.
- **Plot allocation**: this may be a contentious issue, but is an important factor to consider in maintaining social networks. A combination of lottery and allowing households to be considered together as a unit may be considered, but will depend on project circumstances
- **Livelihood programme choices**, based on a range of programmes depending on eligibility

Cash compensation sign-off

The cash compensation sign-off should include both payments for assets and also any additional allowances, such as for transport, which will be paid for by the project.

It is advised that project-affected households are provided with some basic training on money management/investment and supported to establish bank accounts, and that the compensation funds are paid by cheque into these accounts. It is advisable for the company to provide training on financial management so that the impacted households are informed on how best to manage and invest their compensation funds.

Note that international standards require that compensation is paid prior to the company taking possession of the land. In certain circumstances, where there are land disputes, the company may have to acquire land while the legal process to determine ownership of the asset is under way. In these cases the company normally pays the compensation into an escrow account. The amount is paid to the successful party on completion of the legal process. In other cases, the

Figure 13.2: Woman signing off for new house in Africa.

community may prefer to have payments staggered over a number of years so that the funds can be better managed.

Where households are choosing cash compensation in lieu of a resettlement house, the sign-off committee, consisting of government and community representatives, can play an important role in peer reviewing the household's choice, ensuring that they are not at risk of homelessness or increased vulnerability as a result of such a decision. Additional evidence of alternative accommodation may be requested from the household, for example.

Resettlement house sign-off and moves

Resettling households need to **sign off on individual choices regarding available resettlement options, and verify their entitlements**, based on the agreements arising from the negotiation process.

This process can involve a large number of households and needs to be carefully scheduled so that the outcome of the process can inform plot allocations and housing construction at the resettlement site.

A phased approach to development of the site will assist in this regard, and the areas where land access is first required can be prioritised for sign-off and advanced construction and moves.

The timing of sign-off and moves of potentially **vulnerable households** to the resettlement site will need careful consideration depending on individual project circumstances. In some cases it may be preferable to move households early in order to re-establish livelihoods at the new site as quickly as possible, whereas in other circumstances it may be appropriate to ensure the relevant social networks are in place in advance.

Livelihood restoration sign-off

The planning of livelihood restoration programmes is outlined in Chapter 10 and livelihood restoration implementation in Chapter 16. When the packages have been developed, the household should be presented with the support package together with any options, and sign their agreement with the package which also requires them to take personal responsibility for the restoration of their livelihood and their understanding that the support is for a limited time-period.

Compensation and sign-off process: key considerations

- Individual households can reject the RAP compensation and resettlement packages, and so a sign-off process is required to **identify hold-outs as early as possible** in the project cycle in order that a dialogue can be started to resolve their issues.

- Ensure that households **verify baseline survey information** at the earliest possible opportunity in order to identify disputes over ownership of assets which could delay the compensation and resettlement process.

- Ensure that the **sign-off process is witnessed by community and government representatives**, as appropriate, to demonstrate that the household were aware of the record of their assets and the RAP package being offered, and can be counselled on their choices.

- **Involve the wife/wives of the household head in the sign-off process** so that they have an opportunity to also sign off on the resettlement entitlement.

- **Think carefully about the sequence in which you sign off households**: choosing to start the process with households that are influential and clearly willing to sign off can help to ensure that the process starts well and builds early support, trust and momentum.

14

Physical resettlement implementation

Following on from the prenegotiation physical resettlement planning described in Chapter 9, this chapter discusses the key considerations in the construction and bringing to life of new sites, housing and community facilities, including how to sensitively manage the moves of affected households, and measures to ensure the success of resettlement communities post-move.

What are the key components of physical resettlement implementation?

In undertaking physical resettlement construction and moves the following steps or components need to be addressed:

- **Tendering and contracting of works**: following on from the detailed engineering and designs agreed in negotiations, the project needs to develop tender documentation and development of a construction management plan to allow for timely, effective and safe implementation
- **Individual household sign-off** needs to take place, as described at Chapter 13
- **Resettlement construction** of all sites, housing, community facilities and associated infrastructure, to agreed specifications and standards
- **Participatory monitoring and oversight** of the sign-off, construction and moves processes

The land access and resettlement process does not end with the signing of agreements: implementation, successful moves and rebuilding of livelihoods is the key challenge

- **Moves of resettling households** from their existing homes to their new homes at the resettlement site(s), including moves of businesses
- **Final approvals and handover to statutory authorities** including adoption by statutory authorities of all infrastructure and facilities
- **Demolition of existing settlements** to secure and make safe the site for project development
- **Follow up with resettlement communities and households** to ensure a successful transition to the new resettlement site

These key components are discussed further below.

What is the key objective of resettlement implementation?

As referred to in Chapter 9, physical resettlement is one of the major impacts of land access projects on individuals, households and communities as a whole. The process of physical relocation and the demolition of existing hamlets, villages or towns is not just a physical disturbance but can be emotionally unsettling to people.

The issue of physical resettlement therefore requires a **well-planned sign-off, construction and moves process** that ensures as easy a transition to new sites as possible, to allow timely development of the project.

The objective of resettlement construction and moves is to enable the relocation of individuals, households and communities to new locations in such a way that:

- Construction is undertaken as safely and efficiently as possible, maximising the input of local contractors and labour, to agreed standards
- Construction of resettlement sites takes place in a way, with phasing as appropriate, that allows the timely development of the project
- Individual sign-off by households takes place in a way where choices are clearly explained to resettlers and they are clear on entitlements
- Moves of resettling households take place in a smooth and timely manner with minimum disruption for families and businesses
- When existing sites are vacated, they are demolished and made secure and safe as quickly as possible
- Final approval and handover to statutory authorities takes place on completion
- Follow-up occurs with resettlers to ensure a smooth transition to the new sites
- The whole process is overseen by community representatives, resettlers and authorities

The objective of the resettlement construction and moves process is a smooth, safe and timely transition to new resettlement sites

What are the key issues, challenges and risks?

Resettlement construction and moves constitutes a major project in itself, and faces a number of common pitfalls, including:

- **Pressure on construction schedules** from the project
- **Capacity of local contractors and labour**, combined with high expectations of local employment
- Need to construct safely with potentially a large number of local labourers on-site, and a possible phased approach to construction and occupation of areas of the site
- **Resettling households making ill-informed decisions** on resettlement choices and possible increased risk of vulnerability

> Each issue, challenge or risk constitutes a potential opportunity for improved performance

- **Lack of oversight of the process by resettlers and community representatives**, leading to disagreements and delayed moves
- **Delays in handover of key infrastructure** to statutory authorities, with ongoing costs for the project
- **Limited government capacity** to be meaningful development partners

The purpose of this chapter is to help you identify and deal with the issues, challenges, risks and opportunities that will arise.

What are the guiding principles for resettlement construction, sign-off and moves?

Key principles apply regardless of the impetus for physical resettlement or where a project is located:

- **Choice**: to the extent practically possible, all resettling households should have choices regarding plot allocations, house types and time of moves
- **Participation and oversight**: the sign-off, construction and moves processes need to be overseen by resettlers, community representatives and statutory authorities
- **Local content**: the resettlement construction process should maximise opportunities for local employment and provision of goods and services
- **Compliance with laws and standards**: all aspects of the construction process must comply with applicable laws and be guided by agreed best practice standards, including in relation to health and safety

What needs to be considered in tendering and contracting the resettlement construction?

Once all detailed engineering and designs are agreed through the negotiation process, the project needs to develop **tender documentation** and a **construction management plan** to allow for timely, effective and safe implementation of the resettlement site and housing.

The following steps need to be considered in any project:

Consider opportunities to utilise local labour, contractors and service providers

For many projects, resettlement construction offers the first opportunity for employment of significant numbers of unskilled and skilled local labour. Communities will typically have high expectations of employment from the project. In considering the potential for local labour, the project should take the following steps:

- Undertake, ideally with the project's human resources and procurement departments, **an assessment of local labour skills and capacities**. This should in any case be undertaken in the early stages of the project in anticipation of employment and procurement needs for the project as a whole.

> The resettlement construction often provides the first project opportunity for significant utilisation of local labour and services

- **Consider local capacities against construction requirements and project time-scales**, since utilisation of local labour may require more time than utilising a more experienced large-scale contractor.

- Consider opportunities for **capacity-building** of local labour and contractors. This needs to take place as early in the project development as possible, and can be linked to community investment programmes. This is not just applicable to resettlement construction, of course, but the project as a whole. In this way the utilisation of local labour and contractors can be maximised in both construction and operation, maximising the business benefit of community investment spend.

- Given local labour and contractor capacity, **consider management modalities** for the resettlement construction. For example, a project may consider a national- or international-level contractor necessary for major earthworks and use of heavy equipment, but that local contractors can be used for construction of houses.

- In order to further reduce the risk of using inexperienced local contractors, a project may consider an in-house or national/international **construction**

management team overseeing local contractors. It will also be important to use multiple local contractors, to ensure that the level of work awarded can be delivered in terms of local contractor capacity and cash flow. It will be appropriate to allocate significant work to a local contractor only when competence has been demonstrated on-site.

- In order to further assist local contractors, and maintain control on cost, quality and schedule, the project may consider **bulk procurement** of key items (e.g. cement, roofing sheets) and allocating these to contractors.

Development of all tender documentation

This needs to include all engineering and architectural drawings and specifications, and blank bills of quantities, together with information on relevant health and safety standards and regulations, and roles and responsibilities of the project proponent and the contractor.

Depending on decisions related to the use of local contractors, the project may need to consider **comprehensive presentations** on the tender documentation to shortlisted bidders, and assistance with preparation of appropriate bids. In some cases, **fixed-price tenders** may be preferable to control costs and assist contractors.

Development of a construction management plan

Again, the contents of this plan will depend on decisions regarding the use of local contractors, as referred to above, and can be informed by an opportunity and risk assessment.

The construction management plan needs to take into account, but is not limited to, the following:

- **Management and supervision** modalities and personnel requirements
- Opportunities for **phased development** of the site, taking into account project land access needs, and development of a phasing plan
- The **numbers of contractors** on-site and **allocation of works**
- **Health, safety and security** considerations including rules and procedures
- **Transport arrangements** to and within the site in terms of both labour and materials
- **Procurement and storage** of materials and development of lay-down areas
- **Facilities for workers** including sanitation and food, including **opportunities to utilise local providers**
- **Environmental protection** measures during construction
- **Adequate insurances** for the period between construction and handover

Project example

A project in Eastern Europe appointed a local contractor to undertake resettlement site and homes construction. However, no clear tender documentation or construction management plan was in place. As a result, no clear schedule for the works was agreed, and a number of issues concerning specifications and design were faced throughout the construction process, resulting in considerable increased costs and delays.

 Project example

A project in Africa developed detailed tender documentation and undertook several sessions with local contractors to outline the process and assist with development of bids. A fixed-price tender was developed and agreed to standardise bids and assist local contractors in costing. The project proponent procured key construction items in bulk to control cost and quality. The local contractors were assigned units to construct according to capacity and were supervised by an in-house team of construction professionals.

What are the key considerations during construction?

This guide is not an engineering or construction manual, and will not go into detailed consideration of the construction process itself.

However, as discussed above, there are **key social elements to consider** in the process, not least of which is the need for appropriate phasing and utilisation of local labour and services where possible.

Key elements to bear in mind during construction are:

- **Maximising use of local labour and services** (including procurement, food supply, etc.). However, contractors, suppliers and labourers also need to understand the temporary nature of the construction process so as to avoid tensions when work ceases, and the risk that labourers may abandon other livelihoods.

- **Maximising capacity-building of local labour, suppliers and contractors** through on-the-job training, including increasing familiarity with project rules and procedures, particularly relating to health and safety. This will maximise the potential for local labour and services to be utilised during ongoing project construction and operations.

- **Ensuring construction of all elements is in accordance with negotiated agreements**: social teams need to work closely with project managers and construction supervisors to make sure that all sites, housing and infrastructure is being implemented according to agreed designs and specifications. While the construction team should be made aware of all elements of negotiated agreements, personnel who have been intimately involved in the negotiations also need to oversee the process.

- **Management of stakeholder oversight and expectations** in such a way that stakeholders have sufficient access to the site to oversee and monitor works, but in a controlled and safe manner. This is discussed further in terms of handover and maintenance below.

 Project example

A project in Africa fast-tracked the development of a market site in the centre of the resettlement site, with an access road to the nearby host community. In this way local traders could travel to the site daily and supply food and drinks for workers.

Figure 14.1: A resettlement site under construction. Note the emphasis on safety, which required significant capacity-building of local contractors.

Figure 14.2: Before and after: a house (top), mosque (middle) and school (bottom) on projects in Africa, showing the existing buildings (left) and the replacement buildings provided by the project (right).

How is participation of communities and external stakeholders assured?

A key element of the land access and resettlement process is ensuring that participatory monitoring and oversight of the sign-off, construction and moves processes takes place in such a way that resettlers, statutory authorities and other third-party observers are satisfied that implementation is actually occurring in accordance with what was negotiated and agreed.

The project should ensure the following takes place during the construction process:

- An **official ceremony** should be considered to mark both the start and completion of works. This can often be very meaningful to local leaders and communities, and can begin the process of ensuring ownership and pride in the new settlement.

- Regular guided visits by **resettling households** (which can be in groups as appropriate for management and safety reasons) to the construction site to oversee construction of homes and infrastructure.

- Regular updates and site visits by **statutory authorities** of the works. This is particularly important to ensure successful adoption of infrastructure by the relevant authorities on completion, and development of relationships with government as a meaningful development partner. A **handover and maintenance committee** may be formed to focus on these elements, which is discussed further below.

> Delivering the resettlement site and housing on schedule is an essential component in building long-term trust between the project and communities

- Regular updates and site visits by the **negotiation committee**, to ensure that all works are being implemented in accordance with negotiated agreements.

- **Progress updates**, including photographs, etc., can be posted on community notice boards, and regular updates sent to those stakeholders at regional and national levels.

 Project example

A project in Africa undertook a sod-turning ceremony to mark the beginning of construction of a new resettlement community, attended by all stakeholders and traditional leaders, who also undertook necessary traditional rites to make the site ready for habitation. Thereafter regular site visits by a handover committee, traditional leaders, community representatives and resettlers took place to ensure all stakeholders were satisfied that the works were being undertaken to agreed specifications.

How are households moved to the new site?

The movement of resettling households from their existing homes to their new homes at the resettlement site, including moves of businesses, needs to consider the following factors:

- **Phasing**: as referred to earlier, the construction, sign-off and moves of resettlers need to be planned and scheduled in accordance with land access requirements. A phased approach will aid project planning and reduce the numbers of resettlers that need to be moved at any one time.

- **Notifications**: resettling families need to be advised well in advance of **move dates** and what assistance will be put in place to assist them.

- **Final site visits**: resettling families should undertake final visits to their resettlement house in advance of moves. A **final inspection form** should be completed to identify any final finishing required, and ultimately the resettling household needs to sign off that the house is ready for occupation, in the presence of relevant community witnesses.

- **Moving assistance**: on the day of moves the project should provide assistance to families in accordance with negotiated agreements. Normally, this may include provision of **transport** (such as a truck for belongings and car for the family), as well as **payment of allowances** related to disturbance allowance, assistance with moving arrangements and loss of income during moving. This provides another opportunity to utilise local services (such as vehicle hire). Additional specific assistance may be required depending on circumstances (for example, a medical team on hand for vulnerable/ill/disabled households).

- **Moving teams** may be provided by a project to assist families with moving goods. Resettlers may prefer that the moving team consists of people from the community, and this also provides an opportunity for additional local employment, albeit on a temporary basis.

- **Cultural considerations** need to be taken into account in the planning of moves. For example, some communities may not be comfortable with displaying their belongings during moving, and may have a preference to move during darkness.

 Project example

A project in Africa appointed moving teams consisting of young people from the local community, and hired local trucks to assist families with moves. The majority of families preferred to move after nightfall so this was facilitated in the timing of moves to the site.

How does a project ensure final handover of the resettlement site?

A critical element for a project is ensuring timely handover of resettlement site housing, infrastructure and related community facilities to relevant statutory authorities, communities and households.

It is not in the interests of a project, or stakeholders, if a project proponent needs to undertake ongoing management of resettlement sites as this:

- Prevents the development of a real **sense of ownership** by the community and authorities
- **Prevents integration** of the site into the locality as a 'normal settlement'
- Results in **ongoing time and cost** for the project which may distract from its core activities
- **Reduces the potential to spend project resources elsewhere**, such as ongoing community investment

As discussed in Chapter 9 concerning physical resettlement planning, key to both the securing of formal approvals, and ultimately handover, is the need to **engage with relevant stakeholders early**. In many cases local government capacity is likely to be limited, and ongoing engagement will reduce time-scales for agreeing on handover modalities. These should ultimately be agreed in writing, if not explicitly included as a condition of approval. As said, officials who have been properly engaged and given due recognition throughout the process are also more likely to be willing to facilitate speedy approval and handovers as a willing development partner.

A project should develop a **handover committee**. This should include representatives from the key approving authorities and those who will ultimately adopt the various infrastructures (such as the roads authority, electrical authority, etc.). Resettler representatives should also be on the committee.

The following needs to be achieved with the handover committee:

- The **conclusion of detailed agreements** with all relevant authorities on what is required for the adoption and handover of all infrastructures, and when this should take place. This may include specific agreements with power, water and solid waste authorities, school boards, health authorities, church officials, etc.
- Where there is no clear adopting agency, the handover committee should consider **modalities for community management** of infrastructure, such as community halls, markets or a solid waste collection system. Opportunities for employment should be highlighted, as well as the likely need to pay for some services in accordance with national norms. Where services are likely to need to be managed by communities, and/or will require payment for service, this should be discussed and agreed during the negotiations period, as such issues can be contentious.

- Ensure an **ongoing participatory process** in the monitoring and evaluation of both the design and construction process. As discussed above in relation to the construction process, the handover committee needs to be involved in regular oversight of construction works to ensure construction is according to agreed specifications, including the standards of regulatory and statutory authorities.

- The committee can also play a role in ensuring the integration of resettlers to their new environment. Together with the project proponent, the handover committee can ensure all residents and businesses are aware of statutory and personal responsibilities in respect of the completed site, for example maintenance of household plots and control of livestock, and that handover to households takes place in a timely fashion.

- In this regard, resettling families can be given a **welcome pack** to introduce them to their new environment, including information on their house (for example, electricity meters and water supply), any special arrangements in terms of management of their property and communal areas, information on the property registration process and any ownership certificates, copies of house plans, and general rights and responsibilities.

When and how should demolition of existing settlements and housing occur?

The **timing of demolition** of existing settlements and compounds needs to take into account the following factors:

- The need for **land access** in accordance with project planning and phasing
- The **move of resettlers** to the resettlement site
- Minimising the time-lag between moves and demolition to avoid the **potential for squatting** or the potential for **structures to fall into disrepair** and become dangerous
- **The need for resettlers to see the new site as their new home**

The **modalities for demolition** should consider the following:

- The opportunity to use **local demolition teams**, for example young people from the resettling community, to undertake demolition.
- Coupled with this, the need to consider appropriate **health and safety standards**. In this case, the use of local labour for demolition may need to be supplemented with **training and management oversight**.
- In the case of **phased demolition**, safety also needs to be considered in terms of some community members continuing to live on-site while partial demolition occurs.

> ## 👍 Project example
>
> A project in Africa needed to demolish existing structures as quickly as possible to prevent influx and squatting in the old homes. However, moves were occurring in phases and it was considered too dangerous for the existing community to have large-scale demolition ongoing while they remained on-site. Therefore demolition was undertaken in steps, with the roofs of vacated houses being removed initially to render them uninhabitable. The demolition was undertaken by local teams hired from the community, overseen by project construction professionals, with all teams supplied with safety equipment and training.

Figure 14.3: A flooded road in Africa. Investment in transport networks is critical to local development.

What follow-up is necessary with resettled communities?

It is important that engagement with resettling communities does not end with moves to the new resettlement site. A major fear of resettling communities is often that they will be forgotten by the project when they are resettled. This fear can actually lead to resistance to moves, and a belief that they need to negotiate harder to ensure they get all possible advantages in advance.

For this reason, the assurance of ongoing assistance is important, and prioritisation in terms of community investment and employment opportunities may need to be offered to resettling communities, who are in any case by definition those most directly impacted by the project.

As emphasised before, resettlement can be a traumatic experience, and some households will adapt better than others. For the elderly particularly, the transition to a new site may represent a very different environment and way of life. While more modern housing and facilities can offer new advantages and opportunities for families, it also means new ways of living and new personal and communal responsibilities.

> A major fear of resettling communities is often that they will be forgotten by the project when they are resettled

In order to ensure a successful transition to the new resettlement site, the social team needs to schedule follow-up visits with each resettling household and business. The personnel who undertake the follow-up visits should be the same personnel who have followed the households through the process, from baseline surveys to sign-off and moves.

Depending on the assessment of how each household is doing, additional visits and assistance can be planned as required. Where necessary, families may be referred to relevant stakeholders who have participated in the resettlement process to address specific issues (such as social welfare officers).

 Project example

A project in Africa retained the team who had undertaken the sign-off process for a period of time after moves had been completed to perform follow-up visits with households. This proved important in terms of ensuring households understood their roles and responsibilities in terms of management of their plot and the surrounding area, that they took advantage of all assistance being offered, and that any remaining issues with housing could be drawn to the attention of the construction team.

Physical resettlement implementation: key considerations

- The land access and resettlement process does not end with the signing of agreements: **implementation, successful moves and rebuilding of livelihoods is the key challenge**.
- The objective of the resettlement construction and moves process is a **smooth, safe and timely transition to new resettlement sites**.
- Key principles apply regardless of the impetus for physical resettlement or where a project is located: **offering choice; ensuring participation and oversight; maximising local content; and compliance with laws and standards**.
- The resettlement construction often provides the **first opportunity for significant utilisation of local labour and services**. Consider opportunities to utilise local labour, contractors and procurement, including capacity-building efforts as required.
- Develop a **construction management plan**.
- Ensure the **sign-off of households** on available choices and entitlements is **well managed and includes proper oversight** by peer groups and relevant external stakeholders.
- **Oversight of the construction process by all stakeholders and resettling households** is a key aspect of long-term trust-building between the project and stakeholders.
- **Moves** of resettlers to the new site need to consider **assistance required and cultural considerations**.
- **Handover** to statutory authorities and households needs to be **considered from the outset and detailed in agreements**.
- **Demolition** of existing settlements needs to **consider project land access requirements, phasing, community cohesion, and health and safety considerations**.
- **Engagement with communities and households cannot end with moves to the new site**: assurance and follow-up is essential.

15

Community investment and development

Why discuss community investment and development in a book about resettlement?

Projects undertaking CI (community investment) are often also dealing with land access and resettlement at the same time. **In dealing with displacement impacts arising from land acquisition, projects need not only to address their negative displacement impacts, but also to show affected communities the benefits arising from the project.** At the same time, there may also be other communities that will not be affected by resettlement, but which can disrupt project activities if they do not see benefits accruing to them. Apart from benefits such as local employment and procurement, one of the major benefits that can accrue is a company's investment in community development initiatives. It is also the view of the authors that **all of these activities, namely resettlement, local employment and procurement, and CI in its narrow sense, are all, broadly speaking, community investment and development opportunities and activities**. It is for these reasons that we have included a specific chapter on community investment and development.

Those companies and projects that adopt a co-ordinated approach to social issues and activities have the best chance of managing these effectively

Figure 15.1: The place of community investment in the overall engagement strategy.

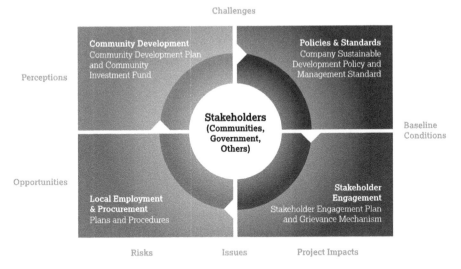

What is community investment?

Community investment (CI) refers to a company's long-term strategic involvement in community partnerships to address social issues chosen by the company to protect corporate interests and enhance reputation. CI comprises of the following components: financial contributions (sometimes known as cash donations); in-kind donations of both goods and services, including the loan of assets such as company premises or resources; contributions of time and skills, known as employee volunteering or EV. (CBL 2014)

The IFC's (International Finance Corporation) *Strategic Community Investment* booklet defines strategic CI as: 'Voluntary contributions or actions by companies to help communities in their areas of operation address their development priorities, and take advantage of opportunities created by private investment—in ways that are sustainable and support business objectives' (IFC 2010b: i).

A project example of where CI fits into a comprehensive overall engagement strategy is shown in Figure 15.1.

Regulatory requirements and best practice guidance

CI is an area where many countries have not legislated a requirement yet, although there are countries where it is specified that certain amounts of taxes and royalties be spent at local level to assist in community development. However, there is a plethora of best practice guidance that has been developed, including by the IFC and World Bank. As well as the experience of the authors, this chapter draws on the guidance of the IFC, as we believe it provides a common sense approach to community investment and development.

Context and importance of CI

One cannot properly discuss community investment and development by companies without putting it in the context of other terms that are frequently used (all with multiple definitions), for example:

- **Social licence to operate**: 'The Social License has been defined as existing when a project has the ongoing approval with the local community and other stakeholders, ongoing approval or broad social acceptance and, most frequently, as ongoing acceptance' (SociaLicense.com n.d.).

- **Sustainable development**: 'Development that meets the needs of the present without compromising the ability of future generations to meet their own needs' (Brundtland Commission 1987).

- **Shared value**: 'In recent years business increasingly has been viewed as a major cause of social, environmental, and economic problems. Companies are widely perceived to be prospering at the expense of the broader community ... The solution lies in the principle of shared value, which involves creating economic value in a way that *also* creates value for society by addressing its needs and challenges. Businesses must reconnect company success with social progress. Shared value is not social responsibility, philanthropy, or even sustainability, but a new way to achieve economic success ... The purpose of the corporation must be redefined as creating shared value, not just profit *per se*' (Porter and Kramer 2011).

- **The TBL (Triple Bottom Line)**: 'consists of three Ps: profit, people and planet. It aims to measure the financial, social and environmental performance of the corporation over a period of time. Only a company that produces a TBL

> Community investment is not something that is just a nice thing for companies and projects to do—it is important for the business. Community investment spending needs to have a clear 'business case' and logic

is taking account of the full cost involved in doing business' (The Economist 2009).

- **Corporate citizenship**: 'is a recognition that a business, corporation or business-like organisation, has social, cultural and environmental responsibilities to the community in which it seeks a licence to operate, as well as economic and financial ones to its shareholders or immediate stakeholders' (Work and Family Researchers Network n.d.).

- **CSR (Corporate Social Responsibility)**: 'the voluntary activities undertaken by a company to operate in an economic, social and environmentally sustainable manner' (Government of Canada 2014).

- **Business case**: 'A business case captures the reasoning for initiating a project or task … The logic of the business case is that, whenever resources such as money or effort are consumed, they should be in support of a specific business need' (http://en.wikipedia.org/wiki/Business_case).

It is not within the ambit of this book to get into a lengthy discussion and debate about all of the above terms, except to say that it is the strong view of the authors that CI is not something that is just a nice thing for companies and projects to do—CI is important for the business. Linked to this is the further point, as discussed in Chapter 2, that CI spending needs to have a clear 'business case' and logic. This perspective does not diminish the need for community investment and development to have a clear 'community case', i.e. to address key community issues and risks, but having a clear business case will ultimately ensure shareholder, board of directors and management support, and the development of sustainable interventions. The bottom line is that money should not be spent unless it makes sense for the business.

More specifically, CI is important because:

- Businesses do cause negative impacts on communities and society, in addition to the positive impacts they make.

- It is no longer enough for companies with significant or perceived significant environmental and social impacts, including the extractive sector, to simply say that they create jobs and pay taxes. Despite some detractors, there is now a strong expectation that companies need to do more, and their social licence to operate depends on this, i.e. getting all the necessary government licences and permits is not necessarily enough to enable a project to be developed, operated and expanded peacefully.

- Other factors that may add to the need for CI include global certification requirements, using it to obtain competitive advantage, trying to ensure customer loyalty, and meeting government requirements.

There is a strong business case for undertaking CI (as part of a co-ordinated approach to stakeholder engagement), i.e.:

- Well-planned and -implemented CI will help a project to develop shared value, thereby helping to obtain its social licence to operate.

- Human nature is such that, if communities feel your project will not give them enough benefits, then they will not support it, or may even actively oppose it.
- Employment is typically high on the agenda for local communities, as is local procurement, but companies often cannot address all employment needs and some (such as opencast mines) are, by their nature, not always large employers of people during their operation phases. Therefore CI is often a necessary way in which to bolster the 'benefit package' for local stakeholders.
- Communities and other stakeholders may be able to delay or stop your project, increase project costs or tarnish your reputation if they think you are not being a good corporate citizen. You therefore need to think what the cost of a project delay will be versus the cost of CI.

At the same time, it is easy to spend money, but not so easy to make a real and sustainable difference. In some companies, executives, while acknowledging in principle that CI is necessary, are jaded when they see little apparent return on the money they spend on CI and feel that the more they give, the more communities, government and other stakeholders demand. There is therefore clearly scope to improve how companies plan for, implement, monitor and report on CI.

What are the objectives of CI?

A project's CI objectives could include the following:

- Overall project goal = broad community and other stakeholder support to enable the project to develop, operate and expand peacefully. (Broad community support is a collection of expressions by affected communities, through individuals and their recognised representatives, in support of the project. There may be broad community support even if some individuals or groups object to the project.)
- Help to create shared value and to obtain and retain a social licence to operate.
- Improve the quality of life of local communities.
- Foster long-term sustainability by enabling communities to help themselves, instead of engendering long-term dependence on the project.

Bear in mind that CI objectives need to be carefully aligned with overall corporate business objectives, and that all spending on CI should have a clear business case.

> Undertaking CI without clear objectives is no different from developing a mine or other project— or undertaking any other human endeavour— without objectives, i.e. efforts will lack focus

What are the key issues, challenges and risks?

Key challenges include:

- **Increasing community, government and societal expectations**: getting people to realise that the 'cake' is limited
- **More media attention**, particularly on the extractive sector
- There is still often a **lack of project realism about the complexity of social issues** and the effort, time and resources required to address these properly
- **Getting project and corporate management to fully appreciate the challenges of, and the business case for, doing social properly**
- **Finding the right spending balance between different communities**
- **Maximising limited project-related local employment and procurement opportunities**: addressing community capacity gaps
- **Sometimes high level of mistrust in and between communities**: getting communities to work more closely together
- While many companies have made major strides in the social arena, including in the extractive sector, the overall **extractive sector is still perceived in a negative light by many**
- **Managing perceptions**: getting more credit for the good things a project does—companies need to get better at showing what they are doing well
- Putting in place the steps to address the above challenges: **making project CI practice less ad hoc and more structured and businesslike**

What are the guiding principles?

Important guiding principles are as follows:

- **Help communities to help themselves** in order to break the cycle of dependence
- **Ensure community involvement, empowerment and ownership**: sustainable development is not possible without a local sense of community ownership and empowerment
- **Process is as important as outcome**: communities need to feel that there has been a process where they have been actively involved, rather than having things merely offered or dictated to them
- **Local context**: the approach needs to be firmly rooted in the local context, i.e. ordinary, practical and sustainable
- **Transparency**: decisions and activities need to be undertaken in a transparent manner, with adequate information disclosed to relevant or interested parties

What are the key components of the process?

Making community investments that result in positive long-term development outcomes is challenging. There are numerous examples of companies that have spent large amounts of money with little long-term benefit to communities and limited mitigation of the social risks faced by mining projects. The reality is that good intent and resources are not enough. Successful community investment and development requires a clear guiding vision, objectives and principles, as well as careful planning and implementation. A comprehensive approach needs to include:

- Early planning, ongoing review and updating
- Investing adequate time and resources (experienced personnel and other resources)
- Setting out a clear short-term and long-term plan for the company's community investments
- Establishing CI objectives that are linked to the overall business case
- Considering both short-term and long-term objectives
- Developing clear guiding principles and criteria
- Identifying target stakeholder groups and specifying eligibility criteria
- Linking the CI strategy to the local context by drawing on socioeconomic baseline studies, an assessment of project impacts, and an assessment of risks faced by the project and local communities
- Selecting clear and focused investment areas: target investment areas that create shared value
- Establishing an iterative process of engagement with local stakeholders and partners on CI: real two-way engagement (listening as well as talking)
- Drawing on the company's/project's core competences and resources to support communities
- Promoting cross-functional co-ordination and accountability for supporting CI objectives
- Integrating CI with other company programmes that involve communities (stakeholder engagement, the grievance process, environmental and social impact and risk management plans, and local hiring and procurement)
- Setting out criteria and guiding principles against which all CI proposals will be screened
- Identifying the key programme areas in which the company will invest
- Identifying the implementation model and decision-making/governance structures
- Defining roles and responsibilities, budget, scope, and time-line

- Describing the company's exit/handover and sustainability strategies
- Describing how project results will be monitored and communicated
- Developing trust and a partnership approach
- Capacity-building of project personnel and stakeholders, as necessary

Tailoring CI to different project stages

CI needs to be tailored to the different stages of a project, as project impacts and risks will vary and the proponent will have differing levels of resources over time. While individual projects will vary, most projects will evolve over time along the following lines:

- **Project concept/scoping/exploration stage**: identifying and beginning to understand stakeholders
  - Engagement is about undertaking a preliminary identification and analysis of stakeholders, gauging potential local support for or opposition to the project, and identifying key issues and risks that could affect project viability.
  - Engagement will be selective and targeted.
  - There will be limited, if any, CI (although some may be necessary, for example, if the project requires an on-the-ground presence to conduct exploration activities).
- **Pre-feasibility study/feasibility study/planning/permitting stage**: detailed planning and engagement to obtain social licence to operate
  - Engagement is progressively at its highest during the components of this stage, bearing in mind the need to:
    - » Undertake detailed stakeholder analysis
    - » Typically go through an environmental, social and health impact assessment process and develop and engage on mitigation measures/action plans
    - » Often undertake a land access and resettlement process
    - » Start spending on CI in a strategic manner to build goodwill without unduly heightening expectations.
  - Failure to address stakeholder issues, concerns and expectations at this stage, when project impacts such as land take start to occur, will generally result in the project not progressing further.
- **Construction stage**: putting words into action
  - Construction is a sensitive time as project impacts necessitate showing affected communities and other stakeholders that issues are being addressed and the project is starting to provide benefits as previously promised in discussions and action plans.
  - Local employment and procurement is typically a very important issue for local communities, requiring careful engagement to manage

expectations: this is the time when project community investment and development initiatives start to intensify.
- Failure to do what it has promised and, critically, to satisfy key stakeholders adequately that this is the case will result in a project losing its social licence to operate: **perception = reality**.
- **Operations stage**: retaining the social licence to operate
  - The operations stage continues to be a sensitive time, as projects will need to continue to show that they are addressing their impacts and sharing benefits.
  - Local employment and procurement is often doubly challenging at this stage, particularly where levels are significantly lower than during the construction stage: this can create major tension with local communities.
  - The danger at this stage is that the project assumes it has obtained its social licence to operate and becomes complacent. Remember that you are not granted your social licence to operate forever—only your actions and stakeholder perceptions will ensure it is retained.
  - At the same time, operating income generally means the project has more wherewithal than ever to engage in CI. However, how this is done is critical, i.e. the project must engage with communities in such a way as to avoid a dependence approach and ensure more sustainable community development.
- **Expansion stages**: doing it all over again
  - Many projects go through expansion phases, necessitating going through the stages mentioned above again.
- **Downsizing and closure stages**: managing the end
  - The downsizing and closure stages of a project are particularly challenging due to a reduction in project benefits.
  - It is important that stakeholders, particularly local communities and government, are carefully prepared for and engaged during these stages.
  - Local employment and procurement will inevitably reduce during these phases, as will a project's ability to invest in community development (unless it has had the foresight to build up a reserve pool in advance for this stage).

Assessment and analysis

Determining who should benefit from CI, i.e. how the 'cake' should be cut and shared between different communities and within each community, is a sometimes difficult but vital step. To assist in determining this, the project needs to undertake:

- A thorough process of stakeholder identification and analysis (with this repeated on a regular basis), including socioeconomic assessment, identification of networks, institutional mapping and identification of potential partners

- A project impact assessment
- An issue, opportunity and risk assessment (in relation to the project and local communities and other relevant stakeholders)

These exercises will help to provide important foundational information on which to base CI planning related to, for example:

- Issues of highest concern to local stakeholders
- Local stakeholders' perceptions of the project
- Community priorities that can potentially be addressed through CI
- The level of risk and opportunity these issues pose for the company (relative to business objectives)
- The availability and capacity of local institutions and potential partners to implement
- Current development initiatives or programmes in the area (including government development priorities at the local, regional and national levels)
- A sense of what other actors—communities, government, donors, NGOs (non-governmental organisations), and other partners—can contribute to a multi-stakeholder development process

Benchmarking

Unfortunately, one does not always have the luxury of developing an approach to CI from scratch at the inception of a project. In developing or updating a CI policy, strategy and plan, it is important to reflect on your project's past CI, i.e. what worked and did not work, what needs to change and what should be retained. It is also useful to benchmark against comparable and appropriate projects in order to see what issues peers are facing, what they are doing and what has worked/ not worked, and draw useful lessons. However, remember that each project is different so do not copy blindly: a 'cookie-cutter' approach does not work.

Government, regional and district development plans

In developing or updating a CI policy, strategy and plan, it is important to take account of what plans the government has for the area. The project should seek to engage with applicable government agencies and levels to try to ensure an aligned and co-ordinated approach that helps to maximise the benefits of the project's efforts.

'Old style' CI

In the authors' experience, and as the IFC and others have noted, the reasons why 'old-style' CI typically underperformed include:

- Limited proponent understanding of the often complex local context
- Insufficient participation and ownership by local stakeholders
- Use of a needs-based assessment of communities approach (instead of an assets-based approach)
- A perception of 'giving' rather than 'investment' created by the proponent and adopted by local communities and government
- CI activities have been detached from the rest of the business
- Proponents responding to local requests in an ad hoc manner
- Lack of professionalism and business rigour
- Insufficient focus on sustainability
- Provision of free goods and services by the proponent that merely fosters dependence
- No exit or handover strategy
- Overemphasis on infrastructure and underemphasis on skills building
- Lack of transparency and clear criteria
- A failure to measure and communicate results

Developing a policy, strategy and plan

Before developing a formal CDP (community development plan), one must first determine what one's policy and strategy is, as these shape the details of the plan.

A policy is a statement of intent, generally adopted by the board of directors or senior governance body within an organisation. The policy will, based on defined objectives, set out the parameters within which planning, implementation and other activities will take place. As with other corporate endeavours, it is important that the company has a clear CI policy to inform its actions, as well as showing external parties that it is committed to acting in a certain way. It is important that a company thinks carefully about what it will be publicly committing to: do not commit to what you cannot achieve on the ground. Probably the biggest issue in

> Undertaking CI without a clear policy, strategy or plan is no different from developing a project without a plan. It results in an unplanned, reactive, ad hoc and incomplete approach

relation to corporate policies is whether actions on the ground, e.g. of a Canadian mining company with a project in Africa, match commitments made in a Toronto office block.

Key parameters of your strategy and plan should include:

- What stage is your project at?
- What are your key issues, impacts, challenges, risks and opportunities?
- What are your key objectives?
- What are your guiding principles?

 Project example

From its exploration stage, a mining project in Eastern Europe adopted a 'donations approach' to community investment and development. At the time, this was felt to be the easiest way to address community requests and demands, given that the project had limited resources and staff. However, once the mine had been developed and was operational, the company persisted with a donations approach yet complained how it lacked a partnership with local communities, who had a dependence mentality and felt that they just had to ask the company for what they wanted. Although the project had a formal community development plan, it was clear that it lacked a clear policy, objectives and principles to guide its community investment and development activities. Putting these in place was identified as a critical step on the road to developing a new partnership-based relationship with local communities, which would not be based merely on handouts from the company.

An example of how to structure a CDP is as follows:

1. Introduction
2. Institutional, legal, standards and policy framework
3. Baseline conditions
4. Community investment and development to date
5. Community investment and development from today onward
6. Work plan and schedule
7. Responsibilities
8. Monitoring and reporting

Bear in mind that a CDP needs to be developed in an iterative process with other project management/action plans. In addition, CDPs are typically not developed once. They should go through a process of multiple drafts prepared by designated personnel (such as the community relations department) working closely with local communities and other relevant stakeholders to the extent appropriate and possible, with reviews by project management, external reviewers and other parties. A CDP needs to be updated on an annual basis, or as appropriate.

The overall annual process of CI assessment, planning, implementation, monitoring and evaluation needs to take place within the context of a detailed work plan and schedule for the year that clearly states who will do what and how the project will engage with other stakeholders relating to CI, and is aligned with other community relations and stakeholder engagement activities and the overall project schedule and key milestones.

Implementation models

A key question is: 'What is the most suitable implementation model for project CI?' Possible implementation models include:

- **Company foundation or trust**: this involves establishing a foundation or trust as a separate legal entity to carry out CI programmes. Foundations and trusts can have grant-making authority (i.e. financing of CI programmes implemented by others) or serve an implementing function (implementing their own projects and programmes).

- **In-house implementation**: this involves creating or using an existing internal department or unit to work directly with communities to design and implement CI projects (this option could include the establishment of an unincorporated fund).

- **Third-party implementation**: this involves engaging a third party, such as a local or international NGO, to work with local communities in designing and implementing CI projects, or support an existing initiative being implemented by others, such as government.

- **Multi-stakeholder partnership**: this would involve establishing or joining a voluntary or collaborative alliance, network or partnership. This implies co-operation between two or more actors in a manner that shares risks, responsibilities, resources and competences, and involves a joint commitment to common tasks and goals.

> There is no one model or approach that is the best. Each project needs to consider what is most appropriate based on its particular circumstances

- **Hybrid**: this approach would utilise a combination of two or more implementation models described above, to deliver various components of the CI programme.

Decision-making around how to deliver CI is driven by both internal and external factors and considerations. Some of these factors may impose limitations on the choice of implementation model in a given setting, or have implications in terms of efficiency and effectiveness. There are three important elements to consider:

- **Time-horizon**: How long will the company be operating in the area and how quickly does it need its CI programme up and running?
- **Budget**: How much will the company spend per year on CI, and how secure is this funding?
- **Local context**: What is the level of local implementation capacity and what is the potential for partnerships? Are there government or legal requirements for establishing certain vehicles to receive or channel funds for local development?

Certain questions are applicable regardless of model chosen. These include:

- Does the implementation model support the company's objectives?
- How will the company maintain ownership, visibility and oversight?
- How will participatory decision-making and governance be fostered?
- Should you pilot before scaling up?
- How will transparency, accountability and sustainability of funding arrangements be ensured?
- What capacity-building is needed to support the chosen model/encourage local delivery?
- What is the company's exit or handover strategy?

Identifying and processing ideas and requests for assistance

Unless a company is intent on a totally top-down approach to CI, which is not recommended, it needs to find a way to engage with relevant parties, in particular local communities and government, in a way that optimises the generation, development and assessment of ideas for projects and programmes where CI can take place. Ideas can come from within the company and from outside stakeholders, but these will need to be evaluated bearing in mind the following:

- Overall CI objectives, policy and guiding principles
- Key issues, risks and opportunities facing the company, local communities and other stakeholders
- The annual budget available as well as what other parties can contribute
- The need to be objective and fair in deciding which programmes to support and the split of spending among different communities and stakeholder groups

Engaging with stakeholders

To what extent, and in what ways, should external stake-holders be involved in CI planning and implementation? As discussed, there are many reasons why old-style CI using a top-down approach does not work. Linked to the type of implementation model that a company chooses, it needs to tailor external (and internal) stakeholder engagement to maximise that engagement to the level appropriate for the location, project and time in question.

> Ensuring adequate stakeholder engagement in the CI process is a critical condition for success

External stakeholder engagement can take place on six basic levels, namely cross-community, community, household, government, with other external stakeholders, and at an individual CI project/programme/initiative level.

A partnership approach takes engagement to a level beyond consultation and negotiation, although these aspects typically remain even where a partnership is developed. This approach seeks to move relations between a project and, for example, local communities, government and NGOs, beyond a situation where the project is seen as merely causing impacts to being the purveyor of employment, procurement and CI opportunities. Issues are seen as everybody's problem, with a move away from an adversarial approach to closer collaboration and solutions leading to win–win outcomes. This approach is based on a pooling of ideas and resources, and joint planning, implementation and monitoring. Characteristics of a successful partnership include:

- Common or sufficiently aligned objectives
- A pooling of resources (time, money, in kind), with a focus on complementarity, i.e. drawing on the core competences of the different partners
- Transparency, i.e. a sharing of information
- Joint fact-finding, planning and implementation
- Sharing risks and opportunities/benefits

Particularly in certain countries such as Canada, broad community development agreements, which come under a variety of different names, are concluded in two main contexts. First, there is a legal requirement: for example, such an agreement needs to be concluded with indigenous people before their land can be accessed. Second, where the project proponent realises the magnitude of the social issues they face and decides to reach overarching comprehensive agreements to try to cover and regulate all social issues with affected communities, rather than adopting a more piecemeal approach.

Before going down this route, project proponents (if they have a choice) need to consider the following:

- Is it feasible and necessary to negotiate such a comprehensive agreement? For example, how many communities and other parties are involved, and are their representatives reliable?

- How widespread would the community development agreement be? For example, will it try to cover all issues, and how large a geographical area would it cover?
- Do the benefits of a comprehensive community development agreement outweigh the risks? For example, is such an agreement implementable over the life of the project?

Implementing CI

How a company implements CI will depend on the implementation model it chooses and the extent to which it involves external stakeholders. A number of parties should and would be involved in aspects of the process (planning and implementation) including, for example:

- Communities: as beneficiaries and active participants
- Local government: as beneficiaries and active participants
- The company: in particular, the community relations department, as well as other departments in charge of employment, procurement and finance
- Other external development partners, such as NGOs

Management structures will depend on the implementation model chosen. For example, the management structure where a company chose a site-specific hybrid approach for a mine consisted of the following:

- Establishment of an unincorporated fund with its own charter
- Establishment of an internal committee to manage the fund, made up of senior company personnel, give final approval to projects to be supported by the fund, and ensure its administration in accordance with a charter
- Use of the mine community relations department to be responsible for the overall day-to-day administration of the fund, undertaking all external stakeholder engagement, processing of all requests and ideas for fund assistance, updating and implementing the CDP, and attending internal committee meetings

How much to spend?

Potential factors to consider include the following:

- The type and level of social risks faced by the company/project and nearby communities
- The negative and positive impacts caused by the project
- What other comparable companies/projects are doing

- The level of profitability of the company/project
- What is required to maintain the company's social licence to operate
- Other contributions the company is already making, such as the percentage of royalties it pays that are being spent by government at a local level
- The need to set aside funds for a 'rainy day', such as years when the company may not generate adequate funds to address key social issues, and to develop a reserve to assist with social issues related to project closure and its aftermath

There are many possible funding formulas/permutations, for example:

- **No fixed formula**: an annually determined amount based on the company's assessment of what social issues, impacts and risks face it and the communities, and what is required to address these and maintain its social licence to operate; and/or an initial endowment; and/or a periodic lump sum

or

- **A fixed formula**: an annual percentage of gross revenue; and/or an annual percentage of pre-tax net profits; and/or some other permutation Or, in the case of a gold-mining company, an amount per ounce of gold (or all minerals) sold; and/or an annual percentage of pre-tax net profits; and/or some other permutation

and

- **Other sources**, i.e. forms of company nonfinancial assistance, such as use of company personnel, facilities and equipment; and sourcing of supplementary funding and resources from appropriate third parties

and

- **Community and government contributions** to approved projects, programmes and initiatives in some form (financial, in kind, time)

Examples from the mining sector include the following:

- **Freeport Partnership Fund for Community Development, Indonesia**: fund receives 1% of mine revenues; 10% of all future receipts are to be invested in a long-term fund
- **Minera Escondida Foundation, BHP Billiton, Chile**: funded by allocation of 1% of pre-tax annual profit based on a three-year rolling average
- **Gold Fields Ghana Foundation**: funded by US$1 for every ounce of gold mined from the Tarkwa and Damang Mines, plus 0.5% of pre-tax profits; includes provision for setting aside funds for a 'rainy day'
- **Ahafo Development Foundation, Newmont, Ghana**: funded through a combination of US$1 per ounce of gold sold, plus 1% of net operating profit (pre-tax) from the Ahafo Mine
- **Mozal Community Development Trust, Mozambique**: funded by 1% of pre-tax profits, plus an initial amount of US$2.5 million

- **Greater Rustenburg Community Foundation, South Africa**: this is a community-developed foundation located in the platinum-rich area of Rustenburg in South Africa. Focused on developing a sustainable future for community members, there is no direct company involvement in the foundation, which relies on donations from individual and corporate donors.
- **Palabora Foundation, Rio Tinto, South Africa**: funded by the greater of 3% of net profit or R2 million
- **Rossing Foundation, Rio Tinto, Namibia**: funded by 2% of all dividends distributed to shareholders after tax

Saving for a rainy day

It is not always possible to perfectly align annual spending on community investment and development with community issues, needs and risks, and company issues and risks. It is also impossible to perfectly predict, for example, the gold price over the life of the mine, or to anticipate periodic economic downturns and other external phenomena. What is certain is that there will

> Make sure you save for a rainy day

be years when spending to maintain the social licence to operate may require resources in excess of those that can be generated by the company/project in the year in question; the project will come to an end one day, and there will need to be resources to manage its social exit strategy (as part of a broader closure plan); and certain longer-term community development projects will, by their nature, require assistance beyond when the project closes.

Therefore, projects should annually review the need and possibility to set aside a portion of the monies available for CI, in order to build up a rainy day reserve. In the case of a mine, this would be a bit like the social equivalent of setting aside monies for environmental rehabilitation and overall mine closure.

 Project example

A company in Eastern Europe determined that the life of the mine was estimated to be no more than ten years. Accordingly, when establishing its community development fund, it decided to stipulate that 10% of the funding accruing to the fund annually would be set aside to build a capital reserve. This would help to offset the impacts of the eventual closure of the mine, and allow programmes and activities supported by the fund to continue beyond mine closure.

Measuring success

Is your CI spend really making a difference as you desired? Possible ways to measure community investment and development outcomes more accurately include:

- Set SMART objectives that can be attributed to CI, i.e. the objectives must be specific, measurable, attributable, realistic and time-bound
- Jointly define indicators and measures of success with stakeholders
- Establish a baseline
- Focus on outcomes and impacts, not just outputs
- Focus on qualitative, not just quantitative, indicators
- Track changes in community perceptions
- Make measurement participatory
- Track results by gender
- Integrate CI into the company's broader monitoring and evaluation systems
- Use the monitoring and evaluation results to drive resource allocation for CI

Participatory monitoring means more than sharing with communities the results of monitoring, i.e. it requires their physical involvement in the actual monitoring process, ideally including the joint development of monitoring indicators. Where communities do not want to be directly involved in monitoring or adequate capacity-building is problematic, another way to address mistrust may be to involve the community in choosing mutually acceptable independent third-party monitors.

Exit strategies

From the inception of a CI project and the provision of company assistance, work out your handover/exit strategy. Doing this at the beginning helps you to determine if you think a project is viable once company assistance ceases. If it is not then you need to think very carefully about, *inter alia*, the design of the CI project, whether the company should be providing assistance at all, and measures that could be taken to avoid long-term community dependence on the company.

Make sure you have a clear exit strategy

Other factors and considerations

Women

It sounds obvious that women form around half of communities and should therefore be critical players in helping maximise community development. Sadly, this does not typically match with the actual role women play in the processes of assessment, planning, implementation and monitoring of community investment and development outcomes. The role of women in these processes needs to increase if the outcomes of CI are to be optimised. To do this, each company/project needs to look closely at ways to involve women more, taking into account the particular circumstances of each site.

Vulnerable people

Programmes and initiatives that assist vulnerable people and minimise vulnerability are an obvious target for CI spending. However, one needs to plan with vulnerable people, rather than merely planning for them, and focus CI appending efforts on measures that will ultimately help vulnerable people help themselves, rather than creating long-term dependence.

Public relations

Is CI spending merely a public relations exercise? There is nothing wrong with companies/projects getting credit for the good things they do. Perception is reality and relations with external stakeholders are largely governed by their perceptions of the company, i.e. the management of social risk and retention of a social licence to operate is premised on a positive perception of the company. If companies do not publicise the good things they do then no one will know about this. However, undertaking CI merely as a public relations exercise is doomed to ultimate failure: poorly planned and implemented CI programmes will eventually fail, leading to negative outcomes and publicity.

Record-keeping and information management

It is all very well undertaking CI, but you also need to be able to show that this has been done: for example, an NGO or the media may allege that the project has not been serious about CI, or a project monitor may ask to see records of CI undertaken. Therefore, ensure that you keep proper records in a suitable information management system.

Capacity-building

It may be necessary to capacity-build not only the project's personnel involved in CI, but also external stakeholders, such as local community representatives and members. Provision of information, explanation and capacity-building will be required to help communities to participate actively in, and enjoy the benefits of, CI. Community involvement in CI planning, implementation and monitoring, where they get the opportunity to work closely together with designated company personnel and other third parties, will also capacity-build local communities (and government). What is required is patience and a realisation that the process of working together and building capacity will take time.

 Project example

A company in Eastern Europe had spent significant sums in the past on community investment and development. However, as they moved into full production, the company realised that it could no longer follow the 'donations approach' that had evolved over time. The move to full production meant that much larger amounts would be available to spend in future. Accordingly, the company decided to put in place a more structured and transparent process for evaluating external and internal requests and ideas for how community investment monies should be spent. This included the development of a set of objective criteria against which each request and idea would be evaluated and scored. The new process also required all applicants to complete a form setting out the basis of the request (in effect a 'business plan'). The company realised that, in order to help the new system work, it would be necessary to capacity-build local communities on the new approach.

Community investment: key considerations

- **Involve communities and local government in CI planning**, implementation and monitoring to develop ownership:
  - Accept that companies sometimes have to do things government or communities should do themselves, but **never take on sole responsibility**
  - Make sure communities and local government also contribute something
  - Never just give—get something in return
  - Develop real tripartite relationships with communities and government
  - Stick to what you are good at

  CI spending should be more targeted to **address key social issues and risks** faced by the company and communities

- **Manage community expectations and perceptions**:
  - Perception is reality: under-promise/over-deliver
  - Be transparent

- – Actions speak louder than words
- – Make sure all company messages and actions are consistent
- – Get credit for the good things you do
- **Sustainability**:
  - – Do not pretend that mines are sustainable, but they can contribute to broader sustainable development
  - – Do not support programmes that cannot continue once company support ends
  - – Ensure the company has a handover and exit strategy
- Apply more **business rigour** to community investment and development activities:
  - – Specific programmes need to be developed within an overarching strategy
  - – Treat these activities like any other parts of the business (they are no different just because they deal with social issues)
  - – Make sure these activities are based on clear objectives, guiding principles and clear plans
  - – All such activities must have a clear scope, objective, work plan and schedule, budget and key performance indicators
  - – All requests for funding and assistance should be assessed using a clear set of suitable and comprehensive criteria
  - – Process is as important as outcome
- **Make sure you can deliver**: do not promise or do things without being aware of what they will cost and the precedent they will set
- Ensure an **appropriate balance** of spending among neighbouring communities
- Make sure the CI programmes and initiatives the company supports are **locally appropriate**
- Develop a **formal CDP** to ensure a comprehensive and consistent approach

16

Livelihood restoration and community development implementation

Livelihood restoration, as outlined in Chapter 10, is key to supporting households to maintain their wellbeing in the face of life-changing impacts on their communities and livelihoods. Despite the best planning, however, poor implementation can render these programmes ineffective, leading to the impoverishment of impacted households.

The objective of this chapter is to provide advice on the practical implementation of livelihood restoration and community development activities to avoid some of the key pitfalls.

> Successful livelihood restoration is a major challenge

What are the key issues, challenges and risks?

- A key issue with livelihood restoration is the timing of activities. Agricultural support programmes often follow compensation payments and clash with project construction when labour is directed towards the project, which limits the uptake of these programmes.

- Many projects are in isolated rural communities where local partner agencies, including government and civil society, have a limited presence or capacity. It may be difficult to bring in outsiders to run programmes and this can cause delays and make many activities ineffective.

- In some countries where corruption is common, there will be attempts by powerful local traditional and political leaders to hijack development projects for their personal needs, leading to conflict with the communities. This is particularly common where the project relies too heavily on powerful local gatekeepers to push agreements through with the local communities.

- It is common for projects to try to implement too many activities simultaneously, resulting in poor project management and ultimately multiple project failures.

- Some projects rely too much on one service provider who may be a specialist in a particular area. This can lead to an overemphasis on one sector. In development, the solution you are provided with depends on the speciality of the agency you ask.

- In some areas the presence of outside experts who may be considered elites can cause tension with the local communities, and this can cause conflict.

- Livelihood projects need to be managed professionally, with transparency around project expenditure.

- Projects generally have limited experience in livelihood restoration and often support projects that promise quick success but which often fail after a short time.

- The role of women in providing for the household is often not properly recognised. This can result in women losing access to key livelihood activities such as gardening, fuelwood collection and petty trading, with a decline in their status and standards of living.

What are the key components of the process?

The main components of the livelihood restoration process are outlined below:

Land-for-land replacement

Experience from the majority of projects is that paying poor people cash for their assets, particularly for land and housing, often results in their impoverishment as they are ill-equipped to manage this windfall and often invest it unwisely. Once the cash is spent, the households find themselves landless and/or homeless and making demands on the project for support. Therefore, the most important principle in land access and resettlement is to try to replace the land if possible rather than pay cash. However, there are many challenges to land-for-land replacement:

- Many projects, particularly for dams and mining, require huge land takes which put considerable pressure on the remaining land resources. It is often impossible to source land to replace all that which is lost to the project. Replacement land should include fallow land which is currently not cultivated and also pasture land and natural resource areas such as woodlands. However, with increased pressure on land it is often difficult just to replace the cropped land area, which leads to changes in local farming practices as fallow systems are abandoned and a greater dependence is created on imported fertilisers.

- The land that is not used around the project and available for purchase is generally of poorer quality than that which was being farmed by the project-affected households, and may need considerable investment to bring it into production.

- As discussed in Chapter 10, replacement land might only be available a long distance from the project area, making it difficult for the resettlement households to access employment and economic opportunities from the project.

> Finding adequate replacement land is often the biggest issue when trying to restore livelihoods

- The available land which is not being cultivated often has an alternative livelihood use such as grazing, hunting, wild food collection or for cultural or recreational uses, so transforming this land into agriculture can be challenging.

- The price of land outside the project area normally becomes seriously inflated due to the presence of the project, making land replacement very expensive.

- Often land which is available for purchase is currently under forestry and the project must clear the land at a considerable cost; this also reduces the natural resource stock in the area.

- Many projects focus on purchasing replacement land for the project-affected households without considering the impacts on the owners of this replacement land by paying cash and somehow considering this a different impact category. It is clear that households that sell land for the resettlement site and replacement land should be considered as project-affected households, and the risks to their livelihoods assessed on an equal basis to project-area project-affected households.

The following are recommendations for managing the challenge of limitations to replacement land:

- Acquire high-resolution satellite imagery for an area up to a 10 km radius around the project area. Recent advances mean that colour imagery up to 50 cm can be acquired at reasonable cost for any project area.

- Digitise the main features on the imagery: houses, roads, rivers, forests, etc. Overlay the project infrastructure map, together with environmental buffers, as a separate layer onto the map. Overlay project-affected fields which have been surveyed as part of the survey process. It is important to identify land owned and managed by women separately from men, including kitchen gardens and rice paddocks. Women will often require small blocks of land on their plot or close by to meet household needs and to have the option to keep small animals such as chickens to supplement household income.

- Establish the area of cultivated land that is being acquired for each project-affected household and cumulatively for each village. This is the target area for land replacement. It is also important to identify the fields that are owned by the project-affected households in buffer areas and outside the project area. The primary objective should be to resettle the project-affected households close to their remaining farmland if feasible.

- From the satellite imagery, identify non-cultivated areas radiating out from the project area boundary and visit these areas to conduct an initial assessment. As outlined in Chapter 9, the resettlement site selection process should be driven by finding replacement land, where agriculture is the main livelihood, as a key project criterion.

- When replacement land areas have been identified, consultations must be held with the existing owners to establish the land use and what livelihood disruption would result from acquiring this land and converting it to agriculture. It is common for projects to buy replacement land from landowners outside the project area, and to consider this as a willing buyer transaction and not to consider the livelihood impact on these landowners. However, those landowners who sell their land should be considered equally as project-affected households, and the same approach taken to ensure that they retain enough land for their livelihoods or can demonstrate alternative livelihood options. As discussed in Chapter 10, the project can try to acquire one large site (blanket approach) or acquire a residential site and smaller parcels of land to replace farms (patchwork approach).

There are two main approaches to acquiring replacement land:

- The project or government acquires the land: this is useful in the case of a blanket approach where there are large blocks of land available close to the project area and all the resettlement land can be acquired at once, as discussed above.

- The project incentivises the project-affected households to find land themselves: this is useful for the patchwork approach where the project-affected households identify parcels of land they want to purchase through their own family and traditional networks. The project must survey this land and verify that the transaction is genuine before payment. The project must also ensure that the seller has enough land remaining, or an alternative livelihood, so that they are not solely reliant on the purchase cash. This approach has the advantage of the project-affected household selecting the quality and location of land that suits their needs.

Quality of replacement land

Land available for sale in many areas is often of the poorest quality and may require considerable investment to make it suitable for equivalent replacement agricultural land. This may require investment in tree removal, ploughing and developing road access and water facilities. The project should not assume available land is suitable, but must get an agricultural expert to assess the land at an early stage, and take soil samples and dig soil profiles before the sites are approved.

Agricultural support packages

It is important that the project-affected households quickly establish basic food production so that they are not dependent on the project for rations. The timing of the move to the new resettlement site must therefore be aligned with the farming seasons to give the project-affected households the opportunity to both harvest existing crops and prepare the new sites and sow their crops. Where it is not possible to harvest existing crops, food rations must be provided to maintain household nutrition until the first crops can be harvested. It is recommended to provide an agricultural support package in kind rather than in case, together with agricultural extension support, in order to ensure that the project-affected households quickly get back to cropping and food production to meet their household needs. It is common for project-affected households who receive substantial compensation money, in their terms, to skip some cropping seasons and this can render them very vulnerable to impoverishment once the money is spent. It important also that the timing of inputs is aligned with the growing season, as there have been cases where inputs arrive late and the farmers lose production.

Figure 16.1: A pasture land development programme.

The agricultural support package must be aligned with the construction schedule of the project: if there are significant short-term employment opportunities at this time, the agricultural support programmes might not work as the project-affected households will not have time to cultivate the land. Instead the support programmes should be limited during construction, focusing on women, and ramped up when construction ends and the men are once more available. The end of construction is often a time of considerable tension on projects as project-affected households lose the regular cash income and status of project employment, and investment in livelihood restoration at this time can reduce community discontent.

Alternative plots in urban areas

Where resettlement is in urban areas and there are few building plots locally, the process of resettling the project-affected households can result in them ending up far from their original homes and livelihoods. This is common in the case of slum resettlements, where squatters move onto unused land close to economic centres in order to take advantage of business opportunities. They are often resettled to outlying areas and, although provided with basic housing, their livelihoods are negatively impacted as they often have to travel long distances back to the city to find work. The only solution is to find sites close to their original settlement area or on good transport networks so that they can find cheap transport to access economic zones.

What if there is not sufficient replacement land?

Where there is not sufficient replacement land, even after the project-affected households have been incentivised to find smaller plots locally, the project may not be able to offer area-for-area replacement of cropland. In this case the company should try to at least provide a minimum threshold for each household of, say, one hectare, so that a safety net is provided. The focus needs to be on maximising alternative livelihood options as discussed below. However, where it is apparent that there is no replacement land and alternative options are seriously limited, the company needs to consider whether developing the project is justified against the negative impacts on the project-area communities.

Livestock programmes

It is often difficult to replace pasture land on projects as these areas are often developed to provide replacement cropland. It is important to establish the dependence of the project-affected households on livestock during the baseline studies as mixed farming systems are often more sustainable, providing a domestic source of manure for crops and a diversified range of products for sale. The project-affected households will want to bring their animals to the new site, and so the design of the resettlement site must make provision for animals to be corralled on the outskirts of the settlement as is appropriate. In many countries herders, such

Figure 16.2: Provision must be made for livestock and herders.

as the Peul in Africa, are employed to take care of animals, leading to a mutual dependence over time. The resettlement can put a considerable strain on these relationships when there is no pasture land near the resettlement sites and the herders have to travel greater distances to find grazing areas.

A common mistake on projects is not properly assessing the impacts of livestock intensification programmes on the remaining pasture areas, and providing incentives to increase production which can end up damaging sensitive grazing areas. Beyond a certain threshold livestock, under certain environmental conditions, can cause severe damage to grazing areas resulting in erosion, silting of dams, flooding and decreases in production. This can be a particular problem where pasture is available as commonage and there are poor management systems to limit overgrazing. In many cases the project-affected households will use compensation money to increase their herd sizes, as this is often a status symbol locally.

There has been a focus in some countries on the concept of the 'tragedy of the commons', where individuals act independently in their own interest and against the communities' long-term interests by depleting some common resource. Many traditional agro-pastoralist systems are sustainable as the herders move the livestock around as the seasons and environmental conditions change, to avoid damaging grazing areas. It is common for nomadic herders to bring livestock to areas after the harvest to eat the remaining stalks and fertilise the land. The animals are then taken away during the growing season so that crop damage is minimised.

It is therefore important to ensure that there is a community management system in place to regulate pasture use before any livestock intensification measures are introduced. An assessment should be made on pasture areas close to proposed resettlement sites to understand current users. It is common for nomadic herders to be ignored, depending on the season when the research is undertaken, and unrealistic assumptions made on the carrying capacity of pasture areas.

Where there is the potential to intensify livestock production, mitigation measures can include providing new watering areas for livestock in nearby grazing areas to allow for increased access. Veterinary extension services can also be provided to livestock owners to reduce mortality and so increase livestock productivity. Intensive livestock raising systems can also assist in taking the pressure off pasture land where animals are stall fed for a few months and fattened for the market with grass harvested from fields.

Alternative enterprises

Support for alternative enterprises can provide additional sources of income to project-affected households and help diversify livelihood income sources. However, projects are rife with failed examples of initiatives to promote alternative enterprises and this can often be a case of raising community expectations only to increase discontent with the project later. Therefore, a proper feasibility study must be conducted before any new initiative is introduced to ensure there is a maximum chance of success. The key lessons are discussed by using specific examples of common initiatives below.

Small animal/chicken production projects

It is common for projects to run initiatives on rearing small animals/poultry. The advantage is that these can normally be raised in small areas and there is always a ready cash market for these in the local area. However, it is important to ensure that training and support is given in animal husbandry and nutrition. In many cases project-affected households already keep chickens running semiwild in their compounds, eating scraps and requiring little care. Where production is intensified a steady source of food is required for the animals and it is not uncommon for whole groups to be wiped out by disease if animal husbandry techniques are not practised diligently; in some cases disease happens anyway. The advice is to develop these micro-projects with the support of local extension services and start small. The expected outcome is that only a minority of these projects will be successful. Once the initial weeding out of unsuccessful producers has taken place, the project can work to scale up those committed to making a success of the business.

Livestock donations

It is also common on some projects to provide improved breeds as starter herds to project-affected households with mixed results. In many cases where these projects coincided with compensation payments the project-affected households were not committed and treated the animals as gifts to be eaten or sold on. In other cases the project-affected households were not equipped to care properly for the animals and many died from poor husbandry as nonlocal breeds are often not adapted for local conditions and need more care. The advice is the same as for small animals/chicken projects, to provide the required training before giving animals, and time these projects to when the project-affected households will be fully committed to their success.

Market gardening

Vegetable production is a skill that already exists in communities and the development of the project often provides opportunities to provide vegetables to the project and associated businesses. There are often committed groups of local men and women producing vegetables for local markets and, in more arid countries, the provision of micro-dams provides an important source of dry-season income. It is important to identify opportunities during the feasibility phase as, if these are planned early, the project can construct the dams by taking advantage during construction of using heavy machinery which might not normally be available in the area. There are also sometimes opportunities to share water from dams created by the company to supply the project with water, but the project needs to be sure that there will be excess water available even in the driest year as the community can become dependent on this resource.

Apprenticeships/skills training

Apprenticeships are one of the most positive initiatives projects can undertake to build real skills in the community. As discussed in Chapter 10, the failure to provide skills training opportunities at the earliest opportunity in the project cycle often results in project-affected households being unqualified for many construction and operations jobs, and leads to resentment towards outside labour being brought into the project area. There will always be a need for specialist skills on projects so it is important that, starting in the feasibility study period, the project begins to train local people in skills required by the project. Even if the project does not proceed, the training will help the participants gain employment outside the project area and will be highly appreciated by the community. It is important to have a fair system for selecting trainees, including pre-selection tests to ensure that local elites do not capture all the opportunities and create community tension. With many projects there will be significant opportunities in relatively low-skill levels such as security, cleaning, cooking, etc., and the project should ensure that all these jobs are first offered to local people.

Project example

A project in Africa failed to conduct any training for local young people prior to project construction. During construction a large contingent of Asian workers were brought into to construct the project which caused considerable local tension and resentment against the company. Since then relations between the project and community have further deteriorated to a point where there is a significant security presence in place, at a huge cost to the project, to enable to the company to continue operating.

 Project example

A project in Africa established an apprentice training programme early in exploration to prepare local young people for jobs with the project. This helped to maximise local employment and, while not all succeeded in getting operational jobs with the mine, many have found jobs with other projects nationally. The project has been recognised locally and nationally for this initiative.

However, the company must carefully assess the potential for employment locally or nationally in the selected apprenticeship areas before embarking on a programme. In many countries there are already evolved local apprenticeship programmes where the local trades (carpenter, hairdresser, electrician, mason, etc.) take on young people for no or low pay to be taught a trade. Where these systems exist it is often better to support these tradesmen with improved tools and capacity-building rather than to start a project programme which might compete with local trades.

Women's groups

Many projects support women's groups to produce goods and services for the project or to the wider public. These groups demonstrate the project's support for women and provide girls with role models in their community. Even where there are limited opportunities to provide the project with goods and services at an economic rate, it makes sense to facilitate the formation of women's groups and support their empowerment. The opportunity for women to meet and participate in training and share experiences can be a powerful force for change in communities, and a forum for the project to have a more in-depth understanding of the issues facing women in the community.

Investments in training centres for women provides an important space where women's empowerment can be fostered in a non-political environment. When establishing a women's centre it is important that membership is offered to a wide group and that the leaders are genuinely interested in the empowerment of local women and willing to work hard to achieve that. Typical support might be the construction or rehabilitation of a building for women to meet, participate in training and produce goods. The project can take advantage of the existence of successful women's groups involved in processing and marketing local produce, such as soap or handicrafts, and support them to reach wider markets. It is important that these groups are supported to engage in meaningful activities and do not become just a group of women who are brought out to sing and dance for visitors, otherwise they will not be real role models for women's empowerment in the community.

Supporting processing/marketing groups

A common source of investment is to provide equipment to processing/marketing groups such as multi-function platforms promoted by the United Nations Development Programme in Africa to reduce the drudgery of common tasks such as grinding grain for women. Other options include providing grain mills and equipment to extract oil from various plants. The lessons are generally that the more simple the technology is to maintain and repair, the more likely it will be to succeed, as major breakdowns often result in project failure or renewed calls for support from the project.

Fishermen

Many projects require port facilities which often disrupt the livelihoods of fishermen both by displacing their landing sites with onshore infrastructure and through creating exclusion zones which reduce their access to fishing grounds. The project should endeavour to find alternative fishing grounds and put in place protocols for allowing fishermen to continue to fish where it is safe to do so. Other options can be to provide support for more powerful engines to allow them to access more distant fishing grounds, and sheds to store their equipment safely. Support can also be provided to women onshore to preserve and process fish so that additional markets can be accessed by fishing families.

Community development interventions

Community investment and development is discussed in more detail in Chapter 15, but the aspects discussed below are mentioned here given their importance in providing support to livelihood restoration and improvement.

Improving access to local services

Before a company makes any commitment to support local services, there must be a dialogue and agreement with local communities and local government on the targeting and sustainability of any support. It is very common for local and national governments to divert support from resource project communities on the assumption that they will fill any gaps in local services. Where local government does not have adequate resources the company will have no choice but to step in to support some local services, but it is still important to develop a handover and exit strategy prior to making the initial investment.

This largely involves two main types of investment:

- Support for local service infrastructure: undertaking improvements to roads, water, schools, health clinics, recreational facilities, etc.; providing equipment to health clinics, schools, etc.
- Support for local services: supporting local government budgets to provide staff to health clinics and schools; providing capacity-building support for local government, including politicians and civil servants to improve the quality of services.

While best practice often points to avoid investing in quick wins in favour of developing longer-term partnerships, the political reality of projects means that upfront investments in local infrastructure are often required to achieve and maintain government and community support. Local politicians will often demand investments in trophy projects, such as road improvements, as these projects are well received in the wider area and increase community pride. It is important to create a structure around community development funding to ensure that the project cannot be cornered into investing in high-cost infrastructure projects in order to maintain political support, but rather to achieve a balance between high-profile infrastructure projects and initiatives to build local capacity.

Water

Direct mitigation

Many resource projects have significant impacts on water resources for a number of reasons:

- Many projects, particularly in mining and agriculture, require significant water storage facilities for production. The construction of water harvest dams can have a major impact on downstream water users as there can be sedimentation and disruption to fish stocks during construction, and the requirement to fill the dam annually can seriously affect downstream availability of water, particularly in more arid areas.
- Many projects resort to pumping groundwater to source water for the project. In addition, the water table may have to be lowered in order to extract resources at depth. This creates a cone of depression which can dry up local wells in the project area.

In these cases the project needs to directly mitigate for the disruption or loss of access to water resources. In the case of dry wells due to groundwater pumping, the project many have to drill deeper wells or bring in piped or tanked water to replace the loss. A more extreme solution is to resettle the impacted households where there are sustainable water resources.

In the case of dams, the impacts can be more difficult to mitigate, and in many cases the downstream water users are not properly considered by the project.

Apart from mitigation for direct impacts on water resources, the project also has to provide water to the resettlement sites. There are two main methods to supply water to the resettlement sites:

- **Boreholes**: this is where boreholes are drilled and a pump installed as a community water point. The number of boreholes required depends on the size of the population and distances from the water point. Boreholes are normally considered a cheaper way to provide water to resettlement sites but this may not be an acceptable solution to communities who want to reduce labour on women and children, who have to carry the water to their houses, and also want access to piped water in their houses. It is critical that the water is tested to ensure that the quality is guaranteed, as it is not possible to treat water using boreholes and hand pumps.

- **Community piped water system**: this is normally achieved by pumping groundwater from boreholes to an overhead tank and installing a piped distribution system around the community where the water can be collected at standpipes or piped directly into people's houses and metered if required. The project may upgrade or extend an existing community water system to the resettlement sites or construct a new system. A community water system may be the only solution where the groundwater requires some treatment prior to distribution to maintain a potable quality. Resettlement site planners must be particularly careful to ensure that the sanitation system provided will not pollute groundwater sources over time.

 Project example

A project in Africa drilled boreholes for the resettlement village without conducting proper water testing. Later it was found that there were natural levels of heavy metals in the water which exceeded World Health Organization standards. The project had to invest in a big upgrade of local water facilities in order to source water from a nearby town at a large cost to the company. The project also had significant issues with the local community accepting charging for water services.

Support for community water supply

The resettlement site water supply system will have to be handed over to the local authorities and/or local community to ensure that it can be managed independent of the project into the future. The project will also often upgrade the local water supply as part of its community development support. The main problem with water systems is local technical capacity to maintain the system and charging structures for water use to pay for this maintenance independent of the project.

Many resettlement communities are reluctant to pay for water where previously it was freely available from surface sources, and they also see it as the project's duty to provide water given they had to be resettled because of the project. It is very important to engage with local government and community leaders early in the project planning stage and work out a sustainable model for managing community water provision. If a payment system is to be introduced, this must be introduced and managed by local authorities/communities and there must be clear handover agreements in place.

Health

Many communities in developing countries are suffering from inadequate health-care. This is an area where the project can make a major impact and win considerable community support. There are a number of key areas where the project should focus based on project experience:

- A number of resource companies have had considerable success with malaria prevention and control programmes. This includes spraying of the interior of houses, providing bed nets, organising a community clean-up to remove breeding sites for mosquitoes, and education campaigns on malaria prevention.
- Companies can also invest in upgrading local health clinics and providing vital equipment to local nurses and doctors, such as ambulances to transport pregnant women/the sick, sterilisation equipment, basic drugs, generators and fridges to store vaccines.
- The provision of and upgrading of housing for health staff and upgrades to health clinic infrastructure can encourage staff to locate in rural areas where there are often significant problems to get people to work.

 Project example

A project in Africa invested in malaria control measures in the local community to reduce the health risks to its employees. The scheme resulted in an over 70% drop in malaria cases and the company has been funded by external partners to expand the project to nearby districts. This is an example of where a focused investment can lead to significant community impacts and positive support for the project.

Education

Access to quality education is holding back development in many communities and any initiative to support children is particularly well received. The development of many resource projects is accompanied by the building of private schools

Figure 16.3: Investment in education is critical, and will be well received.

locally to cater for the children of project employees. The company must ensure that the local community also receive some educational support for their children so that jealousy and resentment does not build against 'privileged' employees and their children. Companies can consider some of the following types of support:

- Investment in upgrading educational facilities, such as repairing existing classrooms and building new school facilities. Any investment in educational facilities must be done in partnership with government to ensure that additional teachers are provided and funded by the state.

- Investing in teachers' accommodation and supporting salaries to encourage quality teachers to locate in rural areas.

 Project example

A project in Africa was reluctant to support education initiatives, particularly requests to provide electricity to local schools and scholarships. After a few years there were strong demands from the community for the company to construct a vocational education centre to train young people in practical skills. The justification for the vocational centre was that students were not achieving pass grades in school and could not progress, and therefore needed to take a vocational route. The lesson is that investments in education are some of the most important contributions a project can make to changing a community and preparing them for the decline of the project.

Project example

A project in Africa focused its small community development budget on educational scholarships for many years. The company consistently won awards for its investment in education as the community placed a high value on their children going to university for the first time, which was credited to support from the project.

Roads

A major benefit of many resource projects is the provision or upgrading of the main access road required to develop and supply the project. Improved road access is critical for farmers and businesses exporting goods from the project area, and for reducing the price of imported goods, including food and raw materials. There will also be considerable pressure, particularly from local politicians, to upgrade local roads. Improving and constructing roads is an expensive undertaking and can divert resources from other activities where the company has already existing commitments, and therefore needs to be carefully considered.

 Project example

The community relations department of a project in Africa had developed a comprehensive community development plan with support for health, education and agriculture. However, there was a security issue at the project and the support of local politicians was important to maintain support from the local police to protect the project. A prominent local politician demanded support for a large road project and the company invested the majority of the community development budget in the road. While the new road was well received by local communities, the lack of investment in committed projects resulted in a deterioration in support from some sections of the community. The lesson is that large investments in infrastructure must be balanced with investment across a number of key sectors in order to win and maintain community support.

Electricity

The provision of electricity to communities surrounding a project is a divisive issue on many projects. Many resource projects are developed in rural areas with no existing power resources, leaving communities dependent on expensive options such as generators. Companies may either invest in generating their own power or install power lines to bring the national grid to the project. Where the company brings power lines to connect to the national grid, it may be possible to have an agreement with government to extend power to local communities and to manage the system. Where the project is generating its own power it is more difficult to reach agreement to provide this to local communities.

Where electricity is already available or being extended to the project area, the company can support local communities by providing transformers on the basis that this is a one-off investment, and the community must ensure that the wires and transformers are not stolen.

The provision of generators to rural health clinics, government offices and schools can also be a good investment in community development, provided that these services can provide the fuel and maintenance costs.

 Project example

A project in Africa reached an agreement with government to take electricity from the national grid on the basis that it invested in a large transformer station to provide power to the expanding local communities around the project. The project also invested in transformers in local communities. The communities were very supportive about the availability of power in their communities and this generated significant positive publicity for the project.

Sanitation

Many communities and local governments do not have the resources to manage solid and liquid waste. This can lead to very unsanitary conditions in local communities and increased disease levels. Companies can partner with local government to develop dumping sites outside population centres and waste collection services. Communities can also be supported to construct household latrines and toilets, and the company can support the construction of communal toilets at markets and also at schools.

Sports and recreation

Communities value recreation facilities, particularly for children, and any investment in community centres and sport and play facilities will be welcomed. The company can also sponsor sports clubs locally as these are often a source of great local pride and will create a positive image for the project.

Communications

Most resource projects bring upgrades to communications services, particularly mobile communications masts, which are a huge boost to local communities. Good communications are important for keeping in touch with relatives abroad and also for trade and commercial activities.

Markets

Local government and communities value markets to facilitate local trade, and so any support for improvements to local markets, aligned with improvements to transport routes, will provide a boost to local trade.

Agricultural support

Projects can provide support for extension services to advise on increasing the quality and productivity of crops through the use of improved cropping methods, including improved seeds and plant husbandry techniques. This extension advice must be linked to a credit support programme, otherwise the farmers will not be able to invest in putting the advice into practice.

In pursuing support for agriculture there should be a focus on the diversification of livelihoods and mixed livestock and crop farms. An ecological intensification approach reduces dependence on external inputs such as seeds, fertilisers and chemicals. However, projects reduce the area of land available for farming, forcing communities to intensify production on the remaining land with reduced fallowing and pasture areas and an increased dependence on fertiliser and chemical inputs.

Project support for the storage, processing and marketing of agricultural goods is an increasingly common community development initiative. This support is best channelled through producer groups, which are often organised separately for men and women, and can involve grant support for equipment, structures and expert advice. While local producer groups can be encouraged to supply food required to feed employees, projects must be careful not to build expectations too high. Projects often subcontract catering services to third parties and have high standards on the quality and quantity of supply required to meet their contracts. The project's drive to cut costs often means that local farmers might not be able to compete on price and quality from more established firms.

Key lessons

Apart from long-term secure employment with the project, which generally only benefits a minority of project-affected households, there are few quick fixes for restoring livelihoods. Therefore, skills training at the earliest opportunity for the local young people to provide them with employable skills is one of the most important interventions that a project can provide. Project-affected young people will generally aspire to paid employment and want to move away from agriculture, but once construction is finished it is better they have a safety net such as a minimum area of family land to meet their basic food needs. It is also needs to be recognised that older men and women generally gain less employment and need to be able to restore their livelihoods. So, land replacement is recommended as the key livelihood strategy.

Livelihood restoration and community development implementation: key considerations

- **Replace project-affected households' existing livelihood activities as a first priority** to provide a baseline safety net to all households to ensure a minimum standard of living.

- **Land-for-land replacement is the most effective livelihood restoration intervention**, but this can be particularly challenging where the project is acquiring large tracts of land in areas with high population densities.

- **Agricultural support must be provided along with replacement land** in order to get impacted households quickly self-sufficient in food again.

- **Skills training must begin as early as possible** in the project cycle to prepare as many locals as possible for direct and indirect employment on the project.

- **Local employment is the highest-priority benefit for local communities** and the project should put in place a fair and effective local employment policy and plan.

- **Local procurement for local businesses builds support for the project.**

17
Cultural heritage

The land access and resettlement process requires consideration of any specific cultural assets, characteristics and norms throughout a project, and these need to be taken into account in all project planning, consultations and implementation.

The IFC (International Finance Corporation), for the purpose of the Performance Standards, defines cultural heritage as:

- **Tangible forms of cultural heritage**, such as tangible movable or immovable objects, property, sites, structures, or groups of structures, having archaeological (prehistoric), palaeontological, historical, cultural, artistic and religious values
- **Unique natural features or tangible objects that embody cultural values**, such as sacred groves, rocks, lakes and waterfalls
- **Certain instances of intangible forms of culture** that are proposed to be used for commercial purposes, such as cultural knowledge, innovations and practices of communities embodying traditional lifestyles

What this chapter focuses on in terms of cultural heritage is **the treatment of tangible, physical forms** of cultural heritage which can be directly impacted by land access and resettlement, chiefly archaeological and historical heritage; traditional, cultural or sacred sites, such as shrines; and also the issue of cemeteries and graves. The replacement of other cultural buildings such as ecclesiastical structures has been dealt with under physical resettlement planning in Chapter 9.

In terms of intangible cultural heritage, projects may need to consider recording of cultural histories, such as music, stories and songs, as well as supporting the protection and enhancement of intangible cultural heritage through the formation of support groups or the provision of cultural centres. The extent to which this is required will vary from project to project, and the primary goal remains to resettle communities in a way in which cultural heritage is retained and community cohesion assured.

What are the key components to be considered?

In terms of physical impacts on cultural heritage, the following key areas commonly need to be addressed:

- **Archaeological sites**: the identification, mapping, investigation and, if necessary, the protection or removal of sites of archaeological significance in advance of works. In addition, the development of procedures in the event of discoveries during project implementation, often referred to as 'chance finds'.

- **Shrines and other traditional sites**: the identification and treatment of locations and structures which may have local or national traditional, cultural and/or religious significance, and which may require relocation or compensation.

- **Graves and cemeteries**: the identification of any graves and cemeteries potentially affected by land access and how to treat these, as well as the need for graves and cemeteries to be incorporated in resettlement planning.

The key steps to take in dealing with cultural heritage, as well as the key areas identified above, are discussed further below.

> While cultural considerations need to be mainstreamed throughout project planning, physical impacts on archaeological, traditional and religious sites require specific planning and treatment

What are the key issues, challenges and risks?

Addressing impacts on aspects of cultural and religious significance is necessarily an emotive issue, and requires careful, considered and respectful treatment. The process may be faced with a range of difficult issues, challenges and risks, including:

- **High degree of external stakeholder interest** and involvement where archaeological or traditional sites are of significant national or international significance.

- **Potential delays to project progress** if significant sites are not identified and their treatment addressed early in the planning process. In some countries there will also be restrictions on when relocations can take place (for example, not exhuming bodies during hot months).

- **Failing to understand fully the significance of cultural norms, practices and sites**, and the potential for damage, disturbance and resulting community disputes.
- **Potential for community disputes and opposition** if all cultural considerations are not fully understood and sensitively handled.
- **Need to understand all legislation** concerning archaeological sites, graves, cemeteries and traditional sites.
- **Lack of planning** for replacement of shrines, graves and cemeteries in replacement sites, and the time required to ensure this.
- **Lack of government capacity** to be meaningful partners.

The purpose of this chapter is to help you identify and deal with the issues, challenges, risks and opportunities that will arise.

> Each issue, challenge or risk constitutes a potential opportunity for improved performance

Is there one definitive standard that provides all the answers?

The IFC's PS (Performance Standard) 8 recognises the importance of cultural heritage for current and future generations. Consistent with the UNESCO Convention Concerning the Protection of the World Cultural and Natural Heritage, PS8 aims to ensure that clients protect cultural heritage in the course of their project activities.

PS8 notes a preference for minimising disturbance of tangible cultural heritage and a preference for leaving sites *in situ*, with necessary protective measures and opportunities for community access. Where this is not possible, relocation and restoration may be considered and, as a last result where this is not possible, compensation for the resource should be considered.

The Performance Standards note that any consideration of the treatment of significant sites requires the informed participation and consultation of communities and relevant regulatory bodies, essentially through the negotiation process.

> While laws and standards provide useful guidance to projects addressing issues of cultural heritage, much of this guidance is of a general nature. The rest of this chapter provides more detailed and practical assistance in dealing with sites of cultural significance

What are the guiding principles in the treatment of cultural heritage?

As identified by the IFC standards, the objective is to protect cultural heritage from the adverse impacts of project activities and support its preservation, and to promote the equitable sharing of benefits from the use of cultural heritage.

The key principles are as follows:

- **Respect** of local cultural norms and traditions, together with knowledge and understanding of cultural requirements, and how this should influence project planning and treatment of cultural heritage
- **Informed participation** by all applicable communities, cultural and religious leaders and regulatory bodies, who need to be consulted and participate in both the identification and agreed treatment of sites of cultural significance
- **Compliance with laws and standards** in all aspects of the treatment of cultural heritage, which must comply with applicable national and international laws and be guided by agreed best practice standards
- **Minimisation of disturbance and preservation** *in situ* as the preferred means of treatment of sites, provided community access can be maintained where required
- **Expert involvement and oversight** is required in the treatment of archaeological and other sites of cultural and religious significance

What are the key steps in the assessment and treatment of cultural heritage?

The following steps need to be considered in project planning and implementation:

Inventory of potential sites

Identification of all sites of potential cultural significance is required, resulting in an inventory of potential sites. This needs to be undertaken by appropriate experts and should identify all archaeological, traditional and religious sites (including identifying graves and cemeteries) that are within or adjacent to the project area, and could therefore be directly or indirectly affected by the project.

The preparation of the inventory should be informed by reference to national records, any previous studies and consultation with key stakeholders, particularly traditional and religious leaders.

Traditional sites that are identified need to have been **utilised in living memory as part of a long cultural tradition**, to prevent proposal of spurious sites in anticipation of compensation. Information received regarding potential traditional sites needs to be triangulated in order to confirm as much as possible the genuine nature of sites.

Assessment of potential impact

Potential sites need to be mapped using GPS and site visits undertaken to obtain photographs and descriptions of each site, and observations regarding usage.

Mapped sites can be overlaid on potential project infrastructure to assess the level of impact on cultural sites, particularly whether sites will be directly impacted by infrastructure. This preliminary review of impacts needs to inform plans to minimise impacts, which may involve relocation or redesign of project infrastructure where possible.

Depending on the outcome of this assessment, proposed treatment of sites can be outlined as the basis for further consultation with all stakeholders.

Consultations and negotiation

If a cultural resource cannot be avoided, a plan should be developed to mitigate any adverse effects, in consultation with traditional authorities, local communities and local or national cultural resource experts.

In particular, in addition to discussions through the negotiation forum, the opinions and inputs of traditional and religious leaders, together with national and international experts, should be sourced.

The sensitivities surrounding cultural and religious sites means that a project will need to consider if the issue is discussed through the regular community negotiation forum, or is best discussed outside this forum with key stakeholders. Even if discussed outside regular forums, the project should ensure adequate feedback is provided to all stakeholders on any decisions reached, in order to avoid conflict later.

Development of proposals

Proposals to mitigate impacts may include any of the following:

- Protection of the site *in situ*, to prevent encroachment during construction or operations
- Access arrangements for communities on a constant or regular basis (such as during traditional festivals)
- Where preservation *in situ* is not possible, arrangements for excavations, examination and recording of the site by experts, in line with recognised practices
- Removal of the site to a new location, or removal of finds to an alternative location (such as a national museum)

- Performance of traditional rites to relocate the site or to remove any traditional significance
- Exhumation of bodies and their relocation, or partial relocation of graves accompanied by religious and/or traditional rites
- Arrangements for the involvement of regulatory bodies and national or international oversight
- Payment of compensation to communities for affected sites where monetary or in-kind compensation can be agreed

Preparation of a cultural management plan

Any agreed treatment of cultural heritage sites needs to be included in a cultural management plan which details the treatment of various sites, together with measures for participatory monitoring and evaluation by communities and key expertise, including national regulatory bodies.

The cultural management plan needs to be widely articulated to ensure that there is broad awareness and support in affected communities, as well as among key informants and experts.

Obtaining necessary permits

Specific permits may be required from national, regional or religious bodies for the movement of religious buildings or graves and cemeteries.

Chance finds procedure

The construction management plan needs to include arrangements for 'chance finds' during project development. Normally, a chance finds procedure will involve the following steps:

 Project example

A project in Africa had a number of sacred shrines on the site, as well as archaeological sites. They employed international consultants, working with the national university, to catalogue all the sites. The location of all sites was taken into account in project design, to minimise disruption to identified sites. The study also formed the basis for negotiation with communities on sacred sites, including extensive negotiation with traditional leaders. Archaeological sites that would be disturbed were catalogued, and key finds were moved in co-operation with the national university and museum authorities. A chance finds procedure was also developed in case of further finds during construction.

- In the event of an inadvertent discovery, work will stop immediately
- The site will be temporarily protected
- Studies should be undertaken by relevant experts
- Consultations with relevant stakeholders
- Appropriate measures developed, agreed and implemented

What options should be considered in the treatment of archaeological sites?

The treatment of archaeological sites may include, but is not limited to, the following options:

- Preservation *in situ*, with measures for protection such as fencing
- Examination of key artefacts and their removal off-site (for example, to a museum)
- Relocation of the site in its entirety
- Recording and removal

What about traditional sites such as shrines?

As referred to above, traditional sites that are identified need to have been **utilised in living memory as part of a long cultural tradition**, to prevent proposal of spurious sites in anticipation of compensation. Information received regarding potential traditional sites needs to be triangulated in order to confirm as much as possible the genuine nature of sites.

Depending on the outcome of negotiations with communities and traditional leadership, the treatment of traditional sites may include the following options:

- Preservation *in situ*, with measures for protection such as fencing
- Ensuring continued access to communities on a periodic or permanent basis
- Relocation of the site in its entirety
- Performance of traditional rites (which the project should facilitate) to allow removal or relocation
- Payment of compensation to communities, combined with the performance of rites

The project should be clear on the ownership of traditional sites, as this will inform methods of consultation and treatment of sites, particularly when payment of compensation has been agreed. In some cases sites will be 'owned' by the community, where modalities for payment of compensation in cash, or in kind in the form of facilities, will need to be carefully considered. In other cases shrines may be family-owned, or related only to a particular subset of the community.

How should cemeteries and graves be treated?

There are two key factors to be considered in relation to cemeteries and graves:

- How to treat cemeteries and graves located within the land area requiring resettlement and development
- How to ensure provision for cemeteries at any new resettlement site

The provision of cemeteries at a new resettlement site can be relatively straightforward, provided the space requirements are taken into account in early planning, and all cultural requirements are considered in advance and incorporated in project planning. Specific stakeholders such as religious and traditional leaders should be consulted. Where households have graves close to their homes, consultations will need to conclude if this should be integrated into the design and layout of plots, or whether these can be transferred to a communal cemetery.

Where graves or cemeteries are located in the area to be resettled, the issue of how to **consult and negotiate** on the treatment of these is important. Depending on the specific community characteristics, it may be preferable either to deal with this in the usual negotiation forum, or to deal with the issue 'offline' with a core

Figure 17.1: Relocated cemetery with resettlement village in the background, eastern Turkey.

group of stakeholders such as community elders, religious leaders and statutory authorities. However, whether the issue is considered in a small group or through the negotiation forum of community representatives, consultations must also be undertaken with the wider community to ensure broad support.

If not directly affected, the potential to leave the graves and cemeteries *in situ* should be considered and discussed with stakeholders. In some cases, it may be acceptable to communities to leave graves *in situ*, especially if access to the area can be secured on a regular basis. In other cases, even where graves are directly affected by project infrastructure, a symbolic ceremony may suffice to 'move souls' from the area to the new sites. In other cases, exhumation and relocation of the bodies may be required. This is a process that will require specialist assistance and close liaison with national and local authorities in order to comply with national legislation and requirements.

 Project example

Two cemeteries and a number of graves were affected by a project in Africa. The project considered it preferable to consult on such a sensitive issue offline with a number of community elders and religious leaders. It was agreed that a traditional ceremony would suffice to relocate the souls of the departed, after which the headstones would be removed and the bodies left *in situ*. However, the consultations and proposed agreements were not sufficiently disclosed to the wider community by either the village leaders or the project. As a result the community protested against the moves, although the anger behind the protests was really due to a leadership dispute within the community. The project needed to spend extra time consulting with the community before the plan could go ahead, alongside acting as a mediator to resolve the leadership dispute.

What about cultural heritage of indigenous peoples?

IFC PS7 makes specific mention of critical cultural heritage with respect to indigenous peoples:

> Where a project may significantly impact on critical cultural heritage that is essential to the identity and/or cultural, ceremonial, or spiritual aspects of Indigenous Peoples' lives, priority will be given to the avoidance of such impacts. Where significant project impacts on critical cultural heritage are unavoidable, the client will obtain the Free, Prior and Informed Consent of the Affected Communities of Indigenous Peoples.

In practice this means following the same steps as already outlined above.

It is worth noting that the IFC also makes mention of the use of **cultural knowledge and innovations** for the benefit of a project, in respect of both indigenous and nonindigenous peoples. PS7, for example, states:

> Where a project proposes to use the cultural heritage including knowledge, innovations, or practices of Indigenous Peoples for commercial purposes, the client will inform the Affected Communities of Indigenous Peoples of (i) their rights under national law; (ii) the scope and nature of the proposed commercial development; (iii) the potential consequences of such development; and (iv) obtain their Free, Prior and Informed Consent. The client will also ensure fair and equitable sharing of benefits from commercialization of such knowledge, innovation, or practice, consistent with the customs and traditions of the Indigenous Peoples.

This is not often likely to occur in the case of natural resource projects, but may, for example, occur in relation to protection of natural habitats which requires resettlement of peoples, and where management of the ecosystem and potential revenues related to tourism may draw on traditional practices and innovations in relation to habitat management.

Cultural heritage: key considerations

- While cultural considerations need to be mainstreamed throughout project planning, physical impacts on archaeological, traditional and religious sites requires **specific planning and treatment**

- **Key principles** include: **respect of local cultural norms and traditions; informed participation by all stakeholders; compliance with laws and standards**

- **Minimisation of disturbance and preservation *in situ*** are the preferred means of treatment of sites, provided community access can be maintained where required

- **Expert involvement and oversight** is required in the treatment of archaeological and other sites of cultural and religious significance

- **Identification of all sites** of potential cultural significance is required, resulting in an inventory of potential sites

- Traditional sites that are identified need to have been **utilised in living memory as part of a long cultural tradition**

- Any agreed treatment of cultural heritage sites needs to be included in a **cultural management plan**

- The cultural management plan needs to include arrangements for **'chance finds'** during project development

18
Monitoring and evaluation

M&E (monitoring and evaluation) of a project is critical in terms of answering the questions: **What constitutes success?** and **When have we finished?** Unfortunately, many projects only get around to thinking seriously about M&E after they have conducted baseline studies and are well advanced in the process of project planning and stakeholder engagement, or are even about to commence implementation. As discussed in Chapter 7 concerning impact assessment, it is critical that M&E is considered and integrated into project planning from the outset, so that meaningful indicators can be developed early and measured in order to answer these critical questions.

Early development of monitoring indicators is important: this should be done before baseline data is collected

The IFC (International Finance Corporation) requires project sponsors to 'monitor and report on the effectiveness of RAP [resettlement action plan] implementation. The objective should be to provide the Company with feedback and to identify problems and successes as early as possible to allow timely adjustment to implementation arrangements' (IFC 2002: 49).

M&E activities should be 'integrated into the overall project management process, and the RAP or other management plan must provide a coherent monitoring plan that identifies the organisational responsibilities, methodology, and the schedule for monitoring and reporting' (IFC 2002: 49).

Ultimately, in order to determine when a project is successful or finished, indicators of success need to be agreed with all stakeholders at the outset, rather than relying on external bodies to declare when projects are successful.

What are the key components to be considered in M&E?

Monitoring can be described as a continuing function that uses systematic collection of data on specified indicators to provide management and the main stakeholders with indications of the extent of progress and achievement of objectives and progress in the use of allocated funds and resources.

Evaluation can be described as the systematic and objective assessment of an ongoing or completed project, its design, implementation and results. The aim is to determine the relevance and fulfilment of objectives, development efficiency, effectiveness, impact and sustainability.

M&E has the following general objectives:

- **Monitoring** specific situations or difficulties arising from the implementation, and of the compliance of the implementation with objectives and methods set out in the RAP, or other relevant management plans.

- **Evaluating** emergent, mid- and long-term impacts of the project on the welfare of impacted households, communities and local government.

- Sufficient involvement of the project-affected persons in **participatory M&E** of short-, mid- and long-term project activities and effects.

- M&E should give particular attention to the project-affected communities, especially **vulnerable groups**, such as female-headed households, sharecroppers and tenants.

- M&E should **take place from the outset** of projects, and occur through the planning and engagement phases, as opposed to only occurring during implementation. It should continue post-move, and monitor the success of livelihoods and vulnerable persons programmes.

The purpose of monitoring is to provide project managers and financiers, as well as directly affected persons, households and communities, with timely, concise, indicative information on whether compensation, resettlement and other impact mitigation measures are on track to achieve sustainable livelihood restoration and improvement in the welfare of the affected people, or that adjustments are needed.

Monitoring verifies that:

- Actions and commitments for compensation, resettlement, land access and development in the RAP or other management plans are implemented fully and on time

- Entitled persons receive their compensation and replacement housing on time

- Compensation and livelihood investments are achieving sustainable livelihood restoration and improvement in the welfare of project-affected persons, households and communities

- Complaints and grievances are followed up with appropriate corrective action
- Vulnerable persons are tracked and assisted as necessary

Monitoring answers the question: Are project compensation, resettlement and other impact mitigation measures on time and having the intended effects?

External monitoring should also be carried out by an independent consultant who can work closely with the project-affected persons.

What are the key issues, challenges and risks?

The key pitfalls that can lead to problems in effective M&E include:

- Poor baseline data-gathering at the outset of projects, with a subsequent lack of baseline data against which to measure progress
- Failure to select an adequate but manageable range of indicators against which to measure project progress
- A focus on outputs (for example, the number of people trained in alternative livelihoods), rather than outcomes (such as the revenue earned by households trained)
- Lack of resources dedicated to M&E: specific staff should be dedicated to M&E
- Failure to include external partners and affected communities in participatory M&E, leading to a risk that results will not be viewed as impartial or be readily accepted by affected households or external bodies
- Measuring whether or not livelihoods programmes have been successful requires a commitment to monitoring longer than two or three years: it may be up to ten years before livelihoods are fully restored in some cases, particularly where tree crops are impacted

What should be monitored?

As noted in Chapter 6, **indicators** need to be determined at the outset of the project, and will influence the gathering of appropriate baseline data. An indicator is a quantitative or qualitative factor or variable that provides a simple and reliable means to measure achievement, to reflect the changes connected to an intervention, or to help assess performance. As such an indicator is the evidence or information that will tell you whether your programme is achieving its intended outputs, outcomes and impacts. Indicators are measurable and observable characteristics. They answer the question: How will we know change occurred?

Indicators that can be monitored may include:

- Delivery of compensation
- Resolution of grievances
- Increase or decrease in household assets/income
- Agricultural outputs/productivity
- Social stability
- Health
- Rehabilitation of infrastructure and public facilities
- Level of satisfaction of project-affected persons
- Number of project-affected persons that benefited from the livelihood restoration programmes

Indicator selection should be guided by the following principles:

- Selecting fewer indicators of significance, rather than attempting to track a host of minor indicators
- Selecting indicators also used by local, regional, national and international institutions in order to be able to compare results with control groups
- Selecting a mix of measurements in terms of quantitative (monetary, asset-based, etc.) and qualitative indicators

How should M&E be undertaken?

Monitoring should consist of:

- Internal monitoring as an integral part of project management
- External monitoring by suitably qualified consultants
- Community and external stakeholder participation

As part of a comprehensive and integrated approach, a project should prepare an overarching **social M&E framework**, which can include an agreed list of indicators and the frequency of monitoring for each component. This will allow for effective monthly and quarterly M&E of activities. The framework should be discussed with relevant project personnel and external partners as appropriate, to obtain buy-in from all actors. The framework should list the mitigation measures which have been identified to address each impact.

A framework allows for succinct and effective identification, monitoring and review of key impacts identified and the various mitigation measures employed through various management plans such as a RAP. At the same time it also allows at-a-glance information according to key project components and departmental responsibilities and interests.

Impacts should be monitored throughout the project life-cycle, from input of resources at the outset, to measuring the final result or change resulting from the mitigation measures employed.

Accordingly, **key indicator questions** in the case of each impact should look at the following:

- **Inputs**: financial, human and material resources
- **Activities**: tasks/personnel undertaken to transform inputs into outputs
- **Outputs/outcomes**: products and services produced and effects of outputs on project-affected persons
- **Results**: change from pre-displacement position

Monitoring efforts can be supported through:

- Review of progress against registered commitments
- Review of progress against agreed indicators
- Sample surveys
- Review of complaints and grievance registers
- Community and external stakeholder participation

The social M&E framework can summarise the current status, together with identification of any key issues or gaps, and recommendations for further action identified as appropriate. Finally, the framework should also note key sources of information to be either consulted or gathered to effectively monitor and evaluate each component.

The framework can be presented in a tabular form. An example format is shown in Figure 18.1.

Internal monitoring can generally take place on a monthly basis by a dedicated on-site M&E officer, while external consultants can undertake M&E on a quarterly basis, utilising the same framework. An internal M&E officer is important to maintain ongoing M&E, and to ensure the project is ready before external monitors, including project financiers, review the project.

In addition to on-site M&E officers, a project may consider having an **expert review panel**, which would be made up of experienced land access and resettlement practitioners, who can advise the project on appropriate M&E mechanisms, as well as identifying key issues and gaps as early as possible in the project cycle, and anticipate issues that may be raised by external reviewers, such as those

Figure 18.1: Example of a monitoring and evaluation framework.

Project Component	Responsible Department	IMPACT IDENTIFICATION & MANAGEMENT				MONITERING & EVALUATION PLAN			
							Quarter 1		
		Project Impacts/Risks/ Aspects	Relevant Management Plans	Mitigation Measures	Aspects to Monitor	Key Indicators (by total and by village as appropriate)	Status Summary	Issues/Gaps/ Recommendations	Sources of Information

providing project finance. This enables the project to address issues in advance, rather than discovering these later through the usual M&E processes.

External M&E needs to be undertaken by independent reviewers, who are experienced in the planning and delivery of land access and resettlement projects.

 Project example

A project in Eastern Europe involved consultants to design a monthly internal M&E process, and a complementary external quarterly M&E process. Both processes used a common framework and indicators. The processes were especially useful as the project was in receipt of commercial bank funding, and regular M&E throughout the project could anticipate issues in advance of bank reviews.

Why ensure external participation in M&E?

Involving affected households and external partners, such as local government and livelihood delivery partners, in M&E has the following benefits:

- Increased transparency and trust-building
- Affected households and communities can see that commitments are being met and how livelihood restoration is progressing
- Community representatives involved in M&E are more likely to be able to confidently report the facts to their constituents
- Involving external partners in M&E, such as livelihoods monitoring, increases their capacity and willingness to be meaningful development partners
- Involving statutory authorities in M&E, such as monitoring of resettlement construction, will ease the process of handover and adoption by authorities of their statutory responsibilities
- External partners and communities can provide insights and recommendations where M&E identifies that corrective measures are required
- Communities and other external stakeholders can more readily appreciate where cumulative impacts beyond the project may be influencing impacts on communities
- All stakeholders can agree what will be measured to determine project success and when the project is 'finished'

In formulating M&E efforts, the involvement of community and external stakeholder representatives should be integrated into the M&E framework from the outset. This will include the various stakeholder engagement methodologies outlined in Chapter 5, but will also involve specific efforts to involve stakeholders at key points in the process.

For example:

- Community representatives and other external stakeholders can be involved in undertaking and overseeing baseline surveys
- Stakeholders can be involved in identifying appropriate resettlement sites and/or agricultural land/fishing sites and agreeing appropriate indicators and measures of success
- A handover committee related to resettlement sites can be involved in regular monitoring of site construction and sign-off and handover of housing and infrastructure, as discussed at Chapter 14.
- A livelihoods committee made up of key stakeholders can be involved in M&E of livelihood programmes
- Communities should be involved in environmental monitoring efforts, especially where there is potential for community impacts arising from construction or operations

Figure 18.2: Focus group as part of internal monitoring and evaluation efforts.

Project example

A project in Africa ensured the involvement of community representatives and impacted communities at key stages of the land access and resettlement process. This included representatives overseeing baseline surveys, the investigation of resettlement site options, development of model housing options, monitoring and evaluation of construction and the roll-out of livelihood initiatives, and follow-up visits with resettlers.

How should M&E be recorded and reported?

The key findings arising from an M&E framework should be summarised in regular, for example quarterly, reports, for action by relevant management and staff. Reports should include:

- Status summary
- Gaps and emerging issues
- Conclusions and recommendations

The report can therefore be used as a summary document, while the framework can provide a detailed breakdown according to mitigation measures and indicators, as well as being the practical tool to monitor the various mitigation measures being applied.

The framework can also provide a useful reference for further information on summary issues raised in the quarterly report, according to the interests of particular departments.

Status summaries should be adapted as required for dissemination to local stakeholders and communities, for example via newsletters, public meetings and community notice boards.

 Project example

A major bank requested a final evaluation of an infrastructure project in Eastern Europe: the audit was a bank requirement but was also requested as the bank was concerned that compensation payments had not been consistent throughout the project area and lifetime. The audit allowed an independent review of the methodologies involved and a set of recommendations to ensure all outstanding grievances related to compensation payments could be addressed.

The framework should be integrated with the project database, which can automate the tracking of several indicators related to compensation entitlements and payments, resettlement entitlements, delivery of resettlement infrastructure, and housing. The database should also track and manage grievance handling and management of the livelihood programme.

When should final evaluation of a project take place?

The schedule for the independent evaluation of project implementation should be agreed with all external stakeholders. The timing of this **close-out audit** should be broadly established at the outset of project implementation, and will have regard to the duration of any livelihood restoration programme. Typically this may be a minimum of three years after project implementation commences, to allow for full re-establishment of land-based livelihoods and the shocks of resettlement to have passed, but this would vary from project to project, and should usually be much longer.

Final evaluation should follow the same format and indicators as identified in the social M&E framework, and may be supported by extensive surveys to measure progress effectively against the baseline. Through this the project can answer the question: **When have we finished?**

Monitoring and evaluation: key considerations

- Ensure **indicators are established at the outset of projects**, and integrated into baseline data-gathering efforts
- Choose a **manageable and meaningful set of indicators** rather than trying to track everything
- **Focus on outcomes** rather than outputs
- Ensure **adequate resources** are dedicated to M&E
- **Include external partners and affected communities in participatory M&E**
- Develop a **social M&E framework**
- Ensure **recording of M&E** is integrated with a project database
- Plan for **final external evaluation** at the end of projects, including a **completion audit**

19

Land management

What is meant by land management and how does it relate to land access and resettlement?

Extractive sector companies, such as mining companies, often hold various forms of title to large land areas. Development of their projects typically does not require immediate company utilisation of the whole land-holding. Projects are often of a scale which may result in progressive periods of land access over time, and result in impacts, positive and negative, which may take place over a wide area, well beyond the project boundaries. At the same time, projects are competing for land with other land uses, and are developed and operated within the context of local, regional and national land-use planning and development priorities.

Whatever the case, once a project has acquired land it needs to manage this for the duration that it controls the land, bearing in mind that, particularly in the case of an extractive sector project, there will come a time when the project is over and enters a closure phase that will culminate in a return of the land to the state or local communities/ previous owners.

Development of an LMP (land management plan) provides an opportunity to draw together key social management plans and considerations, including land access and resettlement, community investment and influx management, and consider how these can be complementary in maximising value and reducing risks through effective social spend.

> Developing a land management plan is part of a more holistic, integrated and co-ordinated project planning process

Life-of-project land management planning needs to take into account:

- Project plans with regard to land requirements for the life of the project, and plans related to closure and rehabilitation of land

- The need to address potential competition for resources in the area and conflict between competing land uses or other operations
- Potential influx and speculation arising from the project, not just in the period when the project is being planned and implemented, but also during the operations phase and at closure
- Project plans with respect to broader community and regional investment
- The need to engage effectively with government and other key stakeholders so that plans are integrated fully with local, regional and national planning and development objectives

What are the objectives of comprehensive land management planning?

A comprehensive approach to land management planning offers the following potential benefits:

- Consideration of life-of-project land requirements at the outset of a project, including consideration of the pros and cons of phased land access and how and when land should be acquired, with a view to minimising impacts and managing land access and resettlement costs
- Consideration of competing land uses, including other major projects, land-intensive activities such as farming, as well as informal and/or illegal activities such as artisanal and small-scale mining, and how potential conflicts or cumulative impacts arising from these activities can be managed, and what opportunities there may be for value creation
- Consideration of potential influx and in-migration to the area, either as a result of increased economic activity or in anticipation of project benefits, and an examination of how project planning and social policies and management plans (including those related to local employment and procurement, land access and resettlement and community investment) might be tailored to address this
- Consideration of wider regional and national development priorities, including government land-use and development planning, and how the project can take account of these and assist in their realisation, while also ensuring that life-of-project plans are acknowledged and protected through such plans
- Integrated community investment and influx management planning can be targeted to reinforce land management measures, for example by directing economic and population growth to key areas

What are the key components of an LMP?

An LMP needs to outline measures to:

- Prevent undesirable outcomes such as the negative impacts of unplanned influx, or speculation in anticipation of benefits, or conflict with existing land uses
- Control and contain land uses such that conflict and impacts are minimised and potential for shared value is created
- Address and minimise impacts over the life of the project
- Co-ordinate on benefits arising chiefly through economic opportunities, local employment and procurement, and community investment efforts, and maximise these cumulative benefits through working with government, NGO (non-governmental organisation) or neighbouring company initiatives

Accordingly, an LMP should include the following components, cross-referenced to other applicable project management plans as necessary:

- **Key issues, risks, challenges and opportunities**: the LMP needs to identify in detail the key issues, risks, challenges and opportunities for effective land management arising from the project in terms of, for example: potential influx and in-migration to the area, including pressures on infrastructure, uncoordinated growth and social problems; increases in informal or illegal land uses such as artisanal and small-scale mining; and speculative building and planting which may occur in the anticipation of project benefits.
- **Institutional and legal framework**: as with a RAP (resettlement action plan), the LMP needs to outline the relevant institutional and legal framework which impinges on issues of land management, including relevant local customs, traditions and law, but with particular reference to land-use planning law and regulations. International standards and best practice in land management should also be considered, in addition to relevant corporate polices.
- **Stakeholder engagement strategy**: a specific LMP stakeholder engagement strategy needs to be considered which will be developed in order to: engage fully with local, regional and national level government and relevant stakeholders; develop a partnership approach to control and management of land; ensure with government stakeholders that mine plans are integrated fully with local and regional development objectives and plans, and that influx management and community development measures are undertaken in a partnership; and address all cumulative project impacts. Capacity-building of government partners and other key stakeholders may need to be considered.
- **Land control measures**: the LMP needs to detail the measures which will be developed to control speculative activities, as well as conflicting land uses that may also occur on the project land, such as artisanal and small-scale mining. Mechanisms may include asset surveys, regular satellite

Figure 19.1: Key components of a land management plan.

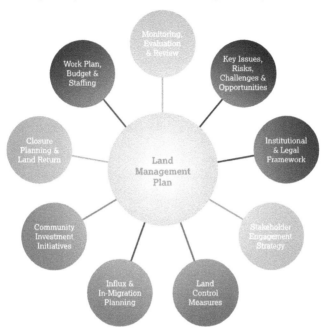

photography, monitoring by 'land teams' (which can include local stake-holders) and the development of policies to engage with and address the needs of competing and illegal land users where possible, while respecting national laws.

- **Minimising and managing influx and in-migration**: the activities which will be undertaken to minimise influx and in-migration should be outlined in an LMP. This may incorporate measures to restrict employment and procurement opportunities to existing local populations where possible through the company's local employment and procurement plan. At the same time a project will need to outline plans with respect to offsetting the impacts of influx and in-migration that will occur in terms of influx management planning. This may include focusing growth in particular areas where services can be most easily provided, in co-ordination with government, and will require integrated planning in terms of a project's infrastructure, community investment and influx management budgets.

- **Wider community investment initiatives**: following on from considerations of impacts as a result of influx and in-migration, the wider community and regional development measures that a project will initiate to further offset project impacts and provide added value and benefits should be outlined. Community investment strategies are discussed in further detail in Chapter 15.

- **Closure planning and land return**: an LMP will need to consider closure planning and land return, and how this will be taken into consideration in project planning from the outset. Opportunities for phased rehabilitation and return of land need to be incorporated in life-of-project land management planning.
- **Work plan, budget and key roles and responsibilities**: in line with other management plans, the LMP needs to be a workable plan with a dedicated budget, integrated with other relevant social management plans as discussed above, and with dedicated personnel overseeing planning, implementation and regular monitoring and review.
- **Monitoring and evaluation**: an LMP needs to detail monitoring and evaluation processes and procedures to be followed, including identification of key indicators which will measure the success of any LMP.

What are the key issues, risks and challenges to be addressed?

The range of risks, challenges and opportunities to be taken into account in a life-of-project LMP will vary from project to project. Typically, the following issues may need to be considered:

Land requirements and phased land access

The project needs to consider land requirements for the life of the project, including access roads, pipelines and other associated facilities. An examination of opportunities to minimise land take is a key requirement, as well as opportunities to phase land access requirements and integrate this into a rolling land rehabilitation and return programme where possible.

The opportunities for phased land access must be balanced between, on the one hand, the opportunities to reduce impacts and stage land access costs, and on the other hand, the risk of speculation, influx and natural growth increasing future land access costs as a result of not controlling all land at the outset. The development of effective land control measures and integration with government development plans and control policies will therefore be an important component of any decision to phase land access.

Resource competition and conflict

Any LMP needs to consider the range of competing land users, both in terms of existing users (such as farms, fisheries, pressure on water resources, etc.), informal and/or illegal activities (such as artisanal and small-scale mining) and other potential projects in the area (such as overlapping exploration licences and mining concessions).

Any strategies developed in the LMP need to seek to address potential conflicts between users, as well as exploring opportunities through increased co-ordination between neighbouring projects or other land users. This will require intensive engagement and negotiation and needs to be incorporated in the stakeholder engagement strategy to be developed as part of the LMP.

Government development plans

Government, at the local, regional and national levels, may have development plans which seek to influence land use, growth and development in the area of a project, as well as policies to control unauthorised development. In many jurisdictions the capacity of government, particularly at the local level, to develop such plans may be limited or non-existent. At the same time, any government plans may be uncoordinated, in conflict or out of date, and information on issues such as plot ownership may be incomplete or non-existent. Projects should work with statutory authorities to develop meaningful development plans and policies which can be enforced, and ensure that the project both influences the outcome of these plans and is recognised in land-use planning initiatives. A project can help to ensure government policies can be realised through the project's own efforts with regard to influx management, community investment and other mechanisms.

Land ownership and legacy issues

The LMP should recognise existing issues which may have created land conflicts or tensions and how these might be resolved through the plan's policies. An initial requirement for development of an LMP may be the identification of all landowners and users in the area through cadastral surveys where this information is not already available or reliable.

Speculation

A key risk to projects is speculation, chiefly through the development of structures or planting of crops in anticipation of project benefits. The LMP needs to consider the risks relevant to a project and develop strategies to address these, as discussed further below.

Illegal activities and encroachment

As referred to above with regard to competing resource users, informal or illegal activities may be pre-existing on a project site or encroachment may occur. Their presence can result in uncontrolled development on a concession, competition for the same resource, conflict and antisocial behaviour, and can quickly make a project unfeasible. Strategies to address illegal users are discussed further below but, in any case, a multi-pronged strategy will be required.

Influx and in-migration

The development of the project can result in influx and in-migration to the area from the wider region and often internationally, in the hope of direct employment or the opportunity to provide services to the project or workers. Such influx, if uncontrolled, can have severe impacts on existing communities.

An LMP needs to consider how various project strategies, including local employment and procurement policies, community investment and government development policies, can combine to reduce and offset the impacts of influx and in-migration.

Community investment and regional development

As referred to above, a project's community investment strategy should seek to address impacts on the surrounding communities while also maximising shared value and meeting the business case for intervention. Community investment can be used in part to enforce land management strategies, for example by ensuring infrastructure investments are focused in areas where the project, and government, would like to focus growth.

Project closure

As referred to above in considering land requirements and phased access, any LMP needs to consider the opportunity for land rehabilitation, often on a phased basis, and how this might allow for land return; it can often offset the cumulative impacts that might otherwise occur on other land uses, particularly agriculture.

 Project example

A project in Africa failed to manage the land on its lease over a 30-year period, which meant that households were resettled onto areas which were subsequently required by the mine, leading to continuous resettlement of communities. This process resulted in disruptions to communities, project delays and also considerable costs to the project.

What institutional and legal frameworks should be considered?

As with the RAP, an LMP needs to consider the relevant national, regional and local legislation and institutions that may impact on the project, but particularly with regard to land-use planning. This will typically include national, regional and local development plans and policies, and any development control legislation.

Is there a specific stakeholder engagement strategy to be followed?

Any LMP engagement strategy may be incorporated into an overall project stakeholder engagement strategy. However, in developing an LMP, the plan should outline specific strategies for how a project will engage with the identified local-, regional- and national-level government and key stakeholders with a clear mandate to influence land management policies and planning, as well as what capacity-building measures may be required.

The strategy will need to identify the key policy-makers in respect of local and regional development and land management, note the relevant development plans, and how and when these are likely to be revised and adopted.

An LMP cannot be developed and implemented by a project alone, since it requires the inputs of competing land users, legislators and planners.

How to address speculation, encroachment and influx?

The LMP will need to identify measures to prevent encroachment and speculation, now and throughout mine operation, including in relation to pre-existing users who may be on the project area such as artisanal and small-scale miners. Often these will not be legally recognised in national legislation, and a project will need to be careful that it addresses these conflicts with regard to users' rights while not being in conflict with national legislation.

As referred to above, a key risk is speculation, chiefly through the development of structures or planting of crops in anticipation of project benefits. The LMP needs to consider the risks and develop strategies to address these. This will typically involve a range of measures, including policing of project areas (often through local task forces made up of community members and project staff), liaison with statutory authorities on development control, and undertaking comprehensive asset surveys, supported by satellite imagery, which may be further supported by entitlement cut-off dates and the declaration of moratoriums on building and cropping, where these can be legally enforced.

In addition to speculative activities, illegal activities may be pre-existing on a project site or encroachment may occur. For example, in mining projects the presence of artisanal and small-scale miners is a key issue of concern. Their presence can result in uncontrolled development on a concession, competition for the same resource, conflict and antisocial behaviour, and can quickly make a project unfeasible. Strategies to address illegal users may include liaison with authorities, although projects need to be careful to avoid the use of force: although such users may be illegal under national legislation, they often have no alternative livelihood mechanisms and, as users of the area, still need to be considered in project development. Other mechanisms may include arrangements for sharing of land on the concession through intense engagement, coupled with access to alternative livelihood programmes and opportunities for employment. In any case a multi-pronged strategy will be required.

The development of the project can result in influx and in-migration to the area from the wider region and often internationally, in the hope of employment or associated service provision. Such influx, if uncontrolled, can have severe impacts on existing communities. These communities may be located in relatively isolated rural areas where in-migration from outside may place strains on the existing society and create social tensions and conflict, often coupled with a rise in antisocial behaviours, including prostitution serving mine workers settling in the area without families and earning regular wages. At the same time, areas will typically have basic infrastructure, including in terms of water supply and waste management services, and significant influx can place severe strain on these resources.

An LMP needs to consider how various project strategies, including local employment and procurement policies, community investment and government development policies, can combine to reduce and offset the impacts of influx and in-migration. The LMP therefore needs a combination of measures that can both prevent influx, and then offset the impacts which do occur from limited influx, such as improvements to infrastructure including water supply, educational and health facilities, and considering impacts and opportunities during resettlement planning, including the potential for provision of new shared resources.

How can LMPs complement other social management plans?

Looking at life-of-project land requirements can identify potential land constraints and conflicts, identify competing users, cumulative impacts, government plans, and where growth needs to be directed to protect the project resource and minimise impacts and potential for conflict.

Figure 19.2: Influencing local development through the land management plan.

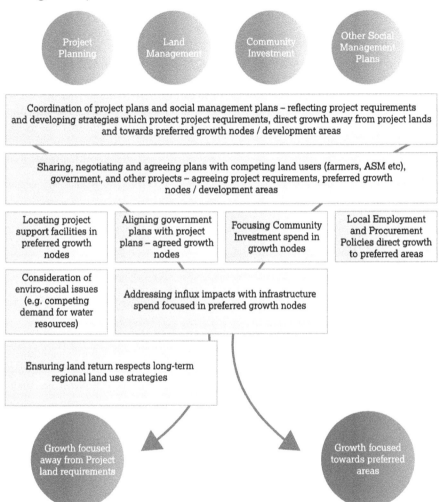

As referred to above, community investment can be used in part to enforce land management strategies, for example by ensuring infrastructure investments are focused in areas where the project, and government, would like to focus growth.

Similarly, as alluded to above, local employment and procurement strategies can assist in directing growth to preferred areas. Figure 19.2 shows how land management planning can work with project planning and other social manage-ment plans to influence and manage land issues over the life of the project.

Taking account of closure and land return planning

As referred to in considering land requirements and phased access above, any LMP needs to consider the opportunity for land rehabilitation, often on a phased basis, and how this might allow for land return; it can often offset the cumulative impacts that might otherwise occur on other land uses, particularly agriculture.

The LMP needs to take account of any statutory requirements with regard to rehabilitation of land and conditions of return. For example, in some jurisdictions land may have to be returned to the state, regardless of the original users. Developing a LMP at the outset of a project provides an opportunity for ongoing negotiation with authorities on the most appropriate use of land post-project.

Developing a work plan, budget, roles and responsibilities

Projects may typically have very long life-spans, which will not be certain at the outset and can be dependent on a variety of factors such as market forces and the outcome of further exploration. The LMP will need to be regularly revised to take account of this changing reality.

Typically, as well as having regard to the potential life of a project, the LMP should have a more focused and detailed 1–3 year plan, with detailed scheduling and budgets, and how the LMP clearly integrates with other management plans related to stakeholder engagement, resettlement planning, influx management and community investment.

Integrating LMPs into monitoring and evaluation efforts

Given the typical duration of projects, the need for regular monitoring and review of LMP efforts will require regular review and assessment as part of wider monitoring and evaluation efforts.

The wider monitoring and evaluation process should include indicators to measure success in implementing actions identified in the LMP, including reducing speculation, focusing growth to key areas, minimising influx and reducing impacts on existing land users.

Key indicators are likely to be required related to:

- Demographic analysis
- Land take and return

- Speculation
- Local and regional development planning
- Capacity-building efforts
- Influx management
- Local service provision and capacities
- Local employment and procurement
- Community investment

Land management: key considerations

- **Consider land management planning at the outset** of projects, even where the duration of the project is not clear
- **Consider life-of-project land requirements**, including the possibility of phased access
- Take into account **all competing land users**, including other projects and the potential for cumulative impacts
- **Work with government** to incorporate LMPs into institutional and statutory planning frameworks, while supporting government planning efforts
- Develop **specific mechanisms to control speculation** and mechanisms to first, prevent, and second, manage, influx
- Use the LMP to **co-ordinate social management planning**, for example using community investment initiatives and local employment plans to focus growth to preferred areas, and away from required lands
- **Develop specific plans to deal with informal and/or illegal land uses** such as artisanal and small-scale miners
- **Consider closure planning from the outset** and possibilities of land return on a phased basis

20
Closing thoughts

As mentioned at the beginning of the book, the authors' aim was not to write a long academic tome, but to provide practitioners with a practical tool to help make a real difference in how land access and resettlement is dealt with in a common-sense manner.

We hope that this book provides advice that is useful on the ground for those undertaking land access and resettlement, and that it also helps at the corporate level as companies grapple with the land access and resettlement challenge.

If you are from an affected community, civil society, government, financial institution or another party interested or involved in land access and resettlement, we hope that the book is useful to you as well. While the book focuses on private-sector projects, chiefly from a natural resource perspective, and infrastructure projects, many of the principles and steps outlined should be useful to those undertaking resettlement projects arising from post-conflict, natural disasters or as part of conservation efforts.

Writing this book confirmed what the authors already knew, namely that there continues to be significant scope to improve all elements of the land access and resettlement assessment, planning, negotiation, implementation, monitoring, evaluation and reporting processes. However, one needs to acknowledge that much progress has been made over recent years by dedicated practitioners across the world. People continue to 'push the envelope' and develop creative and cutting-edge solutions.

Let us never forget that while the process of land access and resettlement is typically focused, from a project perspective, on securing the land to enable a project to be constructed, operated and expanded, ultimately this affects ordinary people. You just have to ask the question, 'How would I feel?' to be reminded that **we owe it to affected communities to ensure that displacement impacts are fully and fairly addressed, while also enabling them to enjoy the benefits that flow from projects.**

Let us also remember that, to be really successful, it cannot be a case of 'us planning their future for them'. Projects need to work closely with affected communities in a real partnership to create a future that works for all.

We close by repeating a few critical points that one should always bear in mind:

- Treat all land access and resettlement exercises seriously, no matter how easy or simple they may appear at the outset
- The land access and resettlement process must result in a win–win situation in order to ensure long-term project land access
- While land access and resettlement is challenging, it can be done properly and cost-effectively.

Glossary of key terms

asset survey A detailed survey of all buildings, farms and crops within a project area, recording various data such as ownership, constructional and crop details, measurements, photographs and GPS positioning.

community Usually defined as a group of individuals broader than the household, who identify themselves as a common unit due to recognised social, religious, economic or traditional government ties, or through a shared locality.

compensation Payment in cash or kind for an asset to be acquired or affected by a project at replacement cost.

completion or close-out audit An evaluation by an independent third party to assess whether the outcome of the RAP (resettlement action plan) complies with applicable policies on resettlement.

cut-off date The date after which people will not be considered eligible for compensation, i.e. they are not included in the list of project-affected persons as defined by the socioeconomic survey. Also known as the **entitlement cut-off date** or **moratorium date**.

displaced persons All the people affected by a project through land acquisition, relocation or loss of incomes, including any person, household, firms or public or private institutions who as a result of a project would have their (i) standard of living adversely affected; (ii) right, title or interest in all or any part of a house, land (including residential, commercial, agricultural, plantations, forest and grazing land) or any other movable or fixed assets acquired or possessed, in full or in part, permanently or temporarily adversely affected; (iii) business, occupation, place of work, residence, habitat or access to forest or community resources adversely affected, with or without displacement; or (iv) loss of access to fishing grounds.

displacement assistance
Support provided to people who are physically displaced by a project. Assistance may include transportation, shelter and services that are provided to affected people during their move. Assistance may also include cash allowances that compensate affected people for the inconvenience associated with displacement and defray the expenses of a transition to a new locale, such as moving expenses.

economic displacement
Loss of income streams or means of livelihood resulting from land acquisition or obstructed access to resources (land, water, forest) resulting from the construction or operation of a project or its associated facilities.

encroachers
Those people who move into the project area after the cut-off date and are therefore not eligible for compensation or other rehabilitation measures provided by the project.

entitlement
The range of measures comprising cash or in-kind compensation, relocation cost, income rehabilitation assistance, transport assistance, income substitution and various other allowances.

expropriation
Process whereby a public authority, usually in return for compensation, requires a person, household or community to relinquish rights to land that it occupies or otherwise uses.

host community
People living in or around areas to which people physically displaced by a project will be resettled who, in turn, may be affected by the resettlement.

IFC
International Finance Corporation, a division of the World Bank Group, which provides investment and advisory services to private-sector projects in developing countries, with the goal of ensuring everyone benefits from economic growth.

IFC PS5
IFC Performance Standard 5, which embodies the basic principles and procedures that underlie the IFC's approach to involuntary resettlement.

involuntary resettlement
Refers both to physical displacement and to economic displacement as a result of project-related land acquisition. Resettlement is considered involuntary when affected individuals or communities do not have the right to refuse land acquisition that results in displacement. This occurs in cases of: (i) lawful expropriation or restrictions on land use based on eminent domain; and (ii) negotiated settlements in which the buyer can resort to expropriation or impose legal restrictions on land use if negotiations with the seller fail. In the event of adverse economic, social or environmental impacts from project activities other than land acquisition (such as loss of access to assets or resources, or restrictions on land use), such impacts will be avoided, minimised, mitigated or compensated for through the social and environmental assessment process of IFC PS1 on social and environmental assessment and management.

land access or land acquisition
The process by which a project acquires land from affected individuals or households in exchange for compensation at replacement value.

livelihood restoration
The measures required to ensure that project-affected persons have the resources to at least restore, if not improve, their livelihoods.

physical displacement
Loss of shelter and assets resulting from the acquisition of land associated with a project that requires the affected person(s) to move to another location.

project-affected person
The same as displaced person within the meaning of IFC PS5 on land acquisition and involuntary resettlement, and means any person experiencing loss of asset or loss of access to income, whether of a temporary or permanent nature, due to the land acquisition process, regardless of whether they are physically displaced or relocated or not.

project-affected household
The family or collection of project-affected persons that will experience effects from land acquisition regardless of whether they are physically displaced or relocated or not.

project area
Usually the area as covered by any licence areas, key infrastructure and access roads, together with required safety and environmental buffer zones.

RAP
Resettlement action plan, the document in which a project sponsor or other responsible entity specifies the

procedures that it will follow and the actions that it will take to mitigate adverse effects, compensate losses and provide development benefits to persons and communities affected by an investment project.

relocation
A process through which physically displaced households are provided with a one-time lump sum compensation payment for their existing residential structures and moved from the project area.

replacement cost
The rate of compensation for lost assets must be calculated at full replacement cost: that is, the market value of the assets plus transaction costs. With regard to land and structures, the IFC defines 'replacement costs' as follows (IFC 2012: IFC PS5, Guidance Note 22):

- Agricultural land: the market value of land of equal productive use or potential located in the vicinity of the affected land, plus the cost of preparation to levels similar to or better than those of the affected land, plus the cost of any registration and transfer taxes.

- Land in urban areas: the market value of land of equal size and use, with similar or improved public infrastructure facilities and services preferably located in the vicinity of the affected land, plus the cost of any registration and transfer taxes.

- Household and public structures: the cost of purchasing or building a new structure, with an area and quality similar to or better than those of the affected structure, or of repairing a partially affected structure, including labour and contractors' fees and any registration and transfer taxes.

- In determining the replacement cost, depreciation of the asset and the value of salvage materials are not taken into account, nor is the value of benefits to be derived from the project deducted from the valuation of an affected asset.

resettlement
A process through which physically displaced households are provided with replacement plots and residential structures at a designated site. Resettlement includes initiatives to restore and improve the living standards of those being resettled.

resettlement assistance
Support provided to people who are physically displaced by a project. Assistance may include transportation,

food, shelter and social services that are provided to affected people during their relocation. Assistance may also include cash allowances that compensate affected people for the inconvenience associated with resettlement and defray the expenses of a transition to a new locale, such as moving expenses and lost workdays.

RPF

Resettlement policy framework, required for projects with subprojects or multiple components that cannot be identified before project approval. This instrument may also be appropriate where there are valid reasons for delaying the implementation of the resettlement, provided that the implementing party provides an appropriate and concrete commitment for its future implementation.

social licence to operate

The concept of a social licence to operate exists when a project is seen as having the approval and broad acceptance of society to conduct its activities. It is not a licence provided by civil authorities, nor a product of an internal corporate process such as an audit of company practices. It comes from the acceptance of the project's development and activities by directly affected and neighbouring communities.

socioeconomic survey

A detailed socioeconomic survey of all households within the project area, recording detailed demographic and socioeconomic data at the household and individual level.

speculation

The erection of buildings/structures or the planting of crops within a project area, with the sole aim of claiming compensation from the project proponent. Speculation may be pre-cut-off (occurring before the entitlement cut-off date has been declared), or post-cut-off (occurring after the entitlement cut-off date).

stakeholders

Any and all individuals, groups, organisations and institutions interested in and potentially affected by a project or having the ability to influence a project.

vulnerable groups

The people who by virtue of gender, ethnicity, age, physical or mental disability, economic disadvantage or social status may be more adversely affected by resettlement than others, and who may be limited in their ability to claim or take advantage of resettlement assistance and related development benefits.

Bibliography and additional resources

ADB (Asian Development Bank) (1998) *Handbook on Resettlement: A Guide to Good Practice*, www.adb.org/documents/handbook-resettlement-guide-good-practice (accessed 27 November 2014).

—— (2009) 'Safeguard Policy Statement', www.adb.org/documents/safeguard-policy-statement?ref=site/safeguards/publications (accessed 27 November 2014).

African Development Bank Group (2003) *Involuntary Resettlement Policy*, www.afdb.org/en/documents/document/bank-group-involuntary-resettlement-policy-11342/ (accessed 2 December 2014).

—— (2013) *African Development Bank Group's Integrated Safeguards System: Policy Statement and Operational Safeguards*, www.afdb.org/fileadmin/uploads/afdb/Documents/Policy-Documents/December_2013_-_AfDB'S_Integrated_Safeguards_System__-_Policy_Statement_and_Operational_Safeguards.pdf (accessed 11 December 2014).

Blaikie, P., T. Cannon, I. Davis and B. Wisner (1994) *At Risk: Natural Hazards, People's Vulnerability and Disasters* (New York: Routledge).

Bowden, A.R., R. Lane and J.H. Martin (2001) *Triple Bottom Line Risk Management: Enhancing Profit, Environmental Performance and Community Benefit* (New York: John Wiley & Sons, Inc.).

Brundtland Commission (1987) *Our Common Future: Towards Sustainable Development*, Chapter 2, World Commission on Economic Development, www.un-documents.net/ocf-02.htm (accessed 1 December 2014).

Carney, D., M. Drinkwater, K. Feefjes, T. Rusinow, S. Wanmali and N. Singh (1999) *Livelihoods Approaches Compared: A Brief Comparison of Livelihoods Approaches of the UK* (London: Department for International Development, CARE, Oxfam and the United Nations Development Programme).

Cernea, M. (1997) 'The Risks and Reconstruction Model for Resettling Displaced Populations', *World Development* 25.10: 1569-87.

Cernea, M., and H. Mohan Mathur (eds.) (2008) *Can Compensation Prevent Impoverishment? Reforming Resettlement Through Investments* (Oxford, UK: Oxford University Press).

CBL (Community Business Ltd) (2014) 'Community Investment', www.communitybusiness.org/focus_areas/CI.htm (accessed 1 December 2014).

Deloitte Global Services Limited (2013) *Tracking the Trends 2014: The Top 10 Issues Mining Companies Will Face in the Coming Year*, www2.deloitte.com/ca/en/pages/international-business/articles/tracking-the-trends-2014.html (accessed 27 November 2014).

EBRD (European Bank for Reconstruction and Development) (2008) 'Environmental and Social Policy', www.ebrd.com/news/publications/policies/environmental-and-social-policy-2008.html (accessed 27 November 2014), including: Performance Requirement 1: Environmental and Social Appraisal and Management; Performance Requirement 5: Land Acquisition, Involuntary Resettlement and Economic Displacement; Performance Requirement 7: Indigenous Peoples; Performance Requirement 8: Cultural Heritage; and Performance Requirement 10: Information Disclosure and Stakeholder Engagement.

Ellis, F., and E. Allison (2004) *Livelihood Diversification and Natural Resource Access*, LSP Working Paper 9, FAO, www.fao.org/docrep/006/ad689e/ad689e00.HTM (accessed 30 November 2014).

Equator Principles (2013) *The Equator Principles III*, www.equator-principles.com/index.php/ep3 (accessed 27 November 2014).

Economist, The (2009) 'Idea: Triple bottom line', *The Economist*, 17 November 2009, www.economist.com/node/14301663 (accessed 1 December 2014).

Government of Canada (2014) 'Corporate Social Responsibility', www.international.gc.ca/trade-agreements-accords-commerciaux/topics-domaines/other-autre/csr-rse.aspx?lang=eng (accessed 1 December 2014).

Henisz, W.J. (2014) *Corporate Diplomacy: Building Reputations and Relationships with External Stakeholders* (Sheffield, UK: Greenleaf Publishing).

ICMM (International Council on Mining & Metals) (2010) *Human Rights in the Mining and Metals Industry: Overview, Management Approach and Issues*, www.icmm.com/page/14809/human-rights-in-the-mining-and-metals-industry-overview-management-approach-and-issues (accessed 30 November 2014).

—— (2011a) *Good Practice Guide: Indigenous Peoples and Mining*, www.icmm.com/publications/indigenous-peoples-and-mining-good-practice-guide (accessed 30 November 2014).

—— (2011b) *Mining: Partnerships for Development Toolkit*, www.icmm.com/mpdtoolkit (accessed 30 November 2014).

—— (2012) *Community Development Toolkit*, www.icmm.com/community-development-toolkit (accessed 30 November 2014).

—— (2013) *Changing the Game: Communications and Sustainability in the Mining Industry*, www.icmm.com/changing-the-game (accessed 30 November 2014).

—— (n.d.) 'Sustainable Development Framework', www.icmm.com/our-work/sustainable-development-framework (accessed 30 November 2014).

ICMM, International Committee of the Red Cross, IFC and IPIECA (2011) *Voluntary Principles on Security and Human Rights: Implementation Guidance Tools*, www.icmm.com/voluntary-principles-on-security-and-human-rights (accessed 2 December 2014).

Inter-American Development Bank (1998) *Involuntary Resettlement: Operational Policy and Background Paper* (OP-710), http://publications.iadb.org/handle/11319/2582 (accessed 27 November 2014).

IFC (International Finance Corporation) (1998) *Doing Better Business Through Effective Public Consultation and Disclosure: A Good Practice Manual*, www.commdev.org/doing-better-business-through-effective-public-consultation-and-disclosure-good-practice-manual (accessed 27 November 2014).

—— (2000) *Investing in People: Sustaining Communities through Improved Business Practice—A Community Development Resource Guide for Companies*, www.commdev.org/investing-people-sustaining-communities-through-improved-business-practice (accessed 27 November 2014).

—— (2002) *Handbook for Preparing a Resettlement Action Plan*, www.commdev.org/ifc-handbook-preparing-resettlement-action-plan (accessed 27 November 2014).

—— (2003) *Good Practice Note: Addressing the Social Dimensions of Private Sector Projects*, www.commdev.org/good-practice-note-addressing-social-dimensions-private-sector-projects (accessed 11 December 2014).

—— (2007) *Stakeholder Engagement: A Good Practice Handbook for Companies Doing Business in Emerging Markets*, www.commdev.org/stakeholder-engagement-good-practice-handbook-companies-doing-business-emerging-markets (accessed 27 November 2014).

—— (2008) *Working Together: How Large-Scale Mining Can Engage with Artisanal and Small-Scale Miners*, www.commdev.org/working-together-how-large-scale-mining-can-engage-artisanal-and-small-scale-miners (accessed 27 November 2014).

—— (2009a) *Addressing Grievances from Project-Affected Communities: Guidance for Projects and Companies on Designing Grievance Mechanisms (Good Practice Note)*, www.commdev.org/addressing-grievances-project-affected-communities (accessed 27 November 2014).

—— (2009b) *Projects and People: A Handbook for Addressing Project-Induced In-Migration*, www.commdev.org/projects-and-people-handbook-addressing-project-induced-migration (accessed 27 November 2014).

—— (2010a) *Guide to Human Rights Impact Assessment and Management*, www.commdev.org/guide-human-rights-impact-assessment-and-management (accessed 27 November 2014).

—— (2010b) *Strategic Community Investment: A Good Practice Handbook for Companies Doing Business in Emerging Markets*, www.commdev.org/strategic-community-investment-sci-good-practice-handbook-companies-doing-business-emerging-markets (accessed 27 November 2014).

—— (2011) *A Guide to Getting Started in Local Procurement*, www.commdev.org/guide-getting-started-local-procurement-companies-seeking-benefits-linkages-local-smes (accessed 27 November 2014).

—— (2012) 'Performance Standards on Environmental and Social Sustainability', www.ifc.org/wps/wcm/connect/topics_ext_content/ifc_external_corporate_site/ifc+sustainability/our+approach/risk+management/performance+standards/environmental+and+social+performance+standards+and+guidance+notes#2012 (accessed 27 November 2014), including: Performance Standard 1: Assessment and Management of Environmental and Social Risks and Impacts; Performance Standard 4: Community Health, Safety and Security; Performance Standard 5: Land Acquisition and Involuntary Resettlement; Performance Standard 7: Indigenous Peoples; and Performance Standard 8: Cultural Heritage.

—— (2013a) *Cumulative Impact Assessment and Management: Guidance for the Private Sector in Emerging Markets (Good Practice Handbook)*, www.ifc.org/wps/wcm/connect/topics_ext_content/ifc_external_corporate_site/ifc+sustainability/learning+and+adapting/knowledge+products/publications/publications_handbook_cumulativeimpactassessment (accessed 27 November 2014).

—— (2013b) *A Strategic Approach to Early Stakeholder Engagement: A Good Practice Handbook for Junior Companies in the Extractives Industries*, www.commdev.org/strategic-approach-to-early-stakeholder-engagement (accessed 27 November 2014).

—— (2013c) *IFC Sustainability Resources Brochure 2013*, www.ifc.org/wps/wcm/connect/topics_ext_content/ifc_external_corporate_site/ifc+sustainability/learning+and+adapting/knowledge+products/publications/publications_brochures_ifc_sustresourcesbrochure (accessed 27 November 2014).

—— (2014) *Addressing Project Impacts on Fishing Based Livelihoods: A Good Practice Handbook—Baseline Assessment and Development of a Fisheries Livelihood Restoration Plan (Draft)*, www.commdev.org/draft-addressing-project-impacts-fishing-based-livelihoods-baseline-assessment-and-development (accessed 11 December 2014).

—— (n.d.) 'Financial Valuation Tool for Sustainability Investments', www.fvtool.com (accessed periodically 2013–14).

IPIECA (International Petroleum Industry Environmental and Conservation Association) (2004) *A Guide to Social Impact Assessment in the Oil and Gas Industry*, www.commdev. org/guide-social-impact-assessment-oil-and-gas-industry (accessed 2 December 2014).

—— (2006) *Partnerships in the Oil and Gas Industry*, www.ipieca.org/publication/ partnerships-oil-and-gas-industry (accessed 2 December 2014).

—— (2008a) *Guide to Operating in Areas of Conflict for the Oil and Gas Industry*, www. ipieca.org/publication/guide-operating-areas-conflict-oil-and-gas-industry (accessed 2 December 2014).

—— (2008b) *Guide to Successful, Sustainable Social Investment for the Oil and Gas Industry*, www.ipieca.org/publication/guide-successful-sustainable-social-investment-oil-and-gas-industry (accessed 2 December 2014).

—— (2009) *Urban Encroachment: An Illustration of Lessons Learned Drawing on Case Studies from the Oil and Gas Industry*, www.ipieca.org/publication/urban-encroachment (accessed 2 December 2014).

—— (2011) *Local Content Strategy: A Guidance Document for the Oil and Gas Industry*, www.ipieca.org/publication/local-content-strategy-guidance-document-oil-and-gas-industry (accessed 2 December 2014).

—— (2012a) *Human Rights Due Diligence Process: A Practical Guide to Implementation for Oil and Gas Companies*, www.ipieca.org/publication/human-rights-due-diligence-process-practical-guide-implementation-oil-and-gas-companies (accessed 2 December 2014).

—— (2012b) *Indigenous Peoples and the Oil and Gas Industry: Context, Issues and Emerging Good Practice*, www.ipieca.org/publication/indigenous-peoples-and-oil-and-gas-industry-context-issues-and-emerging-good-practice (accessed 2 December 2014).

—— (2012c) *Operational Level Grievance Mechanisms: IPIECA Good Practice Survey*, www. ipieca.org/publication/operational-level-grievance-mechanisms-good-practice-survey (accessed 2 December 2014).

—— (2013a) *Good Practice Guidelines for the Development of Shale Gas and Oil*, www. ipieca.org/publication/ogp-ipieca-good-practice-guidelines-development-shale-oil-and-gas (accessed 2 December 2014).

—— (2013b) *Improving Social and Environmental Performance: Good Practice Guidance for the Oil and Gas Industry*, www.ipieca.org/publication/improving-social-and-environmental-performance-good-practice-guidance-oil-and-gas-indus-0 (accessed 2 December 2014).

Japan Bank for International Co-operation (2012) *Guidelines for Confirmation of Environmental and Social Considerations: Involuntary Resettlement*, www.jbic.go.jp/en/efforts/ environment/confirm (accessed 27 November 2014).

OECD (2013) *OECD Framework for Statistics on the Distribution of Household Income, Consumption and Wealth*, http://dx.doi.org/10.1787/9789264194830-en (accessed 11 December 2014).

PDAC (Prospectors & Developers Association of Canada) (2007) *Sustainable Development and Corporate Social Responsibility: Tools, Codes and Standards for the Mineral Exploration Industry*, www.pdac.ca/docs/default-source/public-affairs/csr-sustainable-development.pdf (accessed 2 December 2014).

—— (n.d.) 'e3 Plus: A Framework for Responsible Exploration', www.pdac.ca/programs/ e3-plus (accessed 2 December 2014), with guidance notes and three Internet-based toolkits, including a 'Social Responsibility in Exploration' toolkit.

Porter, M.E, and M.R. Kramer (2011) 'Creating Shared Value', *Harvard Business Review*, January 2011, https://hbr.org/2011/01/the-big-idea-creating-shared-value (accessed 1 December 2014).

Reardon, T. (1997) 'Using Evidence of Household Income Diversification to Inform Study of the Rural Nonfarm Labor Market in Africa', *World Development* 25.5: 735-48.

Russell, C., and T. Smeaton (2009) 'From Needs to Assets: Charting a Sustainable Path Towards Development in Sub-Saharan African Countries', Asset-Based Community Development Institute, www.abcdinstitute.org/docs/From%20Needs%20to%20 Assets%20-Charting%20a%20Sustainable%20path%20towards%20Development%20 in%20Sub-Saharan%20African%20Countries.pdf (accessed 2 December 2014).

Sen, A. (1981) *An Essay on Entitlement and Deprivation* (Oxford, UK: Oxford University Press).

SocialLicense.com (n.d.) 'What Is the Social License?', http://socialicense.com/definition. html (accessed 1 December 2014).

Stakeholder Research Associates (2006a) *From Words to Action: The Stakeholder Engagement Manual, Volume 1: The Guide to Practitioners' Perspectives on Stakeholder Engagement*, AccountAbility, www.accountability.org/about-us/publications/the-stakeholder-1.html (accessed 2 December 2014).

—— (2006b) *From Words to Action: The Stakeholder Engagement Manual, Volume 2: The Practitioners' Handbook on Stakeholder Engagement*, AccountAbility, www.accountability.org/about-us/publications/the-stakeholder.html (accessed 2 December 2014).

SustainAbility, IFC and Ethos Institute (2002) *Developing Value: The Business Case for Sustainability in Emerging Markets*, www.ifc.org/wps/wcm/connect/topics_ ext_content/ifc_external_corporate_site/ifc+sustainability/learning+and+adapting/ knowledge+products/publications/publications_report_developingvalue__ wci__1319577294013 (accessed 11 December 2014).

World Bank (1999) 'Operational Policy (OP) 4.01: Environmental Assessment', http:// go.worldbank.org/RUEQVWD550 (accessed 16 December 2014).

—— (2001a) 'Operational Policy (OP) 4.12: Involuntary Resettlement', http://go.worldbank. org/96LQB2JT50 (accessed 27 November 2014).

—— (2001b) 'Bank Procedure (BP) 4.12: Involuntary Resettlement', http://go.worldbank. org/Q2PR7QE7W0 (accessed 27 November 2014).

—— (2004) *Involuntary Resettlement Sourcebook: Planning and Implementation in Development Projects*, https://openknowledge.worldbank.org/handle/10986/14914 (accessed 27 November 2014).

—— (2010) *Mining Foundations, Trusts and Funds: A Source Book*, https://openknowledge. worldbank.org/handle/10986/16965 (accessed 2 December 2014).

—— (2014) *Environmental and Social Framework: Setting Standards for Sustainable Development*, http://documents.worldbank.org/curated/en/2014/07/19898916/ environmental-social-framework-setting-standards-sustainable-development (accessed 11 December 2014).

Vanclay, F. (2002) 'Social Impact Assessment', in T. Munn (ed.), *Encyclopedia of Global Environmental Change* (Chichester, UK: Wiley), vol. 4: 387-93.

Vanclay, F., and H.A. Becker (eds.) (2003) *The International Handbook of Social Impact Assessment: Conceptual and Methodological Advances* (Cheltenham, UK: Edward Elgar Publishing Ltd).

Van Schooten, M., F. Vanclay and R. Slootweg (2003), 'Conceptualizing Social Change Processes and Social Impacts', in F. Vanclay and H.A. Becker (eds.), *The International Handbook of Social Impact Assessment: Conceptual and Methodological Advances* (Cheltenham, UK: Edward Elgar Publishing Ltd): 74-91.

Wisner, B., P. Blaikie, T. Cannon and I. Davis (1994) *At Risk: Natural Hazards, People's Vulnerability and Disasters* (New York: Routledge).

—— (2003) *At Risk: Natural Hazards, People's Vulnerability and Disasters*, 2nd edn (New York: Routledge).

Work and Family Researchers Network (n.d.) 'Corporate Citizenship, Definition(s) of', https://workfamily.sas.upenn.edu/glossary/c/corporate-citizenship-definitions (accessed 1 December 2014).

About the authors

The authors are the three founding directors of Intersocial Consulting, a firm that specialises in land access and resettlement consulting services worldwide.

Gerry Reddy has extensive experience in land acquisition, resettlement, livelihood restoration and urban and regional development, having planned, implemented and reviewed a variety of projects worldwide. He has worked in private consultancy, local and regional government, the United Nations and international NGOs, including eight years living and working in Africa. Gerry has managed and advised on projects in a variety of locations, including throughout Africa, Asia and Eastern Europe. This has included working with clients in relation to mining, oil  and gas, infrastructure, environmental and refugee-related resettlement issues. His expertise is in project management, planning and implementation, community consultations and negotiations, environmental and social impact assessment, livelihood restoration, and participatory community planning and development. He has also undertaken social due diligence reviews, training of corporate personnel and benchmarking of projects worldwide. Gerry's tertiary education includes a Masters in Urban and Regional Planning as well as a Diploma in Environmental Resource Management. gerryreddy@intersocialconsulting.com

Eddie Smyth has over 20 years of experience working in the environmental and social fields in over 15 countries. The first six years of his career focused on wildlife conservation and environmentally friendly farming in Europe, followed by five years community development fieldwork in Africa. He has spent the past nine years planning, implementing and reviewing resettlement projects in Africa, Asia–Pacific, Europe and South America. Eddie has extensive practical experience in resettlement project management, social impact assessment, stakeholder  engagement, social due diligence, livelihoods restoration and community development. Eddie's tertiary education includes a Masters in Managing Rural Development and a Masters in Wildlife Conservation. eddiesmyth@intersocialconsulting.com

Mike Steyn has over 23 years of experience working with mining, oil and gas and infrastructure projects as a consultant and in a variety of senior management and other positions. He has extensive worldwide experience dealing with land acquisition and resettlement and related issues. He has planned, implemented, managed, carried out due diligence on, reviewed and monitored many land acquisition and resettlement projects in over 20 countries in Europe, Africa, Latin America and Asia.  He helps clients plan, negotiate and implement projects, as well as providing due diligence, benchmarking, review, monitoring and capacity-building training services. He also helps clients at a corporate strategic level and in the development of businesswide social management standards and guidelines. Mike's tertiary education includes an MBA (dissertation title: 'Developing a Global Policy for Dealing with the Community as a Corporate Stakeholder as a Means of Obtaining Competitive Advantage'), Bachelor of Laws (*cum laude*), and Bachelor of Arts (majoring in politics). mikesteyn@intersocialconsulting.com

Index